RICHARD KOLODA

holy ghost
the life & death
of free jazz pioneer
albert ayler

JAW
BONE

I would like to dedicate my book to Jane Zaharias, who was always there and believed in me. **RJK**

HOLY GHOST
THE LIFE & DEATH OF FREE JAZZ
PIONEER ALBERT AYLER
RICHARD KOLODA

A Jawbone book
First edition 2022
Published in the UK and the USA by
Jawbone Press
Office G1
141–157 Acre Lane
London SW2 5UA
England
www.jawbonepress.com

ISBN 978-1-911036-93-7

Printed by Short Run Press, Exeter, Devon

1 2 3 4 5 26 25 24 23 22

contents

preface

Albert Ayler was the spirit that inspired John Coltrane to begin his avant-garde explorations, and that same spirit inspired all of Coltrane's successors as well. But like many geniuses ahead of their time, Ayler was a polarizing figure. Some critics considered him a charlatan, others a heretic for dismantling the traditions of jazz. Some simply considered him insane. His divine messages of peace and love, visions of flying saucers, and the strange account of his final days leading up to being found dead in New York City's East River are central to his mystique, but they are also a distraction.

The mysterious manner of Ayler's death tends to overshadow the blistering impact he had on the direction of jazz to come. Yet while there exists a posthumous cult surrounding John Coltrane, Ayler's spirit, per Peter Niklas Wilson, 'seems to have evaporated into unreality. Albert Ayler was born to the myth, one to be dark and mysterious.'[1]

And that is the shock. Coltrane is a household name. Ornette Coleman is spoken of in legendary terms, and Eric Dolphy is revered as a tragic saint who died before his time. But Ayler's greatest influence today is on rock musicians. At the time of his first released recording, the jazz world considered the outer fringe to be Coleman's 1961 album *Free Jazz: A Collective Improvisation*, Coltrane and Dolphy's interplay on 'Africa' (from Coltrane's fourth studio album of the same year, *Africa/Brass*), and pianist

Cecil Taylor's 'D Trad, That's What' (from 1962's *Nefertiti, The Beautiful One Has Come*). Against even these, however, Ayler's first recording was further out than what many felt was acceptable. Though Taylor was as radical as Ayler, his musical development took place over an extended period of time, allowing the jazz world to assimilate those ideas. Ayler did not have the same opportunity to live a full lifespan.

Ayler did, however, change the course of jazz in influencing Coltrane, and by returning jazz to the roots of collective improvisation. His *Spiritual Unity* was both praised and ridiculed when it was released in 1964. Today it is recognized as a landmark in free jazz. He would also, in what some considered an ill-advised venture into pop-jazz, augur the R&B trend that jazz would follow after his passing. The temptation is to speculate where his genius would have taken him had he been given a second chance by his label of the late 60s, Impulse!, and by life itself.

Within a half-decade of being booted off the stage in his hometown of Cleveland, Ohio, Ayler was headlining the Newport Jazz Festival in Europe. A mere three years after that, in July 1970, he staged the greatest triumph of his career, playing at the Maeght Foundation on the French Riviera, where he was called back onstage for ten encores. Despite the triumphant joy of that evening, captured on tape for the live album *Nuits de la Fondation Maeght*, Ayler had a mere four months left to live.

•

Ayler's story compares to classic Greek tragedy, whether it is the oft-used line about being misunderstood in his homeland or his committing suicide to expiate the guilt he felt over firing his troubled younger brother, Donald, from his band. His story compels us to listen to his spiritual cries.

This first exhaustive English-language biography of Ayler has been in the works for over twenty years. When I interviewed Donald and his father, Edward, for my jazz show on Cleveland State University's WCSB 89.3 FM, my preconceived notions about Albert quickly fell away, and I hope the reader's assumptions about this saxophone giant will fall by the wayside as well. This work attempts to correct a myriad of misinformation, not least the story of his corpse being tied to a jukebox and tossed in the East River. I have also uncovered facts that contradict Ayler's statements to interviewers, such as his claim that he joined the US Army to gain musical experience (it was more likely to avoid paying child support), or that he was born in a ghetto.

Holy Ghost also corrects the historical record. It was convenient for critics to link Ayler with the rising Black Power movement, ignoring the reality that, to Ayler, music held a profoundly spiritual power—it was the 'healing force of the universe,' as he put it. It also dispels the myths surrounding Ayler's mental health that some critics have used to devalue his music, among them reactions to the apocalyptic visions of flying saucers and the sword of Jesus that Ayler shared in Amiri Baraka's magazine *The Cricket* in 1969.

Against critical consensus—and Ayler's own assertions—this book also attributes the later changes in Ayler's musical direction to the limited resources of his trumpet-playing younger brother, Donald, which necessitated the shift from the avant-garde playing of Albert's previous trumpeter, Don Cherry, toward the pop-jazz of his later years.

Since I began working on this book, I have seen reissues that establish Ayler as a creator whose influence is acknowledged by rock musicians such as Patti Smith, who once said that her album *Radio Ethiopia* was 'a lot like Albert Ayler.'[2] John Lurie of The Lounge Lizards wrote a ballet called *The Resurrection Of Albert Ayler*. Saxophonist Mars Williams, who has played with new-wave group The Psychedelic Furs and industrial-metal pioneers Ministry, has a band called Witches & Devils that plays Albert Ayler's music and has established a unique tradition of performing Ayler-inspired Christmas concerts in the US and abroad. A Swedish free-jazz group, The AALY Trio, led by saxophonist Mats Gustafsson, plays Ayler compositions, often in conjunction with Chicago-born reedman Ken Vandermark.

Ayler's work has cast an especially long shadow across New York's own hugely influential rock scene. Ironically, in the years since his death, more guitarists than saxophonists seem to have been inspired by Ayler, among them Tom Verlaine and Richard Lloyd, of the post-punk group Television, and Robert Quine of the Voidoids. Noise-rockers Sonic Youth named their 2000 album *NYC Ghosts & Flowers* in acknowledgement of Ayler's influence, while their New Jersey neighbor (and Tom Waits and John Zorn collaborator) Marc Ribot has also named Ayler as a guiding force and recorded a collection of Ayler compositions on his 2005 tribute album, *Spiritual Unity*. He's not the only one: one-time Captain Beefheart guitarist Gary Lucas and folk-punk firebrands Violent Femmes have also recorded his compositions.

Lou Reed's attempts at free jazz; The Stooges' sonic onslaught in *Fun House*; the guitar maelstroms of Comets On Fire—all bear Ayler's thumbprint. In France, there is even a record label named after him, Ayler Records. Closer to home, Revenant Records, founded by the equally revered American primitive guitarist John Fahey, issued a definitive Ayler box set, the Grammy-nominated *Holy Ghost: Rare And Unissued Recordings (1962–70)*, in 2004, which appeared almost simultaneously alongside Kasper Collin's critically acclaimed documentary film *My Name Is Albert Ayler* (both projects list me as a contributor). And neither has Ayler's stature as a genius diminished among the jazz cognoscenti: *DownBeat* magazine inducted him into its Hall Of Fame in 1983.

Two decades after his death, Ayler's oeuvre finally began to receive the scholarly attention it deserves: in 1992, Bowling Green State University graduate student Jeff Schwartz published the ebook *Albert Ayler: His Life And Music*; the following year, University Of Wisconsin–Madison student Jane Martha Reynolds made him the partial subject of her doctoral dissertation, *Improvisation Analysis Of Selected Works Of Albert Ayler, Roscoe Mitchell And Cecil Taylor*; and English fan Patrick Regan has maintained the long-running website Ayler.co.uk since June 2000. In 2010, several groups marked the fortieth anniversary of Ayler's death with tribute concerts; others chose to celebrate his birth. The First Annual Albert Ayler Festival took place in July 2010 on Roosevelt Island, New York. It had been organized by ESP-Disk', the record label most closely associated with Ayler and his music.

In adding to the wealth of material already out there, the true goal of *Holy Ghost* is to draw attention away from the circumstances surrounding Ayler's death and bring it sharply back to the legacy he left behind. Doing so demands confronting those who have marginalized, maligned, and spread misinformation about Ayler in order to further their own agendas. He was a character as interesting as any that could have been created by a Hollywood screenwriter. It is hoped the reader will enjoy finding out why, just as much as I enjoyed researching Ayler's life.

RICHARD KOLODA
SUMMER 2022

youth

At 1:27am on July 13, 1936, a son, Albert, was born at University Hospital in Cleveland to Edward and Myrtle Hunter Ayler. Albert's mother was of mixed heritage (African American, Cree, and Cherokee) and had come north to Cleveland from Birmingham, Alabama, in 1930, accompanied by her mother, Lula Dalt Hunter. They were just two of what would become millions of travelers in the Great Migration of southern Blacks seeking better lives in the cities of the North, Midwest, and West.

Ayler's lineage through his father was African American and Scotch-Irish. There are two possible origins of his surname. The first is a corruption of the German Öhler, yet slavery was not part of the German tradition in America as much as it was of the Scotch-Irish who settled the South, making the latter the more probable source. Albert's trumpet-playing brother, Donald, who was six years his junior, described his maternal ancestry as 'part white.' The rape and coercion that was a vicious by-product of slavery in Alabama accounts for the part-white ancestry in the family gene lines.

Albert's father, Edward Ayler, came north from Mobile, Alabama, when his mother fled from her abusive husband with her two children, Edward and Nellie. Augusta Ayler entered into a common-law marriage with a laborer, Wright Ceasor, bore three more children, and was claimed to be widowed by 1930, though Cleveland burial records list him as dying in 1963.

Taking his stepfather's surname, Edward Ceasor was attending Cleveland's East Tech High School when he met Jessie Myrtle Hunter—affectionately referred to as 'Mirth,' as she felt her given name was too masculine. He had known her through church. The couple married in 1933, a year after Edward graduated from East Tech and reverted to his birth name. Early in the marriage, tragedy occurred when, in her fourth month of pregnancy, Myrtle miscarried. Albert, who was named after his paternal grandfather, came after the tragic loss of his parents' earlier child.

The family moved frequently during Albert's youth in the Kinsman area, in Cleveland's East Side. His first home was an apartment at 6826 Kinsman Road. As he told German critic Gudrun Endress, 'I arrived in a ghetto to the world—where all what you sensed and felt was the blues.'[1]

Music was important to the Ayler family. Edward's older sister, Nellie Thompson, was involved in the local music scene, singing at Liberty Hill Baptist Church. Edward himself had received violin lessons as a child—his musical idol was crooner Russ Columbo, a rival of Bing Crosby. A serious musician, Edward composed the song 'I Love You' and registered it with the US Copyright Office in 1940; his great ambition was to have one of the contemporary bandleaders record one of his songs. In the early 40s, a friend gave him lessons on the alto saxophone, and Edward became interested in jazz, drawing influence from Charlie Parker, Johnny Hodges, and Illinois Jacquet. But though he became proficient enough to join a nine-man band led by local star Bob McCelvy, family obligations overshadowed Edward's dream of becoming a professional jazz musician. On October 5, 1942, his second son, Donald, was born at the Mary B. Talbert Home And Hospital in Cleveland, all but forcing Edward to treat his jazz career as a pastime. Shortly after Donald's birth, the family moved to 7615 Rawlings Avenue in a racially mixed neighborhood on Cleveland's East side.[2]

As a child, Albert showed a keen interest in music and, when his father switched to tenor saxophone, the fledgling genius inherited the old alto. As Edward recounted for me in a radio interview:

He was a young boy running around, about four years old, and I had Count
Basie and Duke Ellington coming on the radio. And he would go around to
the back of the radio to see where the music was coming from. He was really
excited about it. He'd loved music, and I had bought him a little bench that he
would use, a little stool, and for some reason, he'd pick the stool up and hold it
like it was a horn. And I saw that he was so interested in music, so it was then
that I put him on the alto.

Clearly, Albert grew up in a loving home and benefited from the presence
and support of a musically inclined father who gave him encouragement.
And yet the picture was not as serene as it may have appeared. Many women
experience depression and anxiety after a miscarriage, and the symptoms
can persist for years—even after the subsequent birth of a healthy child.
According to Albert's one-time fiancée, Carrie Lucas, Myrtle's miscarriage
affected her parenting of Albert. Carrie and Albert would laugh and have
fun, but she sensed something else going on underneath—the impact on
Albert of his mother's unresolved grief.

Donald also showed a proclivity for music at an early age, picking out
songs by ear on a piano at his aunt Eva's home. Keen to introduce both
his boys to jazz, Edward took them to see the great bandleaders that came
through town, among them saxophonists Illinois Jacquet and Red Prysock,
and pianist-composers Duke Ellington and Count Basie, who played the
Palace Theater. Albert had trouble sitting through whole performances—
rather, he stood transfixed by what took place onstage.

Back at home, Edward's record collection, which included releases by
Charlie Parker, Wardell Gray, and Freddie Webster, rounded out his sons'
jazz education, and Edward himself taught both Albert and Donald to
play saxophone. After being home-schooled on the instrument from age
seven to ten, Albert received formal tutoring at the Benny Miller School
of Music and the Cleveland Academy of Music, where he studied from
age ten through seventeen or eighteen. During this time, Albert played in
school bands, performing at the local Republican Club, the Liberty Hill
Baptist Church, and Cleveland community centers. He also played with

his father—Edward on tenor and Albert on alto—performing a repertoire built on light classical arrangements such as minuets and Russian folk songs, and French composer Charles Gounod's 'Ave Maria' (a vocal setting of a Bach harpsichord work). But though Albert made astonishing progress and became known as a neighborhood phenomenon, he struggled to master Nikolai Rimsky-Korsakov's notoriously difficult 'Flight Of The Bumblebee,' a big-band arrangement of which had been popularized by trumpeter Harry James in 1940.

The first documented appearance of Albert as a performer was on April 8, 1945, at the Hampton Social Settlement in Cleveland, Ohio.[3] It was quickly followed by one on Mother's Day, May 13, at the House Of Wills funeral home, at a benefit held for the Junior Music Group of the Hampton Social Settlement.[4] The next known instance of an Albert Ayler performance was at the Friendship Baptist Church on East 55th & Central Avenue on July 15, 1945.[5] Five months later, the *Plain Dealer* reported on an 'interracial charity musical' for the Hampton Social Settlement, held at the Public Hall's Little Theater, and gave favorable notice to a saxophone solo by Albert Ayler.[6] Aged just twelve, Albert staged an early solo concert at the Woodland Center on June 13, 1948, appearing on a bill that also included vocalist Maude Stokes and pianist William Appling. Proceeds for this benefit were used to underwrite the musical careers of young musicians.[7]

As one of those young musicians, Albert was on his way. He didn't have much choice. Edward forced him to practice, pushing his own dreams on the young saxophonist and going so far as to beat him with a leather belt when he said he'd rather be outside playing with his friends. Afterward, Albert would lie in bed, terrified. In later years he rationalized his father's behavior in interviews, saying Edward merely wanted his son to achieve more than what he himself had accomplished.

Younger brother Donald recalled witnessing the abuse:

> My father was very strict. And he knew that my brother had a talent. I'd come in there, and my father would be taking a strap to him and telling him he

couldn't go outside and play baseball because he had to practice his horn. Well, they had another kind of relationship to me. Well, Al was the oldest and he had to get his stuff together. I was the youngest, I was spoiled.[8]

Both brothers were educated in Cleveland's public-school system. Albert attended Kinsman Road Elementary School, Rawlings Junior High School, and John Adams Senior High. John Adams was one of the finest schools in in the area, and its alumni included many prominent Clevelanders, both Black and white; at the time of Albert's attendance, it was about sixty percent white. Albert sang in John Adams's Glee Club and choir, and played first alto in the school band, as well as playing oboe in the orchestra. It was here that he began to exhibit an eidetic memory: once he heard a tune, he would be able to play it right back.

•

Far more important to the Ayler children's development was the Liberty Hill Baptist Church. For many avant-garde saxophonists of the era, the church was influential—as Liberty Hill was to Albert, so were the Texas churches for King Curtis; in New Orleans, Ornette Coleman received crucial experience playing in Deacon Frank Lastie's 'spirit church.' But just as Albert was evolving into a solo performer in his own right, his father underwent a different kind of transformation. After receiving a deep spiritual awakening in 1948, Edward left the Baptist church and joined the Pentecostals, but with the boys' mother too sick to leave the house— she had suffered the stillbirth of a daughter, Cynthia, on June 4, 1948, and it has also been suggested that she had developed multiple sclerosis— Edward dutifully took the children to his wife's place of worship.

After service, Albert and Donald would often go to a movie. When they returned home, the boys would sit in the living room and listen to their father read the Bible out loud. These were the days of childhood innocence—the brothers roughhousing until young Donny yelled for his mother to intercede—but Edward had to deal with typical parenting problems. Donald 'was about six or something like that. He was a young fellow then,' Edward later recalled. 'He fooled around with the piano. Then Al couldn't lay his horn down, he'd be runnin' up there and trying to blow into it, and Al would get angry: *That Donny's gonna tear my reeds up.*'

In the early 50s, the family moved to 3587 East 120th Street, so that Donald could attend better schools. It was during this time that Albert met a piano player from East Tech, Bobby Few, in whose home he began to practice. He also hung around with an older friend from Rawlings Junior High, Lloyd Pearson, a tenor sax player. Fascinated by music, the teenagers snuck into bars around Cleveland's East Side, watching the horn players and bar walkers go about their business. Music was all they lived for.

In 1951, Ayler joined Lloyd Pearson & His Counts of Rhythm. One of the group's hangouts was Gleason's Musical Bar, on 5219 Woodland Avenue, where they sometimes sat in with the house band and occasionally picked up gigs as sidemen for visiting musicians. Ayler scored his first paying job in the spring of 1952, and received his social-security card—number 269-32-3410—on May 20 that year. Pearson and his combo (including Ayler) played a gig at the Circle Theatre on December 1, 1954, and they continued in that spot until they relinquished top place at an amateur contest.

Bobby Few recalled picking up little jobs on Woodland Avenue and Quincy, along what they called the 'chitlin' circuit':

> That was really beautiful. We used to play these cabaret parties and big splashy affairs where everybody would bring their whiskey. In Cleveland, there were a couple on Superior, on Kinsman. The names I … wouldn't remember. They were like big beer halls, you might say. People would dance to the music, and then out came the strip dancers—and sometimes we would lose our place in the music, you know [*laughs*]. I remember Albert used to look over and he'd be playing, and he'd look over, and he would shoot his eyes, and, like, 'Wow.'[9]

At Gleason's in late 1953, the group hooked up with Little Walter, a blues giant whose explosive, electronically amplified harmonica style forever changed the direction of blues. At that time, Walter was riding high on the charts with 'Juke,' and he invited Ayler and Pearson to join him on tour.

Edward told Val Wilmer about that first job: 'When he got the job he was so excited he could hardly believe it. He came running home shouting about, They're gonna take me with 'em, they're taking *me!*'[10]

Albert spent two summers playing rhythm & blues with Little Walter And His Jukes. However, still only a teenager, he found life on the road hard:

> The manner of living was quite different, [it was] hard. [We'd] drink real heavy and play real hard. [We'd be] traveling all day and finally arrive and take out our horns and play. It wasn't for me, so I had to think of a way out. But that was part of the development, and I think that this was very important in my musical career, being out there amongst those really deep-rooted people.[11]

Looking on at the musicians drinking and sleeping, Albert wondered whether this was what he wanted from life. He might be 250 miles away from home, playing in Saginaw, Michigan, and then have to travel overnight to the next gig; they spent an entire week stuck in Chicago. Touring lasted several months—too long to stretch the food his mother packed for him—and when Little Walter disappeared, there was little money to buy food. Pearson said Walter had blown their pay on gambling.

After returning to Cleveland, Ayler joined the American Federation Of Musicians Local #550, paying an initiation fee of $40 on December 10, 1954. The federation was still segregated at the time, but it allowed him to spend more time with like-minded musicians. He'd gained crucial experience playing the blues with Little Walter, and learned to develop strength and expression of tone—qualities that were a culture apart from the middle-class Cleveland neighborhoods that had shaped Ayler's life so far. He'd seen a different world from that of his hometown, which had been shaped by the efforts of Progressive reformers like Mayor Tom L. Johnson. Cleveland did not have 'ghetto' districts, nor did it suffer from the race riots that characterized other northern cities such as Chicago and Detroit.

And yet it was on the road that Albert gained his greatest education. After playing with Little Walter, Albert toured with R&B vocalist Lloyd Price, who had big hits in the 50s with 'Lawdy Miss Clawdy,' 'Personality,' and 'Stagger Lee.' Val Wilmer's research first brought to light Ayler's tenure with Price—likely to have taken place in 1956, after Price had returned from his two-year stint with the army—but in subsequent conversations with Wilmer, Price claimed to have no recollection of Ayler. As Val wrote to me, this 'shows the massive numbers of musicians who went through Price's band.'[12] Ayler had better memories of the Price tour, according to Bobby Few, but according to his then-girlfriend he felt ambivalent about playing music to an audience that was not his. He enjoyed the experience, but knew it was not his style. He was finding his own musical voice, and increasingly felt the need to express it.

Though honing his musicianship while playing with other bandleaders, the dominant force in Ayler's stylistic development was Black life in the country—or, as Stanley Crouch put it, the 'country Black intelligence and confidence in individual vision.'[13] This is found in Ayler's freedom from the white notion of pitch, as well as melodies that were not far from the country hymns and marches—all of which were limited to notes used in the pentatonic scales. Black country life was referenced in compositions such as 'Ghosts,' 'Holy Family,' and 'Holy, Holy,' and Ayler spoke often in his music of spirits and heavenly bells. Yet what separates him from sentimentality is, as Crouch wrote:

> The integrity and emotional authority that lifted his compositions above pretension, nostalgia, or the literally maudlin, for what he sought to express was the big-hearted power and warmth of country gospel that invites, laments, dreams and exorcises, finally, with an intensity that brings an unparalleled sensuality to western mysticism—a sensuality that is post-sexual but which uses the body as a root conductor with the shouts, the cries, the leaps, the hip-, knuckle-, and elbow-whacking tambourines, the Holy Ghost dances of possession and the guttural 'language' of the Spirit, the 'talking in tongues' that finally poses the Spirit of God as a passionate music … absolutely liberated.[14]

Bassist and jazz scholar Peter Niklas Wilson has a different perspective. The author of *Spirits Rejoice! Albert Ayler And His Message*, Wilson believes that

Ayler came into contact with the old emotional layers of African American music in the Black church, and that his impassioned saxophone cries 'are an instrumental speaking in tongues.'[15] The latter view makes more sense. Myrtle Ayler's uncle, the Reverend W.D. Hargrove, was a pastor at the United Bethel Independent Methodist Church, an attendee of Tuskegee Institute, as well as a graduate of the theological school of Payne University. Broadcasting out of Alexander City, Alabama, for WSGN, he was one of the first radio preachers in the South. This was part of Ayler's heritage because the church was a constant presence.

Like his church attendance and membership in the American Federation of Musicians, another aspect of local life had a strong pull for Albert. While in high school, he developed an interest in golf—again, taking after his father, who had caddied in his youth. Albert caddied at the Hawthorne Valley Country Club, in Solon, and was captain on the John Adams golf team. The *Plain Dealer* printed the first mention of his golfing abilities, reporting that Albert had finished fourth (scoring a 43 and a 38) in the caddie golf tournament while representing Hawthorne Valley. He also played for the championship of the city at the Seneca golf course, where, on June 5, 1954, he shot an 82 in the *News* Interscholastic Tournament. The local Cleveland paper reported, 'Al Ayler of John Adams … tied for medalist honors on the first nine with 38s.'[16]

That summer, Albert also played in the Sixth City Golf Club Seventh Annual Amateur Tournament, held during the July 4 weekend, again at the Seneca course. The amateur contest was a major event in the Cleveland Black community, drawing such prominent figures as Joe Louis, Ezzard Charles and Marion Motley, and Ayler emerged as that year's champion. Hank Williams, the tourney's registrar, was quoted in the local African American paper as saying, 'Champions of tomorrow lie in the youth of today, boys like Ayler who shot a 79 are to be encouraged and given every opportunity to learn golf.'[17] Years later, as a champion of a different sort, he contended that he could have been a great golfer, but music was in his heart.[18]

After graduating from John Adams in 1955, Ayler joined a rhythm & blues-style band that Pearson told Val Wilmer was 'conventional,'[19] but, much like his experience touring with Little Walter, Ayler's attempts to earn his living as a full-time saxophonist were fraught with difficulty. Yet he realized that he had to do it, even though it was a far cry from the life he was used to. He held hope he could improve his situation.[20]

After Albert's return from the Lloyd Price tour, both he and Pearson began frequenting a barbershop on East 55th Street where the local pimps hung out. Ayler, with his stylish wardrobe, had a reputation as a ladies' man, and he and Pearson began to imitate the style of the macks with the processed hair. If nothing else, he had made a name for himself locally, and it was around this time that Ayler made his putative first recordings, playing with a friend, trumpeter Nathan Horwitz, who owned a wire recorder. In a February 2020 article for *Jazz Podium*, Ben Young speculated on the identity of the alto saxophonist on the two selections, which the magazine posted on YouTube. Ayler played alto prior to joining the army in 1958, and Bobby Few was almost certain he could be heard on the first cut. However, Few believed the saxophonist on the second cut, an interpretation of 'Wimoweh,' could not have been Ayler, as their styles were too different.[21]

Looking to make ends meet, Ayler also held his only non-musical job at the manufacturing firm Thompson-Ramo-Wooldridge, where he polished blades for the lathe. With the money he earned, he bought a green and silver Cadillac. Standing at five foot five inches, he used to place a small stack of pillows on the driver's seat so that he could see through the windshield. Tellingly, he would also put his horn on the front seat in the space between him and his girlfriend when they drove to clubs where he was engaged to play.

Well over half a decade later, these club dates, and Ayler's repertoire, are being lost to the failing memories of participants and witnesses. Looking through the microfilms of the contemporary *Call & Post* tantalizes us with possibilities in the entertainment pages, which carry advertisements for open jam sessions. It's possible that Ayler played at many of these now-defunct clubs.

CHAPTER II

the army

The girlfriend sitting with Ayler in that Cadillac as they bounced from show to show was Carrie Roundtree. Albert had known her since Rawlings Junior High School, and they had mutual friends like Lloyd Pearson. As teenagers, they met through one of Carrie's friends, Greta Howard; Albert and Carrie would spend time together either sitting on the porch and talking or going to the bars and clubs on Euclid Avenue, such as the Key Room. Now they were in love, and Carrie devotedly watched Albert play at different bars, such as the Cotton Club, named after the Harlem venue that had helped put jazz music on the map in the 1920s and 30s.

Ayler was now known throughout town as a disciple of Charlie Parker, as Carrie remembered:

> He would come over and listen to jazz and he'd have his horn—it would always be in the middle. It was his first girlfriend, and I was his second, you know. We listened to Charlie Parker, Sonny Stitt, different jazz albums; 'cause I had all of those. … He loved them, too … and he would never be still … if something came up and a note hit on the album, his horn would be right here in the middle of us so he would do that. All the time. You could be talkin' to him and he'd be chewin' on his lip [reed]. He would always take his fingers and do it.[1]

While Albert had been trying to build a career as a musician, his younger brother, Donald, had only a casual interest in music; he was busy playing outfield for the Cozier Amateur Club, 1958's champions in the Class E league of the Cleveland Baseball Federation. Donald did quite well, hitting a .294 average, and scoring five runs, seven RBIs and five hits in seventeen at bats. He also was on the John Adams track team, running hurdles. But then he, too, began to get serious about music. Somewhere between the ages of thirteen and seventeen, Donald picked up his brother's alto and attended a small music school operated by Samuel Pattie, who ran a studio on East 105th Street, between Euclid and Chester. He began reading duets with his teacher and took his classes so seriously that he would cry when he could not get the music.

As he had with his eldest son, Edward Ayler would then help Donald along. 'He was hot on saxophone,' Carrie remembered. 'I know he could play it, 'cause I heard him play … actually, give or take, he could play the saxophone better than his brother could.'[2] Albert expressed similar opinions in his penultimate interview, with Japanese writer Kiyoshi Koyama: 'When he was thirteen he started playing alto … he could cook on that alto … he could outplay me on that alto. When it comes to playing that space sound.'[3] Several years later, with no desire to compete with his brother, Donald switched from sax to trumpet, an instrument he initially had little skill for.

Meanwhile, as Ayler's relationship with Carrie grew, he began taking an interest in clairvoyancy and became fascinated with a friend of Carrie's named Marilyn, who would use a crystal ball. Albert himself also started to have out-of-body experiences, as Carrie recalled:

> He would like just lay back and he always wanted to travel … Paris, Denmark, he used to mention these places … and he kinda had this thing about water. So, he would visualize that his body would be in those places and could describe things there—and he had never been there before. … The way he would do it … I think he actually did [leave his body].[4]

One explanation for Ayler's interest in psychic matters came from his one-time drummer Sunny Murray, who claimed that Albert had been born with a veil over his eyes. According to Murray, this caul (or afterbirth) had given him the gift of second sight. Another of Ayler's drummers, Milford Graves, also discussed this, telling Daniel Caux, a French journalist, musicologist, and producer:

> People can tell by his tunes … that he was very involved with this sort of spiritualism, and this spiritualism made him very understanding of himself. … He felt that as though he was communicating with a higher supreme being … and certain things did happen, you know, that he'd seen before they actually happened. … Lots of times we personally played, I can say that everything else sounded just like a spirit—no common form or shape—just all over the place. I mean Albert really mentally left Earth. … Albert didn't do this off no drugs. If he did, you know, I didn't know about it. For all my experiences, he did it off belief … and he only did it because he was trying to reach something through his music, you know, to convey a feeling in a person. It takes people away from just ordinary things they're hearing.[5]

In September 1957, Carrie fell pregnant, and the twenty-one-year-old Albert proposed in early 1958. His mother was not happy. Carrie recalled:

> His mom straight up told me that she wanted him to marry a girl like the girl next door. I was pregnant with Curtis, but I had a daughter that was two years old … And when his mother found out, I was standin' in the living room … she had a fit and that was that. … After I seen how they were, I just left 'cause I didn't have to go home to that.[6]

On April 7, Carrie filed a bastardy complaint against Albert in which she stated that she 'is now pregnant with a bastard child.' An arrest warrant was issued for Ayler two weeks later and served to him on April 30. At a preliminary examination, Ayler pled guilty to being the father of Carrie's unborn child and agreed to pay twenty dollars a week to the court, plus legal costs, with the first payment scheduled to be made on May 9. The warrant was recalled, but after Ayler missed his first payment, a second warrant was issued.

Curtis Darnell Roundtree was born June 28, 1958, at St Luke's Hospital in Cleveland. On July 18, Ayler was arrested at his parents' home; a month later, his parents posted a property bond of $500. On August 20, Ayler agreed to pay eight dollars a week child support, starting September 19, as well as covering $221.31 of maternity expenses accrued at St Luke's Hospital.

The day before his first support payment was due, Ayler signed up for the standard three-year enlistment in the US Army. His application described him as a brown-eyed, black-haired man, blood group B, sixty-six inches high, and weighing 138 and three-quarter pounds. There were, however, several omissions, with Albert claiming he had no dependents, and that his only arrest was for a speeding ticket issued in August 1957. Joining the armed forces was a typical escape for young men who had legal problems, but Albert told others such as Val Wilmer that he enlisted in order to get himself together. His friends said he was crazy, that he would die on a battlefield, but Albert saw an opportunity to make music with like-minded people in an institution some felt doubled as a national music school for Black musicians.

On September 27, Ayler arrived for induction at Fort Knox, Kentucky. He received specialized training in the code of conduct, the Geneva Convention, and survival training, and by October 23 he was qualified to use an M-1 rifle. By November 28 he'd completed two months of band practice, and on December 1 he advanced from basic combat training to advanced individual training.

The records state that Ayler was part of the Company A, 9th Battalion, United States Army Training Center Armor, and a photograph from the time places him in the #3 Training Regiment big band. Dated November 9, 1958, it's unusual because Ayler is the only Black band member, though Stanley Turrentine—later to find his own fame on tenor saxophone—was supposedly also in the band. Other future stars at Fort Knox were drummers Chuck Lampkin and Beaver Harris, and bassist Lewis Worrell. Almost immediately, the fashion-conscious Ayler impressed Harris with his red sports coat and Cuban-heeled shoes, as well as his advanced technique on his instrument. While on leave, Ayler played gigs in nearby Louisville, but his official band duties took up a lot of time. During breaks from playing concert music for seven hours a day, Albert practiced scales in an unusual manner, playing them fast and exploring trills and different progressions. As he had hoped, he received a complete musical education in the army, learning marches, classical and operetta arrangements, and dance music alongside the jazz he already knew.

It was here that Ayler also switched from alto to tenor sax, telling Nat Hentoff in a *DownBeat* interview, "It was at that time that I switched to tenor. It seemed to me that on the tenor you could get out all the feelings of the ghetto. On that horn you can shout and really tell the truth. After all, this music comes from the heart of America, the soul of the ghetto."[7] Ayler had, however, studied at a white school and lived in a middle-class neighborhood, and it is more likely that he simply liked the tenor because he had the embouchure to get a bigger sound from it. His style of playing also changed while he was stationed in Kentucky, with Beaver Harris recalling that he started out with more of a big, honky-tonk sound, but had begun to develop his more spiritual style of playing by the time the company made its first trip to Europe, in the spring of 1959.

From November 29, 1958, through March 3, 1959, Ayler was in the Special Training Regiment of Company E, and on March 4, he left Fort Knox for New York City, setting off from there to Europe. Immediately after arriving at Bremerhaven, on Germany's north coast, on March 21, he travelled onward to his ultimate destination, Orléans, in France. There he was assigned into the 76th Army Band, stationed at Coligny-Kaserne.

Already developing at a rapid pace, Ayler's style changed even more in Orléans, where he soaked up French military music along with cutting-edge jazz in the shape of Ornette Coleman's debut album, *Something Else!!!!* While playing with the band, however, Ayler suppressed his individuality. It was only while sitting in with friends that he allowed his true style to shine through, even while soloing on standard commercial fare such as 'Volare' and 'Bernie's Tune.' Along with bassist Lewis Worrell, Ayler was moving in the direction that Coleman had just begun to signpost. However, Ayler would never condescend to be a follower. Even at this early juncture, he understood that Coleman may have pointed the way, but there were many creative avenues to explore in the new neighborhood.[8]

As a lasting marker of his time in Orléans, the French national anthem, 'La Marseillaise,' reappears throughout Ayler's oeuvre, almost as a signature. The saxophonist never forgot how the military director led the 76th Army Band parade down the Champs-Élysées, in Paris, on Bastille Day, and he wrote letters home, recounting other formative experiences in France. His father later recalled:

> At the first time in the Army Band they were … supposed to play. He was smart. He didn't have his music, and the instructor told him: now, if you can't play this you're out of the army. And you know, he just played it. He just knew what to play. If he made a mistake he'd be kicked out of the army band. But he got it perfect.[9]

Ayler falsely claimed to have never learned to read music, but it would have been a mandatory part of his army training. Still, he cut a wayward figure: the band's commanding officer told the musicians that Ayler was insane and that they should stay away from him. But Ayler often jammed in the barracks with his closest friends—bassists Chalmer Adams and Lewis Worrell, and alto saxophonist Lucius White among them—and with some of the many combos that came by seeking gigs at the base's enlisted-men's clubs. According to Adams, the repertoire consisted of blues and popular tunes of the era, yet Ayler maintained his individualistic style. The self-taught musicians practiced together, and Ayler continued long into the night, exploring tones and changes in intensity, and exercising around a single sound as he pushed forward the possibilities of his instrument. Ayler's notion of focusing on sound had its genesis in a simple notion—return to the notes. He also began to be more influenced by John Coltrane, whom he witnessed in action with Miles Davis at the Paris Olympia March 21, 1960. He duly purchased a brand-new, top-of-the-line Selmer Mark VI sax after seeing Coltrane play one.

Even though Ayler had high artistic aspirations, contemporary witnesses have said his playing became more mannered. He made numerous appearances at various clubs in Orléans and Paris throughout 1959–61, sitting in with bands uninvited, but he lacked the musical etiquette to wait for his solo, much less attempt to fit his playing within the context of the group's style, or even the piece they were performing. It became a source of tension in the jazz scene: if the audiences were Black, Ayler incorporated idioms from Black popular music of the time—riffs from songs such as the R&B hit 'Night Train.' However, Paris attracted Ayler because he could play with musicians of a professional caliber in front of audiences largely made up of civilians, as opposed to GIs.

Ayler had hoped that a more cosmopolitan crowd would be more receptive to his burgeoning style, but critics who had heard free-form jazz in various incarnations, from early practitioners such as Sonny Rollins and Ornette Coleman, were not prepared to accept it from a newcomer. Audiences behaved in a similar manner. French journalist Daniel Berger heard Ayler in a GI club at Coligny-Kaserne in October 1960. Ayler played a long version of Sonny Rollins's 'Sonnymoon For Two,' accompanied by bassist Lewis Worrell and pianist Jean-Luc Vallet. The audience broke into laughter.

Despite this hostility, many of Ayler's fellow-GIs had fond memories of him and his talent. Tony Viscomi, also stationed in Orléans at this time, recalled how the saxophonist's individuality shone through during jam sessions in the different service clubs, even when they were playing jazz standards:

> When I met him, he was playing with a R&B band, and then they had all these jazz musicians in jam sessions on Sunday. … He lived upstairs in the barracks. Everybody called him 'Bop.' [Bassist] Leroy Vinnegar was playing in Paris, and he was playing down at the club with a piano player … but nobody

played but Bop. He came out of the kitchen with a green leather coat and Ray Charles-like sunglasses.

They would play records from Viscomi's collection, especially liking Coltrane (in particular his work on Cecil Taylor's *Stereo Drive*) and Coleman, while Ayler expressed a fascination with New York. Viscomi not only heard Ayler in the jam sessions, but also in rhythm'n'blues combos in which Ayler played pieces similar to those found on his final Impulse! albums. Viscomi remembered: 'It didn't matter what he played, it was different—he was always on the outside.'[10]

Drummer Jerry Webb recalled playing with Ayler in a combo called The New Yorkers, alongside bassist Fred Choice and Master Sergeant Sam Brown on piano. 'Bop'—or 'Bop-Daddy'—was very popular, and he made a number of other friends among his fellow GIs, Charles W. Taylor and Jorge Thompson among them. Thompson in particular remembered Ayler playing in an avant-garde style at this time.

Besides playing in the Bastille Day parades, the 76th Band toured France and Germany from June through September 1960. When the band returned, they recorded a rehearsal that now provides evidence of Ayler's style in the early 60s. Dated September 14, the tape captures Ayler soloing on 'Leap Frog' and 'Tenderly'—(recordings that would not surface again until the release of Revenant's *Holy Ghost* box set). In the *Village Voice*, Francis Davis described the two selections as the 'sweetest of flashbacks … he isn't himself yet. The lurching, operatic vibrato isn't there, and neither is the altissimo speaking-in-tongues. He's GI Joe Cool, breezy and efficient and not yet tragic.'[11]

Ayler took occasional leaves to further explore Europe musically. On one trip he travelled to Stockholm, where he sat in on a jam session; on another he went to Spain, where he bought three leather suits, establishing the look that would become his trademark. Clarinetist Perry Robinson recalled Ayler sitting in with the house band at the Jamboree Club in Barcelona. The group consisted of Robinson, pianist Tete Montoliu, tenor saxophonist Vicho Vicencio, drummer Luis Sangareau, and bassist Antonio

Vidal. Ayler borrowed Vicencio's sax, unleashing a big-band sound as the group began with 'All The Things You Are.' Some audience members got up and left, while Robinson and his bandmates freaked out. Ayler hung out with them for the next few days, talking to them about Ornette Coleman and asserting, 'I have something original to say as well, as I have my own thing and I'm going to do something special.'[12] Neither disparaging nor being egotistical, Albert was simply sure of his place in the jazz pantheon.

Ayler's path was, however, unusual—the avant-garde offered many different paths while other saxophonists were still looking to bop and other jazz forms for inspiration, some slavishly imitating the likes of Charlie Parker. However, Ayler found enough sympathetic ears to validate his new sound, among them German saxophonist Peter Brötzmann, who played with Ayler during this period, in a session at a Heidelberg club (Brötzmann himself would develop a style of extraordinarily powerful tenor playing, obviously influenced by Ayler).

Ayler also performed with saxophonist Roscoe Mitchell, of future Art Ensemble Of Chicago fame, who was also in a different branch of the army band. Mitchell recalled the occasion as if it were an epiphany: 'I was stationed in Heidelberg, Germany, and there was a club there called the Cave … but at this one session, Albert led off with three or four choruses of the blues and then went off into his own thing, with that awesome sound he had, and everything became clear to me.'[13]

Toward the end of his time on leave in Copenhagen, Ayler played a divisive version of Art Blakey's 'Moanin'' that elicited different reactions— some hated it; some respected it; some considered it too far out for their tastes. Jazz writer Marc Chaloin, in an essay included in the *Holy Ghost* box set, noted that the audience's restraint may have later convinced Ayler to travel to Scandinavia; on another leave of absence, Ayler visited Sweden, and was greatly impressed by the way audiences accepted his inner self, as expressed in his music. He felt that Sweden offered a home where he could formulate his ideas and not face the possibility of rejection.

•

Ayler's tour of duty in Europe ended on February 13, 1961. It took him two months to travel home to the US, but finally, on April 13, 1961, he arrived at Fort Ord, California, to play in the 52nd Army Concert Band. There he met Harold Budd, who later gained fame as a minimalist composer. Budd and Ayler played in the marching band, which performed weekly radio broadcasts. They also hung out in the hip jazz clubs of Monterey and Oakland; someone in California was impressed enough to give Albert a silver soprano sax that he brought back with him to Cleveland.

Ayler was discharged from the regular army in California on September 15, 1961, but he would have to remain in the reserves for an additional three years; Fort Hayes, Ohio, being his home base. Army life seemed to have agreed with him—so much so that his only problems seemed to be dental. He had received a marksman qualification on the M-1 at Fort Knox, and a sharpshooter qualification on the Carbine, while he was stationed in France in 1960. Ayler also came out a bit heavier, weighing 152 pounds.

Newly discharged, Albert struggled in Los Angeles, where the cool Californians were less receptive to his recasting of gospel into the harmonies and rhythms of free jazz. However, comic Redd Foxx, who had gained a reputation in the Black community for his controversial, cutting-edge humor, encouraged Ayler to continue following his path. Like Foxx's jokes, Albert's style was new to some, though it was maturing every time he played.

Albert returned to Cleveland for a bit, staying with his parents at their new home at 2978 Ripley Road. His sharp dress—those leather suits from Spain; a Cossack-style Russian hat—took on a new aura when he returned to the old neighborhood, and was topped off by Ayler's newly acquired habit of smoking, something he'd been against until he picked it up in the army; his brand of choice was Kool.

Inevitably, he also started hitting the local bars and participating in jam sessions. Musician and jazz scholar Bill Cole could have been describing the Cleveland clubs Ayler frequented when he writes about a Detroit club in the 50s that played host to a fledgling John Coltrane:

It was a place where minors were almost openly served alcohol, where drugs were passed between peddler and user without anyone so much as blinking an eye, and where 'ladies' were always around—and more than willing to be picked up. Most of the women who visited this bar were underage and were interested in musicians that were playing. So there was a lot going on besides the music itself.[14]

Guitarist Jimmy Landers, who by now headed the house band at Gleason's, recalled the time when Leo's Casino could still be found on Central Avenue. Everybody, including Albert, played at the clubs on Central. Bobby Few recalled: 'Albert had a thing where he wouldn't tune up his horn like other horn players do. They tune up in B-flat. He would just put his mouthpiece on and go—and it worked.'[15] However, his new style met derision on the local scene. Lloyd Pearson, who'd enlisted Albert for his Counts Of Rhythm, in the early 50s, at first hearing, thought Ayler was rusty, wondering if hadn't even touched his horn while he was in the army. But while audiences laughed at his new style, Pearson hid his shock, even letting Ayler lead his band at a few gigs. And yet, the way Albert played spirituals disturbed him and dampened the spirits of his audiences. Soon enough, Albert was banned from the 100 Club at 10020 Euclid (sometimes misidentified as the Esquire). He was supposedly ejected from the bandstand by another avant-garde evangelist, Rahsaan Roland Kirk, in 1961.[16]

Mutawaf Shaheed, a friend of Donald Ayler, remembered those days and the various clubs they used to frequent when he was known as Clyde Shy, such as the Tangiers on Kinsman; the House Of Blues; Cleo's; the Kabongo Village on 105th and Quincy; and the Dome Club, also on Quincy—Albert frequented. A lot of jam sessions were also held at musicians' homes and apartments, and Albert often jammed with Clyde at Shy's apartment on 105th and Elk, down near the Dupont Loop.

Ayler told his brother that he was thrown out all over because people did not understand him. After one notorious jam, he was no longer welcome to sit in with Joe Alexander at the 100 Club. Cleveland's top saxophonist,

Alexander was not happy when Albert refused to play the chord changes, and later insisted to Coltrane it was impossible to play a soprano sax in that manner. Coltrane simply responded that Ayler had done so.

Pearson believed Ayler's deep connections to God and religion is part of what made him sound so strange: his huge tone impressed listeners, but his divergence from the melody line caused people to question his talent.

Howard Johnson, a fellow Ohio musician, related such a story to Peter Niklas Wilson about a November 1961 jam session which likely took place at the Loop Lounge. Johnson sat in with members of a band, who were impressed when Ayler walked in with his leather outfit and matching leather saxophone case at odds with the wooden cases most other saxophonists used. Johnson had heard warnings about Ayler, but the band respected him because he had played in Europe. The group began 'Green Dolphin Street,' and Johnson was immediately impressed with Ayler's loud tone and metal mouthpiece, noting that Ayler played unbelievably fast, with the speed of machine-gun fire. He seemed lost in his own world, his eyes rolled back so that only the whites were visible.

Ayler began moving to the edge of the stage with tiny steps, until only his heels were onstage, the points of his Stacy Adams—the 'it' shoe for Black gentlemen of a certain generation—hanging over the edge. Playing unbelievably loud, Ayler almost drowned out the rest of the band until the rhythm section came to a stop, leaving Ayler playing alone. Possibly thinking they had taken a break, Ayler launched into a chorus; the rest of the band thought he had not rehearsed and was playing a joke on them. Remembering how good he was before he joined the army, the band simply thought that Ayler had lost his touch.

Yet Ayler was searching for the freedom of a soul's release; his father felt his son's army years had not only changed him musically, but also spiritually. Speaking to Val Wilmer, one of his earliest champions, Ayler said:

I always had thought of free music, even when I was still small. I'd be playing a ballad and my father would say, 'Get back to the melody, stop playing that nonsense!' But I knew there was something there. I'd be standing in a corner playing and trying to communicate with a spirit that I knew nothing about at that particular age.[17]

But what was Ayler trying to communicate? He had loving parents who would always let him return home to work on new music if he was in financial trouble. He had a magnificent talent, too, but it seems not to have been enough. After Christmas, he left Cleveland. On February 10, 1962, he travelled to New York, where he crashed with bassist Lewis Worrell, a buddy from the army. Sometime in February or March, Albert sat in at the Village Gate with Thelonious Monk, a pianist whose own radical music had startled the jazz cognoscenti the previous decade. Shortly afterward, he flew to Sweden, a country where he always felt at home.

scandinavia

Ayler arrived in Sweden on Good Friday, April 20, 1962. The country had appealed to him ever since he'd played there with the army band; he still had fond memories of its friendly atmosphere, and he desired to live in a place where artists were accepted for what they were.

In one interview, Ayler said his mother had suggested the move; however, he gave a radically different explanation to French journalist Daniel Caux in what would be his final interview, in 1970. In this telling, he claimed his mother tried to dissuade him from going overseas because she needed him at home. And yet the urge to find people who would understand him and his music, as well as to continue his own self-discovery, compelled him to go. The search for receptive audiences would occupy him throughout the remaining eight years of his life.

Ayler's first live performance in Sweden was at the Jazz Jamboree in Gamla Stan, Stockholm's Old Town. Admission was 50 kroner per person, and Ayler blasted and blew. Initially, though, he found Swedish audiences to be as unhip as those he'd left behind in Cleveland. As overseas musicians often did, he enrolled in a Swedish institute called the Folk Paks and played typical commercial gigs in small towns—routine affairs that saw him performing for dancing couples. Ayler attempted to go all out and received friendly admonishment from his bandmates: don't play complex music at a dance. In retrospect, he had misjudged Sweden. According to

Marc Chaloin, the Swedes were not necessarily receptive to his music; rather, they were too tolerant to openly boo a musician playing something off the beaten path.

At the Bobadilla Club in Gamla Stan, Ayler joined bassist Bill Houston's group. There, in May or possibly June, he met Anna-Britta Westerman, the vocalist who became his girlfriend. He also joined various jam sessions that became scenes of controversy. Prior to his arrival in Stockholm, there had been a clash of styles between younger musicians who embraced modernist styles and an older generation of traditionalists. Unfortunately, Ayler alienated both parties by joining in jam sessions without any regard for their underlying stylistic ideologies.

In late June, while still part of Houston's group, Ayler played at a club in Vasa, Finland. Around this time, he made the acquaintance of Finnish guitarist Herbert Katz. A heavily respected figure since the late 40s, Katz had been influenced by the godfathers of jazz guitar, Eddie Lang and Charlie Christian, and often assembled backing bands for visiting musicians. Under Katz's leadership, Ayler made his first Scandinavian recording session, along with some July gigs in Helsinki, and the main selling point was that Ayler was Black. On June 30, 1962, he entered Yleisradio Studio 2 in the Finnish capital, as part of the Herbert Katz Quintet. Though the guitarist led the session, Ayler chose the tunes, settling on those he was familiar with, such as 'On Green Dolphin Street,' 'Summertime,' and 'Sonnymoon For Two.' Perhaps inevitably, however, he strayed from the tunes so that only the contours remained, though he started and finished each chorus at the correct time. Ayler later admitted that he disliked playing commercial music such as calypsos and would rather have been playing music for a younger crowd.

While in Helsinki, Ayler reconnected with the clarinetist Perry Robinson, whom he'd met during one of his army leaves within Europe. Robinson was on the bill at the World Youth Festival of late July/early August, playing in a group with saxophonist Archie Shepp, trumpeter Bill Dixon, bassist Don Moore, and drummer Howard McRae. After the festival, Robinson and his group (minus Shepp, who had gone on to

Russia) went to Stockholm and got some gigs in Gamla Stan. Things were beginning to change, and audiences were becoming more receptive to the new style of music that Ayler was developing. According to Don, they used to call him 'the orchestra.'

The change didn't happen overnight: in a replay of scenes from Cleveland, one Stockholm promoter pulled Ayler off the stage; he wound up playing in the subway for children who would appreciate his music. Two years later, in 1964, Danish critic Boris Rabinowitsch of the *OrkesterJournalen* remembered that, though Ayler was well known in Swedish music circles, he was considered too far out to be of any value. One of Rabinowitsch's colleagues, Dick Idestam-Almquist, said that jazz fans considered Ayler crazy because his free playing ignored the rules that they held dear.

Nevertheless, Ayler made appearances at the Nalen, *the* place for jazz musicians to play in 60s Stockholm. Nalen's legendary jam sessions were held in a side room called Harlem and were tightly restricted—hopeful participants had to apply in advance. However, Ayler was apparently given special treatment because he was American, so he may have been able to bypass the application process. He claimed to have played there a few times before being pulled off the stage, but he also may have exaggerated the incident when he told others about it.

Most importantly, Ayler made the acquaintance of several Swedish musicians and fans, among them Bengt Nordström—who, by a strange coincidence, shared Ayler's birthday. An individualist in the Swedish jazz scene, Nordström was not beholden to the bebop tradition. Even though he had come up as a clarinetist in a traditional jazz group, Nordström was open to the new sounds as exemplified by Sonny Rollins and Ornette Coleman—he even played a white plastic alto, as Coleman did, and, in 1959, had shared Nalen's stage with Rollins on a rendition of 'St Thomas.' Nordström was a major supporter of new music and, in particular, Ayler. He also came from a wealthy family and had money to indulge his hobby, launching his own private record label, Bird Notes, from his living room.

Everyone was aware of Nordström—he could be found wherever music was played. Known as 'Frippe' to the jazz community, he was a fantastic listener, and he often climbed onto the stage and tried to play with groups. Normally, most of the musicians walked off, leaving him to play alone. Like Ayler, Frippe was often refused entry by some club owners, but he showed Ayler around Stockholm's various venues, among them the Gyllene Cirkeln (Golden Circle), a new club that welcomed both avant-garde and traditional musicians. Ayler first played there around September 1962. That evening, clarinetist Gunnar 'Silja-Bloo' Nilsson was playing; his drummer, Sune Spångberg, had yet to arrive, and someone else was sitting in for him. Frippe saw an opportunity for Ayler to play with two musicians who would be attuned to his style, so he persuaded Ayler to bring his sax to the club.

According to photographer Nils Edström, Ayler was everything Frippe had promised:

> He more or less shot out of his saxophone. Not only sideways like this famous Lester Young position, but he would turn it upwards and at the same time, I'm not going to say he twisted and turned, fawning and bowing, that would be nasty. But he saw to it that the sound roared out in all directions, from the acoustic aperture outlets of the saxophone as well as from the sides and the bell itself, and the mouthpiece, too.[1]

As was his custom, Ayler ignored the tunes and instead focused on the sound, described by Edström as 'a raw blast coming from nothingness via the primeval backwoods and forests.' It was probably the first time those in attendance had heard music at that volume, as Ayler played through the falsetto register, utilizing pedal tones and dirty effects on his horn. The band was playing a jazz standard when Ayler joined them—eventually, he was alone onstage, Frippe shouting encouragement from the floor.

Word of Ayler's appearance spread throughout Stockholm's jazz community, and those who heard about it secondhand considered it an embarrassment. Again, people questioned whether Ayler, whose soft-spoken manner was at odds with his sound, could even play. They had failed to see that he was still working within the cycle of fifths, but in a different way. The controversy provided Nordström with a golden opportunity to publicize Ayler as a radical alternative to what passed for jazz in Stockholm in 1962.

Within a week of that appearance, Frippe took Ayler to Nils Edström's photography studio for a shoot that would provide the cover of Ayler's debut album. The photos were taken in a park near the public library, Edström using a flash in his attempt to capture Ayler's lightning that grey, rainy morning.

Frippe had to cajole Ayler into recording his music. Though he did not feel ready, Ayler agreed to step in for saxophonist Bernt Rosengren, who had to pull out of a booking at Stockholm's Academy Of Music, on October 25. Frippe purchased a Revox G36 tape recorder—a rare and expensive item at the time—and captured Ayler as he led Rosengren's bassist Torbjorn Hultcrantz and drummer Sune Spångberg through the session in the academy's Main Hall. The recording is almost stripped bare: lacking a harmonic instrument, Ayler focuses on variations of the melody, drifting in and out of tempo. The influence of Ornette Coleman's early recordings is evident (indeed, the album would be called *Something Different!!!!!*, its fifth exclamation mark upping the ante on Coleman's debut, *Something Else!!!!*), yet the style is distinctly Ayler's. He focuses hypnotically on individual motifs so that they break up into individual parts.

Spångberg had met Ayler at the Gyllene Cirkeln. He recalled:

> The hall where we played was desolate and empty, with an echoey acoustic. Passers by peered in curiously from time to time, but for the most part, they soon disappeared elsewhere in the building, to where there was music that was more danceable and easier to listen to. One exuberantly intoxicated jazz fan did manage to hold out through the entire proceedings, singing and yelling, and whistling ecstatically.[2]

There was no advance planning, and the trio played standards that were familiar to most jazz musicians. Spångberg felt like they were flying, yet Ayler's playing remained close to the ground:

And all played with a big sound that was mature and ruggedly roughhewn, but also with a glistening saxophone sound that was rich with overtones and filled with expression, like a living being. He was a preacher on fire! His sermon simultaneously a challenge and an act of love. Audacious phrasing and capricious rhythmic groupings, often with unexpected leaps and displacements, made it so that the form itself was broken up to float in suspension. Ayler moved with superb freedom in a music that was transparent and seemingly without bar lines. What deliverance and release to yield to all this, as a participant! Like being lifted up high and empowered to discern unending possibilities! A spontaneous and unhesitating flood of inspiration, at the same time conscious and unconscious. Like a blessed gift of grace—it isn't I who is playing—I allow myself to be played.[3]

Lars Werner reviewed *Something Different!!!!!* in the February 1963 issue of *OrkesterJournalen*, writing:

The musical development in his playing almost exclusively appears to be limited to tonal aspects. In this sense his approach to melodies plays no role, and the rhythm is very common and does not appear very interesting in this study. … Yet Ayler has much to do about his rampant wildness and to restrain rough experiments. He has a fondness for voiced sound effects to which he always returns. The first few times it is very cool to hear it, yet on repeated listening it is meaningless. I believe in every case it is something in Ayler. He has a fresh and uninhibited manner in presenting his music. He believes in what he does, and in the different noises and sounds that he transforms, and that is certainly not easy to produce. It gives much to discover in a tenor saxophone.[4]

Even though later critics, such as Jeff Schwartz, would note Ayler's poor interaction with his bandmates, the recordings seem to have captured a typical Ayler performance of that time. Rosengren's sidemen were seasoned musicians who knew how to follow: they had been the house band at the Gyllene Cirkeln, and they had backed bebop pianist Bud Powell on live albums recorded there. They also had been members of a Swedish band that had released an album in the US in 1960, and bassist Hultcrantz later became a member of Don Cherry's Swedish-Turkish group. Rather than struggle with Ayler's sound, they likely knew enough to stay out of his way, as Richard Cook later noted: 'Not called on to keep time, Hultcrantz and Spångberg occasionally resort to marking it, but they seem mostly unfazed by Ayler's primitivism.'[5]

In his analysis, German musicologist Ekkehard Jost felt the framework of the rhythm and Ayler's defamation of standards to be so dramatically opposed that the results sound absurd; in attempting to escape the rigidity of the material, Ayler distances himself as far as possible from the tunes through melodic distortion. Though Ornette Coleman, through deviations from fixed intervals, had done this earlier, Ayler's style is more to the point—he totally negates pitch relationships.[6]

A better assessment is that Ayler was only slightly removed from the Euclid Avenue jazz clubs that had expelled him. His style was still developing—as he later told Kiyoshi Koyama, he was treating sound as space. At the time *Something Different!!!!!* was released, he explained, 'Free music is a new blues, the new truth as seen by musicians who want to take a modernistic view … geometric shapes and forms conveyed musically.'[7] Other characteristics that first appear here and continue to be found throughout Ayler's work are his hard, gigantic tone and fragmentary phrasing.

There might have even been another explanation for Ayler's explosive playing. As the recording took place, the Cuban missile crisis held a terrifying grip on the world: everything could end in a blaze of nuclear fury. What must have been going through his mind as he thought of all his relatives and friends facing the threat of imminent annihilation?

•

Released in early 1963, *Something Different!!!!!* was not intended for public distribution. Privately pressed on Frippe's Bird Notes label (as BNLP 1), Ayler received fifty copies of the album, which he later sold on Cleveland street corners. An original copy sold for $3,950.53 on discogs.com in 2021. The album was given a wider commercial release in 1969, when it was reissued by Sonet Records as *The First Recordings*. At that time, critics compared it to contemporaneous jazz releases—or, even worse, to Ayler's own recordings of the era—rather than listening to it in the context of the time it was recorded. If approached as a product of its era, *Something Different!!!!!* demands to be rescued from the stiffs bin of history.

By playing standards, Ayler stayed close to his roots: opening the album, 'I'll Remember April' comes from the bop canon, as placed there by Charlie Parker's late-40s recording. Reviewing *The First Recordings* in 1970, *Jazz Monthly*'s Brian Priestley gave this cut faint praise, writing, 'the best part of the album is the five minutes following the last recapitulation of "April," a long cadenza, stringing together a fantastic collection of rhythmic cliches and half-remembered melodies.'[8] For Cook, the tune emerges 'virtually unrecognizable.'[9] Critic John Litweiler, in his book *The Freedom Principle: Jazz After 1958*, describes the recording as 'amazing and perverse' because Ayler's 'pitch is so imprecise that the themes he plays … are recognizable only from their rhythmic configurations—definitely not from any melodic features. His discontinuous phrasing is short, blunt, and bop-shaped.'[10]

And yet the form and harmony of the theme are irrelevant here— the primary focus of Ayler's improvisation is the rhythm. On a more positive note, Litweiler found that Ayler's 'huge tenor sound' was 'full of resonance, split tones, overtones, R&B techniques come to madness.'[11] Ayler's characteristic sound is, however, present at this beginning: that is, intonation, interpretive style, melodic line distortion, and the individualistic vibrato.

The second cut, 'Rollins' Tune' (a take on Sonny Rollins's 1953 composition 'No Moe'), is likely a repertory staple. Again, Priestley was somewhat sarcastic in his review:

> Albert comes in at the wrong place in bar 24, having been thrown by the simple but stodgy beat of his accompanists, and with great uncertainty—sorry, magnanimity—he twice adjusts his phrasing to theirs. The other thing is the clear derivation of his whole style from Rollins (minus Rollins's sense of time, of course), even down to some of the vocabulary and the approach to quotation.[12]

It is parodied by the phrases taken in an uncommonly slow tempo.[13]

Something Different!!!!! also contains 'Tune-Up,' an early Miles Davis composition. Like 'April,' it is notable for its interesting chord progressions. For this reason, 'Tune-Up' shares with the previous songs a rapid tempo that challenges the player to make the changes. The album's closing piece, 'Free,' differs because it lacks the tension generated in the others by their underlying harmonic structure. Writing in *Albert Ayler: His Life And Music*, Jeff Schwartz felt this composition to be a 'false clue' because it focuses on Ayler's improvisational abilities through his virtuoso timbre rather than his compositional abilities.[14] Other writers disagree, among them critic Barry McRae, who wrote:

> Due to the unyielding rhythmic support, Ayler makes a greater number of thematic references than usual. Even on 'Free,' which lives up to its name, the opening motif serves as a starting point for every new idea, if not at first hand, at least as an extension of an earlier variation. This was the essence of his style.[15]

On 'Free,' Ayler plays a Middle Eastern-inspired melody—a possible signpost toward his later explorations of folklore—the likes of which also appears in 'I Didn't Know What Time It Was,' a Rodgers & Hart composition (from the musical *Too Many Girls*) recorded at the same October 25 session, alongside three more selections that later received a release on *The First Recordings Vol. 2*. Writing in *Cadence*, Scott Yanow noted traces of Rollins's style in Ayler's playing when he reviewed the second volume, stating, 'There is an abstract connection between his tenor playing at this early date ... and Sonny Rollins that would not be apparent at all on Ayler's later recordings.'[16]

Of the second batch of songs, 'I Didn't Know What Time It Was,' along with a take on pianist and one-time Clevelander Tadd Dameron's 'Good Bait' and Sigmund Romberg's 'Softly As In A Morning Sunrise,' from the musical *New Moon*, originally only made it as far as the test-pressing stage—five to ten copies on Bird Notes (BNLP 2)—leading to a confusion that was finally cleared up by Mats Gustafsson. Despite Bengt

Nordström's denials that a second collection had been released, a 1989 discography listed the record, and the error was subsequently perpetuated. A third volume, identical to the second but with the addition of 'Moanin',' also received a test pressing; it was not until Japanese label DIW issued *The First Recordings Vol. 2* in 1990 that these four recordings received an official release.

The entire session was a radical departure from what was then considered jazz, but many critics have felt these initial recordings fail to capture what Ayler was capable of. Reviewing the CD reissue of the Sonet collection in 1991, Barry McRae, writing in *Jazz Journal International*, observed:

> Unfortunately, Ayler's first recording does not quite live up to expectations. The essence of his style is on show but at times he lapses into over-romanticism and throughout he is hampered by some sadly inappropriate drumming. The upside is that this album allows an easier examination of his improvisational methods than the more finished recordings.[17]

Yanow came to nearly the same conclusion:

> This music is neither conservative nor accessible. A major problem is that neither ... Hultcrantz [nor] Spångberg seem to have the slightest idea what to play behind Ayler's advanced explorations, and there is very little musical communication of any kind. ... Ayler plays well enough ... [the] value is much more significant historically than musically.[18]

Until *Something Different!!!!!*, Ornette Coleman was considered to be working on the furthermost reaches of jazz, but Ayler's debut surpassed Coleman's in its departure from tradition. Schwartz viewed this through Ayler's rejection of the bebop aesthetic, which focuses on medium rather than rapid tempos. The architects of bebop denied harmony by utilizing a stream-of-consciousness style of playing, focusing on the 'hook' of the song and then elaborating upon it through improvisatory free association. Yet other listeners have noted that jazz tradition remained present in the wide vibrato of Ayler's gospel phrasing, as well as in the selection of standards he recorded. Albert's exaggerated vibrato can be considered a legacy from Sidney Bechet, a clarinetist whose popularity dates from the Roaring Twenties.

•

Sometime between October 14 and 27, Ayler revisited the Gyllene Cirkeln in the company of his Swedish girlfriend to see Cecil Taylor. The pianist's band lacked a bassist to provide a harmonic function, while his drummer eschewed the traditional role of timekeeper. Ayler was impressed by the way Taylor ignored the old concepts of solos and rhythms: Taylor's notion was that the melody contained enough rhythm and energy to stabilize the music and move it forward. Because of this, the drums could elaborate on the melody while other soloists improvised on those elaborations—that is, each instrument could perform melodic and rhythmic roles, timekeeping losing its importance amid the flow of continuous energy.

In an interview for *Paris Transatlantic* magazine, Taylor's drummer Sunny (né James) Murray told Dan Warburton how Albert Ayler first came to jam with Taylor's group. While playing in the free idiom, Murray and alto saxophonist Jimmy Lyons left the bandstand and approached Ayler, who was wearing a leather suit and had brought his brand-new Selmer sax to the club. Ayler told them they were the kind of musicians he had been looking for, and asked to sit in with them. Lyons had to ask Taylor, who was very particular. Taylor refused his request. Murray, however, told Ayler to join them on the bandstand anyway. As the audience ate their meals, oblivious to what was happening onstage, Taylor, Murray, and Lyons fitted into what Ayler played. Though Ayler and Taylor were reticent at first, the two began talking. As Murray recalled, 'Cecil started to laugh and said, "What is *that* shit you're playing?"'[19]

History is divided over whether this incident happened in Sweden or Denmark. Bengt Nordström was at the Gyllene Cirkeln on October 27, the final night of Taylor's residency at the venue, and told Nils Edström about it, but it was at the Jazzhus Montmartre, in Copenhagen, that Ayler became a member of the group. Ayler had followed Taylor to Denmark in the hopes of joining the group, but Taylor, though impressed with Ayler's playing, kept his feelings to himself—likely because of the limited pay his band was receiving. It was Taylor's style to keep people—bandmates included—at a distance, but he did have a lot of respect for Ayler; he recalled that Ayler could play anything, even imitating Sonny Rollins to the point that Taylor could not tell the difference.

Donald Ayler later explained the tremendous influence Taylor had on his brother: 'He taught him forms, shapes and forms on the instrument.'[20] The pieces they played together can probably be deduced from the track listing on Taylor's album *Nefertiti, The Beautiful One Has Come*, recorded live in Copenhagen in November 1962, and the Ingo label's release *The Early Unit 1962*. They also played the Swedish folk song 'Den Bloomstertid Nu Kommer.' Ayler's apprenticeship came at a price, however, as these gigs were marathon performances under less than ideal conditions—Taylor would think nothing of holding four-hour sessions, which took their toll on Murray in particular.

This line-up's only documented appearance—which unfortunately has not survived in its video incarnation—occurred on the Danish television station TV Byen on November 16, 1962; Ayler was still an unofficial member of the group at the time, so he was not compensated for his performance. According to Taylor, Ayler officially became part of the group during this broadcast. In celebration of his eighty-third birthday, Taylor told *JazzTimes* that Ayler had claimed to be the best saxophonist Taylor had ever heard—but Taylor was not interested in the best; he needed to know how his musicians' music would fit into his style. When the show's recording engineers told Ayler he could not be part of the performance, Taylor insisted that Albert was part of the band.

Murray was very close to Ayler, and the pair were often in each other's company. Until Albert found a girlfriend he could live with, he survived by crashing with Sunny. They would run and race together in the parks, and go to the bakery for Danish pastries. Along with Lyons (but not their bandleader), the musicians would hit the local jazz scenes and participate in jam sessions; the drummer would later note a connection between Ayler's personal charm and the eroticism of his playing. Despite their closeness, however, Ayler's largely apolitical stance sometimes set him apart—he could not, for instance, fathom Murray's Marxist girlfriend.

Ayler continued to find other outlets for his music. Danish saxophonist John Tchicai, who would play alongside Ayler in the summer of 1964, on the score for a short film called *New York Eye And Ear Control*, remembered sessions at the Jazzhus Montmartre and at a bar called Vingården, on Nicolai Platz, where they would sit in on Sunday afternoons. These Sunday sessions often featured baritone saxophonist Max Brüel, pianist Niels Brønsted, bassists Benny Nielsen and Lars Malther, and drummer Jørn Elniff, and the bop standards they played together differed from the usual Dixieland fare usually performed at the bar. Tchicai also recalled that Ayler talked about the religious basis of his music. The influence of Liberty Hill Baptist Church could always be heard in his playing, whether in the spiritual 'When The Saints Go Marching In' or in his own composition 'Ghosts.'

As ever, Ayler's powerful sound astonished the participants, though he also polarized the Danish musicians who, like most of the audiences he had encountered so far in his career, were either enthusiastic or antagonistic toward his playing. Though the likes of Archie Shepp and Bill Dixon had toured there in the summer of 1962, and Cecil Taylor had staged his earlier engagement at the Jazzhus Montmartre that fall, Scandinavians had had less exposure to jazz's latest developments than the Americans who rejected Ayler and his fellow travelers in the free-jazz movement.

The Danish engagement came to an end, but despite the arrangement settled upon during the November 16 broadcast, Cecil Taylor had yet to extend to Ayler a formal job offer. His group returned to Sweden, where they had a gig at the Erikslust, in Malmö, on November 26, but it is doubtful that Ayler played that evening. As 1962 rolled into 1963, he scored a gig with Texas blues pianist Candy Green, earning himself two meals at a restaurant called the Don Pedro in Gothenberg. But he was hungry for more: his future lay in America, playing with Taylor.

my name
is albert ayler

As Cecil Taylor's group left for New York, Ayler returned to Copenhagen, where his second album resulted from an appearance on Danmarks Radio's *Jazz '63* show on January 14, 1963. Ayler had hoped to have Taylor's group as his band, but scheduling problems prevented this. Instead, he was backed by two Danes—pianist Niels Brønsted, bassist Niels-Henning Ørsted Pedersen—and the American drummer Ronnie Gardner.

For this studio broadcast, Ayler recorded what would be his first album intended for public release, a scant nine weeks after the Stockholm recordings that had resulted in *Something Different!!!!!* As *DownBeat's* Bill Mathieu described it, the album became a 'planned, perverse irony' in which Ayler's attempts to break free from the bebop tradition were stifled.[1] This was because Brønsted set the mood for the session, and, as a result, the rigidity of the increasingly antiquated bebop sound, focusing on what Jeff Schwartz calls 'neat centered comping,' overwhelmed the saxophonist.[2]

Writing about the recordings three years later, poet, critic, and essayist Amiri Baraka praised the 'surprisingly good' rhythm section, noting:

> Albert's work on soprano is almost as valuable as his work on tenor. ... The bassist, Niels-Henning Ørsted Pedersen, shows up very well on this album ...

his playing on 'C.T.' is very fine (Ayler's fantastic). But the entire group had some strong empathy for Ayler, whose mad runs, and huge exploding sound, sound even wilder with a listening rhythm section.[3]

Released in 1964 as *My Name Is Albert Ayler* (and under the title *Free Jazz* in France), the album opens with a spoken-word introduction by Ayler and includes four more traditional standards—'Bye Bye Blackbird,' 'Billie's Bounce,' 'Summertime,' and 'On Green Dolphin Street'—as well as 'C.T.,' an original composition named for Cecil Taylor that lacked a main theme. Like its predecessor, *My Name Is Albert Ayler* utilizes hard-bop idioms that Ayler inserts into improvisations as if they are out-of-context quotations, as on 'Billie's Bounce,' on which each twelve-bar chorus begins with a melodic figure that quickly becomes fragmented when, as Ekkehard Jost put it, 'cliches' are played against the harmonic foundation.[4]

Reviewers such as Terry Martin, writing in *Jazz Monthly*, failed to see what Ayler was trying to accomplish:

'Billie's' theme gets a rather brusque dismissal and the accompaniment who seems to think it knows how the piece *should* be played is at its worst. Ayler makes one step towards appeasement—he blows a 'High Society' quote (after Bird)—then continues with some catching blues fragments though never really evolving a unified structure.[5]

Martin noted the same stylistic idioms in 'On Green Dolphin Street,' stating that the song 'is similarly compromised by the clash of personality, but the contrast between the tenor's distant but suggestive references to the progression and the pianist's grim orthodoxy is illuminating. There's an entirely acceptable arco bass contribution and Albert throws in an Ornette Coleman quote to round things off.'[6] On the other hand, the absurd dichotomy of Ayler and the rhythm section works to his benefit in a composition like 'C.T.,' just as it did on *Something Different!!!!!*'s 'Free.' Here, the melodic line is broken through short flourishes, isolated staccato tones, and wide-ranging leaps. Slurs connect the tones, and these slurs form sound spans which allow the overall context to benefit from Ayler's explorations. The musical communication between Ayler and his rhythm section is strong—as a result, 'C.T.' transcends stylistic differences as well as time.

Still impressive to Amiri Baraka's ears in 1966, Ayler's playing was radical for 1963. 'C.T.' marked the first time that he stepped into improvisational territory that lacked any structural harmony, meter, or form. The tune opens with a call and response in which Ørsted Pedersen and Gardiner respond to Ayler's opening declamation. Then a metrically unconnected passage alternates with a pulsating passage.

In *DownBeat*, reviewer Bill Mathieu (himself a composer and arranger whose works were performed by the Duke Ellington and Stan Kenton orchestras) declared that this cut alone made *My Name Is Albert Ayler* more than a historical curiosity.[7] Terry Martin, however, found fault with it:

> One or two Coleman passages also crop up on 'C.T.' … and the only nominally *free* performance included (one wonders if the pianist refused to play). The item is full of interest even though the drummer is completely out of his depth and makes a lot of noise drowning. Pedersen, who is a sensitive bassist and who acts throughout as if he is at least not openly against the main soloist, is understandably less than perfect here, drawing too heavily on flamenco cliche.[8]

Though the response to the album was mixed, each reviewer identified a different masterpiece within it. For some it was 'C.T.'; others highlighted 'Summertime.' In his landmark analysis over four issues of *Jazz Monthly*, critic and musicologist W.A. Baldwin called *My Name Is Albert Ayler* the 'weakest of Ayler's recordings,' stating that, even though each track had ideas that were attractive and original, the use of clichés left them feeling unsatisfactory.[9]

While Bill Mathieu was of a similar opinion, he found that Ayler, 'even under impossible conditions, is a wild, stimulating player':

> In 'Billie's Bounce,' Ayler sounds as if he is deliberately trying to play directly from the Parker tradition. Though his ideas are not spectacular, his point of

view is. … Ayler's truest impulses (some nihilistic) are operating behind these
wobbling, whimpering comments on the music he grew up in. … The record
is true in the sense that it shows Ayler growing out of his boyhood.[10]

Terry Martin agreed that *My Name Is Albert Ayler* captures the saxophonist
in a crucial stage of development:

Ayler had by this time almost reached maturity and the breadth of his talent
is clearly apparent. Already a completely individual musician whose influences
are almost beyond detection, he was evolving a style with implications leading
out beyond the Coleman barrier. … Two musical details that catch the ear
are his use of a continuous … rather than a particulate (scalar) pitch, and the
attempt to suggest numerous melodic lines by rapid alternation of extremes
of pitch or intensity. Also worth noting is the fact that despite the apparently
arhythmic atmospheric style, careful attention reveals a complex division of the
beat and some of his cadences are as subtle as any yet played in jazz. Needless
to say, he reveals tremendous confidence and authority.[11]

Despite the album containing the first stirrings of Ayler's own original
material, 'Summertime' remains the standout cut that forces us to pay
attention. Baldwin noted that, because Ayler stayed close to the melody in
his solos, it was his expressive phrasing that brought out the lyrical quality
of Gershwin's melody. Ayler's use of intonation, dynamics, rhythmic
inventiveness, and control made it the outstanding performance on the
album—one accepted as a classic in his own lifetime, 'stately yet full of
pathos and a flavor new to jazz.'[12]

And yet Ayler's music was also in a state of crisis. 'Summertime' contrasts
the notion of the standard setting against Ayler's conceptualization of sound
and a wandering feeling of tonality to create what John Litweiler felt was
a 'long, tragic masterpiece … of layered complexity' with 'a Shakespearean
sense of feeling and wholeness … that he would never equal again.'[13]

What makes the piece so special, however, is that Ayler uses the rhythm
of life to create the ascent and fall of the dynamic structure. A string of four-

bar statements opens with Ayler's big tone, but he becomes almost inaudible by the final beat of the phrase. Additionally, the wide, primitive vibrato, though strong at the phrase's opening, bends and blurs the succeeding tones such that the opening of the phrase is modified as an afterthought, as 'Summertime' progresses through and into a realm of distant harmonies. Ayler's precise timing is disguised by 'bent and ambiguous sounds [which] are perfectly played even as long tones extend into slurs or when vibrato is so extreme that pitch is indeterminate. The performance is too extravagant to permit a conventional climax, though the arches of sound that lead to the concluding cadenza are indeed conclusive; in place of resolution, there is only a final subsidence of sobbing.'[14]

The beauty of 'Summertime' was lost on some reviewers who felt Ayler simply played 'music that is pure sadness,' made more so by 'a cocktail rhythm section [that] makes him seem more suppliant, more lonesome.'[15] Ironically, according to his brother Donald, Albert recorded the song in order to afford a return ticket home.[16]

•

Writing three decades later, Jeff Schwartz would note four key differences between the Stockholm session that produced *Something Different!!!!!* and the Copenhagen session that resulted in *My Name Is Albert Ayler*, beginning with the configuration of his band. The presence of a pianist restricted Ayler's attempts to break free of chord progressions, with Schwartz noting that the structural rigidity of 'On Green Dolphin Street,' which consists of alternating sixteen-bar sections, forced Ayler to return to form and abandon explorations.[17] Writing in *Jazz Monthly*, W.A. Baldwin concurred, comparing Ayler's album to Ornette Coleman's *Something Else!!!!*, in which pianist Walter Norris 'was a hindrance rather than a help.'[18] In Ayler's case, the pianist made it worse, since the fixed harmonics of the chords made him seem even more out of tune.[19] (Another theory is that Ayler never understood chord progressions. His long-ago acquaintance, trumpeter Nate Horwitz, believed that while Ayler could play the solos of Charlie Parker, for example, he did not understand the underlying chordal concepts.[20])

Schwartz also notes Ayler's use of the soprano saxophone, instead of the tenor, during the Copenhagen session, in particular on 'Bye Bye Blackbird.' Compared with the roaring deepness of his tenor-playing, the soprano brought a new timbre into Ayler's expressive world. This is especially evident in 'On Green Dolphin Street,' in which other critics felt they could hear Ayler both laughing and crying.[21] Ayler described further differences to musician and jazz historian Frank Kofsky, saying, 'It was like a natural thing, because the soprano has a different, an Eastern feeling— somewhat of a natural feeling to the *sound* of it.'[22] Like many progressively minded Black musicians of the late 50s and early 60s, Ayler was drawn to Indian and Middle Eastern musical traditions, which offered a contrast to music that was Western and white, but which was not necessarily African.

Schwartz's third observation is that, having previously absorbed traits from John Coltrane and Charlie Parker, Ayler's style becomes his own on *My Name Is Albert Ayler*. His 'frenzied blowing at the highest velocity possible, or in melodramatic balladry,' Schwartz writes, is consistent with that of his later work.[23]

Lastly, Schwartz identifies the Copenhagen session as marking the first instance of Ayler's being recorded with musicians who were hip to his style, as when the bassist extends the register and utilizes extreme techniques in bowing. Such backing allowed a characteristic Ayler trait to emerge. Writing in *JAZZ*, Frank Smith described it as a 'simple straightforward format … a very lyrical tune with an old timey feeling is set forth and then the playing gradually gets into something more intense and ferocious until the listener is practically overwhelmed.'[24]

In other words, Ayler's improvisations were based on a gradual heightening of complexity. Kofsky also gave equal weight to composer Gunther Schuller's notion of thematic improvisation, which is 'the construction of spontaneous variations which reflect the contours of the theme as well as its underlying harmony.'[25] The concept is best heard in 'Free,' which closes *Something Different!!!!!*, the opening figure becoming a point for the emergence of every new idea. What is important is that, despite what McRae called 'lapses into over-romanticism,' Ayler can be heard moving away from the influence of Sonny Rollins, whose style was to close pieces with 'flourishing phrase-ends.' However, the 'wild declamatory shout' at the end of 'I Remember April'—also from *Something Different!!!!!*—breaks the mood hinted at by the romantic runs.[26]

•

Shortly after the radio broadcast that resulted in *My Name Is Albert Ayler*, Albert would meet bassist Henry Grimes and trumpeter Don Cherry, who would form the nucleus of one of his great groups. They were part of the Sonny Rollins group that toured Europe in early 1963, appearing at the Copenhagen Konserthuset on January 15.

Cherry remembered meeting Ayler:

> He was waiting on the sideline from the stage after the concert, and he asked me did I want to go to a session at the Montmartre. So I said sure, and so then we went to Montmartre and at this session was [saxophonists] Don Byas [and] Dexter Gordon, I think Niels-Henning was playing bass. … Albert didn't play on the first tune … but then they played a medley of ballads, and everybody played a ballad … and then I heard Albert Ayler, his sound come. As I remember it—now me and Billy Higgins, we argue about it, 'cause he was there, too—and I thought he had played 'Moon River' like [sings opening line], but it was like the primal scream. … But at this particular session, I heard him, and chills went up my spine. Billy Higgins says that he played 'Summertime' … but I remember that it was 'Moon River.'[27]

The audience was stunned by Ayler's slow, intense performance, and he was starting to win the respect of long-standing jazz musicians, such as Don Byas and pianist Erroll Garner, who had been around since the late 20s and achieved prominence in the 40s. Byas even told drummer Sunny Murray 'that he had wanted to play like Ayler since he was a boy.'[28] Now finally gaining acceptance into the traditional jazz fraternity, Ayler followed Rollins's band to Stockholm before making a return to America—a land that had yet to embrace him.

CHAPTER V

back to the usa

B ack in Cleveland, Ayler made trumpeter Norman Howard's home at East 75th and Kinsman one of his first stops. The pair had been friends since before Ayler's army days—growing up on the same block, they had often jammed together—and they were ready to hit Cleveland's jazz clubs together. Ayler also played big brother to Donald, who was now working on the lathe at TRW, just as Albert had done. However, Donald quit after three months, becoming a meter reader for the Cleveland Electric Illuminating Company—his only other non-musical job in the years prior to his following in Albert's footsteps.

Albert took Donald to see John Coltrane at the Jazz Temple during the week of February 9, 1963. He sat in with Coltrane and later, on April 14, with Sonny Rollins. According to Errol Henderson, a pianist who would later switch to bass and cut some sides with Ayler in February 1964, Ayler and Howard thought they would blow Rollins and Don Cherry off the stand. But Henderson felt that Rollins messed with Ayler's head, as Ayler did not say anything about it.[1]

It was during this period that Ayler was quoted for the first time in the US press. In a *Cleveland Call & Post* article titled 'Free Music … Discorded Chaos?,' he offered the prophetic observation, 'People are going to the moon. It's time for music to change, too … It is undeniably time for a change, but you have to be ready for it. Everybody's not. Some people don't want to be Free.' Expressing his views on local taste, Ayler also admitted that the negativity Cleveland's musicians showed toward free jazz made him consider moving to New York, where his music would be accepted.

He postponed any such plans, however, when a few players began to show an interest in his work. No longer exclusively viewed as weird, and with the memories of his past rejections dimming, the prophet of a new sound found some disciples on the local scene. If it weren't for Val Wilmer's research into Ayler's associates at a time when there was little interest, these early stories would have been lost to history; her work is particularly important, as she seems to have been the only Ayler scholar to have had contact with Errol Henderson.

One of these musicians was Frank Wright, a one-time bassist who was influenced enough by Ayler's playing that he, too, started playing tenor in the new style. Another was a former schoolmate of Ayler's brother, Donald Strickland, a saxophonist who would also fashion his sound on Ayler's, and who later adopted the name Mustafa Abdul Rahim.

Errol Henderson was impressed by Ayler's European life, and especially his classy threads—a green leather suit, a Cossack-style hat, and slipper-like shoes whose tongues pointed back. Ayler's look indicated success, but Henderson also felt that Ayler had not taken on airs during his continental sojourn.

More than Ayler's look, Henderson was drawn to his sound: no longer derivative of Sonny Rollins, he had come into his own. One of the few Clevelanders who could compare Ayler's playing before and after his trip to Europe, Henderson wrote to Val Wilmer:

> Smooth, oh so smooth and easy did the music ease from the tenor's bell, with such tone, with such feeling. The melody was a haunting little ditty, not remarkable technically but moving. But when he began to improvise, this is when I became startled by his music's style. It was like the wind sometimes, moving fast. At other moments it hovered, and at others it oscillated back and forth with sounds that would strike the earth to its center, or soar until

the penetration of the sound would clear the sky of clouds. The sound was so pure, the disposition of the feeling so obvious, that I was entranced. He, the music, went directly to the feeling. He was speaking from or with his very soul, for himself and for me and for all other people. … Norman [Howard] and I looked at each other and said nothing aloud, but the expression on Norman's face and the expression of my heart said, 'Yeah, man, yeah, Albert; you got it.'

The rest of Cleveland could not have cared less about Ayler. Though he jammed with Henderson and Howard, still the nightclubs had no use for his unique style, and his other only known appearance at this time was at Esquire Bar, where he sat in with the band of Eddie Baccus, a blind organist. Ayler attempted to sell copies of *Something Different!!!!!*, but his clothing typically got more attention than his music.

•

Whereas Scandinavia had once been his promised land, Ayler now set his sights on the jazz capital of the world. Heading to New York City, he crashed at Sunny Murray's place on 9th Street, south Manhattan, before renting a place in his maternal cousin's home in Harlem, on 454 St. Nicholas Avenue. Ayler's maternal cousin, Beatrice Hargrove, was a prominent American educator who held a master's degree in education from Columbia University, and it was while renting from her that Albert met Call Cobbs Jr, a fellow tenant and a musician with a past. Older than Ayler's father by two years, Cobbs was a humble and modest individual who brought with him a wealth of experience of playing with bandleader Lucky Millinder, saxophonist Wardell Gray, and singer Billie Holiday, as well as recording with saxophonists Johnny Hodges and John Coltrane. He later told Val Wilmer how they met:

[Beatrice] knew I was a musician and she wanted me to meet her relative. Albert said, 'I hear you play piano,' and his aunt [*sic*], who plays piano also, had a baby grand so I played some things for him. He said, 'That's beautiful.' He didn't have his horn with him at the time, so a few days later he brought it over and he played. I will say that when he first played, I had never played free music before and it was odd, but I could look at him and the way he was playing, and I knew that he knew what he was doing. And I felt something.[2]

After several jam sessions, Ayler asked Cobbs to be in his group.

Murray showed Ayler the city's jazz haunts, and Ayler got acquainted with Ornette Coleman, Archie Shepp, and others. Initially impressing them with his stylish clothing and good manners, when Ayler took to the stage with them it was the beautiful, warm feeling of his playing that made them take notice. It was likely at this time that Ayler and Murray made a little-known duet recording that is now available to hear at the American Jazz Museum, in Kansas City.

Though Ayler's situation was better in New York, reliable engagements were few. The restructured Cecil Taylor group—featuring returning bassist Henry Grimes, who had passed on the European shows because the pay was too low—lasted for a short time in March 1963, playing at the Take 3, a Greenwich Village club at 149 Bleeker Street. After Eric Dolphy and John Coltrane came to see them following their own sets at the Village Gate, Ayler acknowledged that, even though they did not grasp the music Taylor was playing, they realized that a new sound was developing.

Ayler himself performed several times at the Take 3, likely on October 20 and/or 27. Frank Smith covered an appearance in *JAZZ* 'one cold Sunday afternoon':

> The playing was still overwhelmingly beautiful and ferocious, but … there was a lot of nervous shuffling going on. … Unfortunately, Albert wasn't feeling too well that day and cut his playing short because of it, but … what he played was marvelous.[3]

•

Just days after the assassination of President John F. Kennedy, Donald Ayler travelled to Sweden to join Clyde Shy, his friend from John Adams. Though Donald claimed he was seeking freedom and wanted to further his musical knowledge, in reality he wanted to hook up with Albert's former girlfriend, Anna-Britta Westerman. Now in a new relationship, she was not receptive to Donald's advances; her family owned a timber company, and she suggested the pair go north to Kiruna, where they could find jobs in coal mining. Stalked by timber wolves and encountering severe cold, they made it as far as Jokkmokk, where they expected to get a job cutting trees. Surprised by the trees' diameters, they quit and hitchhiked back to Stockholm.

Looking back on the trip, Donald recalled, 'I wanted to free my mind from America, and I wanted to find my own form—not only in music but in thought and in the way I used my imagination.'[4] He did a little more than imagine: Donny contracted gonorrhea from one lover, and he also had an affair with a German-Polish ballerina named Katerina Scholz, who had a thing for Black American musicians. He also may have fathered a son. Several months after his trip, Donald received a letter from her, including a picture of their supposed child together. He never responded.

•

Meanwhile, back in New York, Albert Ayler met other Cleveland expatriates in Harlem. Errol Henderson and saxophonist Charles Tyler (alleged to be Ayler's cousin, though Donald denies this) lived nearby, at 130th Street and Lenox Ave. Sometime around December, they began to visit Ornette Coleman at his apartment near Washington Square. Coleman, like Ayler, was rooted in the blues—while Ayler had started out with the Chicago harmonica-player Little Walter, Coleman had an early apprenticeship in Fort Worth with guitarist Pee Wee Crayton, before moving west to Los Angeles. Tape recordings of jam sessions document Ayler and Coleman's musical relationship, but where a legendary session between two giants of avant-garde sax could have occurred, Coleman instead played violin and trumpet—his first appearance on either instrument. Coleman still had the tapes but never released them in his lifetime.

Ayler's last session with Coleman was recorded by a 'rich white friend,' as Val Wilmer originally described him in *As Serious As Your Life*. The benefactor was subsequently identified by Wilmer as the acoustic bass builder and recording engineer Fred Lyman, who played banjo on the session. Other musicians at this jam were Norman Butler on alto sax, Errol Henderson on bass, Coleman on trumpet, and Charles Tyler on C-melody sax. According to Henderson, the tapes were freely circulated around Europe.

Writer Frank Smith, who was at one of the sessions, described how Ayler:

> took out his horn after a while and started playing all this lovely and unbelievable music. The most striking thing at first was his incredible speed and the way he played the high and low notes … Albert plays these with a clarity and force that make them sound like a trumpet train coming down the line, and [Amiri Baraka's] term 'electronic foghorn' is perfectly apt as a description of his low note sound. It was simply devastating. It was so fresh that I couldn't then, and can't now even begin to compare it to anyone else's playing.[5]

Ayler continued to gig around New York. The Baby Grand in Harlem usually attracted anyone who was anyone—boxers Joe Louis and Sugar Ray Robinson and Congressman Adam Clayton Powell Jr. among them— but its Christmas Day engagements were minimally attended, usually only by the wives and girlfriends of the musicians. On Christmas Day 1963, however, after playing a set with bassist Richard Davis and pianist Elmo Hope, Ayler met the man who would change his life.

In the audience was a New York attorney, Bernard Stollman, who later recalled, 'Albert Ayler blew the saxophone for twenty or thirty minutes nonstop … I was blown away—I'd never heard anything like it.'[6] Then and there, Stollman decided to sign Ayler as the first artist on his fledgling record label ESP-disk'. Though Stollman had initially launched to release Esperanto records (its first release was a disc titled *Ni Kantu En Esperanto*), Ayler's performance planted the idea in his head to change the direction of ESP-Disk', which would now be run as a co-operative: the artists and the company would co-own the masters in an equal partnership, the musicians contributing the talent and Stollman contributing money for studio time, manufacturing, and distribution. This arrangement precluded typical record-company practices of licensing material to other labels and reissuing outtakes and other material in compilations to compete against any product an artist may have on a rival imprint. With Stollman paying session fees, the musicians would get royalties from actual sales, instead of waiting until the label had recouped its expenses, while Stollman also co-published and administered the publishing rights with his artists.

But what impressed Stollman so? Though he was an attorney for several musicians—among them Dizzy Gillespie, Cecil Taylor, Ornette Coleman, Mary Lou Williams, and Bud Powell—and had handled the estates of Billie Holiday and Charlie Parker, Stollman had little interest in jazz. He was, however, floored by the cascades of sound coming from Ayler's horn. Along with Davis, Hope, and the audience that day, he realized something special had just taken place.

'When he finished, covered with sweat, he came down from the stage,' Stollman later remembered. 'I went over to him and introduced myself, and I said, "I'm starting a record label and I want you to be my first artist." This voice in the back of my head said, "Oh you are, are you?" But I made the commitment, I set things in motion. I had a cause, as this man was incredible.'[7]

And so ESP-Disk' was on its way to becoming one of the world's most legendary independent jazz labels. Future greats who recorded their first albums as leaders for the label include saxophonists Gato Barbieri and Pharoah Sanders, and singer Patty Waters. They owe it all to a twenty-minute Ayler solo. ESP-Disk' was at the forefront of the avant-garde in the early to mid 60s, and it made hip America aware of hipper America.

•

On New Year's Eve, Ayler appeared with Cecil Taylor's new quintet at Lincoln Center, playing to an audience of 1,500. Though the Taylor portion of that night's concert was recorded, it has never come to light, despite extensive efforts by Revenant Records and others. But in a prophetic review for *DownBeat*, Amiri Baraka—then still going by the name LeRoi Jones—captured what the audience heard that night:

> Lyons and Ayler played very lovely unison passages on Taylor's 'In Fields,' 'Octagonal Skirt,' and 'Fancy Pants.' … [Ayler] is already playing himself completely, and the music he is trying to get together is among the most exciting—even frightening—music I have ever heard. He uses, I am told, a thick plastic reed and blows with a great deal of pressure. The sound is fantastic. It leaps at you, actually assails you, and the tenorist never lets up for a second. The timbre of his horn is so broad and gritty it sometimes sounds like an electronic foghorn.[8]

Albert did, indeed, use a tough plastic reed—a Fibercane No.4—which contributed to his hard tone. It failed to win over the *New Yorker*'s Whitney Balliett, who was hostile in his assessment of Taylor's performance. A drummer himself and an admirer of Sid Catlett, rather than merely being a reporter, Balliett had an extraordinary eye for detail and literary virtuosity that made reading his reviews fascinating, even if one had no interest in jazz. But despite having championed both Coleman and Taylor in 1957—while simultaneously lamenting the physical abrasiveness of their new music—he stated that the Lincoln Center show:

> passed from the unendurable (Coltrane and Taylor) to the matter-of-fact (Blakey). The first two groups had a wildness and passion that came close to holocaust; in places their playing was supramusical, or perhaps amusical, for it took on distinct and disturbing human characteristics—defiance, anger, and bitterness. … Taylor's group reached even bolder climaxes [than Coltrane]. He played … just one number. It lasted close to an hour, and it was an abrasive experience. The tempo shifted continuously … sporadic ensembles came and went, Taylor soloed, his horns soloed, Taylor soloed again, his horns returned, Taylor returned, and so on. Taylor's excursions were demonic and breathtaking … he used mass upon mass of dissonant chords, usually executed in staccato passages so rapid that his hands … assumed the blurred vibrations

of 'Nude Descending A Staircase.' The rest of him vibrated fearfully, too, and in time. Ailer [sic] proved a cautious, but promising follower of Ornette Coleman.[9]

Many assume that this was the final Taylor-Ayler concert, but there was one more: a benefit for the Cooper Square Community Development Committee at the Five Spot, at 2 St Marks Place, on January 12, 1964. After that, Taylor and Ayler never again appeared together onstage. According to Murray, Taylor distanced himself from the saxophonist; Murray suspected that Taylor was jealous of Ayler's playing, harboring fears that Ayler could undermine his own dominance. For his part, however, Ayler still respected Taylor's talent and ideas.

•

Sometime between January 13 and 16, Ayler returned to Cleveland for a short visit. After an article about him appeared in the *Call & Post*, Ayler once again left for New York, this time with Donald, who himself had recently returned from Stockholm.

Ayler was moving on. He sat in with other avant-garde musicians at the Take 3 that winter, among them were Bill Dixon, trombonist Roswell Rudd, pianist Paul Bley, and bassist Gary Peacock. As Bley later wrote:

> One cold February in the Village, I got a call from Gary Peacock. 'Paul, I've got a gig at the Take 3 for two bands. You and I will play in both bands. One band will have [saxophonist] John Gilmore and [drummer] Paul Motian, and it will be followed by a band with Albert Ayler and Sunny Murray. It starts on Friday. It pays five dollars a night.'[10]

There is some dispute over the nature of the group. According to John Gilmore, the regular group involved him, Bley, Peacock, and Motian, meaning Ayler and Peacock were really guest performers.[11] However, Jeff Schwartz points out that, by the time of the recording of Bley's *Turns* on March 9, 1964, Gilmore and Motian had been permanently replaced by Ayler and Murray.[12] Peacock also claimed to have led another quartet comprising of Bley, Ayler, and Motian. He also recalled that the musicians had to guarantee to bring in an audience, or else they would have to pay the club owner themselves. The engagement lasted for a few weeks in January and February, with the group sharing the bill with composer Carla Bley (Paul's then-wife). According to Ben Young's chronology, the quartet evolved yet again when Murray replaced Motian; this line-up played four dates at the Cellar Café between April and June 1964, with John Gilmore, saxophonist with the Sun Ra ensemble, also part of the line-up.[13]

spirits

B y 1964, Ayler was in the thick of New York's avant-garde scene. Sunny Murray later noted that he would often bring hometown musicians east with him after a visit to Cleveland, and on his latest trip, Ayler returned with Norman Howard. One of Ayler's most committed Cleveland acolytes, Howard had picked up some of Ayler's style—though he wasn't as lyrical a player, he was just as interested in exploring the tonal resources of his trumpet, and he used elements of linear discontinuity as the basis for his improvisations. He would make for a good match with Albert on Ayler's first recording sessions as a bona-fide bandleader in New York.

The two sessions, arranged by Ole Vestergaard of the Denmark-based Debut Records, took place at Atlantic Studios on the same day, February 24, 1964, and saw Ayler lead two slightly different groups through two very different types of material. One of the resultant albums would be shelved for almost two decades, its expressionistic reading of spirituals—pieces such as 'Goin' Home,' 'Ol' Man River,' and 'When The Saints Go Marching In'—lacking the improvisatory character expected of jazz. Ayler played soprano and tenor saxophones on the recording, which also featured Call Cobbs on piano, Henry Grimes on bass and Sunny Murray on drums, and which finally saw release as *Swing Low Sweet Spiritual* almost a decade later, in 1981, on Osmosis Records.

The second album to emerge from the sessions was, however, a landmark for Ayler. Issued on Debut as *Spirits* (Debut 146) and later re-released on Freedom Records as *Witches & Devils* (FLP 40 101), it was his first official studio recording with musicians of his caliber, and for which he had full control over the material. Norman Howard was called upon to provide trumpet, Sonny Murray reprised his role on drums, and Grimes—who was a veteran of bands led by Sonny Rollins, Cecil Taylor, and saxophonist Gerry Mulligan—shared bass duties with Errol Henderson.

Writing in the Canadian jazz magazine *Coda* in 1976, Barry Tepperman contextualized this session within the entire Ayler oeuvre:

> When he recorded *Witches & Devils*, he was still an unknown quantity, never having been afforded the opportunity to record the music he wanted in settings of his choice. ... This meant not only that he could choose his most sympathetic cohorts, but that he was free to concentrate on his spiritual preoccupations and the themes he drew from them rather than randomly include errant 'standards' and blues as before. ... But for such a large group, and especially compared with the constant barrage of his later quintets, the textures of this one are amazingly diverse, and frequently have a sparse, almost desolate quality. This was a 'free' ensemble in which, although collective improvisation was not yet a major concern, each instrument had an independent and simultaneous melodic role to perform. The textural drones of his later years were not yet in evidence. Not yet having learned the uses of musical power/violence through brother Don, Ayler is free to concentrate the relaxation in his lines. The tension that built emotional ambiguity was to come later. Here is the tenorist's conception at its purest—the reconstruction of melody through the elasticizing of parallel layers of fragments, a huge tone drawn from a relaxed embouchure ... and a compositional optimism that was naive almost to the point of saccharine. ... But one of the great virtues of the open freedom of this quintet is that it allows creation and hearing on several levels.[1]

Nine years after Ayler's death, *Spirits* remained a force to be reckoned with. That year, *Melody Maker*'s Michael James wrote of how 'the uncompromising expressionism of Ayler's first maturity is brilliantly captured here. His re-interpretation of the tenor saxophone's role in jazz sounds as drastic today as it did then.'[2]

Bassist Henry Grimes was himself very impressed by Ayler and his command of the session, calling him 'a fantastic improviser, amazing musician. He would come up with things completely out of nowhere, and from, everywhere … Albert had all these sounds going on. … The music had a spiritual element, but I didn't want to get too caught up in it and overplay, do too much. … Didn't want to over-contribute.'[3]

Spirits opens with what Gary Peacock referred to as 'shapes': providing the basic material of the improvisation, these musical structures are the key to understanding Ayler's music. Ayler had first discussed them in the *Call & Post*, when he described his music as 'geometric shapes and forms displayed musically.'[4] His brother Donald explained that these shapes arose from playing two notes simultaneously—rather than consecutively—and inclusive of all that is in between.[5] He elaborated further, 'Yeah, smear notes together in a shape. I took geometry. I made shapes with music like geometry—I saw my brother was into making pyramids. I got them all together and I played them in my music. Circles, rectangles, spirals.'[6]

Albert's view was similar: to him, it required a great ability to conceptualize transforming notes to sounds. It is believed that his 'shapes' were a development from or a response to Cecil Taylor's piano techniques in performances with Archie Shepp and with Ayler himself; Shepp's improvisations were described by the late German music scholar Ekkehard Jost as 'Klangbogen,' or 'Sound contours.'[7]

The notion of a shape is comparative to the sound block—a shape being a smear of sound. The structural value comes not from specific pitches, but the total shape or contour. *Village Voice* jazz critic Gary Giddins described it as a 'kind of playing whose dynamic impetus arose not from off-beat phrasing, but from combining the parameters of time, intensity, and pitch, thereby creating a new musical quality, energy.' This energy replaces the old notion of 'swing' with velocity and urgency. The resulting tension creates a sense of constant motion through accelerations and decelerations.[8]

Gary Peacock elaborated on the notion:

Here improvisations are no longer based upon melodies. In their place melodies are replaced by shapes (forms, figures) and produced through the difference between one tone and the next on the instrument, where the tone is no more an integral factor. There are no more pure tones. Albert Ayler does not interest himself in pure sounds anymore, he interests himself in all the possibilities that he could produce in one single sound. These shapes are basically contours of pure sound and not defined by the beat.[9]

Though Ayler's exploration of shapes was thoroughly modern, they have always existed in the jazz tradition, in which 'blue notes'—dramatically sharpened or flattened notes—were played. Pianists such as Thelonious Monk, Herbie Nichols, and, more specifically, Cecil Taylor, who felt themselves limited by the piano's fixed tonalities, invented harmonies that distorted the notion of pitches within a certain chord. Saxophonists such as Ornette Coleman used the overtone structure to stress notes that seemed detuned. However, rather than use such concepts for effect, Ayler based his music upon them. In his critiques, John Litweiler has cited George Russell's theories that African music was atonal and arhythmic—a style also heard in the blues of Lightnin' Hopkins and John Lee Hooker—and, therefore, that Ayler had reverted to the roots of Black music.[10]

In these shapes the harmonic center disappears. Musicians such as Taylor and Ayler accomplish this by overlaying chords upon chords, and key upon key, so that the effect is *pantonal*, as opposed to atonal. This is the one element of Ayler's music that is not linked to New Orleans but rather to modern jazz. The lack of defined tonality can also be heard in the African instruments that are not played to conform to the Western notion of scales, such as the mbira. Lacking scales, one lacks harmony—and, therefore, chord changes.

Ayler had surpassed Ornette Coleman, who had moved away from chord changes, bar lines, white (or Western) intonation, and a regular beat. Instead, Ayler had substituted the notion of sound as the basis of musical structure. In doing so, he redefined the saxophone, as Louis Armstrong had done for the trumpet, achieving this through a series of screeches, 'sound scales,' and rhythms. Ayler's melodies of sound colors consisted of improvisations built upon the 'shapes and weights of his compositions.'[11] Val Wilmer likened it to 'the playing of chords on a saxophone,' via the overtones and harmonics usage. Citing the *New York Times* critic Robert Palmer, she also noted that the 'one-voice chording' stretched back to a West African tradition, and to soul screamers such as Wilson Pickett and James Brown, who 'chord' with one voice.[12]

Speaking to Wilmer, Ayler described the importance of playing around the beat—something that can be traced back to New Orleans and the lack of a steady beat in the collective improvisation of the city's bands: 'It has changed so much from when Ornette Coleman started, this playing around the beat which is neo-avant-garde music. This beat will be eliminated.'[13] To music critic Nat Hentoff, he explained, 'One way not to [listen] is to focus on the notes and stuff like that. Instead, try to move your imagination toward the sound. It's a matter of following the sound. You have to relate sound to sound inside the music. I mean you have to try to listen to everything together.' Donald added, 'Follow the sound, the pitches, the colors. You have to watch them move.'[14]

Jazz Monthly critic Don Locke felt that this 'freedom' gave Ayler's music a tighter organizational structure than seen in traditional, harmonic-oriented jazz, since the composition (and interaction with other musicians) is the basic element, rather than individual soloists performing improvisations over a series of chords.[15]

Equally as important as the abandonment of chords, Ayler's rejection of standard scales (he focused on a five-note pentatonic) permitted a greater freedom—less material allowed for greater imaginative possibilities. We can understand this notion better if we compare his music with that of classical music minimalists such as Philip Glass and La Monte Young, who used cells (the interaction of two or more lines of different lengths being played and repeated at the same time) as the basis for major works. Ayler's themes are incredibly simple, and often derived from the spirituals and folk songs he heard in his youth. He discussed this source material with Val Wilmer in 1966:

I like folk music and march music and so forth. You have to build a solo around something, and different folk songs would be back there in my head, and New Orleans marches would come to me when I'm playing. This is the way I'm trying to form my music. Always a person should have something to go by. It can't be one thing anymore, any one emotional level, but before we were just *playing*, and at that time there weren't too many people who could do that. Now everyone has come to that, they just open up and start playing.[16]

As Barry Tepperman put it in his *Coda* review, white and Black musical aesthetics are differentiated by simple diatonic melodies yet shaped by total freedom. This contrast is best exemplified in the creative possibilities open to the quintet format Ayler explored on *Spirits*—using two bassists opened up 'the great breadth of harmonic feed it allows the front-line soloists.'[17] For Ayler, this enabled the group to simultaneously take two different harmonic directions, connected in an 'organic unity.'[18]

The African rhythmic tradition can be heard in the interplay between the bassists and drummer Sunny Murray, as described by Tepperman:

But the bassists are no less prominent in the sound of the music, and their intricate pizzicato interplay is at least as important as Murray's non-repetitive drumming in establishing the proper rhythmic setting for the horns. Murray is the other really dominant player on *Witches & Devils*, one whose approach to his kit was brilliantly new—and not just a matter of avoiding the cliche in playing time. Rather, Murray uses the expected timbral qualities of his kit in personal combinations to establish a tonal atmosphere for the music. He was in no sense a timekeeper.[19]

In the absence of a steady beat, the free horn/rhythm interaction permits the music to proceed at a natural pace, focusing on some aspects and rushing through others as it is driven on by its own energy.[20] Listening to *Spirits*, it is possible to detect fragments of traditional spirituals and other songs rearranged into an expressionistic collage. One critic, W.A. Baldwin, referred to the album's 'archaic' phrasing as 'the almost anti-modern approach,' while noting that it also included a parody of a New Orleans dirge.[21]

Val Wilmer was the first critic to notice this source in Ayler's music. It was the coalescence of all that preceded him—spirituals, funeral dirges, bugle calls, the blues, and marches of the past. His growls, she wrote, would 'produce coarse, gutteral effects' that hark back to the sounds of Earl Bostic and Illinois Jacquet.[22]

Ayler was stylistically closer to trumpeter Bubber Miley and trombonist Joe 'Tricky Sam' Nanton of Duke Ellington's Cotton Club bands than he was to the bebop tradition. Yet some of the controversy surrounding him came about because critics ignored the historical elements of his music. Even *DownBeat*, in its obituary of Ayler, would erroneously state that his recordings 'bore little resemblance to any other jazz, past or present.'[23] In fact, Ayler's scream can be traced back to the New Orleans rhythm & blues tradition. Wilmer writes that he encompassed the 'fire and passion' of Ornette Coleman and Charlie Parker, as well as the poignant sadness of Miles Davis and Billie Holiday, yet it was in the Crescent City's musical history that Ayler found the future of jazz.

Ayler admired the work of Sidney Bechet, particularly the strengths of his tone and his vibrato. He felt Bechet was the true spirit of jazz, as evident in the old, rejoicing music of New Orleans and lacking in the music of his contemporaries. As Donald Ayler explained, 'The thing about New Orleans jazz is the feeling it communicated—that something was about to happen, and it was going to be *good*.' The notion of collective improvisation which pre-dated even King Oliver found its modern incarnation in the Ayler brothers' free jazz: it was spiritual music that demanded musicians listen to each other, rather than being concerned with what they themselves were playing. It was 'free' music in the sense that it was built on the relationship of free sounds.

•

Three years after its release, *Spirits* was acknowledged by W.A. Baldwin as the first on-record example of Ayler's mature style. The medium-tempo tracks 'Spirits' and 'Holy, Holy' clearly illustrate the 4/4 character of his playing, and Sunny Murray's driving percussion deepens that character. Ayler, on the other hand, settles into a more relaxed mode—even the solo in 'Spirits' seems to die away, as if he has run out of ideas.

Some contemporary critics felt that the solo was poorly constructed because it was composed of separate units that lack any connection with each other. (In contrast, Norman Howard's trumpet solo moves toward a climax; gaps do exist, however, because Howard's solo was weak in both melody and rhythm.[24]) However, for Michael James in *Melody Maker*,

> The slower items, 'Saints' and 'Witches,' best show how Ayler's unique handling of sound enabled him to draw unprecedented implications from what were really quite simple melodies. Fear, frustration, and outright anger jog elbows within the teeming confines of these performances, yielding impressions comfortless in their detail yet healing in their overall effect.[25]

Ayler's phrasing, particularly on the track 'Witches And Devils,' is reminiscent of classic blues singers, whereas the song's theme sounds like it originated from a New Orleans dirge. The New Orleans connection was also noted by Jack Cooke in *Jazz Monthly*:

> The big surprise here is 'Witches And Devils,' the first time Ayler has broken away from his race-track tempos; here he has produced an out-of-tempo dirge, with a simple theme full of long notes that becomes extremely affecting on repeated hearings. … [Howard] seems to be trying to create a parallel idiom to Ayler's, and his style will provide some headaches for those brought up on normal jazz trumpet techniques. At fast tempos he produces a spluttering, jerky line in which, as in Ayler's own work, clarity of articulation and control of pitching and vibrato are entirely dispensable … he matches Ayler remarkably well, the two of them producing a sound astonishingly like that of a New Orleans brass band; the control he shows in his work here, though always of a somewhat non-academic character, should be enough to prove he's no faker. He's going his own way to his own ends, and he's not yet entirely master of his style, but for all that he's a good musician.[26]

In reverting to the raw antiquities of the likes of Jelly Roll Morton and Louis Armstrong, Ayler renounced the fake sophistication that modern jazz had acquired. In reverting to pure emotional playing, Ayler was denying both the intellectualization and elegance of Gil Evans and Miles Davis and the 'polished glibness' of J.J. Johnson and Cannonball Adderley.[27] In a near-contemporaneous article in *Vogue*, Nat Hentoff described it as a move into feeling, as opposed to knowledge-based playing. To find ourselves, we must find our feelings, and the new jazz of the mid-60s was built on introspection and a continual self-exploration, without regard for what old critics or night-club owners would think or care.[28]

This is especially clear in the phrasing that Baldwin characterizes as 'archaic.' Here Ayler often creates cross-rhythms or overlays a contrasting rhythm on top of the 4/4 beat. This rhythmic complexity illustrates just why Ayler's relaxed style of playing is so impressive: the solos utilize greater tonal resources, and continual interest builds because of his rhythmic and melodic inventiveness; yet solos without shape and abrupt endings detract from the power of Ayler's playing.

Despite his imaginative and sensitive constructions of lyrical statements, Howard's solos also lack shape toward the end, yet his blowing resurrects memories of the brutal velocity of his New Orleans forbear Buddy Bolden.[29] Howard also impressed Amiri Baraka, who wrote in his 1966 *DownBeat* column, 'Apple Cores,' of how Howard 'will make a lot of people sit up and listen. His runs are piercing staccato blasts that leave little room for charming ready-made notes or fake displays of easy virtuosity.'[30]

It has been said that Howard's playing on 'Witches And Devils' is Ayler-like—he utilizes the same blurred lines, slow and wide vibrato, and primitive textures.[31] However, it is arguably the case that Ayler's playing is more Howard-like, since Howard wrote the piece, even though it was credited to Ayler on the album.

Mutawaf Shaheed relates the story behind it:

That was a sore spot in that relationship. Because Norman actually wrote 'Witches And Devils,' and Norman was a Black Muslim—and that was dealing with people and not the spiritual essence of evil. At the time he was a follower of Elijah Muhammad … their music was based on their belief system … Elijah Muhammad's, uh, philosophy was white people were devils, and, you know, the males were devils, and the women were witches, and so this is—you know, the exploitation piece, the nationalist philosophy of Elijah Muhammad. … This all played into that music—you know, but when Albert dealt with it, he didn't deal with it like that because he wasn't racist. He wasn't a bigot, more or less, you know, so his thing was always, 'People are people and I'm about the music, and I'm not about the rest of it.'[32]

And yet some, Amiri Baraka among them, understood the piece's deeper implications:

One of the tunes, 'Witches And Devils,' should frighten anyone given to mystical involvement or even simple impressionistic reaction. It is a scary tune, going deep beneath what we say is real to that other portion of our selves that is, finally, realer and much less familiar.[33]

Here, Howard is the theme's interpreter—he plays the first theme, and, unusually for an Ayler recording, there is a two-voice arrangement led by Howard. For Baldwin in particular, the solos are a problem: Howard's goes on too long, while Ayler's final solo stops in mid-theme, similar to the abrupt ends of his other solos on the record.[34]

It's clear from Baraka's review that he found 'Witches And Devils' impressive, and so too 'Holy, Holy'—a composition that shows early Ayler at his best, disproving critics who claimed he couldn't construct a melody. As Michael James wrote,

If melodic resourcefulness was never his strong suit, the long solo in 'Holy' proves he could meet that challenge when he wished. Musically paramount, though, was the play of tension and relaxation within the whole ensemble, and concentrated listening to the bass, and drum parts in the light of Ayler's or Howard's lines, solo, or intertwined, will bring rich auditory rewards.[35]

Baldwin had a similar opinion, feeling that Howard's solo would be regarded as a classic of its era. He was also impressed by the flow of ideas and mood changes in Ayler's solo.[36] Elsewhere, shortly after Ayler's death, critic Barry McRae wrote, 'He is motivated by a good basic melody and where he shows how well he can construct a continuous solo without reference to each thematic contour.'[37]

Taken at an extremely fast tempo, Ayler leaves behind any notion of playing notes. He 'blares a slurred line that breaks often into the extreme heights and depths of his range, in spasms of multiphonics and overtones. His phrase differentiation is … distinct … there is a flow and contrast to phrase shape, even thematic improvisation, in his music that are not merely freakish sounds played at overwhelming speed.'[38]

After this classic solo, *Spirits* ends on a weak note: the excessive vibrato that gives such power to Ayler's solos elsewhere on the album seems inappropriate on the final cut, 'Saints,' detracting from its brilliant moments. The tune is further harmed by what Baldwin called an 'incoherent' solo by Howard.[39] Their interplay throughout the album, Baldwin noted, is marked by Ayler's rhythmic ease and Howard's arhythmic solos, just as the lyricism of Ayler's solos are sharply contrasted against his instrument's tonal character. These contrasts are heard in the strong vibrato that creates a sense of sentimentality against the 'strength and conviction of Ayler's lines.'[40] The album's lighthearted nature—something that's lacking in Ayler's subsequent work—is a result of his utilization of 'purely rhythmic ideas.'[41]

In a sense, the rhythmic and lyrical development of his solos makes their formal development less important—an unusual trait, since Ayler's later recordings focus on developing motifs throughout the duration of his solo. However, on *Spirits*, Ayler's solos have more in common with those of Lester Young, because of what Baldwin calls 'the long lines of unpredictable length,' built from repeated riffs without changing the interval, as well as the addition of an afterthought to a line that is seemingly complete. Baldwin's conclusion is that *Spirits* is 'a very fine record' because of Ayler's assuredness, despite a lapse or two, and that it can be compared to classic jazz records, not merely be considered a classic of new jazz.[42]

CHAPTER VII

swing low, sweet spiritual

t might be seen as strange that a recording session held in the same studio, involving almost the same personnel, and on the same day, could yield such different results; and yet, the iconoclastic interpretations of spirituals that made for the posthumously released *Swing Low Sweet Spiritual* (a.k.a. *Goin' Home*) were not as radical as some reviewers have claimed.

Half a decade before Ayler held his February 1964 session at Atlantic Studios, Little Richard had forsaken the riches of rock'n'roll for gospel music, and he was followed swiftly by Elvis Presley, whose first gospel album, *His Hand In Mine*, came out in 1960. Jazz music, too, had its own precedent: Count Basie's early days consisted of 'playing buckets of blood Saturday night, and churches Sunday morning';[1] Louis Armstrong had issued his take on the traditional hymn 'Goin' To Shout All Over God's Heav'n' in 1938; and, twenty years later, Mahalia Jackson's performance at the 1958 Newport Jazz Festival illustrated the common roots of jazz and spirituals.

This relationship had always been loosely connected in the American psyche: the spirituals gave birth to the blues, and the blues became the root of jazz, whose church-derived chords and backbeats eventually became the basis for a style that looked back to its origins: hard bop. Heard in classics such as Cannonball Adderley's 'Sermonette' and Jimmy Smith's 'The Sermon,' it would not have been a stretch for Ayler to continue the bop tradition of adaptation. Just as Ayler had freed himself from the constraints of his early training, on the recordings that made up *Swing Low Sweet Spiritual*, he found liberation in the old spirituals of his childhood. The interpretations on this album exhibit the simple melodies that later characterized his work, as well as the cosmic-spirit viewpoint that runs through his work.

The influence came from his mother's birthplace, Birmingham, Alabama, from which Arthur Turner & The Dunham Jubilee Singers arrived in Cleveland, in the late 1920s. They were soon followed by others until Ayler's hometown played host to a couple of dozen gospel quartets by the time of his birth. Radio regularly broadcast these groups, as well as the forty-to-fifty-voice Wings Over Jordan Choir. Another influence was the rise of contemporary groups such as The Soul Stirrers, who started a trend for vocal outfits to move away from close-harmony singing. Also from Birmingham came The Kings Of Harmony, who thrilled local audiences with their powerfully emotive performances. Because of Cleveland's status as a home for the finest gospel groups, few outsiders dared tour the city.

From gospel and the spirituals, Ayler adapted the rich vibrato and declamatory style of his playing. From the so-called 'Holiness churches'—storefront Pentecostal churches—Ayler adapted the 'false-voiced' shouts of sermonizing preachers and the outbursts of worshippers talking in tongues.[2] Gospel worship pushed the body beyond its physical limits; it screamed to the spirit as it rose beyond vocal registers to an otherworldly existence. Ayler used the saxophone in the same manner, and the elevated consciousness he brought to his music is evidenced in the titles of some of his later albums, *Ghosts* and *Spirits Rejoice* among them. However, the Pentecostal church was a vicarious influence; Ayler more directly drew from the Baptist tradition.

All the gospel traditions are present in *Swing Low Sweet Spiritual*, belatedly released in 1981 and later reissued in 1994, on Black Lion, as *Goin' Home*. Described by Ayler's first biographer Peter Niklas Wilson as 'a rare and fascinating view of the roots of Ayler's anarchistic music,' its eight spirituals were recorded by the quartet of Ayler, pianist Call Cobbs, and

Grimes and Murray (reprising their roles on bass and drums, respectively).[3] According to Murray, the group hallucinated and saw remarkable things in the air throughout the recording.[4]

The Ayler family had sung the album's opening piece, 'Goin' Home,' in church in Cleveland; Albert's aunt, Nellie Thompson, had performed it in a 1947 concert at Liberty Hill. Arranged as a duet between Ayler and Cobbs, however, 'Goin' Home' exposed weaknesses in the group. As Barry McRae later noted, 'The choice of Cobbs as the pianist was a strange one … Cobbs's genteel, almost cocktail lounge style was always unsuitable for the stark reality of Ayler's music. Here it seems especially so, because the saxophonist treats each selection in a straight, almost terse manner.'[5]

Elsewhere, Wilson cited the ill-fitting nature of Cobbs's 'romantic arabesques' against Ayler's vibrato,[6] while another reviewer wrote that his 'tremolo-laden playing is almost too proper; his tinkly intro chorus … could have been recorded in the '30s.'[7] And yet, Cobbs's 'ability to slide into the melody line, to play with it, to bring it in and out of sharp focus at will,' as reviewer John Sutherland put it, made him the perfect foil to the rhythm section, his introverted stylings allowing Grimes's powerful bass to interlock with Sunny Murray's drums.[8] In particular, the group's second take on 'Ol' Man River,' a Hammerstein-Kern composition from the musical *Showboat*, reveals how Grimes was free to use Ayler's sax lines as a sounding board for his own contrapuntal improvisations.[9]

Ayler once told his father, 'Dad, when I play, I'm just in another world,' and the other selections on *Swing Low Sweet Spiritual* capture him in transcendent form.[10] Two takes of 'Ol' Man River' were recorded, with the second making it onto the album's original issue. Writing in *Coda*, however, John Sutherland preferred the second because of the way Ayler wrenches Kern's melody from the instrument, as if he were an unpolished singer baring his soul.[11]

Kevin Whitehead of *Cadence* concurred:

> The session's masterpiece … is a perfect vehicle for Albert's haunting tenor.
> On his a cappella intro to the second version, he plays with the vulnerability

and emotion of a lone singer in the choir loft, and when he swings low into the bridge on take 1, it sends a chill up your spine. Here Cobbs's harmonic conservatism and melodramatic trappings … are perfectly at home.[12]

The balance of the album's material is lifted from traditional spirituals: 'Nobody Knows The Trouble I've Seen' (another Cobbs-Ayler duet), which Sutherland described as 'warm-toned, ironic in its stated mood'; 'When The Saints Go Marching In,' in which Ayler 'reaches a full falsetto voice to a rhythm & blues-like tempo' that would have fit in perfectly in a New Orleans ensemble.[13] On the album's title cut (otherwise known as 'Swing Low, Sweet Chariot'), Ayler 'quavers the melody against the overlay of trio support,'[14] and the contrast between Ayler and Cobbs is demonstrated by an Ayler solo whose earthiness is balanced against Cobbs's cocktail piano styling.[15] Following directly after, 'Deep River' recalls Sydney Bechet's playing, as Ayler explores 'the wide register of the instrument.'[16]

Six takes of 'Down By The Riverside' were recorded, but only the final one was originally released, with take five later appearing as a bonus cut on the Black Lion reissue. Long unknown, this alternate rendition finds Ayler, per Wilson, 'well detached from the melody, yet is satisfied with it in the strict components of all harmonic, metrical, and melodic vocabulary.'[17]

•

Shelved after its recording, it was only a lack of Ayler product that led to *Swing Low Sweet Spiritual*'s release in the early 80s. Yet Ayler devotees were shocked to hear him in a less adventurous frame of mind, Barry McRae among them:

It is as if he wants to nurture each of these tunes, rather than rebuild them. His playing on 'When The Saints' and at the end of the first take of 'Old Man River' is falteringly poor, and throughout, his poignancy of tone, production of imaginative phrase shapes and his unique sense of timing, do not fully compensate for his lack of true improvisational commitment.[18]

Indeed, improvisation can only be heard on 'When The Saints Go Marching In,' a work that harkens back to the Sidney Bechet tradition, as Grimes and Murray create a New Orleans feeling behind Ayler. Yet the album also suffers from Grimes's 'non-timekeeping, commenting style,' which, as Kevin Whitehead claimed in *Cadence*, largely 'succeeds here on a conceptual level—answering Ayler's pleas and prayers like a congregation responding to a preacher … but this band's sound needs a firmer backbone which more conventional bass support would have given it.'[19]

Overall, *Swing Low Sweet Spirituals* is best heard as a straightforward collection of songs played by a great musician who is 'respectful, humble, and simple … yet full of the gigantic tone, the vibrating pathos that you knew from his free ballads.'[20] And yet Ayler's conservatism brings out the best in his overpowering tone: the spread of low notes is offset by the high squeals; the sudden and extreme changes in register and dynamics, plus the great breath control and unceasing intensity, show that this album's strengths lay deeper than at first glance.

Creatively speaking, 1964 would become one of Ayler's most productive years, both in terms of the quality and the quantity of his music. Personally, too, his life was expanding. On March 3—just one week after the landmark recording sessions that produced two albums in one day—Arlene Benton, Ayler's Cleveland girlfriend from shortly after his discharge from the army, gave birth to their daughter, Desiree. Now a father twice over in the literal sense, Ayler was poised to engender further revolutionary changes in modern jazz.

prophecy

Along with other radical musicians such as Archie Shepp, John Tchicai, and Marion Brown, Albert Ayler was taking the old models and using them to construct a new identity for jazz. As bassist Gary Peacock's then-wife, the electronic-music pioneer and free-jazz exponent Annette Peacock had a front-row seat from which to witness these developments. She later described the environment that New York City's avant-garde creatives worked in: 'This was a time of serious people working alone in their lofts, dedicated to personal expression. A small circle of people who recognized each other.'[1]

This work was often carried out through the time-honored jazz tradition of jam sessions. Ben Young's *Ayler Seen*, included in Revenant Records' *Holy Ghost* box set, documents much of what took place, drawing on fleeting memories and other recollections that left a more lasting impression among participants. Marzette Watts, a painter and later a saxophonist and recording engineer, remembered one of the early gigs:

> I think the first place he played in New York … was at my loft, and it took a long time after the concert to be able to paint there again. It was just literally hitting the walls, the vibrations, you know?
>
> I've never been as shocked by anyone as by Albert—just an electrifying experience. … We were sitting in the Half-Note … and John [Coltrane] wasn't

feeling well. So he called Eric [Dolphy], and Eric walks in with this strange little man with a green leather suit on. John was bent over, wrapping his soprano sax in a towel, and putting it in his tenor case, and Eric motioned for this little guy to come up. Well, they must have played for forty-five minutes to an hour, and John stayed in that position, that's how shocked he was with Albert. That sound stayed in my ear for two weeks! ... They had been practicing all day, probably in that loft on Jefferson Street [on the Lower East Side]; you could tell they had been playing together. It was incredible ... we were all in a total state of shock.[2]

Those who heard him were still undecided as to whether Ayler was renouncing jazz conventions or returning to the music's origins in order to revitalize it. Musicologist Ekkehard Jost felt that Ayler not only continued the evolution of jazz that Ornette Coleman had pioneered in the late 50s, but veered off into a new 'ever greater degree of freedom in improvising.'[3] It was both a combination of Coleman's forward-thinking ideas and the tradition's simplest forms, with stylings reminiscent of the early innovators King Oliver and Louis Armstrong.[4]

Pushing jazz forward were Ayler's 'melodic deformation' (first seen in the Scandinavian recordings, these are 'sound-spans' or contours of a series of overblown tones lacking pitch definition); his rough, low-register tenor sound, with traits of the harsh staccato found in R&B music; and the hectic nature of his music, which lacked clarity and relationships (as seen in the music of Ornette Coleman). But Jost also noted that Ayler's music, particularly his thematic material, is loaded with melody—a strange mixture of folk-song happiness and sadness that's also present in traditional jazz—and that the upper register of his tenor sound is thin, yet possesses an extremely wide, rapid vibrato of the kind that listeners can hear in vintage recordings of Sidney Bechet and Freddie Keppard. Jost also felt that Ayler's music was transparent and simple, much like the early jazz recordings.[5]

These contradictions are what make Ayler's work so controversial. Even though he had just recorded *Spirits*, it would be the ESP-Disk' recordings that truly ushered him into the avant-garde.

•

Ayler's brother, Donald, warned him away from the label's founder, Bernard Stollman. Other artists did, too. As pianist Burton Greene, who would release his own titles on the label, later reflected, 'Bernard was a New York lawyer, so everyone thought he was smart, but he was a foolish idealist like the rest of us. The only reason ESP survived at all was because of his parents' money.'[6]

Stollman himself effectively admitted as much in a 2005 interview with *All About Jazz*'s Clifford Allen:

> I didn't have the education or the preparation to take on being a patron in the arts. I didn't have the money and wasn't affluent. But I did go to my mother at just about that point [1964] and I said, 'I've found what I want to do (I was thirty-four, so you can imagine I wasn't a kid), I've found my calling. I'm going to document this whole community of desperate composers of improvisational music.' When I went to her I had an idea to start a record label, and I wanted my inheritance. She gave me $105,000, which in those days was a fortune. … I wasn't what you'd describe as an aficionado of the music; it was something I could do that was meaningful. I could document it, and the choices I made—well, in most cases I didn't know what [the artists] sounded like [before recording them].[7]

Stollman was a hands-off producer, too, telling journalist John Kruth, 'I wasn't going to second-guess the artist's work, he's the expert on his own music. … They could never say later that they had some great ideas, but that son-of-a-bitch producer got in my way. So the opportunity was there for them to wail. And that is just what they did!'[8]

Though musicians signed to ESP-Disk' were paid a small advance against potential royalties, it is doubtful that anyone, much less Stollman, made money from the endeavor: he supposedly signed artists on an album-by-album basis, and even landmark releases in the free-jazz world sold next to nothing. In light of the label's poor distribution, it's likely that Stollman's artists saw little beyond the $695 advance they initially received—an easy figure to forget among those who felt Stollman was exploiting the musicians he worked with.

And yet Stollman gave Ayler and his contemporaries an important chance to document their visionary music. ESP-Disk' labelmates Sun Ra and Milford Graves realized that Stollman was the only person who showed an interest in recording them—and, unlike other label heads, he invested any money he did make back into the label. As Stollman told Tom 'Tornado' Klatt in the liner notes to a CD reissue of vocalist Patty Waters's 1966 album, *College Tour*, 'The artists came to ESP from all over America. They had widely differing educational, cultural and economic backgrounds, but they lived in the realities of their time. ... You may ... consider ESP to have been an attempt to document in a journalistic fashion, and with integrity, the music of a time.'[9]

In a later interview with John Kruth of the now-defunct magazine *Signal To Noise*, Stollman expanded a little on this. 'These people needed to be recorded or their work would be lost. They were in their prime. While Impulse! Records recorded John Coltrane they were totally loath to go near the new generation. There was a big gap. Nobody would touch them and yet they were ripe, mature and ready to go.'[10]

Ayler's views aligned with Stollman's, as he later explained. 'I felt my art was so important I had to get it out. Most musicians had begged me, like Cecil Taylor and other musicians begged me not to make records for Bernard Stollman, that it would be a bad deal. But at that time, I was musically out of this world, and I knew I had to play this music for the people.'[11]

To some of his friends from home, such as Clyde Shy and Bobby Few, Ayler suggested that he wasn't satisfied with Stollman. Others, like Roswell Rudd, spoke favorably of the label's founder. But what shouldn't be forgotten is that Stollman was in the right place at the right time to capture Ayler's music for posterity. Though Cecil Taylor and Amiri Baraka questioned his business practices from the very beginning, Jeff Schwartz's studies support Stollman's claims that no ESP-Disk' release ever made any profit after production costs and royalty advances (some of which were quite substantial). In his history of ESP-Disk', *Always In Trouble*, Jason Weiss further chronicles Stollman's naive (and altruistic) business practices, revealing how he was ripped off by various parties, among them foreign distributors and record stores with dubious accounting practices.

Issues of Stollman's credibility also partially stemmed from the apartment he lived in—but which his parents owned—on Manhattan's Riverside Drive (whose upscale housing sharply contrasted with the poorer conditions in which many ESP-Disk' musicians dwelled), as well as a distrust of Jewish businessmen by the nascent Black civil rights movement in jazz.[12] But when bassist Alan Silva and Paul Bley tried to launch their own individual record labels, they too learned the hard way about the financial difficulties that came with running such an operation.

•

The music that Ayler recorded in 1964—the year he cut his first ESP-Disk' sessions—can be separated into three different strands, though they are connected by a common thread, as Jost notes:

> This conscious archaizing of thematic material is musically reflected in Ayler's choice of the most elementary melodic, harmonic, and rhythmic forms. In general, Ayler's melodies are strictly diatonic and are frequently triadic. Their rhythm is simple and by and large confirms (or helps establish) the meter, while their harmonic groundwork is limited to cadential patterns like I–IV–V–I.[13]

Of the three strands in these recordings, folk themes predominate. This is especially notable in the five versions of 'Ghosts' that Ayler recorded. Ornette Coleman's influence is heard in these pieces' themes, if not in Ayler's actual playing: as heard on *Spiritual Unity*, 'Ghosts' has a South-West blues-folk sound in common with Coleman's 'Ramblin'' (from 1960's *Change Of The Century*).

The avant-garde's interest in folk themes was not limited to Ayler alone. Don Cherry also utilized folk music as a basis for improvisation, and Ayler believed that the tradition had been in existence since before creation; that 'the music we play is a prayer … coming from God.'[14] These motifs functioned as thematic starting points in his improvisations, while techniques of playing folk music allowed Ayler to blur the clarity of his pitch.

Cherry expressed a similar notion about the folk source of Ayler's compositions:

> For one thing, we must understand that like the melodies that Albert played. … They can have the familiarity … you had never seen this before, but you would still feel this … and where it was so strong, you know that the melodies would ring—even though you could go and improvise. You could still hear the sound of the melody ringing … he was one of the first persons that I know that played melodies that he loved that were dear to him, you know, and now it's happening. … He wasn't doing it to be popular—to being in a band wagon, and all that you know. … These melodies were something that was passed to him, I believe, by a spirit … I think he's only a filter … and these melodies are a part of this preservation of quality that happens in its purest form. … It was incredible.[15]

Contrasting with the folk-music source is the ballad material Ayler drew from—particularly in melodies overloaded with pathos, almost to a point of approaching pomposity. These long, sustained melodies, lacking a strict tempo, are especially evident in cuts such as 'Mothers' from the live album *Ghosts*, released in 1965 on Debut. Here, the sentimentality derives not only from the banality of the melody but also from Ayler's phrasing and tone production.

Pieces such as 'Holy, Holy' and 'The Wizard'—the latter also from *Spiritual Unity*—make clear the third strand of Ayler's music from this era: dense, high-energy motifs. The simple, almost predictable nature of these pieces' themes is, however, offset by the unpredictability of Ayler's improvisations.

It is these thematic models that provide the template for Ayler's improvisatory patterns; the sound-spans follow the underlying thematic structure.[16] These three elements of Ayler's music were in evidence in June 1964 when the newly formed Albert Ayler Trio—consisting of Ayler, bassist Gary Peacock, and drummer Sunny Murray—played at the Cellar Café, a small basement bar with a capacity of sixty-five that had opened just two months earlier in the uptown area of 91st Street. Bill Dixon had booked the group. Fresh like Peacock from the Take 3 sessions, trumpeter Dixon had been hired by filmmaker and Cellar Café co-owner Peter Sabino to be the bar's musical director, and he set about booking artists on the outer limits of jazz. This concert was presented as part of a series that featured musicians who were struggling for work at other New York clubs, and which placed the Café at the center of the white avant-garde world of artists such as pianist Carla Bley, drummer Paul Motian, bassists Steve Swallow and Barre Phillips, and trombonist Roswell Rudd. Ayler's outfit rehearsed in Gary Peacock's 22nd Street apartment, playing music that Sonny Murray described as a combination of styles he had heard in the US Army and in Europe. If the improvisation was based on a known tune, Ayler would tell the band about it and what he felt about it.[17]

Archie Shepp had a similar impression of Ayler's approach to composition, explaining, 'Ayler did not say, "We are going to play this or that piece." Rather, he said things like, "Let's play sadness. Let's play hunger."'[18]

Bill Folwell, another bassist who would play with Ayler in 1966, told a similar story to Marc Chaloin of the online magazine *Point Of Departure*:

> I didn't know what Albert wanted. So, I just played the bow and he said, 'Hey, that's great, yeah! Keep that up. Just play that.' And I was just holding on for dear life, you know, I was just trying to play something that I thought was right. I didn't get any guidance or anything from him. ... The little tunes, and the, you know, going out, the energy. You know, 'Give me more energy, more energy, more energy.'[19]

With Ayler's permission, writer Paul Haines recorded the trio's set at the Café on June 14, 1964, five cuts of which—'Spirits,' 'Wizard,' 'Ghosts (First Variation),' 'Prophecy,' and 'Spirits (Version Two),' incorrectly labelled on the record as 'Ghosts (Second Variation)'—were posthumously released in 1975 as the ESP-Disk' album *Prophecy* (ESP 3030). An extra hour's worth of material remained unreleased until *Albert Smiles With Sunny* was issued two decades later on the InRespect label, adding 'Sweet Variation (1),' 'Ghost,' 'The Truth Is Marching In,' 'No Head,' and 'Sweet Variation (2)' to the material fans were already aware of. The set is now available in a (mostly) complete version as *Prophecy Revisited*.

Effectively an early version of Ayler's landmark album *Spiritual Unity*, hindsight already tells us that the music on *Prophecy* is great, but, at the time of its performance, it was merely just another gig for the Albert Ayler Trio. For a group that made such an impact, Ayler utilized them for only a short time: it allowed for the largest number of instruments that could be used without getting in the way of his own drive, yet also the smallest group of instruments that could effectively offset him. Writing in *Coda*, Barry Tepperman noted the advantages of utilizing a small group:

> In the trio a maximum of sympathy in countermotion was joined to a minimum of restriction, leaving only the tenorist free to move his lines in several directions at once. This in fact is the course of development of his solos, moving not only linearly and rhythmically but timbrally, achieving in the two trio albums the greatest critical momentum of any of his work.[20]

This contrasts with the music on Ayler's earlier albums, where each selection represented a different aspect of his expression, whether that be in the choices of instruments or in the compositions he played. The traditional jazz line-up limited the multi-directional movement that Ayler could explore, but Ayler's celebrated trio can be viewed as an extension of the musical laboratory Cecil Taylor had led across 1962 and 1963, and which had 'proved the total irrelevance of the European structural orders.'[21] Jazz music's early innovators, such as pianists Earl Hines and Jelly Roll Morton and trumpeters King Oliver and Louis Armstrong, created a 'sound of surprise' that was accomplished by 'shifting structures, tempo modulations, key shifts, and a wild humor.'[22] Ayler's group did the same.

In this setting, bassist Gary Peacock combines a command over his instrument with imagination: the structure of Ayler's compositions permits Peacock to focus on tonal and rhythmic aspects, instead of focusing on supplying the harmony. After he opens each composition with a bass solo, it's Ayler who then slowly drives the band to the melody. Around the time that Peacock joined the trio, he had been on the verge of accepting an invitation to join Miles Davis's band, but his wife told him that his future lay with Ayler. Indeed, the two were blessed with a mutual understanding that seemed almost telepathic. Toward the end of his life, Ayler stated that Peacock was the best bassist he had ever played with.

On drums, Sunny Murray also supplies a timbral rather than a mere rhythmic feed to Ayler, reinforcing the notion of 'shapes' that Ayler began exploring on *Spirits*. Murray had abandoned rhythm after his work with Cecil Taylor; he now focused on a cymbal-snare interaction with the lead instruments, responding to Ayler's horn lines in a dense and intimate manner. It also left him free to interact with solos without having to tend to the rhythm. As such, Murray contributes to the pure creation of sound and atmosphere—like Miles Davis and Thelonious Monk, his approach was minimalist. Rather than adding the sort of complexities that can be heard in the polyrhythmic style of drummers such as Tony Williams and Elvin Jones, Murray focused on the rhythms of Native American music, seeking, as Stanley Crouch put it, to 'fuse them with an unpredictable range of accents and paraphrases that were defined as much by duration as they were by rests, and this, in turn, made silence take on an importance totally new to Black American music.'[23]

Bassist Sirone (born Norris Jones), who would sit in with a different Ayler outfit in 1968, had another view on what Sunny Murray brought to the trio: 'Sunny is the master of sounds. Natural sounds. Controlled sounds. Just what he can do with a cymbal. Just a cymbal; trills, ascents, and sustained sounds against the time. Multiple rhythms with a space that's a mutha!'[24]

•

There are several discrepancies common to *Prophecy* and *Spiritual Unity*. The first and second variations of 'Ghosts' are different compositions; the second variation of 'Ghosts' on *Prophecy* is actually 'Spirits' from the *Spirits* album; and 'The Wizard' on *Prophecy* is called 'Holy, Holy' on *Spirits*. [25] *Prophecy* almost parallels *Spiritual Unity* (discussed later), only differing in the title cut.

Critics are divided over whether the presence of an audience on *Prophecy* makes it a more intense listen than *Spiritual Unity*, or whether the freshness of the trio's early days gives the compositions a looser feeling, but the one-month difference between this June show and the July recording session that produced *Spiritual Unity* is negligible. Ayler was peaking as a musician, driving his band to fame and possibly sowing the seeds of his own destruction.

As Annette Peacock later observed, 'He was coming from a place in the heart, a wordless place, one heart speaking to another. That's what he was about … It broke his heart when the people didn't respond. People often seemed stunned by the music, I think it was a question of timing. He came too soon after Ornette Coleman. People hadn't had time to assimilate what Ornette had done. They weren't ready for total freedom, for music that did completely without time and changes. Albert was a soldier on the battlefield in a war he couldn't win.'[26]

CHAPTER IX

spiritual unity

Though Bernard Stollman had offered Ayler a premier place on his fledgling ESP-Disk' roster the previous December, he'd yet to get his new charge into the studio. Already committed to the Atlantic Studios session that produced *Spirits* and *Swing Low Sweet Spirituals*, Ayler had promised to call Stollman when his schedule cleared up. Stollman later said:

> I was frankly quite skeptical that he would ever bother—he was diffident—but in June the phone rang. It was Albert Ayler, and he said, 'I can record now, it's fine.' I didn't ask him any questions, but I said, 'I know this studio near Times Square, Variety Arts it's called, why don't you meet me there.' He did, and the other guys showed up—Gary Peacock and Sunny Murray—I met them, they went in the studio to record, and I sat out on the steps.[1]

The small Variety Arts facility was used by Moe Asch, the owner of Folkways Records, and was more often a spot where Latin groups demoed their music. But it was here, on July 10, 1964, that Ayler made his first official recording session for ESP-Disk'. As Stollman later told Val Wilmer, Ayler walked in, accompanied by 'a tall, very slender white American, very emaciated-looking, named Gary Peacock, and a large, corpulent jolly walrus who turned out to be Sunny Murray,' plus Gary's wife, Annette, and Stollman. Unaware that this wasn't a demo session, the studio engineer recorded the group in mono, but that didn't stop the power of the Albert Ayler Trio in full flow. The engineer ran from the control room, presumably in shock; when the tape reel was almost empty, he returned, and Stollman began to dance around the studio, saying to Annette, 'My God! What an auspicious beginning for a record label.'[2]

It was. Titled *Spiritual Unity* and given the catalogue number of ESP 1002, the album was readied for release the following year alongside two other records—self-titled works by the Byron Allen Trio and the Giuseppe Logan Quartet—as a way of establishing the label's artistic integrity. Given a red-on-white silk-screened cover with an image of a saxophonist cradling his saxophone sitting in between the group name and album title, Ayler's record immediately stood out on any racks it found itself in. 'I decided that silk screening them would have a primal quality, suitable for this enterprise,' Stollman recalled, adding, 'We worked together doing the screening.'[3] The rear sleeve pictured head shots of the trio placed around a large 'Y'—a symbol that existed before recorded history and which represents the spirit of mankind rising to God—presumably in unity.

Three years later, Ayler explained his concept of spiritual unity:

When we let the will of God produce itself in us, we will work with Him, and will be blessed in all our actions. He will also help us to think justly and kindly. When all the people understand what links them spiritually to one another, Peace will reign on earth. All men will be men of good will. Spiritual Unity will reign then.[4]

As somewhat foretold by *Prophecy*, the groundbreaking compositions on the initial pressing of *Spiritual Unity* are 'Ghosts (First Variation),' The Wizard,' 'Spirits,' (7:49 version), and 'Ghosts (Second Variation)'. An alternate pressing (ESP-1002B) was also made, and became the common release, with a different 6:46 take of 'Spirits (called 'Saints' on *Witches & Devils*) in place of the initial 7:49 version—which was subsequently retitled 'Vibrations' on the album of that name, though Stollman could not later recall why this was. All of these compositions were included on the album's fiftieth-anniversary CD reissue.

However *Spiritual Unity* is configured, it is a classic—a record that speaks about Ayler's life. As John Litweiler wrote, 'Here are the conflicts of a Hamlet, more fantastic because Ayler lived amid the incomprehensible chaos of an age more betrayed than the ancient prince's, asserting his lonely nobility despite the certainty of its denial.'[5]

It was also controversial from the moment it was released, with reviews sitting at opposite ends of the spectrum—either positive in up-and-coming jazz publications such as *Coda* and *JAZZ*, or damning in conservative titles like *DownBeat*. Writing in *JAZZ*, Frank Smith—himself a white free-jazz saxophonist who sought to emulate Ayler—provided the first favorable US review of the album:

> All of the tunes on this album and all of Albert's playing that I've heard follow the same simple straightforward format: a very lyrical tune with an old timey feeling is set forth and then the playing gradually gets into something more and more intense and ferocious until the listener is practically overwhelmed. … There is nothing far out about the tunes themselves, they have an immediate and direct appeal. … But as he moves more and more away from the tune many listeners are bound to be scared by what comes on. This is just where it's necessary to understand that you're supposed to be overwhelmed by his playing. He's playing so strong just because what he feels is so strong and he wants you to feel it and come alive too … the main thing listeners will have to adjust to is the dissonance level of the music, which is another way of saying that they have to adjust to the strength of these feelings coming at them. … Just the power and love of his humanity, that's all Albert's trying to sell.[6]

Stuart Broomer of *Coda* was probably the first critic to place *Spiritual Unity* within the wider context of jazz history:

> The repercussions of Coleman's ideas can be seen in Albert Ayler, who, arriving only a few years after Coleman, is playing in a manner that few musicians and

fewer critics could have imagined. His music can be described in a sense as a combination of [Cecil] Taylor's and Coleman's in that it combines the textural density of the pianist with the altoist's use of timbres and pitches that have little to do with European formal music. The result is incredible … Ayler plays a virtuoso music—music that demands control of the instrument in a personal direction … for Ayler's music is obviously contained—he plays clearly what he intends to play and playing things I doubt any other tenor saxophonist could touch—speed, range, sound, that are completely musical and completely beautiful.[7]

Continuing a practice it began with Ornette Coleman's *Free Jazz* in January 1962, *DownBeat* ran two reviews of Ayler's record—an approach instigated by the magazine's then-editor, Don DeMichael, who felt that major avant-garde statements would be given fairer treatment with a positive and a negative critique. Though *DownBeat*'s humor columnist George Crater continually disparaged avant-garde music—the recurring theme being that the artists did not know what they were doing and that listeners later developed an appreciation for the music after experts explained the logic of the 'strange music'[8]—the dual-review format also allowed the magazine to cover both bases and save face if they were wrong about landmark developments in jazz, as they had been when they missed the boat on bebop.

Kenny Dorham—a respected hard-bop trumpeter who had recorded several classic albums for Blue Note and had already indicated a bias against the avant-garde ever since appearing on Cecil Taylor's 1959 album *Stereo Drive*—gave *Spiritual Unity* no stars and described it as 'a satirical comedy' in which Ayler is putting the listener on. His sarcastic review reeks of denigrating humor, concluding that Ayler was so far out that he 'passed the moon and the stars.'[9]

But there was more to Dorham's review than meets the eye. In a question-and-answer session in Rotterdam, free-jazz drummer Milford Graves recalled asking Dorham why he was so negative:

I saw him on 125th street—I was with Albert Ayler and a few more people—

and we went up to him, out of respect, and I said, 'Well, why did you review that recording like that?' He said, 'Well, to be honest with you … I didn't understand what it was, and I thought I was supposed to be analyzing it, and I couldn't.'

Jazz historian Frank Kofsky has claimed that, because of the revolutionary nature of the albums ESP-Disk' was putting out, conservative Black musicians were hired to pen negative reviews in order to both avoid the appearance of racism and to limit the album's impact (and sales). Indeed, Kofsky felt Dorham was a 'nice, safe, domesticated neo-bopper' who felt economically threatened by the work he had been asked to review. However, it is important to note that Dorham was also one of the few Black writers—let alone musicians—to be on *DownBeat*'s reviewing panel, and that many jazz icons who weren't *DownBeat* critics (Miles Davis, Cannonball Adderley, and Dizzy Gillespie among them) had openly derided the avant-garde scene ever since 1959, when they were faced with Ornette Coleman's *Tomorrow Is The Question!*

A champion of Black cultural nationalism who was influenced by Marxist thought, Kofsky also wrote biting criticisms filtered through his Trotskyite Fourth International lens against white jazz critics who he felt were in league with the white capitalist record companies and club owners. And yet, ironically, the early champions of the avant-garde were white critics such as Martin Williams, Nat Hentoff, and Gunther Schuller.

DownBeat's more sympathetic coverage was penned by Bill Matthieu, who reviewed *Spiritual Unity* alongside the Byron Allen and the Giuseppe Logan discs:

These three records are best heard as a document from the center of contemporary jazz, not as finished, definitive performances. The music, however, is not merely experimental. It is fundamental to the lives of the many men making it. The ability to form rounded judgments of the music seems less appropriate than the ability to suspend that judgment willingly. … The primary thing is this: many men are suddenly laboring very hard to find a new language that will express a new grace within the human condition. ... Ayler makes a great wobbling noise. Notes disappear into wide, irregular ribbons, fragmented, prismatic, wind-blown, undetermined, and filled with fury. Though the fury is frightening, dangerous, it achieves absolute certainty through being, musically, absolutely contained. Ayler seemingly rarely hears one note at a time—as if it were useless ever to consider the particles of a thing. He seems to want to scan all notes at all times and in this way speak to an expanded consciousness. ... Ayler's music, as well as most avant-garde music, is at best, difficult to listen to. It is nevertheless a very direct statement, the physical manifestation of a spiritual or mystical ritual.[10]

•

After Ayler's death, six years later, *Spiritual Unity* still commanded respect as what *Melody Maker*'s Richard Williams called 'a perfectly executed trio album ... the three reaching new heights of freedom and empathy.'[11] This freedom can be heard on three separate rhythmic planes. In contrast with what Jost called Ayler's 'negation of fixed pitches,' Murray and Peacock negate the beat, with Murray's cymbal playing creating color, as opposed to keeping time, while Ayler's improvisations take the form of extended sound spans as Peacock focuses on impulses.[12] Other commentators have noted the inherent contrasts in the music, with Val Wilmer writing that the album was 'shockingly different—Ayler disquietingly harsh and brutal but at the same time deeply tinged with pathos. Peacock listening as he played monumental bass figures, Murray behaving... as though he might just want to disappear—but its conclusions seemed so simple when you listened to it. Ayler, Murray and Peacock had created the perfect *group* music.'[13]

As Ayler put it, listening to each other was the highest level of interaction: 'Most people would have thought this impossible, but it actually happened. The most important thing is to stay in tune with each other, but it takes spiritual unity to do this. ... We weren't *playing*, we were listening to each other.'[14]

This is evident in the increased systematic approach the band takes toward their solos, in which, according to Baldwin, each one 'seems to be almost an exercise in this kind of [linear] development.'[15] Those on 'Spirits' build via 'motivic' or thematic development, while the linear development in 'Ghosts' sees each phrase relate back to the preceding phrase—this is most clear in the second variation; the first variation of 'Ghosts' suffers a little as the development is broken by the insertion of unrelated material.

As Ayler once said, it's all about feelings, which grow as each musician tunes into what is being played and then builds upon it. This is the key to understanding Ayler's music: the themes function not so much as source material, but instead as structural markings that lead the band in and out of improvisational sections.

Despite his admiration for Ayler's use of structured form, W.A. Baldwin considered it secondary to the message in his music—that is, the strength of the 'argument' corresponds to the strength of the message. In evidence, he would cite 'Ghosts (Second Variation),' which 'builds up to a tremendous sustained climax of shifting emotions held together by the almost inexorable logic of the development.'

'Ghosts' is the most revealing composition on the entire album—a piece that John Litweiler in *The Freedom Principle* felt was the most autobiographical work on an autobiographical record. 'Ayler's dark shattering of the theme and central passages in a welter of "unknown" pitches, booms, cruel rising phrases,' he writes. 'The passion and the extreme internal disorder of this catharsis are among the most intense moments in the career of this most intense of artists.'[16]

Utilizing the harmonic structure of the Swedish folksong 'Torparvisan' (also known as 'Little Farmer's Song'), the two takes of 'Ghosts' are illuminating in the way that they invite comparison with each other, as well as with the Cellar Café performance recorded a month earlier. Most critics first look at the differences in the development of Ayler's solos, comparing them as a means of quality assessment, with Barry McRae noting how ideas that are thrown out in 'First Variation' become extended in 'Second Variation':

This latter piece is a superb example of fleet saxophone playing in its own right, but it is the way which he improvises at such a crippling tempo that is really impressive. Each individual discovery belongs to the parent melody, even when used to extend it, and every one is cogent and well formed.[17]

Opening the album, 'Ghosts (First Variation)' begins with a chromatic introduction played by Ayler alone. The tones resulting from his overblowing contrast sharply with the succeeding phrase—a plain statement of the melody, shorn of any embellishments, repetitions, or temporal differences heard in his variants. Ayler plays with the song by blowing long screams that match the direction of the melody's contours; the rhythm of the piece is imitated by honks and screams in a dissonant mix. As a result, the composition's individual elements are synthesized into a single noise wave.

When Peacock begins his bass solo, he utilizes the high-register arpeggiated figures that previously accompanied Ayler and then elaborates these figures into his own solo. These simultaneous solos, delivered on a horizontal plane, characterize the entire album, and, when seen as a whole, are examples of consistently free improvisation. Jeff Schwartz compares it to an extreme of the New Orleans tradition of collective improvisation, while Peacock felt that playing through inspiration allowed the musicians to overcome the lack of understanding of what they were doing—the end goal was to learn to listen.[18]

Pure emotionalism marks *Spiritual Unity*'s second track, 'The Wizard,' as a contemporary reviewer, Mort Maizlish. wrote:

'The Wizard' is based on a pretty simple line that sounds like a spoken sentence: duh DA duh duh duh DAH DAH DUddlelah—Ayler shouts it to you from his pulpit, but he doesn't just repeat it. He mulls over the notes, examines it like [Charlie Parker] used to do with those tired old 'standards,' finds such a variety of intricate variations that you feel ashamed of yourself for not having seen what might have always been there. Ayler works 'The Wizard' in and out and finds some fantastic possibilities in it, and at the same time brings it to a hair-raising emotional peak. Then, there he is, way up at the top, wailing his message to the wind, and you can still hear his statement in there with all of that fire and ecstasy.[19]

Writing in *Coda*, Stuart Broomer also noted the simplicity of the piece, calling it 'a terse phrase which Ayler spits out four times, but at the end he tacks on a simple resolution that is hilariously effective when coupled with the rhythmic figure which he plays.'[20] Others saw a more complex structure in 'The Wizard' (a variant of 'Holy, Holy,' from *Spirits*), with the solos moving further away from the themes, giving the piece a looser feel. This composition is based on a series of one- or two-measure phrases played at a fast pace and in numerous repetitions that trigger off the improvisations. Again, the melody's contour is parodied by Ayler's long screams. Yet these pale in comparison to those heard on 'Spirits.' Writing in *Jazz Monthly*, W.A. Baldwin praised Ayler for delivering an extraordinary performance in which each solo begins with a theme before departing and then returning to the theme. In turn, each of these become longer and more distinct in their thematic relationships.[21]

Because this is done in stages, it is not immediately apparent to the listener, since the first solo is a paraphrase of the theme which stays close to the original melody while differing in intervallic relationships and rhythmic reorganization. The second solo develops in a linear fashion, with each phrase relating to the theme before Ayler gradually returns to it. However, the third solo completely abandons the theme before once again returning to it, setting the fourth solo up to rapidly depart from the theme and never come back.

Noting that Ayler was 'in a warm, exquisite mood' on 'Spirits,' Mort Maizlish recognized the importance of this piece to Ayler's development:

It's slow and piercing, reminding you of something long past that was wanted but never attained. He almost sounds like he's playing a viola or cello, with his notes long and slightly curving as if they were bowed by a master. Peacock increases the effect with an *arco* introduction, then goes into some of his finest accompaniment work on the album. This is a crying, soaring piece, very earthy and sexy if you hear it one way, but it could be called 'ethereal' or 'searching' if you had to describe it.[22]

The idea that Ayler's music was 'sexy' was challenged by *Jazz Monthly's* Brian Priestley, who did not consider *Spiritual Unity* to be a great album:

> Any music worth assessing by jazz criteria should have a strong erotic content, the rewards here are disappointing. On this level, Ayler sounds like an impotent exhibitionist compared ... with Sonny Rollins. And on a rhythmic level (which is obviously closely connected) Ayler shows here ... that his sense of timing is more ... elastic than his accompanists! And the lack of variety or ... singlemindedness which causes him to quote from 'Ghosts' during 'Spirits' and from 'The Wizard' during 'Ghosts 2,' limits him emotionally.[23]

The 'Saints' version of 'Spirits' was described by Schwartz as a 'rubato ballad' on which Ayler deploys a wide vibrato that runs deeper than any used by Louis Armstrong or other musicians playing in the New Orleans tradition in which it was extensively employed.[24] The sobbing that can be heard offers an emotional antithesis to the detached coolness of vibrato-less players such as Paul Desmond and Lee Konitz.[25]

In revisiting 'Ghosts' for *Spiritual Unity's* final cut, Ayler brings the album's message of spiritual ecstasy to the forefront. The piece opens with an ornate theme that bears no relationship to the solos that follow, but while Peacock's accompaniment is similar to what he delivered on the piece's opening counterpart, it is here played an octave lower, more like a traditional bass part. As an album closer, 'Ghosts (Second Variation)' was praised by Maizlish for the emotional force of Ayler's playing:

> It is the most exciting, exhausting solo on the record for sheer emotional intensity and the levels that he reaches with high and low notes. That wide tone is always there at the bottom while Ayler climbs and screams his strings of high notes, as if he started at point zero and is playing a duet with himself,

going up and down at the same time. He plays both 'sides' (it really does sound like two simultaneous lines, like the old 'tenor battles') of the solo with magnificent control and intensity. The lines themselves are beautiful, melodic, all of them using previous ideas while contributing new ones. This man has complete knowledge of his instrument and of his music. Like Coltrane, and Cecil Taylor, he forms his ideas and resolves them at such a rapid pace that they sound incoherent unless you can hear *all* of the notes and think about them, examine them, *with* him, while he's getting them out.[26]

CHAPTER X

new york eye and ear control

J ust a week after recording the epochal *Spiritual Unity*, the Albert Ayler Trio were recording another new work, this time augmented by alto saxophonist John Tchicai, whom Ayler had met during his time in Copenhagen; trumpeter Don Cherry; and trombonist Roswell Rudd. The six-piece were booked to record the soundtrack for Michael Snow's black-and-white experimental film *New York Eye And Ear Control*, which was then released on ESP-Disk' as ESP 1016. Rather than have the band create a score that would match the mood of the film, however, Snow, a major figure in avant-garde cinema, shot the thirty-four-minute, 16mm film *after* the soundtrack had been recorded, fitting his images and ideas to the music.

The idea stemmed from a commission Snow had received from a Toronto concert organization, Ten Centuries Concerts, who wanted Snow to make a film that utilized jazz music. The director—who had himself played jazz professionally—had heard Ayler at a club (likely the Cellar Café) and was blown away. 'I simply said then that I wanted to buy a half hour of music,' Snow later recalled of his initial conversations with Ayler. 'But it did have some stipulations, which were that I didn't want any previously played compositions, and I wanted it to be as much ensemble improvisations as could be with no solos.'[1]

Snow wanted the film to be about polar opposites, and he elaborated further on the role of its soundtrack with ESP-Disk' historian Jason Weiss:

> It's like the music is a particular kind of experience, and the film is something quite different that you see simultaneously. That's why the title is *New York Eye And Ear Control*. It is actually being able to hear the music and being able to see the picture without the music saying, the image is sad, or this image is happy—which is a way that movie music is always used. … It's as if the image part of it is very classical and static. In fact, most of the motion is in the music, actually. So, they're kind of counterpointing and being in their own worlds but happening simultaneously.[2]

Elsewhere, Snow explained how he 'tried to make it possible for the "improvised," spontaneous, raw "vocal," raucous, expressionist, emotional, "romantic" music of Albert Ayler, Don Cherry, etc., to co-exist with the "classical" measured, refined, considered, composed, "intellectual," temporal images. That's what the title means.'[3]

The film featured the 'walking woman,' a cut-out silhouette that was a recurrent image in Snow's films, performances, paintings, and sculptures throughout the 60s. In *New York Eye And Ear Control*, he uses positive and negative exposures of the woman in various permutations in order to explore the ways a two-dimensional figure can be placed and manipulated in a variety of settings. Louis Dompierre, who edited a collection of essays celebrating Snow's work, considered the results a 'portrait and landscape study' based on the interaction between sound and image.[4]

Still frames from the film appear on *New York Eye And Ear Control*'s album cover. The record itself was recorded in a loft owned by the poet Paul Haines, who allowed the group to drill a hole in the floor of their makeshift studio to feed the microphone wires down to the floor below. In the context of Ayler's oeuvre, this album continues his trend of changing his style for each new work, and it was a radical departure from the *Spiritual Unity* session from the previous week. Roswell Rudd described it as 'free counterpoint … the basis of what we do, and Albert's music was a regeneration. He went back as far as back goes, and all the way up to the moment … but he had many sounds. Such a range of colors and dynamics. There were many spirits in the mix there.'[5]

Following a brief intro, titled 'Dons Dawn,' each album side consists of a twenty-minute collective improvisation—'AY' and 'ITT,' respectively—without themes, just as Michael Snow had requested. As the band played, the director shaped the music according to how he envisioned it in his film. Roswell Rudd recalled instructions such as, 'Don, would you play something kind of lyrical, and you other guys just play softly around Don?' Or, 'We just need something a little more rubato, sweeter, toned down.'

Ayler once explained what collective improvisation meant to him, calling it 'a thing of rejoicing collectively to the spirits—or a prayer.'[6] On this record, however, it could best be characterized as 'disorganized,' suffering from the characteristics common to much free collective improvisation: a low degree of self-discipline and the lack of a unified conception; creating a collective character under these conditions is nearly impossible, as the music becomes the realization of each individual's strengths combined to create a collective weakness.

Despite the group's intentions, *New York Eye And Ear Control* is not a true collective free improvisation, since Ayler's playing dominates while the other five musicians follow him, or are carried along with his flow. Rudd described trying to keep up:

> It was just the force of his thrust. He had such a strong sense of purpose that the music kind of gravitated toward him. Then his dynamic would change, or he would drop out for awhile, and then something else would happen. But by and large, when Albert was on the scene, he was blazing the trail, so to speak. He had a great quality that way. So, playing an accompaniment to him was like playing in a Dixieland band to me, with a strong trumpet player or something. It was kind of a natural, reflex action that happened.[7]

Yet an analysis by Ekkehard Jost suggests that the contrasting temperaments of Tchicai, Cherry, and Rudd are what gives the album its artistic success: that the three horn players inspired Ayler to absorb their styles into his own musical idiom and give a 'new direction to the flow of ideas.' Jost highlights Tchicai's use of repeated melodic patterns as the source of the music's 'motivic linkage' and notes that Rudd used stylings from the old 'tailgate trombonists'—those who sat over the back of a horse-drawn carriage while the rest of the group faced forward during a procession—such as fragmentary flourishes in the higher register, as well as growl sounds intermixed with glissandos. For his part, Cherry's improvisations are, Jost writes, composed of 'broad melodic lines' or 'sharply accented staccato passages.'[8]

According to W.A. Baldwin—who, writing in 1967, put forth the idea that the album's three pieces simply ended when the tape ran out—the works suffer from a lack of both 'overall shape' and of 'rhythmic continuity,' problems which render the performances failures saved only by the musicians' talents.[9] Baldwin's negative appraisal is based on Ayler's occasional lapses of taste, such as his low-register honks; in tandem with Tchicai or Cherry, Ayler builds his solos strongly and maintains an assurance of rhythm, but he swings only occasionally. For Baldwin, the other musicians' performances are also at fault: Rudd's phrasing is stiff, and bassist Gary Peacock loses the beat because of the excessive freedom; even though he sometimes recovers it, he more often concentrates on bowing his instrument.

Not all critics shared this opinion. Writing in 1974, Jost was better positioned to place *New York Eye And Ear Control* in a more advantageous context in the history of free jazz, and he claimed the record as one of Ayler's best recordings—one that provided an important link between Ornette Coleman's *Free Jazz* (which was released in 1961) and John Coltrane's *Ascension* (which would follow in 1966). Feeling that the give-and-take between the musicians is what controlled the form of the music, he also concluded that the quantity of variation on all levels across 'AY' and 'ITT' is what differentiated Ayler's album from the uniformity of emotional content found on Coleman's.[10]

The album's first piece, 'Dons Dawn,' focuses on trumpeter Don Cherry, who puts his solo on a subordinate level to the rest of the group.

Indeed, all the solos on the record are secondary to the collective effort. This is seen best in the two long pieces, in which short individual solos serve as transitional phases—ür-motifs for the next collective improvisation. These improvisations are self-generating, being, in Jost's description 'a-thematic.' The sole exception is a short quote by Ayler, from his own 'Holy, Holy,' that acts as a trigger in 'ITT.'

The differences arise when the motifs interact with one another and each musician takes turns in attempting to break out of his envelope of sounds in order to bring himself into a different sound unit. In these instances, fast, pulsing passages lead into slow, melodic passages, full of glissandi. Cherry's staccato notes arise independently from the rhythm and are then mimicked by the other horns, resulting in a pointillistic chain. Tchicai, in contrast, draws Ayler's atonal sound spans to a tonal center by utilizing fragments of scales and ostinatos. In Jost's assessment, several levels of emotion are simultaneously present, coming together as they alternate between calm and agitated; the rhythmic plane alternates via a constantly changing rhythm between arhythmic accents and a complete stop.[11]

Appraising Ayler's legacy in *DownBeat* in 1971, John Litweiler pre-echoed Jost's view, noting, 'It might have been a disaster like Coltrane's *Ascension*, but the more sophisticated shared principles of free time and harmonic basis guarantee part of the music's success.'

Outside of *New York Eye And Ear Control*, Ayler used collective improvisation only minimally, usually at the beginning or end of a piece. With this album, however, he proved himself adept at working on different and more complex levels of improvisation, expanding on his trio work in order to move to a freer setting.

ghosts

D uring the summer of 1964, Ayler made a few club appearances, on one occasion making an informal cameo with the Pharaoh Sanders Trio, most likely at the Anderson Theater, a now-defunct venue in the Bowery. Recalling some of the frostier treatment he received in Scandinavia, Ayler wasn't actually welcomed onstage—instead, he stood at the back of the theater and played anyway.

Despite having made their way into the studio and onto record, the avant-gardists were still largely barred from playing the New York City clubs—owners preferred to stick with moneymakers such as Dave Brubeck and others—so sympathetic entrepreneurs set up private concerts in lofts and coffee houses. Advertising was minimal, limited to placing an occasional ad in the *Village Voice* and passing out handbills. Some venues served coffee and sandwiches, but without alcohol licenses, many patrons came with pre-prepared hip flasks. Other fans organized weekend jazz clubs, meeting in lofts where they would sit on the floor or in wooden folding chairs. Though far smaller in scale than anything the established clubs offered, such activity helped give the avant-garde scene a kind of formal structure.

Ayler appeared in at least one of these loft sessions at the closed-up Jazz Gallery—now renamed the Ski Lodge and completely outfitted in ski trappings—in August, his core trio augmented by Don Cherry, who joined the band for most of the set. A private recording of the performance, which contained the pieces 'Children,' 'Ghosts,' and 'The Wizard,' is supposed to have been made, but its existence today seems extremely doubtful.

Ayler played another of these jam sessions with bassist Alan Silva and pianist Valdo Williams after walking into a club on West 4th Street and asking to join them. As Silva recalled, Ayler played an old Charlie Parker piece:

> So he plays 'Ornithology' perfectly, I mean, really in a bebop mode, incredible. He takes this first, very strong bebop chorus, second chorus, and then he starts to do these fantastic things on the saxophone. Screaming qualities, and vocal qualities, on this lower and upper registers, and it was really cooking, we were really burning. With perfect pitch, his intonation was incredible. I said, 'This guy's brilliant, what is he doing?' I was really impressed.[1]

The club's owner, however, was not impressed. After another dispiriting encounter with a hostile businessman, Ayler told Silva that he was headed to Denmark with Sunny Murray. He later explained, 'American-minded people are not listening to music any more … we wanted to leave to give some of our love to someone who would really sit and listen and be quiet.'[2]

Ironically, if Ayler had stayed in New York, he would likely have achieved recognition earlier. Saxophonist Marzette Watts told *Cadence* interviewer Larry Nai that Amiri Baraka had conceived of a plan to take all other avant-garde music off the market and to focus solely on recording and promoting one artist: Ayler. The idea was that Coltrane would then take the tapes to producer Bob Thiele, who had worked on records by Coltrane, McCoy Tyner, and Charles Mingus, and was then the head of Impulse! Records. But just as Baraka was about to put his plan into action, Ayler went to Denmark. Instead of being pushed as the leading light of the avant-garde, his spot was taken by Archie Shepp, whose *Four For Trane* album emerged on Impulse! later in the year.

•

Ole Vestergaard of Debut Records had offered Ayler a one-way ticket to

Copenhagen. According to Sunny Murray, Eric Dolphy was supposed to join the band on tour, but Dolphy died on June 29, of complications from diabetes, two months before the tour began. The expanded line-up would have given Ayler more name recognition, as Dolphy was an associate of both Coltrane and Mingus. In the event, however, the engagement was successful enough to be extended, and the Albert Ayler Quartet (with Peacock, Murray, and Cherry) also toured the Netherlands and Sweden.

Bernard Stollman felt that Vestergaard's offer was inadequate for a group such as Ayler's—not to mention that he wasn't footing the bill to fly them home—but because Ayler had had previous dealings with the Danish impresario, he accepted. As Stollman recalled:

> I walked with Albert—it was a sunny day, I think it was a Sunday—Albert said, 'We're going to Europe in a few days. I know what's going to happen. We'll tour, and then Sunny will get into trouble … and we'll have to bail him out. And we'll have to make a record in order to get the money to come home.'[3]

On August 31, bassist Gary Peacock, who had been fasting for fifteen days, was dragged from his bed, and the band caught a flight to Copenhagen. Their engagement at Jazzhus Montmartre began the following month. Audiences were not specifically hostile, but they were reserved, yet the group gradually developed a clique of European fans. One Montmartre employee, Bill Hess, recalled these shows as if they were transcendent experiences, describing Ayler as 'very gentle, very friendly person who never said a bad word about anyone.'[4]

And yet Stollman's concerns were somewhat justified, as Ayler did record for other labels while in Europe, and at least two radio broadcasts were given posthumous release. A broadcast from Montmartre, dated September 3, 1964, consisted of 'Spirits,' 'Vibrations' (mistitled 'Holy Spirits'), 'Saints' 'Mothers,' an incomplete 'Children,' and 'Spirits'; a performance from Radiohuset Studio 2 a week later featured 'Vibrations,' 'Saints,' and an incomplete recording of 'Spirits.' Both were eventually given posthumous release across an array of collections.

When three of the Montmartre tracks ('Mothers,' 'Children,' and the mislabeled 'Holy Spirits') were first issued, in 1990, on the Italian label Philology, as part of a free giveaway from *Musica Jazz* magazine, the disc was reviewed by avant-garde multi-instrumentalist Milo Fine in *Cadence*, who noted 'a heightened sense of organic interplay' between the band, adding:

> With the exception of 'Mothers,' where Murray's drums literally whisper and Ayler majestically sticks with the theme to make his statement, solo passages are featured, but they seem to simply ripple out of and back in to ensemble dialogues as the moment demands. Ayler and Peacock are particularly potent, the former with his soaring cries and the latter with his intense, lurching, pulsating lines. Murray personifies rhythm as vibration, embracing and cushioning his associates in waves of undulating percussion. Cherry sounds a bit hesitant, adding only asides on the opener, but finds moments to shine on the closing tunes.

All six of the songs broadcast from Montmartre were eventually collected on *The Copenhagen Tapes* and later again on Revenant's *Holy Ghost* box set, giving listeners a fuller picture of the music Ayler played in Copenhagen that fall. James Beaudreau of *Signal To Noise* magazine praised the recordings for offering 'a beautifully detailed look at Ayler's most famous group.'[5]

Ayler also recorded two classic studio albums while overseas with this quartet: *Ghosts* (aka *Vibrations* and *Mothers And Children*) and the posthumously released *The Hilversum Sessions*. Recorded on September 14, 1964, while Ayler was still engaged at the Montmartre, the former entered the canon almost immediately after its release, in 1965, on Denmark's Debut Records. Views differ as to where it ranks among his work. The dividing line seems to be whether critics were writing during Ayler's lifetime (when they assumed Ayler would be able to develop even more as an artist) or whether they were writing after his death (when the supply of Ayler recordings was running thin).

Those early reviews were negative. As Brian Priestley of *Jazz Monthly* wrote in 1966, 'I am not unduly impressed by this record. ... It is perhaps the best Ayler record yet, by which I suppose I mean the least boring, and there are some quite pleasant moments; in particular, Don Cherry.'[6]

Jack Cooke, writing in the same title, felt that, though Ayler 'had at this time a remarkable purity of style,' his music

> was at a rather early stage of development when this was made … it was non-European in its elements, though it had not yet incorporated some of the more conscious primitivism that came later; it was rich melodically and rhythmically, easily approachable through the simple song-forms of the theme lines, yet demanding in the concentration it asked of listeners once the performance got under way.[7]

Yet jazz critic Barry McRae, writing in *Jazz Journal* two years after Ayler's death, opined that his style had developed fully by this stage, and that all the notable characteristics of his playing were present, though he acknowledged that the album presented 'a real clash of ideals as Cherry's dancing figures jar with Ayler's busier and more earthy approach,' leaving listeners with 'the obvious conclusion that becoming part of the highly individual jazz community is not an overnight task.'[8]

Three years after this, *DownBeat*'s Ira Steingroot considered *Ghosts* to be 'a classic of the new music,' thanks in large part to the presence of simple themes that run throughout the quartet's performance. He praised Ayler's sax as 'the most direct emotional presentation in jazz' because of a 'lush lyricism' that linked to a 'dark anima, the world of witches, devils, spirits, ghosts, vibrations, and wizards,' which contrasted with Peacock's bass 'moaning in the background,' and concluded that 'what distinguishes this music is the group creation and interplay … This album presents that music at a peak moment of power and beauty.'[9]

Jack Cooke had similar opinions about the way the band interacted:

> He was supported by a fine bassist and a brilliant drummer who stuck with him for a long enough period to become totally convincing in what they did; adventurous in themselves, yet so completely a part of the whole that their

innovations were at times mistaken for more conventional responses than they actually were. Into all this Don Cherry fits extremely well with his bright sound and sharp-angled lines; his solos are good and along with Ayler he provides a feast of invention and wit.[10]

As heard on earlier Ayler recordings, the album's title cut, 'Ghosts,' harkened back to the New Orleans tradition of collective improvisation, as well as a preaching style of the church that Ayler had grown up in. It is also notable that the piece appears in two different versions here—'short' and 'extended'—as it had on *Spiritual Unity*, and was clearly now important enough to Ayler to have named the record after it. Ayler's brother Donald later explained that this was Albert's way of making the same statement with different words: 'Music, to us, is like talking.'[11]

The differences in the performances are immediately apparent, however, while the notion of parody continues on *Ghosts*. In comparing the two 'Ghosts' on the album of the same name with the two versions that had appeared on *Spiritual Unity*, W.A. Baldwin found that the first lacks any real improvisation and is simply a thematic statement alternating between slow and fast tempos, and that on the second Ayler avoids the serious nature of the theme, and merely plays with it.[12] Ira Steingroot also compared the two versions on *Ghosts*, finding the first to be played in a 'variety of tempos' and the second to show Ayler 'reconstructing the melody, rhythmically and tonally' while retaining the beautiful tone of his horn.[13] Jeff Schwartz later observed that, in this version, Cherry (and to a lesser degree Peacock) imitates Ayler's greatest frenzies.[14]

A dark humor had become prevalent in Ayler's work that is especially evident on the album's next cut, 'Children,' when, at the end of a rather serious solo, Don Cherry adds a trumpet squeak—a lighthearted touch of de-emphasis. Based on variations of Ayler's themes, Cherry's solo opens the piece, the trumpeter supporting the saxophonist. Unfortunately, the music goes downhill after that: Cherry's solo is rhythmically weak—only Peacock's bass solo prevents it from dying out—though great momentum is generated from the piece's 4/4 time signature.[15]

The next composition, 'Holy Spirit,' impressed *Melody Maker*'s reviewer, Steve Lake, who heard evidence of 'master musicians in a sensitive almost reverential mood. Cherry loosing blue notes against the breathy almost fragile textures put down by the tenorist.'[16] Cherry's solo also impressed Baldwin, who described it, in *Jazz Monthly*, as 'well-developed and beautifully expressive.' Baldwin also noted the intense lyricism on display: Ayler utilizes a cry which is developed out of a motif and seems to mock himself, in a form of black humor, by not articulating the leaps in the upper register in the way he usually would.[17]

In a 1966 interview with Val Wilmer, Ayler seemed to explain the meaning behind 'Vibrations,' saying that 'the true artist feels the vibrations of what he is living around, and this has held true all through the past, from Louis Armstrong and Lester Young up to Coltrane.'[18] The piece, which follows the extended 'Ghosts,' also bears similarities to 'Holy Spirit.' In that tune, a cry originating in the theme is repeated as a leitmotif; in 'Vibrations,' Ayler uses the intense motif to rejuvenate the performance when it seems to be flagging. Yet for Baldwin, the latter is also 'the most successful performance on the record.' Even though the tune was a new version of 'Spirits' (from *Spiritual Unity*), it had become a quite different composition as 'a collective improvisation between Ayler and Cherry. ... The sheer momentum generated is tremendous, and the rhythm section, maintains it during its own "solo" spot, instead of combining the usual out-of-tempo improvisation.'[19]

Closing *Ghosts*, 'Mothers' has a slow, simple theme that reviewers considered to reveal 'the other Ayler'—awash in sentiment, as heard in the quavering rubato. It is, however, notable for its mood changes, as the romantic atmosphere is broken by shrieks and cries before the performance turns serious as the piece ends.

In this cut, the interplay between Ayler and Cherry's emotions perfectly illustrates a unity created from differences, as John Litweiler notes:

> The Victorian sentiment of the tenorist's quavery vibrato is heartfelt. ... Much of Cherry's ensuing solo is a haunting, clear-toned statement emphasizing the

theme's yearning lyricism without Ayler's grotesquerie. … Self-pity is a most unlikely source, for … a major jazz performance … *Mothers* is one of Ayler's finest works.[20]

So, is *Ghosts* the parodic work that Baldwin later believed it to be, or the transitional album that Jack Cooke reviewed during Ayler's lifetime? Baldwin's opinion came in the framework of a chronological analysis of Ayler's oeuvre, allowing him to observe that, 'Of all Ayler's records, this is possibly the most disturbing and least satisfying' because of its 'confusing aspects.' Despite his reservations, Baldwin still liked the record, praising the 'tremendous force and energy behind Ayler's playing' and concluding, 'It should in fact be clear enough that in its way this is a great record, in spite of its faults … in this case having a vitality which makes up for an occasional lack of discipline or taste.' Feeling that *Ghosts* was a transitional work between *Spiritual Unity* and the albums recorded the following year, he noted, 'The change in style is in fact a considerable one to have taken place in such a short time.'[21]

•

After their residency at Jazzhus Montmartre came to an end, the band then played an engagement at the Gyllene Cirkeln, in Stockholm, from October 5 to October 10. However, serious problems began to arise within the group, largely because of drug use. In Stockholm, Don Cherry tried to compensate for his heroin dependency by drinking Schnapps—with mixed results. Finally, under Murray's guidance, he attempted to kick his habit by spending two and a half weeks locked in his room, but while experiencing withdrawal he deceitfully took well-measured dosages of marijuana. Cherry eventually emerged full of strength but also seemingly full of hate for Murray, which he blew out furiously onstage, night after night, in Murray's face.[22] Cherry and Ayler would soon part ways—a studio session in November 1965, for Murray's solo album *Sonny's Time Now*, marked their last performance together—leaving these superior shows both a creative high-water mark and a disappointing reminder of a collaboration cut too short.

Peter Niklas Wilson claims that the band returned to Copenhagen without Cherry, but the LARM.fm website lists a 'Jazzkoncert fra Radiohusets koncertsal' on the afternoon of Sunday, October 11, with Ayler, Cherry, Murray, and Peacock all booked to appear. It is possible that the listing was created in advance, and that the group never showed up for the broadcast, but it is also plausible for them to have flown in from Stockholm following their final performance at Gyllene Cirkeln. What is clear is that, following their return to Copenhagen, the trio, without Cherry, took up another residency at the Montmartre, probably beginning on October 18.[23] Sometime during this latest engagement, Peacock, who had pre-existing health problems prior to the tour—put down to 'moving too fast, physically and mentally'[24]—broke down onstage in heavy pain, but continued playing.

By November 5, 1964, the final night of the residency, Cherry was back in the fold. The band then moved on to the western Netherlands, and their November 6 gig at the Sheherazade, a club on a narrow street in Amsterdam, was reviewed by Michael James of *Jazz Monthly*. Though he focused on the influence of Ornette Coleman upon Ayler's music, James also noted their differences—primarily a lack of rhythmic pulse in Ayler's work. Peacock's bass lines were played arco, in detached figures, as opposed to 'walking,' and his playing intensified in order to contrast between Cherry's thin tone and Ayler's full tone. On the other hand, Murray did not supply a continuous rhythm but rather focused on the sound-energy, which would grow in volume and intensity through arhythmical figures. Ayler and Cherry, according to James, linked musically, creating 'a peculiarly attractive kind of violent beauty' through Cherry's shrill tone and Ayler's 'rasping tenor ejaculations.' James concluded, 'This … is a band in which carefully graduated dynamics help to bind together the extremely diversified melodic, rhythmic and tonal substance. The music was most rewarding when passion and group control were fused in this singular but nevertheless effective way … the audience reaction was favorable; the applause was not deafening, but it was more than merely polite.'[25]

Another contemporary review, by the Belgian jazz bassist Benoit

Quersin, appeared in the Parisian publication *Jazz Magazine*. Though praising Ayler for 'using his instrument in a way nobody thought of before,' Quersin felt that:

> Rather than talk about a new approach, we should probably talk about a total, absolute deconditioning, to the point that one could almost think that he has never heard any Western music. … Once the profound feeling of alienation that grabs you when listening to this music has been accepted, or set aside, one can follow Albert Ayler's astounding narrative. The unspeakably dramatic climate of certain moments should be enough to alert you: the time has come for the exploration of new territories. … Albert Ayler is taking hearty bites into reality, as unpleasant as it may be, and this is a reality too radically new to be in line with frameworks that were used, wonderfully in a previous universe. … Freedom is not the exclusive privilege of painting anymore.[26]

After Sheherazade, the band played at various Dutch clubs, with a November 7 show at the B-14, in Rotterdam, starting two and a half hours late because Peacock was ill. Following the show, Cherry played the piano for about two hours, accompanied by a local drummer and bassist. Riding with Ayler to his next engagement, Dutch saxophonist Hans Dulfer learned of a lesser-known spiritual side of Ayler that would emerge more in the coming years, and later recalled Ayler telling him:

> My manner of playing comes not from inside—but on the contrary from without. All what comes from inside stands in comparison to the measurements and possibilities of the human body. The sound of a musician who performs from within can never be greater than his physical body, just as music can never be greater than its spirit. With me it is different, the stress that I receive from out of music is so great, that the sound that I have, and the music that I make cannot be physically endured very long, so that in approximately ten years my body will be completely consumed. So I will die then, but I remain, so my parents and relatives will be provided for. I remain here until I have earned enough money.[27]

There has been confusion over whether this next show, on November 8, was at Alkmaar or the nearby village of Bergen. Peter Niklas Wilson claims it was at the former, and that it suffered from Sunny Murray's refusal to play for the $25 fee, forcing the group to perform as a trio. Ben Young, however, writes that the concert was at the Extase Club—normally a dance club—in Bergen, and that the full quartet appeared. A contemporaneous article by Bert Vuijsje, in the weekly *Vrij Nederland*, seems to confirm Wilson's view: 'Last weekend Peacock suffered three bouts of stomach trouble and on Sunday afternoon Murray demanded an extra 50 guilders for the performance in Alkmaar. The owner, Paul Karting, refused, and the group therefore played without a drummer in Extase.'[28]

The following night, the band played a concert for the weekly jazz program *Jazz Magazine* in Studio A of VARA, the Hilversum radio station. Dutch journalist Bert Vuijsje was again on hand to document proceedings, noting that the group performed five Ayler originals, among them 'Angels,' 'Ghosts,' and an untitled piece, alongside Thelonious Monk's 'Light Blue' (on which Don Cherry played piano) and Cherry's own 'Infant Happiness,' the latter of which saw Murray lose a drumstick four times. Vuijsje noted the intense physicality of their playing:

> Don Cherry hardly moves, only during high passages he sometimes bends his knees … He alternates between fast and nervous runs of notes and quiet and strongly melodic lines. Ayler's violent movements are reminiscent of Johnny Griffin. Like Griffin, he gives the impression of permanent and complete involvement. … Peacock's amazing speed, the effortless way in which he uses double stops and the sheer unbelievable certainty with which he plays even the highest notes, demonstrate that the technical advances in playing the bass in the US during the past few years have proceeded even quicker than was suspected in Europe. … Sonny Murray constantly makes strong movements with the mouth and accompanies himself with a piercing buzz that becomes irritating after a while.[29]

The taped portion of the evening lasted for forty minutes, and the whole thing was over by 9:35pm. In the Hilversum audience, saxophonist Herman Schoonderwalt and bassists Arend Nijenhuis and Ruud Jacobs listened with varied responses, only Nijenhuis seeming appreciative enough to applaud.

Later that evening, while Vuijsje drove Ayler back to his hotel in the Geldersekade, the saxophonist shared some of his own opinions about his contemporaries—as well as revealing how pleased he was to learn that John Coltrane had played *Spirits* in its entirety:

> Ayler does not seem to like Mingus at all: 'Much too commercial. I never understood what made Dolphy play with him. Miles, Rollins, Coltrane, they *know* who's playing.' Although two Danes played on his first record, he now could not work with European musicians anymore. He tells that he lived in Harlem for six months ('Do you know the word *tension?*'), and that most musicians did not have the guts to visit him there. 'Only Ornette sometimes passed by; he had a girl there.' … Suddenly he asks what kind of records I have. My answer (a lot of Parker, some Mingus and Coltrane) seems to disappoint him. Apparently, Ayler does not belong to those musicians that have much interest in older (nowadays a rather relative adjective) jazz forms.[30]

Issued in 1980 as *The Hilversum Session*, the *Jazz Magazine* recordings surfaced at a time when Ayler's genius largely went unquestioned. *Melody Maker* reviewer Brian Case described it as 'some of the most extraordinary music ever devised, and indispensable,'[31] while the *Boston Phoenix*'s Bob Blumenthal felt that it showed 'all three hallmarks of Ayler's style: tonal distortion, melodic naivete, and tumultuous group improvisation.'[32] *Cadence*'s Walter Horn felt that Don Cherry could never 'have been much better than he is here' and praised Ayler's 'tunes and improvs' for 'their ingenuity and their depth … Ayler's anthems provide wonderful backdrops for these brilliant improvisers … his stuff is both deep and funny.'[33]

Even a decade after his death, however, Ayler still divided opinion. Recalling *DownBeat*'s dual-review approach to *Spiritual Unity*, Canadian jazz publication *Coda* ran two opposing critiques. Where Art Lange heard in it 'all the makings of an instant classic,' Roger Riggins focused on its uneven musical mood. Despite stating that Cherry, Peacock, and Murray were the best group Ayler had assembled, he believed the album fell short of Ayler's standards, lacking the textural focus that would have provided a source for the improvisations, and failing largely because Peacock and Murray didn't adequately embellish the rhythm.[34]

Jazz Journal's Barry McRae blamed *The Hilversum Sessions'* shortcomings on Ayler and Cherry, writing:

> This was never Ayler's most happy partnership. The rhythm team of Peacock and Murray could not have been bettered. They bring vibrancy to the group, they genuinely boost the horns and they cooperate with each other in an uncanny manner. Cherry and Ayler, for all their individual talents, never quite gelled when together. Ayler was an idiosyncratic player and his music was best served by players prepared to enter his world totally. Cherry never did this … Ayler, for his part, seems unruffled. His own contributions move from his deliciously ponderous theme statements, highlighting his unique vibrato, to the superbly linear solo masterpieces to be found on 'Ghosts,' 'Infant Happiness,' and 'Spirits.'[35]

Yet John Litweiler felt that Cherry's stylistic differences worked, because they acted as a 'leavening agent' among Ayler's intensity:

> His blasts of punctuation, his joining in ensemble improvisations, his broken phrase responses lend the music the intimacy of sympathetic, recognizable emotion, as opposed to Ayler's extravagance. The melodic beauty of his long, graceful tones in … 'Angels' convey emotion as profoundly as Ayler's overstatements of timbre and range.[36]

In all of Ayler's Scandinavian recordings, Cherry was often singled out for his differences. Though he struck a balance between Ayler and the other musicians, he also added aspects of his own: his cool, narrow-centered tone counterbalances Ayler's emotional lines and also contrasts sharply with the big tones of the other trumpeters Ayler worked with.

Of the six compositions on *The Hilversum Sessions*—'Angels,' 'C.A.C.,' 'Ghosts,' 'Infant Happiness,' 'Spirits,' and the untitled piece—opener 'Angels' defines the album. It is, as Schwartz writes, 'more like a live performance in the openness of the players' approach, with more energy in the rhythm section and more simultaneous blowing by the horns.'[37]

Brian Case gave a lengthy description of the piece in *Melody Maker*:

['Angels'] opens to an unbearably tragic, ragged, juddering unison of horns over standing bass strokes and snare rushes. There is little accuracy in any of Ayler's theme statements, which wander off pitch, backfire, and howl; detail seems not to interest him, here or during his solos. He has a broad, dramatic shape in mind, and will gabble repetitively, albeit with great projection and momentum, until he has blocked in what is necessary as a counterpoise to his grand moments. He delights in the tumble of pell-mell, the high held yell over hugely pulled bass strokes, the heavy bounce between the extremes of register, the demise of a truculent note into a pleading, the movement of a motif out of focus, either by the use of a flattening speed, an unusual pitch or a grotesque busker's vibrato. An obstacle course—and then some—it is a measure of his spirit that the melodic material not only avoids parody, but actually gains nobility.[38]

On 'C.A.C.,' Ayler and Cherry's contrasting stances complement each other as they quote previous Ayler tunes—a common theme throughout Ayler's work. Where the saxophonist dropped elements of 'Ghosts' into 'Angels,' Cherry here interpolates into 'C.A.C.' a quote from 'Holy Spirits.'[39]

Also looking to the past, 'Ghosts' is characterized by a dovetailing of neo-bebop phrasing that truly shows the genius of cornetist Cherry, whose own original composition on the record, 'Infant Happiness,' would later be recycled as 'Awake Nu' on his legendary album *Where Is Brooklyn?* Like 'C.A.C.,' 'Infant Happiness' reflects the Ayler-Cherry relationship, with Cherry's folksong composition flowing seamlessly among Ayler's themes.

Another recycling—this time of Ayler's 'Spirits'—opens with Cherry quoting from a different composition before finding himself 'overruled' by Ayler, who delivers what Case called 'one of those unstoppable "Ghosts, Second Variation" exorcisms, deftly interrupted by the cornetist, and continuing to climb, honk in the bass register, and combine the two extremes in a split-note advance.' Cherry's solo is equally marvelous: 'as vestal and hysterical as a witch-hunt.'[40] The final cut, 'No Name,' is similar to 'Mothers' in that they both are characterized by Ayler's tragic ballad style.

•

Despite the group's artistic success, the European tour had its share of problems. As Bernard Stollman had predicted, the money wasn't as Ayler imagined it would be, and Ayler once again found himself on the sharp end of critics' barbs. Even his contemporaries could be unkind, with saxophonist Hans Dulfer, who'd sat in the Hilversum audience, later recalling how they mocked Ayler for using a plastic reed and Murray for playing with knitting needles, with which he could affect a very soft sound in his drumming that evoked running water.[41] The day after the Hilversum show, the quartet separated. Peacock and Cherry rested in Belgium with a friend; Ayler and Murray went back to Copenhagen, where Ayler stayed until mid-December. While he was there, he recorded an interview for *Afterbeat*, and, on December 16, played live with the Per Aage Brandt Trio (Brandt on piano, Simon Koppel on drums, and Steffen Andersen on bass), performing 'Angel Eyes' and 'The Living Spirit.' After that, he was soon on a plane back to Cleveland.

Meanwhile, Murray, having sent much of the little money he'd made back to his family, had to go to the US Embassy in order to secure a boat ticket home. When Peacock returned to the US, he relocated to Boston, where he became involved in a Zen macrobiotic group to improve his health until he resumed playing a few months later. Only Don Cherry remained in Europe, starting his own group and eventually settling in Sweden.

This latest European sojourn left Ayler convinced his music needed a second horn, but if Cherry was no longer available, he had to look closer to home. He had already convinced his kid brother, Donald, to switch from saxophone to trumpet: 'He told me one day, "You practice that trumpet, and me and you can go places," so that's what I did do,' Donald recalled.[42] For his part, Donald felt that the trumpet provided a greater range, giving him the ability to 'deliver a more personal feeling.'[43] He also recalled his father encouraging him to switch instruments:

> My father said, 'Well, Al's playing all the reed instruments. Don, I see you have the ear and technique for playing the trumpet. Why don't you play trumpet along with your brother?' I went down to a pawn shop and I needed a horn really bad, so they gave me a horn for so many dollars—I think it was $7. I put a patch, one of those band-aids, over the hole in the trumpet and I played it. Well, I wrote my chromatic out. I got the lowest note which I could hit, which was F-sharp, and then I played up and hit the highest note I could hit, which was F-sharp.[44]

Donald had begun practicing for up to nine hours a day. Before leaving for Europe, Albert had asked saxophonist Charles Tyler to bring Donald's playing up to a professional level. Another Clevelander who'd moved east, Tyler had already been acquainted with Donald, Clyde Shy, and former Ayler sideman Norman Howard: back home, they would jam at Tyler's place, the Pizza Projects, at 75th and Kinsman; Albert had first struck up a conversation with him after noticing Tyler was carrying a sax. Now that Albert was back in his hometown, Donald would be his new trumpeter.

Donald had some musical influences, such as Clifford Brown and Freddie Webster. Webster was a Clevelander who had played in Jimmy Lunceford's band, and he had also been a major influence on Miles Davis, who appropriated Webster's 'meditative trumpet tone and calm notes.'[45] His mother was a friend of Myrtle Ayler, and Donald recalled a time when 'Mother was gonna give me a mute Freddie had.'[46] It seems unlikely the gift occurred, however, as Don would have mentioned it in other interviews.

Some critics, such as Ben Young, have disputed Webster's influence on Donald, citing the Aylers' lack of exposure to Webster's recordings (the trumpeter's solo work was incredibly rare, even at the time it was made), plus Donald's age, which meant he would have been too young to have seen Webster live. However, it is possible that Donald heard the more readily available recordings Webster made as a soloist with Lunceford. It's also likely that Donald knew of the influence Webster had had on the other trumpeters that had influenced him.

As Don Cherry had before him, Donald would go on to shape his older brother's music: the emotional expression would become even more intense, and a more directly forceful style would replace the rhythmic subtlety of *Spiritual Unity*. This new style was evidenced by what Baldwin described as 'more straightforward accenting' and a 'more obvious motivic development' in Ayler's music, along with an increased tension due to a rapid articulation in his playing (as opposed to the slurring of note lines that characterized his previous work). As the articulated notes were played with greater clarity, the ambiguities in Ayler's music disappeared, the earlier shading of tones now possessing a 'strident, imperious quality,' with Ayler's use of the extreme high register intensifying the emotional climate.[47]

According to Peter Niklas Wilson, this stylistic change may have grown out of an emotional crisis: Ayler's quartet had broken up, and his dreams of a successful European tour were over. The weeks he spent in Cleveland were filled with despair and the uncertainty of his existence—a year that had begun in a tumultuous world populated by *Witches & Devils* should have ended in a terrestrial paradise of spirits and angels.[48] It didn't. Extremely frustrated, Ayler no longer knew where he was headed. He continually practiced music in his room, yet even his family did not seem to understand him—his mother even told him she believed that he had been switched with another infant at the hospital.[49]

It was from within these circling crises that Ayler created a new group—one that would only fuel his enigma. From here on out, critics would be even more divided than before. To some his music entered a decline; for others, it took another great advance.

CHAPTER XII

c'est la belle epoque

E xpanding in number as he expanded his sound, Ayler's next group would be a quintet, and he made the first significant move toward his new style at a house party in Cleveland, on New Year's Eve, 1964. Backed by Donald on trumpet, Charles Tyler on alto sax, Clyde Shy on bass, and Larry 'Skeeter' Hancock on drums, Ayler played for about three hours.

For Hancock, who was about seventeen years old at the time and still a student at John Adams High School, this was just a one-time gig. For Donald, however, the party was more significant: it was here that Albert officially asked Donald to join the group, telling him, 'What you don't know, I'll teach you.'

As Donald recalled, there were some things Albert did not want him to learn. 'He said, "Stay natural. All [sight-]readers are devils." I told him I didn't read too good … but he wanted me to learn it naturally through execution.'[1]

Though it may seem strange that an established jazz musician would ask a beginner to join his group, Albert put importance on Donald's ability to communicate with an audience—his decision had more to do with personality than it did musical talent. And yet some critics have believed Albert was making a 'willful effort to deny listeners the pleasure of recognizable melody and music.'[2] Amiri Baraka, for example, felt that the beauty within the obvious ugliness led to an aesthetic that required a new standard of listening and awareness. Other critics, such as Martin Williams, questioned whether the musicians could be responsible enough in this new 'freedom,' or skilled enough to truly express their musical ideas.[3] When Sunny Murray questioned Ayler about it, he came away with the understanding (from Ayler) that 'he's got the spirit … and the spirit is what it's all about. … Murray, he wants to do it, I feel he can, and I want him to be with me.'[4] As drummer Milford Graves put it, Albert was 'the big brother who always protected the little brother.'[5]

Albert also wanted Donald to adapt the stylistic characteristics he had picked up by himself—the strong, blaring tone and powerful attack—to the role of trumpet in his band. Graves best described both the strengths and weaknesses of Donald's playing when he said, 'If he played only six tones, these were so full of strength they just shot out.'[6] Cecil Taylor expressed similar views, observing, 'I found out that Donald had a way of playing all the notes condensed into one octave. Man, the brilliance of that funkin' sound.'[7] Other trumpeters would have had more experience or greater variations in phrasing, but, as Graves also observed, 'What good would it do, if the sound didn't carry?'[8]

Some of the musicians who played with Ayler, such as bassist Bill Folwell, dismissed Donald's talent, going so far as to say that Albert was 'babysitting Don, pretty much. They rehearse him and rehearse him, they work him out, and they're playing together, and … he wasn't there. You know, the stuff before Donald … he wasn't … you know, just doing something else, it was really just a different place.'[9]

According to Murray, Albert wrote music that expressed his philosophy and echoed what had happened in his life. As such, both Donald and Charles Tyler would fit into the new ideas that Albert was exploring; though they could not play the feelings he had developed with Don Cherry, they could play the new feelings that were emerging.[10] In one of his final interviews, Albert expressed as much, telling Kiyoshi Koyama, 'When my brother started playing with me, that's when I really started stretching, start stretching out—really where it was at. He was very far ahead.'[11]

Indeed, the Ayler siblings complemented each other, as Bobby Few told me: 'He was out there. When you heard Don and his brother together—they were like two peas in a pod. … Don was more simple in form, less note and more vibrato.'[12]

•

Returning to New York, Albert moved back into his cousin's place in Harlem, this time with Donald in tow. Before he left Cleveland, however, Albert took an important step in another direction when, on January 14, 1965, he applied for a marriage license with Arlene Benton. Two years his junior, Arlene had been born on March 1, 1938, to Frances I. (née Bertrand) and Cassie C. Benton; she lived with her parents at 10711 Garfield Avenue and was a waitress at the lunch counter at a local Kresge's store. Not much is known about their marriage—Ayler spoke very little about her, except to tell Koyama that Arlene believed that she was marrying a musician who would be a star and make money—but records show that it took place on January 26, 1965, at Cleveland City Hall, in front of Judge P. White.[13]

Ayler's former fiancée, Carrie Lucas, described Arlene as being 'like his mother,' who had always 'wanted him to marry the girl next door.'[14] But even though Albert was wildly in love with Arlene, their marriage was off to a rocky start. She had given him $300 to find an apartment in New York; Albert proceeded to blow the money on marijuana, which he and Don smoked.[15] The couple eventually found a spot together on Jefferson Street, on the Lower East Side, moving into the heart of the downtown scene. In 1965, downtown New York reflected a new diversity as well as the richness of talent in the booming folk scene, the second wave of the British Invasion, and the new free jazz. Musical boundaries were crossed in the nightly gatherings in the East Village clubs that provided a haven for cutting-edge artists of all types of the new music.[16]

It was a year of revolutions and retrenchments; acknowledgements and recognitions; crownings and inaugurations; raisings of manifestos and reassessments of cultural mores played out across Harlem and Greenwich

Village. Harlem—a place of 'competing philosophies, religions, and politics; the Garveyites, the Nation Of Islam, the Communists, the Christians, of course, but also the Yoruba Temple and the Egyptian Coptics, all of whom debated in front of the Hotel Theresa, or in front of Michaux's Afrocentric bookstore'[17]—witnessed Malcolm X's assassination on February 21, and, two days later, the torching of the local Nation of Islam mosque. Just as musical boundaries were being pushed, the philosophical boundaries in these neighborhoods were also being stretched, and it would be hard to believe that they did not have a vicarious influence on Albert to start challenging his old style and replacing it with new ideas that were influenced by Don.

Recognizing his brother's talent and how it affected him, Albert began really stretching out after Donald joined the band, spurred on by a feeling that his younger sibling was way ahead of him on alto. One night at Slugs' Saloon, an East Village venue known for its brick walls and for having sawdust strewn on the floor, Donald blew a fifteen- to twenty-minute sax solo while sitting in with Coltrane's drummer Elvin Jones. According to Donald, it shocked everyone; Albert later called it 'a heck of a night.'[18]

Adding Donald to his group aided Ayler's shift toward ensemble playing and the expansion of theme-based material in his repertoire (as opposed to the collective improvisation heard on records such as *New York Eye And Ear Control*). Ekkehard Jost argues that the group became more popular at this time by playing 'music that people can hum,' although he also felt that the 'increasing triteness' of his music signaled the beginning of Ayler's decline. For Jost, whereas previously the thematic elements of Ayler's music could be considered to be of equal importance to the improvisational aspects, those two strands now formed two sides of a triangle alongside an additional third element 'grounded in contemporary European music.'[19]

W.A. Baldwin was undecided about whether Ayler's shift was a temporary decline or an advance. He recognized the limitations of the new style—such as a diminishing range of ideas in his solos, or a loss of imagination in the melodies and rhythms—but he also heard advancements in the music, among them sudden register changes, as well as a more straightforward approach to rhythm. Just as important to Ayler's latest development was his diminished use of tonal effects in favor of an 'extremely sensitive use of dynamics,' which was superseded by a constant blowing at full volume.[20]

ESP-Disk' founder Bernard Stollman secured Ayler's new group some gigs, and, though the money was poor, they started to make a name for themselves. As Donald later reflected, 'He had gotten us a few things together for us so we could at least work. But at the time there wasn't much money to be made. You know, we were just being recognized and we had to take it no matter how much the money was.'[21]

Sometime in January (likely the 31st), Ayler joined the Ornette Coleman Trio at the Village Vanguard for the very last set of their month-long engagement at the venue. Jazz historian Milan Simich recalled what took place:

> I was sitting by the drums and I see Ayler come in with Charles Tyler and Sunny Murray. [Bassist David] Izenzon stayed, Murray sat down, Ornette picked up one of the instruments he couldn't play and off they went. I remember how huge Albert's tenor sound was, being that close … Albert was not a jazz musician. He played gospel sax, all the weepy vibrato for Jesus![22]

Ayler's own group played some gigs in February 1965 in a loft that probably belonged to saxophonist Marzette Watts, who had been hosting jam sessions at 27 Cooper Square since 1963. The likes of Don Cherry, drummer J.C. Moses, bassist Juini Booth, and former Ayler sideman Henry Grimes had all passed through Watts's door for the sessions, which expanded to become bona-fide concerts after the intervention of Amiri Baraka, who used his influence and reputation to encourage other (presumably Black) musicians to come to this encounter. However, one unfortunate by-product of these get-togethers was the use of heroin. Though Donald Ayler claimed that neither he nor Albert themselves had ever used heroin (and there is no proof to refute this), many of their musical associates, including Sunny Murray and Don Cherry, snorted the drug at these jam sessions. Albert, however, was clear in his stance on drugs, telling Nat Hentoff:

Since we are the music we play, our way of life has to be clean, or else the music can't be kept pure. I couldn't use a man hung up with drugs, because he'd draw from the energy we need to concentrate on the music. Fortunately, I've never had that problem. I need people who are clear in their minds as well as in their music, people whose thought waves are positive. You must know peace to give peace.[23]

The Cooper Square group consisted of the Ayler brothers; an old army acquaintance, bassist Lewis Worrell; and drummer Sunny Murray. During one memorable performance in early 1965, Ayler's group played with drummer Rashied Ali; John Coltrane was in attendance, pulled a chair from the row, and placed it in the middle of the aisle, so that he could get an unobstructed view.[24] On other nights, Albert played with The New York Art Quartet, as well as with Roswell Rudd and Pharaoh Sanders.

The first reviews of Ayler's new group soon started coming out. Writing in *JAZZ*, Frank Smith referred to Donald as 'another monster' musician:

As usual [Albert] turned me and everyone else in sight upside down, as did his brother Don and the rest of the group. At one point Lewis [Worrell] got so carried away with the power and beauty of the music that he was actually sing-howling along with it, a wonderful thing to hear. … When I heard Albert and his brother Don improvise together at the Cooper Square loft I wasn't always sure who was playing what because of the force and clarity with which he hits these high notes.[25]

In later years, some critics would either forget or play down Don's contribution to jazz. Even though he adapted to Albert's concept of 'sound-span,' he did so while conforming to stereotypes—focusing on the middle register, creating a bawling tone, playing music that consisted of 'extremely fast chromatic or diatonic runs to form phrases' that were limited by his breath supply. With these techniques, Jost concludes, Don invented new clichés as fast as he discarded old ones.[26] And yet, if Donald's playing is viewed in the traditionalist sense, in line with critics such as W.A. Baldwin, it is also clear that it embodies traditionalist notions set out by forebears such as Buddy Bolden.

At the time that Albert and Donald began playing together, initial indications were that another jazz great had appeared. Though New York's loft scene was not documented by ads or recordings, memories exist, such as Mutawaf Shaheed's:

> [Amiri Baraka] lived in the Village, and everybody would go by his house and jam until early in the morning. Pharaoh Sanders was there … Albert would come, Donny would be there, I'd be there, the Shorter brothers [Alan and Wayne] would be there. … You had all kinds of drummers. Everybody who was anybody in the music, back at that time, would come to [Baraka]'s house. They played all night long. … Sometimes there'd be a couple of bass players there—a lot of horns, a lot of trumpets.[27]

Prior to Smith's article, Albert had received limited coverage in major publications such as *DownBeat*, with Baraka immortalizing him as an 'electronic foghorn.' A brief mention also appeared in *Playboy*, in an article written by critic Nat Hentoff. However, Smith's *JAZZ* article, 'His Name Is Albert Ayler,' devoted four pages to the saxophonist, and Smith was the first critic to place Ayler in the pantheon of jazz greats:

> Albert's playing in general is very similar to Armstrong, Lead Belly, Billie Holiday, Charlie Parker, and Ornette Coleman in overall feeling and intent, because to me all of these people have a burning intensity, love, yearning, joy, and beauty in their playing and singing that is matched by most others only on rare occasions.[28]

Smith's writing was prescient, not least because Ayler's records, largely recorded in Europe, were literally not available to buy in the US, with the exception of *Spiritual Unity*, which had then just been released by ESP-Disk'. As such, Smith was describing Ayler's playing at this crucial point in his career to those who only could vicariously experience the future of jazz, building on Baraka's legend-enshrining phrase:

It was simply devastating. It was so fresh that I couldn't … even begin to compare it to anyone else's playing. … He will suddenly light onto the low B-flat (the saxophone's lowest note) when you least expect it, giving all his force with his teeth on the reed and the mouthpiece halfway down his throat. More than an electronic foghorn, you might feel that a streamliner is coming down the tracks just twenty feet away from you, and the high notes coming out are really the whistle screeching at you, 'cause when Albert hits that low note he can go right on to that high note like he never stopped the low one … the emphasis is on the unexpected … no player before Albert really got up above the C and then played there. … [Albert is] playing the hell out of these notes, making them clear as a bell every time.[29]

Smith also felt that Albert's playing made him sound faster than any other saxophonists, an effect created in part by 'a continual shaking and trilling' of his horn. He would keep listeners off guard through the 'element of surprise he creates by suddenly changing direction when you least expect it,' such as switching octaves and 'thus the entire sound of what is coming at you.'[30]

•

With the civil rights movement providing a political backdrop to the music coming out of the New York City lofts, a new Black nationalism also began to emerge from Harlem, further pushing artists to explore new territory and galvanizing the young Black critics who wrote about them. In the wake of Malcolm X's assassination, Amiri Baraka became more radicalized; moving north from Cooper Square to Harlem, he founded the Black Arts Repertory Theatre/School. Launching it as a space to provide Black studies and drama programs, Baraka felt the school would inspire Black people toward a revolutionary unity.

Baraka would be one of the greatest champions of free jazz as a political music. Linking its artists together with Black nationalism in powerful diatribes written against white avant-garde musicians such as Frank Smith and Burton Greene, he believed that white musicians had to *learn* jazz as, unlike 'The Blues People,' they could not be born into it. He also believed that white jazz critics did not understand the music's social implications. In his 1963 *DownBeat* article 'Jazz And The White Critic: A Provocative Essay On The Situation Of Jazz Criticism,' Baraka—then still using his birth name of LeRoi Jones—wrote that music was only secondary to the expression of an attitude about the world. In other words, jazz was a state of being more than a genre of music.

In his book *Where The Dark And The Light Folks Meet: Race And The Mythology, Politics, And Business Of Jazz,* Randall Sandke writes that Baraka further railed against Black musicians who were formally trained, implying that they were being 'whitened.'[31] Ironically, however, some of the musicians Baraka championed did not view free jazz that way—Ayler included. In a short story titled 'Now And Then,' published circa 1965, Baraka presents his own views on the Ayler brothers in a fictionalized version of their time in New York. Even though he is awed at their talent, he can't fathom their spirituality, and is disgusted at their girl chasing—especially when the girls are white. By the end of the 60s, Baraka had turned against the music of Ayler and Coleman, claiming that they 'now describe bullshit so are bullshit.'[32] However, in his 1963 book *Blues People: Negro Music In White America*, Baraka had claimed that the music the Aylers—and others like them—played was an expression of freedom after centuries of racism and the struggle against it. But to the musicians themselves, the music was an expression of their spirit and its search for freedom.[33]

Even a cursory look at the titles of some of Albert Ayler's best-known compositions—'Truth Is Marching In,' 'Ghosts,' 'Our Prayer,' 'Holy Family,' 'Infinite Spirit'—indicates that his music speaks to a liberation of the soul rather than the mind or the body. Bringing what *DownBeat* called a 'shamanistic, spiritual gravity to jazz that simply wasn't there before,'[34] Ayler sought to reaffirm the spirit in a music that had been taken over by those who had repackaged it as something sexy and cool. Don Cherry had felt this firsthand, later recalling, 'The feeling in the Baptist-Holiness type Church is that everyone feels the spirit in the room … It's this whole feeling of spirit playing and a feeling of bliss, and it happened in me hearing Albert Ayler play.'[35]

It is also important to remember that the relatively affluent Aylers attended a high school that was predominantly white, where they participated in integrated sports teams. At that time, Cleveland did not have the ghettos and race riots that plagued other cities in the north, such as Chicago and Detroit. It was only when traveling with Little Walter that Ayler began to experience inner-city poverty.

Sources close to the brothers always denied Baraka's influence on them. Hometown friend Jon Goldman spoke of their lack of interest in Baraka's agenda, as did Mutawaf Shaheed. In any case, Baraka used the pair to further his ideals as much as they relied on him to give them exposure, and one of the ways the Aylers became involved with Baraka was through a fundraising concert for the Black Arts Repertory, held at the Village Gate on Sunday, March 28. Ayler's group didn't make much money—only $25 a man—but the concert introduced listeners to their chaotic, folk-styled jazz, along with other emerging forms of Black music, such as the blues-based work of Archie Shepp, the hard bop of the Charles Tolliver Quintet, the space jazz of the Sun Ra Arkestra, plus emerging talents such as trombonist Grachan Moncur III and bassist Cecil McBee. Most importantly, John Coltrane played. Though his commercial success and his origins in more traditional jazz styles—dating back to Dizzy Gillespie's Big Band and the Miles Davis Quintet—meant he could never be a part of New York's free-jazz scene, the ever-questing Coltrane had now chosen to associate himself with musicians who lacked commercial success and began playing in their revolutionary style.

Ayler's quartet—minus Charles Tyler, whose flight from Cleveland had been grounded by fog—was augmented by cellist Joel Freedman, whom Ayler had met in the Contemporary Center, the meeting point of the Jazz Composers' Guild, two floors up from the Village Vanguard. Freedman, however, had only known Ayler through secondhand accounts, and he was nervous when Ayler called on the morning of the concert and convinced him to come and play. They met at the Fat Black Pussycat on MacDougal Street, where Freedman persuaded Ayler to have a quick rehearsal, and later walked over to the Village Gate. But though Freedman wondered what he was in for, Ayler's certainty and confidence put him at ease.

Onstage, however, this calm quickly grew into a frenzy, as Freedman recalled:

> We got out on stage, and suddenly I felt like I was in a tornado, the vortex of sound. One of my thoughts was that no one would ever hear my cello, I'm just going to be blasted into oblivion in the sense of being totally surrounded between the power of the drums and Albert's horn. I heard him complete his solo … there's no real conscious thought but somewhere I thought I'm gonna pick up where he left off his solo and see where I can go with that. When we finished playing, I felt that my life had been absolutely and permanently altered for the better.[36]

Two of Ayler's songs, 'Holy Ghost' and 'Saints,' were recorded at the benefit, but only the first was issued, on *The New Wave In Jazz*. (No master tape of 'Saints' is known to have survived.) Though he was right in the heart of Amiri Baraka's new Black Nationalism, Ayler had chosen to perform one of his most spiritually minded pieces, later saying of it:

> A good many people are not touched by the Holy Ghost. The Holy Ghost will lead all of us through the world someday … The Holy Ghost has been favorable to me. Music is one of the gifts God has given to us. It should be used for good works. We should always thank the Lord; then, we will understand how rich His blessings are in spiritual value and in truth. We must let the sacred spirit of God enter our bodies and keep it there preciously. That's why a creator … is a being in spiritual communion whose ideas are in total harmony with God. For me, the only way I can thank God for His ever-present creation, is to offer Him a new music imprinted with beauty that no one before had heard.[37]

Released by Impulse! Records in 1966, *The New Wave In Jazz* collected highlights from the Village Gate show, presenting them as a compendium of New York's avant-garde styles. In a *Time* magazine review, Ayler's contribution was described as 'even farther out' than Coltrane and consisting of 'hysterical, sizzling squiggles of sound played fast and high, while a drummer beats insistently, as though knocking on a locked door.'[38] Even less understanding was *DownBeat*'s Gilbert Erskine, who called the record 'a bizarre artifact—not art' while suggesting that Ayler's abandoning melody, meter, and harmony was restrictive in a way that convention never would have been.[39]

Ayler supporter Bill Mathieu understood what he heard, writing:

> There is no moment on this record when the spirit falters … Albert Ayler's 'Ghosts' ['Holy Ghost'] is to my ears the top of the crest of the wave. To an astonishing degree it commands the suspension of critical judgment and succeeds in presenting itself full face forward to the listener on a level above quality, above personal like or dislike. It simply *is* what it *is*; it arrives at *mere* experience.[40]

Reviewing a reissue of the album six months after Ayler's death, British critic Richard Williams also recognized the path Ayler had been blazing during the show:

> This is Ornette taken to the logical extension, the mould for every free-blower in 1971. [Sunny] Murray keeps up a keening wail in the distance as Albert writes those frenzied Gothick squiggles with his own insane logic. He put his lines together as logically as Ben Webster, but how many could hear it?[41]

The Village Gate performance of 'Holy Ghost' opens with a simple rhythmic figure that is used for its theme, and which Donald Ayler expands upon without making it the basis for his solo. Instead, he seems to play a string of his favorite phrases, ending his solo on a stop-time figure, which Albert then picks up for his solo. Lewis Worrell plays a strongly rhythmic figure on the bass before cellist Joel Freedman performs a solo with a strong Bartók influence. Not as intense as Ayler's solo, it is nonetheless, well-sustained. In contrast, Worrell's solo hints at a Latin flavor while maintaining a strong yet subtle beat—it's his bass that gives the rhythmic support, freeing Murray to adds only percussive effects. The piece ends on a collective improvisation that, according to W.A. Baldwin, was 'little more than noise,' added as an afterthought, since the emotional level of the performance has been fully developed through each bandmate's solos.[42]

•

The Black Arts Repertory Theatre/School opened on April 30 in a four-story Harlem brownstone at 109 West 130th Street, its opening celebrated the next day with a parade down 125th Street that featured the Aylers, Milford Graves, and Sun Ra's group, along with writers, artists, and members of Baba (Ofuntola) Oserjeman's Yoruba Temple (a group that called for a return not only to African religions but to an African way of life in its entirety). They marched with the Black Arts flag: a black-and-gold banner with Afro-centric 'comedy' and 'tragedy' theater masks designed by William White as the new standard for a Black revolution.

This parade encapsulated everything the Black Arts movement was supposed to be about. The organization sent trucks—'Jazzmobiles'—to playgrounds, parks, and vacant parking lots in order to introduce communities to Black music, dance, drama, paintings, and poetry. 'Albert didn't play catchy melodies,' Milford Graves recalled. 'People were on the sidewalks of Harlem, they were looking out their windows! I had a drum tied around my waist. It was Don Ayler, Albert, and me. Amiri Baraka in front with two other guys carrying the Black Arts and American flags with a police car escorting us. Sun Ra was behind us with his band.'

Although Ayler was never fully committed to Baraka's cause, the association worked to his advantage by giving his music exposure in contemporary interviews, which in turn gave him a platform to express his opinions over the primacy of spirituality in his music. But the Black nationalism and Black awareness that Baraka espoused alienated many conservative critics, among them the *New Yorker*'s Whitney Balliett and *DownBeat* writers Dan Morgenstern and Martin Williams, who expressed concern about the political overtones implicit in the new music. One-time *DownBeat* editor Ira Gitler criticized the avant-garde scene for its overt 'racial propaganda,' citing Abbey Lincoln's Candid LP *Straight*

Ahead, 'Pride in one's heritage is one thing, but we don't need the Elijah Muhammad type thinking in jazz."[43]

And yet freedom and jazz music had once been linked, and scholar Frank Kofsky—who had pilloried Kenny Dorham for his no-star review of *Spiritual Unity*—pushed the belief that listeners were either in sync with the music and the burgeoning political movement, or against it—no middle ground. But though Kofsky was aware of the connections between some Black musicians, African independence, and the civil rights of African Americans, he failed to realize that not all musicians were united in support of the music, even if they aligned with the progressive politics. Dorham had played on Cecil Taylor's *Stereo Drive*, but he did so because Taylor's record company had insisted on it; trumpeter Freddie Hubbard had delivered commendable performances on Ornette Coleman's *Free Jazz* and John Coltrane's *Ascension*, but the music he released under his own name would be forever rooted in bop idioms.

The advent of Black Arts marked a new beginning of Black artistic development in New York, as well as the re-establishment of Harlem as the center of black politics and creativity. Though there were predecessors, Baraka's group was a landmark, and a tremendous inspiration to those who followed, in no small part because Baraka had been able to synthesize many ideological influences—leftist, Black nationalist, and avant-garde, plus the newer Black countercultural movements such as the Yoruba Temple and the Nation Of Islam—into the first major Black nationalist art group.

In contrast to the literary stylings of writers such as Whitney Balliett, Baraka attempted to turn jazz criticism into a performance of 'sound, feeling, and movement' that matched the music he was writing about. But while some musicians, such as Bill Dixon, questioned whether he was trying to advance the cause of jazz, or merely stir up controversy (Cecil Taylor felt Baraka was opportunistic as well as lacking in knowledge), Baraka's name would be forever synonymous with the artists he championed. Meanwhile, his polemics on race made the establishment take notice of him (as opposed to the music he was describing), and his attempts to utilize the new culture to push the Black community to liberation fostered a 'Blacks only' attitude toward jazz that Ayler did not believe in, and which some saw as a reaction to the rise of The Rolling Stones and other British bands who had taken so much from Black music history.

This presented a conundrum for Black avant-garde musicians who had cultivated white audiences but now had to remain relevant in contemporary Black culture. Black Arts critic A.B. Spellman noted that the majority of Black audiences preferred soul music to the avant-garde jazz they did not understand: 'The reality is that it was Greenwich Village which heard the evolution of the New, not Harlem. The man standing in line for the Otis Redding show at the Apollo almost certainly never heard of tenor saxophonist Albert Ayler, and wouldn't have the fuzziest idea of what he was doing if he did hear him.'[44]

Baraka scorned the idea, however, writing in his *Autobiography*:

> It was really a great program, running that entire summer. … We brought new music out in the streets, on play streets, vacant lots, playgrounds, parks. I think perhaps the Jazzmobile came from our first idea. We had trucks with stages we designed from banquet tables, held together by clamps … and Pharaoh, Albert, Archie, Sun Ra, Trane, Cecil Taylor, and many other of the newest of the new came up and blew. … So that each night throughout that summer we flooded Harlem streets with new music, new poetry, new dance, new paintings, and the sweep of the Black Arts movement had recycled itself back to the people. We had huge audiences, really mass audiences, and though what we brought was supposed to be avant and super-new, most of the people dug.[45]

While Spellman has noted that Black Arts performances were favorably received, at least one truck was pelted with eggs.[46] It's possible that the crowd may not have been as appreciative of the music as they were of the simple act of musicians coming to their neighborhoods and playing for them.

bells

G aining recognition and renewing his association with Bernard Stollman, Ayler finally seemed to be getting his dues in New York. Though Cecil Taylor allegedly tried to talk him out of making any more recordings ESP-Disk', Ayler felt trapped by circumstance: he had a wife and a one-year-old daughter, so he needed to record and perform when he could. Already booked in to participate in an evening event on Saturday, May 1, honoring what Baraka was calling the 'New Black Music,' Ayler made an afternoon appearance at a showcase for ESP-Disk' artists that took place at the Town Hall and featured Bud Powell, Giuseppi Logan, and Byron Allen. It would also result in his next album for the label.

Reviewing the concert for *JAZZ*, Frank Smith noted Charles Tyler's return, after being stranded in Cleveland, along with the addition of an unknown musician playing a set of finger bells:

> The effect of these little light bells cutting through the powerhouse music of the rest of the group was quite lovely. Lack of sufficient promotion had kept the audience to about 350 people, but it didn't prevent the audible gasps that were emitted throughout the crowd as the curtain rose on this group giving off music like a waterfall of scarifying friendly swords. … The reaction was extremely favorable. … I hope this concert stands as a symbol and turning

point of Albert's career, because if anyone deserves success, he should get it just because of the sheer humanity of what he's doing.[1]

Even *DownBeat*, which usually kept a distance from his work, praised Ayler's set as 'the strongest and most unusual music of the afternoon.' Noting how Tyler fit Albert's 'drawn-out notes, glissandi, sentimental melodic emphasis' and Donald's 'loud, staccato, and broadly emphatic' if elementary playing, Dan Morgenstern continued:

> The music that goes with this definitive instrumental approach is no less personal. It resembles at times … the music of a village brass band or a military drum-and-bugle corps. In spite of its abrasiveness, the music is quite gay and friendly. … The harmonies are stark and almost primitive. … Ayler's group played two pieces. The first, quite brief, ended with a prolonged bombardment by the full ensemble; a flurry of repeated notes played strictly on the beat. The effect was not unlike a surrealistic parody of those famous Jazz At The Philharmonic finales, replete with screaming trumpet and honking saxophones. Or perhaps the image was of a rhythm-and-blues band gone berserk. The second piece, though sprawling and too long, was nevertheless filled with exciting passages. … To this listener, there seems to be a great deal of wild humor in Ayler's music. Though often vehement, it is celebration rather than protest; much of it has the sheer 'bad boy' joy of making sounds. … Some may dismiss it as untutored, primitive, or merely grotesque, but it certainly has the courage of its convictions and is anything but boring or pretentious.[2]

Ayler's portion of the concert was issued later in the year as the album *Bells*. Almost as radical as the music was the physical record itself, which was pressed on transparent vinyl with just a single, twenty-minute track (actually three compositions: 'Holy Ghost,' the unnamed composition from The Hilversum sessions, and what later would be called 'Bells') cut into one side of the record. (French critic Philippe Carles later expressed the opinion that the transparency of product paralleled the transparency of Ayler's music.) Characterized by the concise nature of its solos, the recording exposed a new aspect of Ayler's music: the influence of the old New Orleans marching bands. Ironically, however, jazz aficionados who wished they could have seen Buddy Bolden in his prime derided his musical descendants such as Ayler, and while some viewed Ayler's use of the marching-band sound as a parody, others saw it as homage—perhaps even a reinvention of collective improvisation.

Group dynamics now became central to Ayler's music. Though he and Donald exhibited a noticeable stylistic compatibility, the most important factor was Murray's interactions with the group as a whole, as he left it to the bassist to provide a regular beat—if one were provided at all. For his part, Murray played rhythmic figures that varied in subtleness and wildness. By holding back the emotions and letting them build behind Ayler's arhythmic lines, Murray produced a tension that worked as a traditional chorus division.[3]

However, reviewing *Bells* at the time of its release, *DownBeat*'s Pete Welding did not view Ayler's music this way, writing that the album was:

> perhaps the most formless, incoherent, and quite possibly the most ineptly stated pronunciamento from the outer (and outré) reaches of the 'new thing' I have heard. The first half of the work is a sprawling, turbulent devil's brew of unrelated sounds, squawks, bleats, cries, whinnyings, etc—a musical gobbledygook that is almost impossible to describe. It sounds like a henhouse gone berserk. Ayler surely is capable of wresting a wide variety of effects from his instrument, but music is more than a catalog of effects. The mere airing onstage of a sequence of unrealized emotions through a musical instrument does not in itself amount to the creation of a coherent musical design … The second half of the composition employs a number of simple, folkish motifs to which the participants return from time to time. … What bridges these segments, however, is more of the inchoate, feverish disorder that marks the first part; again, no coherence.[4]

Bells was, however, influential on up-and-coming groups of the time. As Val Wilmer later observed, 'The intense, braying ensembles and raggedy

bugle-calls and marches—the younger Ayler's idea on this occasion …
became standard practice for any ensemble of the period that considered
itself hip.'⁵ But though Terry Martin, of *Jazz Monthly*, praised Ayler, calling
his music 'the most strikingly original to have arisen in the post-Coleman
era,' he found fault with other aspects of the album:

> Structural development does not play much part in this essentially static style,
> yet the emotive power and perverse humor combine with technical consistency
> to produce a unified art. His themes are equally part of the expression, strange
> often brilliant fusions of half-remembered folk-tunes or common martial airs
> that underline the child-like aspect of his approach and call forth a nostalgic
> response to complicate the trenchant darkness. … Technically he has continued
> the constant expansion of the saxophone's range to hitherto unheard extremes.⁶

The band opened their Town Hall set with 'Holy Ghost,' which had been
played five weeks earlier at the Village Gate, starting off with a brief,
unremarkable passage of collective improvisation that serves as a basis to
launch Donald's solo, which was a development of his limited world of
ideas—restrictions based on Ayler's rhythmic reorganization rather than
on any melodic inventiveness. Donald builds his solos not by coming up
with new melody lines but rather by increasing the intensity of his playing.
Albert's solos are founded on similar material, until he breaks away for a
build-up.

The emotional message as well as the construction of the solo so
impressed British critic W.A. Baldwin that he analyzed its twenty-two
phrases in detail, writing, 'This solo, I feel, merits close examination, for
it expresses as coherently as it does its very powerful emotional message
because of its fine construction, which relies mainly on strictly motivic
development, as well as to some extent on traditional "call-and-response"
patterns.'⁷

The band then moved into the untitled piece that Ayler had performed
at the Hilversum radio session the previous November—a work that
Danish critic Erik Raben felt was based on Black folk themes, and that

alternates between the lyrical and the grotesque. Opening with a slow solo of beautifully developed, constantly shifting moods, Ayler links phrases through themes and utilizes a recurring motif. His ideas are emphasized by repetition: though he ends his solo with what Baldwin called a 'very fine, lyrical phrase,' any finality is strengthened by a return to improvising a variation on the piece's earlier development and then coming back to the same phrase.[8] A bass solo by Lewis Worrell follows before Albert returns, playing a bugle call. This passage leads into a full-band rendition of 'Bells.'

Lending the album its title, 'Bells' was in fact Donald's composition, as Albert confirmed in his final interview:

> Yeah, that was his idea to do that. Because at that time, like I was kinda like tired of the whole situation. He was like of the new generation coming with new ideas. He had that march-type feeling, so it was his idea. It wasn't mine. Truthfully this is what nobody knows. … Then I put in the intricate parts in between to carry it over. That part's mine—but the beginning was my brother's idea to give that march-type feeling.[9]

Donald explained the idea behind the composition: 'We was talkin' about the heavenly bells, church heavenly bells,' he recalled. 'The Bells of heaven.'[10]

Albert had similar thoughts. Coming from a strong spiritual background, he told Val Wilmer that his fellow musicians at this concert were playing in a 'spiritual dimension.' Expanding a bit on this, he added, 'We can get a divine harmony or a divine rhythm that would be beyond what they used to call harmony.'[11]

'The bells of heaven' are not in any Bible passages, and yet the idea has taken hold in music. There is an old hymn called 'Ring The Bells Of Heaven,' which is about the return of a repentant sinner. Another reference can be found in an old Flatt & Scruggs song, 'Prayer Bells Of Heaven,' as well as in an early 1927 country tune cut at the legendary Bristol sessions, Alfred Karnes's 'When They Ring Those Golden Bells.' The only Biblical mention of bells is the 'golden bells' of *Exodus*.

'Bells' opens as Ayler plays a solo based on a theme the likes of which was played by a New Orleans brass band at a funeral—described by Baldwin as 'quite as well developed, although a little too repetitive in parts.' Tyler's solo follows ('a little disorganized but shows promise in his melodic inventiveness'), and then Donald's, which Baldwin felt was 'more inventive in the conventional sense than his first solo [on the album], not being based on such restricted material and showing a considerable melodic gift.' A section of wild collective improvisation follows before Tyler ties the whole performance together by introducing a motif from the first selection, 'Holy Ghost,' to unify the separate entities. This motif leads into what Baldwin described as a brief recapitulation based on the brass-band-styled theme.[12]

Besides the analyses and reviews, Ayler's own words in an interview with Robert Ostermann of the *National Observer* expressed what the band sought to achieve with their performance:

> We're not just sitting down and trying to create beauty. We're making more than pretty, melodic forms. Follow this, please. We're musicians and we're asking the whole world to listen—and understand. We're all together, everybody, and there has to be peace. That's what we're saying. … Don't move. Consider who you are and what you are, where you are and where you're going.'[13]

•

Free jazz reached a milestone on June 28, 1965, when John Coltrane recorded *Ascension*. A masterpiece of the genre, it provided the final piece of the free-jazz triptych—alongside Coleman's *Free Jazz* and Ayler's *New York Ear And Eye Control*—when it was released the following February. Clearly, Ayler had been an influence on Coltrane's latest music, as he recalled:

> After I made *Ghosts* and *Spiritual Unity*, I would send albums to Coltrane to help give him the direction, because he's a spiritual brother. He's one that can really hear music, all different kinds. After I sent him those records, the next

thing I heard was *Ascension*. It was beautiful, everything was building ... and that's about the freest thing that's going. I thought that Coltrane was going in this direction: to play a prayer.[14]

According to Mary Parks, Ayler's final girlfriend, Coltrane called Ayler and told him, 'I recorded an album and found that I was playing just like you.' Ayler is said to have replied, 'No man, don't you see, you were playing like yourself. You were just feeling what I feel and were just crying out for spiritual unity.'[15]

Similar sentiments were expressed by Coltrane himself, who told Frank Kofsky, 'I think what he's doing, it seems to be moving music into even higher frequencies ... he filled an area that it seems I hadn't gotten to.'[16]

Certainly, Ayler and Coltrane traveled similar paths—which also often crossed. Their first encounter took place at the Jazz Temple in Cleveland, where Albert had taken his brother and ended up sitting in with Coltrane, in 1963. Others recalled seeing Coltrane watch Ayler's performances with Cecil Taylor at the Take 3 later that year, and catching Ayler and Eric Dolphy together at the Half Note—where, in March 1964, Coltrane would invite Ayler onstage. And then there's the Cooper Square loft show with Rashied Ali, at which Coltrane ensured himself a prime spot from which to witness Ayler as he developed his new sound.

And yet there was a vast difference between the two: Coltrane's musical contradictions became brilliant conflicts that found satisfaction only in the violence and continued agitation in his playing. For John Litweiler, 'He is usually considered the greater artist, yet Ayler's broad vision and the humane responsibility of his musical philosophy are the more life-sustaining principles. As listeners we recognize and internalize Coltrane's passionate conflicts, yet as modern men and women we need Ayler's bitter humor, his resigned sorrow, his fully sensitive tragic awareness as a condition of our lives at their most ideally humane.'[17]

Shortly after the recording of *Ascension*, Albert, Donald, and Charles Tyler visited Cleveland, where Albert saw his son, Curtis—now seven years of age—for the third and final time. Calling over to a group of children playing football and asking which one was Curtis, Ayler introduced himself and gave the child a dollar before moving on.

That same summer, Albert composed some songs for Amiri Baraka's play *The Dutchman*—contracts were signed and the score was finished.[18] Built on the idea that jazz music is a displacement of Black rage, *The Dutchman*'s message is that, if one truly listens to jazz, one hears a more accurate account of the Black experience in the United States.[19] Baraka, however, claimed that it was another one of his plays, *Home On The Range*, for which he sought Ayler's music, actually giving directions on the title page that the work would ideally be performed with Albert Ayler soloing in the background.[20]

For an eight-week period leading from August into October, Albert and Donald participated in some Harlem Youth Opportunities United events in Harlem, along with Archie Shepp, John Coltrane, Pharaoh Sanders, Sun Ra, and Cecil Taylor. Organized by the Black Arts project, these 'Jazzmobile' gatherings attracted huge audiences, according to Baraka, but conflicting accounts claim that it was actually the white scenesters in Greenwich Village that truly embraced the new music, not the Black communities that Baraka felt it should serve.[21]

CHAPTER XIV

Spirits Rejoice

B y now, Ayler's music was less about individual notes than it was about overall sounds, and his next album, *Spirits Rejoice* (released on ESP-Disk' as ESP 1020 before the year was out), would offer an opportunity to hear how his latest developments sounded when transposed from the live stage to the studio. Musicologist Ekkehard Jost notes a stylistic change in Ayler's ensemble playing throughout 1965, writing that his compositions now showed a very limited variety of themes. Though Ayler still maintained his stylistic traits, such as low-register honks and repetitive passages, he had now moved away from collective improvisation to focus on themes (limited as they may have been) and also exhibited an increased tendency toward triteness that would come to mar his final creative period. W.A. Baldwin heard another reason for this, suggesting that Ayler's music had become more European in content, with marching songs like 'La Marseillaise' indicating a trend away from Black influences and toward white ones—a trend that led away from the solos and their impact upon the listener.

The title track on *Spirits Rejoice* would highlight some of these changes, with Jost observing that the thematic material is equal in quantity to the improvisational passages. After opening with a four-minute march section in which the same motifs are repeated several times, it then sees Ayler perform a brief one-minute solo that leads back to the march material. Throughout the piece, this 'clash of mood' between the brass-band passages and the solos is not thematically based, apart from in each of Donald's solos, which use the main theme as their starting point.

Recorded on September 23 at Judson Hall on 57th Street, *Spirits Rejoice* would also see the return of bassists Gary Peacock and Henry Grimes to Ayler's line-up, which otherwise remained the same. Guy Kopelowicz, a correspondent and photographer for the French magazine *Jazz Hot* who sat in on the session, later recalled the experience, noting, among other things, that Sunny Murray used a simple setup of one bass drum, one snare, one hi-hat, and a single cymbal, and that he played with 'metal drumsticks that looked to be made out of aluminum':

> While waiting for him [Peacock] to show up, Albert and Don Ayler and Charles Tyler rehearsed music in unison. The music they were playing turned out to be the French national anthem 'La Marseillaise.' … Albert Ayler was blowing and marching around the studio. The engineer stopped him to indicate how far he could move around the premises when the recording session would actually take place. … The full band assembled for a quick soundcheck and at 4:30pm the recording proceeding started. Two hours later, all the music for the album had been recorded.[1]

Bernard Stollman also sat in the recording booth throughout, watching on as Ayler moved quickly between tunes, with just a few indications to the musicians as to what would follow. For Kopelowicz, nothing could equate to witnessing him perform his music in the moment:

> The full blast of his (and his players') sound just about shattered one's ears and had your mouth wide open in amazement. The impact was overwhelming. You loved it or you hated it … there were no second takes. 'It's always like that with Albert,' Murray told me. When the tunes were done, the musicians went to the control booth to listen to the tapes. They seemed happy with the music.[2]

As ever, reviewers were less sure. Max Harrison of *Jazz Monthly* felt that Ayler was starting to come into his own on *Sprits Rejoice*, and that he would achieve recognition as a great figure in post-Coltrane jazz. Harrison heard what he felt was a rejection of jazz's European experience and a renewal of focus on the pre-harmonic innocence of Black music—a simple music of bugle calls that caricatured military phrasing.[3]

W.A. Baldwin felt that Ayler's performance on *Spirits Rejoice* was 'something of a disappointment' after *Bells*, which he had declared 'Ayler's greatest achievement.' Indeed, Baldwin believed that Donald Ayler's solos 'pretty convincingly cut' those of his brother on the title track, though he praised Ayler's solo on the track 'D.C.,' despite highlighting that awkward opening phrase. While acknowledging that the record had brilliant ideas, Baldwin claimed that Ayler overdid the repetitive passages as well as the low-register honks, and that the band's performances failed in some rhythmic aspects, especially on 'Spirits Rejoice' and 'Prophet.'

'Spirits Rejoice' is a long march medley that differs from 'Bells' because of its defined thematic order and begins with a long solo by Ayler on tenor sax. Tyler then plays a brief thematic passage on alto saxophone and is followed by Donald on trumpet. A bass duet by Grimes and Peacock then leads back to the theme. But while Baldwin criticized Tyler's 'rather tiresome'[4] solo, if the piece is heard as Donald has suggested it should be— by paying attention to the overall sounds rather than the individual notes— then the meaning behind 'Spirits Rejoice' becomes readily apparent. In a letter to German critic Gudrun Endress, Albert elucidated, 'The true spirit was in New Orleans jazz, that's what I'm trying to bring back into music, the true spiritual feeling or jubilation, a prayer to God. ... The artists who play this music are beyond the civilization that exists today.'[5]

Baldwin dismissed the next cut, 'Holy Family,' as enjoyable light relief.[6] The late critic and comic-book writer Harvey Pekar held similar views, describing it as 'a simple, trivial piece, sounds a little like hoedown music.'[7] Schwartz, too, calls it 'all theme.'[8] Indeed, the only improvisation in the piece is by drummer Sunny Murray, though interpretations differ as to why it's there: Schwartz believes it to be Murray's futile attempt at challenging the composed horn and bass lines, while Baldwin felt that it provided a 'more dramatic than musical effect.'[9]

The final three cuts on *Spirits Rejoice* form a trilogy. 'D.C.,' which is dedicated to Don Cherry, is based on measures five and six of 'Infant Happiness,' the Cherry composition that made it onto the Hilversum radio broadcast. Donald Ayler later revealed that Albert wanted to invite comparison between his two trumpeters ('He was letting them hear what I sounded like, compared to Don Cherry'[10]), but the tune also led Baldwin to suggest that Donald could outperform his brother, thanks to an imagination that could do wonders with limited material. Baldwin also singled out bassist Henry Grimes for his 'strongly rhythmic accompaniment' and highlighted 'a couple of good bass solos,' which he attributed to Grimes and then Peacock.[11]

'D.C' is followed by 'Angels,' which revisits Ayler's earlier composition 'Prophecy.' Opinions differ as to its worth. Baldwin felt it was as lightweight as 'Holy Family,' but John Litweiler writes coyly of a 'frilly lace harpsichord' part performed by a guesting Call Cobbs. Last heard playing with Ayler on *Swing Low Sweet Spiritual*, here Cobbs provides accompaniment to a 'tenor solo aching of nostalgia for cranky grandmothers who bake apple pies and quietly fart a lot; the tenor vibrato and the big theme tones, with their little trailing away decorations, are charming and elephantine.'[12]

Litweiler obviously caught the humor, though another reviewer in *DownBeat* thought the humorous elements were 'almost certainly unintentional,' and that the piece sounded 'like a put-on in various spots.'[13] Val Wilmer, meanwhile, heard 'luxuriant waves of tinkling sound,'[14] while Schwartz feels that 'Angels' captured 'a powerful performance,' thanks to Ayler's soloing near the theme. With the other horns, Don and Tyler, laying out, a bowed bass anchors the piece, and Murray and Cobbs provide embellishments in the higher register.[15]

Interestingly, Ayler originally wanted Cobbs, a pianist, to play vibes on the piece, but relented when Cobbs told him that the harpsichord was the first piano:

> So Stollman rented one from a studio—I think he paid ten dollars an hour
> for it. … [The sound] wasn't too much different—course I had a classical

background. The touch has to be precise—you can't slide over it—and I like that because my fingering and my dexterity was right. … So I rehearsed on it for about a week and saw how we were coming along, and Albert and I, we wrote some things together and then there were several tunes that he wanted that I wrote down for him. So when the group came together as a whole, I played four or five numbers with him, some on piano.[16]

Whatever preparations Cobbs and Ayler had made, Cobbs did not play on the rest of the session's selections. It would have been a waste if he had—Cobbs's harpsichord part on 'Angels' was poorly recorded.[17]

Bringing *Spirits Rejoice* to a close, 'Prophet' suffers from the same defects that plagued the title cut, among them an overuse of lower-register honks, moments of weak rhythm, and indulgent repetition. Yet Baldwin felt this repetition was important as a structural feature of the piece's theme, which—based on elements of 'Holy Ghost' and the initial part of 'Bells'—holds the piece together. While Albert's solos 'alternate between mediocrity and brilliance,' Donald's seem to be 'more dependable and consistent,' even if he doesn't match his brother's peaks. Together, the solos generate a tension which contrasts with the 'not very coherent' sections of collective improvisation in the piece.[18]

Speaking to this author, Donald revealed why he and Albert sounded off: 'Some stupid ass, Charles Tyler, gave … both me and my brother some heroin.'[19] Apparently, they thought they were scoring some cocaine instead.

After the session, the band dined at an Indian restaurant, and then went back to their apartment, where they talked deep into the night. The evening had a vital impact on Cobbs, who told Val Wilmer:

That was a beautiful thing. Somebody else was there and they were talking about the free music. I was very quiet because I wanted to listen. Everything was new to me, I really didn't have the connection then, but I could hear. From then on we were inseparable.[20]

•

After the Judson Hall session that produced *Spirits Rejoice*, Ayler played a few gigs around New York. Archivist Ben Young uncovered evidence of one performance under the name The Special Quintet, in late 1965, and there is also mention of an October performance at Slugs'. His band may also have played at the Black Arts Theater in December, and/or at Slugs' on Sunday, December 19, at 4pm.[21] Ayler was also one of twenty-six musicians included in a roundtable discussion by *Jazz Magazine* in France, although he provided a written essay instead of answering the submitted questions.[22] His contribution was translated into English and published fifteen months later in the British magazine *IT* (*International Times*).

Ayler made one more studio recording before 1965 came to a close, this time as a sideman on a Sunny Murray record financed by Amiri Baraka. Also on the session were Ayler's former trumpeter Don Cherry and bassists Henry Grimes and Lewis Worrell. Baraka was involved too, reciting his poem 'Black Art' on the closing track of the same name. Murray remembered how, though they 'tried not to be concerned about the text'—which contained lines like 'Setting fire and death to whitie's ass. Look at the Liberal Spokesman for the jews clutch his throat & puke himself into eternity'—the group 'had worries that our careers would be ruined.'[23]

An anonymous friend of Don Cherry told *Jazz Monthly*'s Max Harrison that the session only came about because Ayler, Cherry, and Murray got drunk at a Christmas or New Year's party, and Baraka hustled them into a car and took them to the Black Arts Theatre. Cherry claimed not to remember the session but recognized his own style of playing when he heard it, while Harrison doubted whether Ayler and Cherry could have been at all under the influence—if they were, they would never have been able to play as well as they did.[24]

Ayler attempted to clarify things in an interview with Daniel Caux:

> That was around Christmas time, and I had a little baby—I didn't necessarily want to make [the session]. It was Sunny Murray's. He said, 'OK, I'll give you guys some money, if you come and play.' And he had money, and you know, we had to make this record, because the kids had to have food … I don't know

if I was sad about it, or what … I didn't necessarily want to do it, because I wanted to do my complete thing. I didn't want to be part of anything.[25]

Despite the potentially fallible memories of the participants, Ben Young's research indicates that the session could have taken place anywhere between early November 1965 and February 1966 but gives its most probable date as November 17, making it unlikely that the musicians were drinking at a holiday party. As well as 'Black Art,' three other compositions were recorded that day: 'Virtue,' 'Justice' (split across the end of side one and the beginning of side two on the original vinyl), and 'The Lie,' all of which except 'The Lie' were released on Murray's debut album as a bandleader, *Sonny's Time Now* (Jihad 663). Scarce even at the time of its release, the album attracted few reviews, but John Litweiler found a copy to review in his book *The Freedom Principle*:

> Trumpet and tenor improvise in opposition to the grim Murray tides, and the two rumbling basses in 'Virtue,' and an intense LeRoi Jones poem … are answered by the flutter of drums and the tempoless, free-form quintet. Ayler does not dominate this recording … and he opens up in the 'Justice' collective improvisations, responding to Cherry's longer lines with snapping and snarling.[26]

The album was also reviewed favorably by *DownBeat*'s Bill Quinn. As well as feeling it held 'excitement for those attuned and is something of a representative selection of the New York new scene,' he wrote:

> The new music still seems to be locked in a glacier of audience approval, its potential energy unrealized for the majority of jazz listeners. This LP, an icicle with a rather pointed tip (that being the poem 'Black Art,' read by Jones), is an all-star effort by the new musicians and should contribute something to the kinesis. Murray has gathered some formidable exponents of the genre. Cherry appears to be the strongest soloist. His sound is lean and curvilinear on 'Virtue'—dagger thrusts that seem to pierce Ayler's vibrating shards of sound … Ayler moves into a soaring chase with Cherry on 'Justice I.' The

tenorist wrests sound from the horn's entire range—nervous, schizophrenic sound cycles … Ayler is the Ayler of his other albums. Though his work is exciting, its framework could stand more latitude, more diversity to transcend what by now is becoming a somewhat too customary approach.[27]

Max Harrison felt the album was a case of the emperor's new clothes, however, with Baraka—imitating the noises of an airplane and a machine gun, and speaking of 'dagger poems in the slimy bellys of the owner Jews'— sounding like nothing so much as 'a prurient schoolboy trying desperately hard to be shocking.' Regretting that Ayler and Cherry were associated with the album, he noted that the two horn players, along with Murray, at least recaptured some of their old magic: they were 'excellent foils to each other.'[28]

Phrases such as 'slick half-white politicians,' 'jewladies,' and 'fire and death to whitie's ass' abound in Baraka's poem, raising the question of whether Ayler's appearance on *Sonny's Time Now* indicated a growing alignment with Baraka's political outlook. Many people who knew him, such as Danish saxophonist John Tchicai, violinist Michel Samson (who joined the band at La Cave), and Clevelander Jon Goldman doubt it, asserting that Ayler's message was always spiritual. The closest Ayler himself ever got to explaining his position was in his *DownBeat* interview with Nat Hentoff:

I think it's a very good thing that Black people in this country are becoming conscious of the strengths of being Black. They are beginning to see who they are. They are acquiring so much respect for themselves. And that's a beautiful development for me because I'm playing their suffering, whether they know it or not. I've lived that suffering. Beyond that, it all goes back to God. Nobody's superior, and nobody's inferior.[29]

It would be naïve to believe that Ayler, living in New York at the height of the civil rights movement of the mid-60s, did not have a sense of Black awareness, and it's possible that he felt it was expedient to downplay his political leanings in order to keep attention focused on his music in an industry that was still largely segregated and dominated by white gatekeepers. Indeed, it would be a few more years before Black artists began to feel comfortable speaking out about Black politics; according to Frank Kofsky, even *DownBeat*, which had long supported the Black arts, sought to downplay the impact of Black nationalism through certain articles such as Brooks Johnson's 'Racism In Jazz,' as well as Gus Matzorkis's 'Down Where We All Live: Today's Avant-Garde Seen In The Light of Jazz's Long History of Internal Strife.'[30]

But many critics besides Baraka, such as the German Ekkehard Jost, understood the relationship between free jazz and political revolution, with Jost noting, 'As a rule, wholesale judgments on free jazz focused on its sociocultural and political background.'[31] For his part, Baraka picked up on avant-garde jazz's rejection of harmony—which he rejected as a Western, and therefore white, innovation—when he began calling it 'New Black Music,' and Kofsky also tried to push the avant-garde into a racial-revolutionary niche, writing, 'Today's avant-garde movement in jazz is a musical representation of the ghetto's vote of no confidence in Western civilization and the American Dream.'[32]

And yet Ayler consistently avoided talking about race in public, other than to disassociate his music from the word jazz. 'Jazz is Jim Crow,' he once said. 'It belongs to another era, another time, another place. We're playing free music.' Charles Mingus and Cecil Taylor expressed similar sentiments—they saw their music in universal terms—and Donald Ayler once claimed that he and Albert weren't 'selfish enough to limit' their music to parameters of race. However, in *Coltrane And The Jazz Revolution*, Kofsky claims that many Black musicians avoided speaking out after seeing the change in fortunes of Max Roach and Charles Mingus, who were accused of reverse-racism in an October 1962 *Time* magazine article entitled 'Crow Jim.'[33] Elsewhere, Ira Gitler of *DownBeat* referred to Roach's wife, Abbey Lincoln, as a 'Professional Negro' in his review of her album *Straight Ahead*, adding, 'I hope that she can find herself as a militant but less one-sided American negro.' Lincoln did not make another album for a dozen years. Fear of being labeled a 'Black radical' silenced many musicians, according to Kofsky, but, based on interviews with associates who no longer needed to protect the career of a deceased friend, it's doubtful that Ayler himself had such sentiments.

Meanwhile, in the wake of the Office For Economic Opportunity's withdrawal of funds from the Black Arts Theater—and Black Arts' subsequent closure in March 1966 after a police raid turned up a cache of weapons—Amiri Baraka relocated to Newark, New Jersey, where he opened a new Black cultural center under the name the Spirit House. From here, he developed a theater, bookstore, and a publishing house, Jihad, which put out the Sunny Murray record.

•

According to Barry McRae of *Jazz Journal*, Ayler's style was 'completely formulated and boasted all of the features that have become his trademark' by the time 1965 drew to a close. Highlighting the *Spirits Rejoice* track 'Angels' as an example of this, McRae noted the 'exaggerated vibrato which always appears on his slower material and which brings his work deceptively close to bathos.'[34]

John Litweiler believed that Ayler planned his shift away from collective improvisation and toward performing thematic material as early as the 1964 European tour, noting that the themes in 'Spirits Rejoice' were based on 'La Marseillaise,' while its bridge drew upon 'Maryland, My Maryland,' the official song of the titular US state. The music that Ayler began playing in 1966 would see him borrow themes from the nineteenth-century composers Stephen Foster (whose 'Oh Susanna' was used for 'Truth Is Marching In') and Edward MacDowell (elements of whose 'To A Wild Rose' were interpolated into 'Dancing Flowers'), plus Christmas carols ('Omega'), and even a Thanksgiving hymn ('Our Prayer'). The new themes he wrote would be played straight with a compelling energy, leading critics to refer to his band as offering 'echoes of New Orleans marching bands,' or sounding variously 'like a Salvation Army Band on LSD' or 'the music of central European firemen's bands.'

The simple melodies that Ayler spoke of to Nat Hentoff in 1966 would unfold into complex textures before returning to simplicity:

I'm using modes now, because I'm trying to get more form in the free form. Furthermore, I'd like to play something—like the beginning of 'Ghosts'—that people can hum. And I want to play songs like I used to sing when I was real small. Folk melodies that all the people would understand. I'd use those melodies as a start and have different simple melodies going in and out of a piece. From simple melody to complicated textures to simplicity again and then back to the more dense, the more complex sounds. I'm trying to communicate to as many people as I can. It's late now for the world. And if I can help raise people to new plateaus of peace and understanding I'll feel my life has been worth living as a spiritual artist, that's what counts.[35]

In this cycle, the simple parts became progressively so, while the complex part became even more dense. These new densities led John Litweiler to describe the music as:

> a rasping like the attack of a giant mosquito; it's Donald Ayler playing trumpet in a small range of a few imprecise notes, each buzz lasting as long as breath permits. [Charles] Tyler's little solos sound wild, primitive, with short, internally varied phrasing. The fast solos are almost static elements in the performances, sometimes too brief and too poorly recorded to communicate much more than sonority and range in what sounds like almost unbroken spasms.[36]

Whatever Ayler's avowed political leanings, Litweiler also believed that his music was a reaction to mainstream America:

> True, we live in a time of progressively increasing disorientation, social destruction, institutional malice, with the result being, for us, and even for great creators such as Ayler, increasing fear, ignorance, violence, escapism. Albert Ayler daily struggled for professional existence against the most hardened attitudes, the most inhuman reactions and conditions. It is most important in hearing his music to understand that he visualized life in more open, more sensitive, ideally even simpler terms. His entire career was totally opposed to the mainstream of modern American existence.[37]

CHAPTER XV

la cave

I n moving toward an increased simplicity, Ayler's music emerged as a combination of naivety and grandiosity. Though the solos strayed from a common theme, they were now subtler and mixed into the flow of the melody. Often criticized for this development, Ayler merely compressed into four years what jazz greats such as Louis Armstrong and Lester Young did over the course of their entire careers.[1]

Some have suggested that Ayler developed so quickly either because he knew his time was running out or because he had once faced death and understood how short life could be. The closest he ever came to saying as much was in conversation with Val Wilmer:

> My music is the thing that keeps me alive. But I must play music that's beyond this world. … If I can just hum my tunes and say, live like [Thelonious] Monk and live a complete life like that, just humming tunes, writing tunes and just being away from everything. … If I could do this, this would just carry me back to like where I came from. And that's all I'm asking for in life. I don't think you can ask for more than that, than just to be alone and create from what God gives, 'cause I'm actually getting my lessons now from God.[2]

And yet his radical evolution was in keeping with similar developments elsewhere in music: Bob Dylan had gone electric; The Beatles had become sonic pioneers. Just as Ayler changed personnel to accommodate a new style of playing, so did Miles Davis—who would continue to do so for his entire career, keeping up with changing trends regardless of critical concerns. In the lineage of jazz, pop, and rock music, Ayler's choices were nothing out of the ordinary, even if his music was.

•

In January 1966, Ayler may have played some evenings at Slugs'. What's certain is that, beginning January 24, he began playing Monday nights at the Astor Place Playhouse in the East Village, at 434 Lafayette Street. Ayler's group initially consisted of Donald, Charles Tyler, cellist Joel Freedman, and Sunny Murray, although he was about to split from his long-standing drummer.

Though Murray was led to believe they'd be playing a second concert, Ayler told him it had been cancelled. Two hours later, a friend called to tell Murray that Ayler was, indeed, playing another show. When Murray arrived at the venue, he saw Ronald Shannon Jackson in his place. Ayler apparently looked sad onstage, and when Murray began to cry, Ayler comforted him.[3] But terminating relationships without warning or communication was Ayler's style. Going back to the late 50s, he had gone out of his way to avoid confrontation, failing to stand up for his former fiancée Carrie Lucas in the face of his mother's disapproval, then enlisting in the army in order to avoid paying child support.

It's possible that drummer Charles Moffett played with the group on January 31. He was definitely onstage with Ayler on February 7, though he drew derision from the *East Village Other*:

> [Ayler's] mastery of his instrument was obvious, and his solos were intensely beautiful; his group, which sounded best when playing 'tutti' [in unison] often had as many things going as there were men on the stage. … Trumpeter Don Ayler and alto saxophonist Charles Tyler were extremely inventive in full ensemble passages, but did not come near measuring up to their leader's soloist ability. Cellist Joel Freidman [*sic*], an astounding musician, often couldn't be

heard over the rest of the group ... something should be done to insure that his brilliant playing will be audible. Drummer Charles Moffat [*sic*] ... was, unfortunately ... an incredibly poor drummer who is best off hiding behind the 'percussionist' moniker. ... His constantly choppy and very obvious use of two-measure, 4/4 phrases, during passages in which a steady pulse was maintained, made his work seem out of place with that of his cohorts. However, the concert was enjoyable as a whole, and Albert Ayler's work is always to be commended.[4]

Moffett would soon join the increasing list of former Ayler bandmates, as the saxophonist exhibited a pattern that would take greater hold with each change of style. According to Peter Niklas Wilson, Sunny Murray—who harbored no bitterness toward Ayler—believed that ESP-Disk' founder Bernard Stollman was involved in Ayler's decision to drop him, but Donald stated that his brother simply wanted a drummer who could play march rhythms for his new music.[5] (Stollman was a hands-off label owner, and it is doubtful that he would have dictated who his artists should play with during live engagements.)

However, Ayler's decision to hire Ronald Jackson occurred because Ayler was in attendance at the February 4 session that was booked for Charles Tyler's own debut album, *Charles Tyler Ensemble*. Ayler was impressed enough to ask Jackson to join his group. Though Jackson was an unknown quantity at the time, Ayler's decision to drop a great drummer like Murray in favor of the untested newcomer was in keeping with his decision to bring his brother, Donald, into the group.

This was to be Jackson's first job with a name performer, and it would prove to be a pivotal experience:

> Soon I realized that with Ayler I was able to play the way I played back home when I wasn't playing for people at a nightclub. I could play as the people at the Holiness Church did—through the instrument. ... Ayler was the kind of person who recognized that there was a spiritual reality—and music was just a vehicle for what was trying to be expressed spiritually.[6]

John Norris reviewed one of the Astor Place Playhouse concerts in *Coda*, finding that it was comparable to Ornette Coleman's music of the 50s because of its individualism and a strength that engulfed the audience. Though noting the similarity to New Orleans jazz through the parade music they played and feeling that the themes, drawn from folk music, were simple, Norris concluded that the band produced a great richness of sounds whose intense beauty eliminated old hackneyed ideals.[7]

Ayler's next live appearance was as part of the 'Titans Of The Tenor' show at Lincoln Center's Philharmonic Hall, February 19, 1966, sharing the bill with an array of saxophonists, among them the veteran Coleman Hawkins, Zoot Sims of the West Coast 'cool school,' his hero Sonny Rollins, and John Coltrane. Despite his best efforts, Coltrane had failed to convince the show's promoters to include the Ayler brothers, so he paid them out of his own funds. As Ayler later told Frank Kofsky for *Jazz & Pop* magazine, 'He called me … and said, 'If you can't play there, then you wait for me. I don't want anybody but you and your brother.'[8]

Now a bona-fide giant in the jazz field, Coltrane made a point of helping talented young players to gain exposure. Though he had recorded albums such as *Ascension* and *Meditations* the previous year, neither had yet been released, so the Lincoln Center audience likely expected him to play standards such as 'Chim Chim Cheree,' from his 1965 album *The John Coltrane Quartet Plays*, and the landmark 'A Love Supreme,' also released in the previous year—but Coltrane astonished them by playing in the style of the music that would appear on the next year's release, *Ascension*. They should have known things would be different when they saw two drumkits onstage. Bassist Jimmy Garrison was the only member of the quartet to play that night, alongside drummers Rashied Ali and J.C. Moses; pianist (and John's wife) Alice Coltrane; and—the shock of shocks—horn players Albert Ayler, Donald Ayler, Pharoah Sanders, and Carlos Ward. A tape of their performance may be in the possession of Coltrane's son Ravi, and many of those present still remember that night like it was yesterday, with Blue Note discographer Michael Cuscuna recalling, 'Standing at the apron of the stage, they erupted into a spiritual, frenetic sound that scared me half to death, yet stimulated every aspect of my being. I don't know whether I loved it or hated it, but I knew that I was not indifferent to it, and I knew that I did not understand it.'[9]

Also looking back with years of hindsight, the *Village Voice*'s Gary Giddins remembered how he 'left the hall angry' and 'in a state of confused elation,' but feeling that 'a door of perception had swung open':

> The joyful, terrifying noise lasted about an hour. Except for a snatch of 'My Favorite Things,' melodies were not apparent, though the Rodgers and Hammerstein echo was itself momentous. Coltrane inserted it amid a squalling solo, played with more than a few deep knee-bends, and the shock of recognition elicited an explosion of approval. ... The rhythm section was not a thing apart, providing a swinging foundation, but a collusive force. The collective assault either focused your attention or dispersed it. In the absence of melody and harmonic progressions, it relied on the fever of the players, and while this shattering din could never be the sole future of jazz or of any other kind of music, it could—and, in fact, already did—represent a new way to play and experience music. The sound spread evenly, like the dribblings on a Jackson Pollack, yet the wall-to-wall harangue allowed for plenty of individual details as each player emerged from the ensemble for an *Ascension*-like salvo ...
>
> Yes, the saxophonists squealed and screeched, but they found individual ways to squeal and screech. I recall Sanders playing for a long stretch with his fingers splayed outward, never touching the saxophone keys, rendering an unholy and unbroken wail, and Donald Ayler offering little more than listless tremolos spaced within an octave's range. Albert's solo was something else: a hurricane of raw emotion and radiant luster. I had not paid much attention to Albert Ayler previously, and immediately resolved to make up for it.[10]

Less convinced was Dan Morgenstern of *DownBeat*, who hated the whole affair, reserving his deepest disdain for Albert and Donald:

> When it came to screaming, however, Sanders met his match in Albert Ayler, whose noises at least had some movement. Squeaking and squealing at lightning

speed, he gave a convincing musical impression of a whirling dervish seized by St Vitus dance. Trumpeter Don Ayler came to bat next. Because he played with his horn's bell pointed at the floor, most of his solo was inaudible. ... What was decipherable seemed to be a series of rapid spurts of disjointed notes played with considerable frenzy but little else. ... The Ayler brothers ... fashioned a weird duet, a bit like the screaming contests little children sometimes indulge in; it was scarcely more pleasing to the ear. ... As for Ayler and Sanders, they made a mockery of the use of the term 'titans' in the concert's title ... to ride on the reputation of others is deception.[11]

The set closed with the Sanskrit chant of 'Om mani padme om' ('Praise to the jewel in the lotus'), a compassion mantra. As Ayler later told Frank Kofsky:

[Coltrane] walked up to me while I was playing and he said, 'If you feel like saying something, go ahead and do it.' And like I was playing the 'Holy Ghost' from *The New Wave In Jazz* ... and I turned around to see what it was, and it was *John*, just standing there, man. Singing, singing. Chanting, you might say.[12]

Having blown that night 'like the world was on fire,' as Amiri Baraka later wrote, Ayler continued to play around New York.[13] A *Village Voice* advertisement for Slugs' Winter Jazz Festival on February 24 lists him on the bill, and Ayler joined the Burton Greene Quartet for a date in March 1966, playing on the final piece of the night. Writing in the jazz magazine *Sounds & Fury*, Joe Pinelli described Ayler 'generating still another dimension' with the 'contrast of his horn,' and 'actually pushing the already incredible tempo another notch further, blowing way up there in high register joy sounds, now and then ripping off a riff at the other end, something like the call of a bull elephant in heat maybe.' But though Pinelli wrote of 'the crowd at the bar now on its feet, mesmerized,' the audience's reaction was, in reality, mixed: some refused to applaud, some laughed, and some yelled. Others were too stunned to react at all.

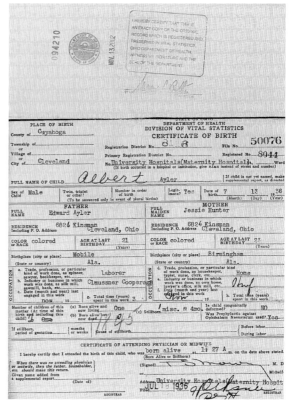

ABOVE LEFT School ID-card photographs of Albert (*top*) and Donald Ayler. *Courtesy of the Cleveland Metropolitan School Board.* **ABOVE** Albert's birth certificate. **LEFT** July 29, 1949: Jimmy Sanders & His Musical Cats entertain children at the Rawlings Playground. Donald is bottom left; Albert is in the middle, to the right of Sanders's elbow. *Photo by Schaeffer, courtesy of the Cleveland Call & Post.*

TOP Albert Ayler and Charles Tyler at the
Bells concert at New York City Town Hall,
May 1, 1965. *Photo by David Holzman,
courtesy of the Jazz Institut Darmstadt.*
ABOVE An undated portrait of Ayler.
*Photographer unknown, courtesy of the Jazz
Institut Darmstadt.* **RIGHT** Print advertisements
for shows at the Village Gate and Astor
Playhouse, New York City.

RIGHT & BELOW The Albert Ayler Quintet—Albert Ayler, Donald Ayler, Bill Folwell, Michel Samson, and Beaver Harris—at the Philharmonie Berlin Jazzfestival, November 3, 1966. *Photos by Manfred Schaeffer, courtesy of the Jazz Institut Darmstadt.*

ABOVE Albert Ayler, Donald Ayler, and Michel Samson at De Doelen, Rotterdam, November 8, 1966. *Photo by Bob van Grevenbroek, courtesy of Jaap de Klomp.*
RIGHT Albert and Michel at the same concert. *Photographer unknown, courtesy of the Jazz Institut Darmstadt.*

OPPOSITE A contact sheet from De Doelen. *Courtesy of Pieter Boersma.*

ABOVE Albert Ayler and Milford Graves outside St. Peter's Church on the day of John Coltrane's funeral, July 21, 1967. *Courtesy of Walter Ohlemutz.*
RIGHT & BELOW Donald and Albert Ayler (with Beaver Harris and bass players Bill Folwell and Clyde Shy in the background) at WHK Auditorium, Cleveland, Ohio, February 4, 1967. *Photos by Frank Kofsky, courtesy of Bonnie Kofsky and Special Collections, University Library, University of California Santa Cruz.*

RIGHT Albert Ayler at Saint-Paul De Vence, July 1970. *Photo by Friedman, courtesy of the Jazz Institut Darmstadt.*
BELOW *Left to right:* Juini Booth, Albert Ayler, Call Cobbs, Milford Graves, and Donald Ayler at the Albright-Knox Gallery, Buffalo, New York, March 9, 1968. *Photo by Sherwin Greenberg, courtesy of the Albright-Knox Art Gallery's Archives & Digital Assets Collection.*

ABOVE An advertisement for the 1970 Nuits de la Fondation Maeght festival, featuring 'free jazz et underground' performances from Ayler and others.
RIGHT Albert Ayler's death certifcate.
BELOW LEFT Allen Blairman, Steve Tintweiss, and Albert Ayler at Saint-Paul De Vence, July 1970. *Photo by Claude Gaspari, courtesy of Archives Fondation Maeght, Saint-Paul De Vence (France).*
BELOW RIGHT Blairman, Ayler (in the background), and Mary Parks at Saint-Paul De Vence. *Photo by Claude Gaspari, courtesy of Archives Fondation Maeght, Saint-Paul De Vence (France).*

Ayler also hit the clubs with his new drummer, Ronald Jackson, in tow, particularly the now-defunct the Dom, on St Marks Place, across the street from the Five Spot Café. Jackson recalled an incident during a Kenny Dorham show:

> Albert took out his horn between the compositions they were playing and started playing 'Summertime.' And the whole place became … mesmerized, transformed. Cash registers stopped ringing, the waitresses stopped where they were … the band didn't play. Everything just transcended the place …, and went to where he took the song. It was like we were on some kind of ship. And when he got through, he brought us all back. And then the band started back up and kept on going. But that was the kind of power he played with. When he played, you'd have to stop and listen. He sucked all the air out of the room and turned it back into a wonderful … lightness.[14]

Clarinetist and bandleader Tony Scott recalled Ayler sitting in on the jam sessions he led with his band, which consisted of Henry Grimes on bass, Eddie Marshall on drums, and, on occasion, an array of pianists:

> Albert came to the Dom many times and I invited him to jam … So he played with his band—trumpet player and all. … They sounded like a marching band. One day he sat in with my band playing 'Summertime,' and then he went the way out you know. I turned to [clarinetist] Perry Robinson and said, 'Does he know "Summertime"?' He said, 'Forget that and listen to what he's playing.'[15]

•

No longer being kicked out of clubs as he had been years before, Ayler was gaining professional recognition, but his private life was in disarray. Living the precarious life of a musician in New York City had taken its toll on his marriage, and Arlene had moved back with their child to her parents' home in Cleveland. As much as Albert loved his daughter—Sunny Murray remembered how he would play lullabies for her as she slept—his reluctance to pick up regular gigs as a jobbing musician failed to provide for his family. Mutawaf Shaheed observed how this affected the marriage:

> [Arlene] was all for Albert … and what she wanted was for Albert to be a
> regular guy, and he just wasn't. And he had a child—I remember when she got
> pregnant, and she was all for him. She would go to the concerts, and she would
> do what she could for him. But she really wanted him to be a regular guy. …
> He was never one, and he couldn't be one. Arlene was always in the picture,
> even afterwards … because she had his child. Albert was a free spirit—I'll just
> leave it at that. He loved his music.[16]

All Arlene ever said about the experience was, 'It was hard in New York.'[17]
Meanwhile, Ayler himself returned to Cleveland in April, hoping to bring his
music to his hometown. Fortunately, La Cave, the local folk club at 10615
Euclid Avenue, became available after a cancellation by Tom Paxton, and
Ayler staged the venue's sole jazz engagement, across April 15, 16, and 17.

Once again, however, the band's line-up had changed. Trying to escape
being labeled an Ayler disciple rather than a creative musician in his own
right, Charles Tyler had left the group during rehearsals for the show. He
would later reveal frustrations with the way Ayler's music was evolving:
'Albert started to change his mind about things. A lot was going on. And
people started to convince Albert that he could get an even larger audience
if he changed certain things in his direction. I couldn't watch that happen.
So that's when we parted.'[18]

According to Ayler's friend Jon Goldman, Tyler was unhappy that
Ayler had added the classical-trained Dutch violinist Michel Samson
to the group—something that diminished his income while also taking
Ayler's music in a direction he considered unhip. Mutawaf Shaheed (then
still known as Clyde Shy, and Ayler's bassist at the La Cave shows) told me
that race may also have played its part, as did a disagreement over a song
credit and Donald's credentials as a musician:

> He just didn't like the fact that this guy was coming in there, you know, under
> the influences that he and [former Ayler trumpeter] Norman Howard came up

under [Elijah Muhammad and the Nation of Islam], you know, and also there was a song that he felt Albert had taken from him—this 'Poppy.' … In reality what happened is, 'Poppy' was some variation of what Albert had done … and he had a little beef with Donny. He didn't feel Donny had the talent and that he had gotten in because … Albert was his brother, and he didn't know music.[19]

Donald offered a different opinion. 'Coltrane said that he wanted just [me and Albert] to play at Lincoln Center. See, my brother caught on from there—and told Charles he would have to do something else, and besides Charles was recording on ESP as a leader so he couldn't carry him anymore. Yeah, there were hard feelings.'[20]

At first, Albert attempted to find a replacement for Tyler, trying out Clevelander Terry Hynde, who passed on the gig. In the event, Michel Samson would fill in for what had once been Ayler's dual-saxophone sound. A child prodigy who began playing the violin at age six, he had taken lessons at the Academia di Musica da Camera in Rome and Mannes College in New York, and from classical violinists Henryk Szeryng and Alberto Lysy. As a teenager, Samson became interested in jazz and hung out with the Dutch avant-garde crowd; he had once played for (but not with) Ornette Coleman in Coleman's hotel room in Amsterdam. Eventually, Samson wound up studying with violin tutor Ivan Galamian at Julliard in New York, where he became acquainted with Peter Bergman, a Yale film student who would go on to found the Firesign Theater.

Samson was in Cleveland to play at the opening of a haberdashery on Shaker Square owned by Bergman's father. Jon Goldman was there and struck up a conversation with the violinist, inviting him to La Cave. Samson arrived while Ayler and his group were rehearsing. Mentioning that he had played with Ornette Coleman at the Concertgebouw in Amsterdam (on October 30, 1965), he asked to sit in, and quickly slotted in with Ayler's approach to practicing 'soundwise'—that is, with the musicians having a dialogue between themselves on their instruments, rather than relying on figuring out chord patterns. As Ayler told Nat Hentoff, 'From the beginning, we hit it off musically.'[21]

Samson concurred. 'From that moment on we hit it right away. That night I played in his band and the following night again, at the same club. Obviously, I was wearing my new suit that I had been allowed to choose at the fashion shop the other day.'[22]

Opening for Ayler at La Cave was 'Folk Balladier' Dick Wedler, who'd originally been booked to support Tom Paxton. Though Cleveland as a whole took little notice of the La Cave shows, Jon Goldman claims the 250-capacity venue was packed every night, attracting 'the entire Jazz community of the city, Black and white, all of whom came to get their first taste of the new sounds that had only been something to read about.'[23] According to Wedler, the club was not sold out, but the crowd—'pretty well coiffed, lots of jewelry, furs'—extended to the back rows of the club's seating, leaving just the standing-room area empty.[24] The Cleveland gig featured the Ayler brothers, Samson, Don's friend Clyde Shy on bass, and Ronald Shannon Jackson playing percussion. Saxophonist Frank Wright joined them on the final night.

Goldman recorded the Saturday and Sunday shows, and the Friday set may have been have recorded surreptitiously by La Cave's owner, Stan Kain, on a professional machine hidden in a sound booth.[25] A twenty-five minute excerpt of the Friday set survives, but as La Cave was a folk club, it is doubtful that Kain would have recorded the balance of a weekend's worth of music that did not fit into his musical interest. It is more intriguing because there is some confusion as to what day Samson joined. In the *Holy Ghost* box set, he is stated to have played at the haberdashery on Saturday, April 16. That means Tyler would have played on the Friday night and walked out on Saturday afternoon. But it could very well have occurred that the haberdashery opened the previous Saturday, and that Samson met Goldman and stayed the week with Bergman in Cleveland. The Kain tape would clear up any questions about the personnel.

Feeling the musicians would not have approved, Ayler had originally rejected Goldman's idea of recording the shows but changed his mind shortly before performing on Saturday. In the event, all the sets were similar because, according to Goldman's recollection to Ronald Jackson, Donald and possibly Michel Samson were incapable of playing the complex music Ayler had run them through in rehearsal.

Following one of the shows, the band had a late dinner at a house owned by a woman named Beatrice. The group played a little, and Beatrice's daughter, Ann, who was about fifteen, asked Albert to play 'Auld Lang Syne.' After first begging off, Ayler finally relented and played the old chestnut. As Mutawaf Shaheed recalled, Ayler typically avoided playing songs such as these because he associated them with being square, but he would occasionally set aside his concerns for someone for whom he had a deep liking. (Shaheed also remembered how Ayler had once charmed his father with a very straight rendition of 'Moonlight On The Wabash.')[26]

Stranger still, on the Sunday morning in nearby Mantua, Ohio, several police cars chased a UFO into Pennsylvania. Unlike the La Cave shows, the incident was the talk of Cleveland for the following week and was used by Stephen Spielberg in the movie *Close Encounters Of The Third Kind*.

In a published letter to Amiri Baraka, written in 1969, Ayler put the event in a different light:

> In this vision there was a large object flying around with bright colors in a disc form. Immediately I thought of the flying scorpion that I had read about in the chapter of Revelation from the Holy Bible, but when the object started turning I saw that first it was flat then it turned sideways and started to shoot radiant colors at first then it would turn back to the same position. I was running with my brother when it aimed at us but it didn't touch us at all. I guess this is what they are calling the flying saucers.

During the week, the band gigged at Adele's Lounge Bar, a notorious University Circle hangout on 11605 Euclid Avenue that never checked the age of its clientele, and which had become famous as a hangout for the poet d.a. levy.

The addition of Jackson and Samson further signified Ayler's move away from what was considered traditional Black music and into abstraction. Ayler appreciated the violinist's sensitive playing and the folk-style notes that he brought to the group sound, as well as the dignified image he afforded them among intellectuals. Art Lange described the changes when he reviewed the Revenant box in *Coda*:

> The material had changed once more, too, now featuring more of the short, catchy melodies that Ayler hoped listeners would go out of the concert humming to themselves. … But, rather than sounding hermetic, the simple themes have been inflated to anthem-like proportions through emphasis and repetition: the music is more theatrical with arrangements—shorter solos, repeated motifs … more varied with instrumental colors and ensemble textures. The rousing colors are more compact though no less intense—Donald's trumpet blaring, sputtering, and raising pitch-by-pitch from sheer urgency with almost no range or contour…and guest tenor saxophonist 'Reverend' Frank Wright following Albert's example by chewing and spraying fractured notes. Though the music's coarse, propulsive ensembles, tumbling rhythms, and high-energy sound projection may alienate as many listeners as it seduces.'[27]

These changes were also noted by Tony Herrington in *The Wire*:

> Hearing these performances back to back with those taped two years earlier it feels like a shift of seismic proportions has occurred in the conceptual designs and constructions of the music. It wasn't that way in reality, but unfortunately there is no music here to complement that already archived on the *Spirits Rejoice* and *Bells* albums, both taped in 1965, which documented the slow dissolution of the ideas the saxophonist was working through in the 1964 trio and quartet, and the formulation of a new approach to his group music, one that was forced on him … by the eventual departure of Peacock and Murray, and the need to accommodate a number of very different forces that were introduced into that music … while violinist Michel Samson, a Paganini for the ESP set, spun thick webs of harmonic expansions and inversions, creating a new atonal centre within the music.
>
> But here at least … where Ayler first begins to make overt the links between his concept of group music and a reconfigured model of that which ruled in

the cradle of jazz, New Orleans, at the turn of the century ... That the most revolutionary musician of his generation should suddenly turn away from the breakthrough concepts he has made in the company of some of the other most radical musicians of the time ...

But if elements of this music felt sepia-tinted, it was all simultaneously coated with thick layers of cosmic dust. Just as Ayler's solos draw a line connecting the raw vocalized cry of R&B saxophonists like Illinois Jacquet with images of 31st-century Afronauts. ... Jackson's drums tear a wormhole in time, shifting the location of the music dramatically up and down what Amiri Baraka would refer to as the changing same of the Afro-American blues continuum. ... Jackson reroutes the kind of parade ground snare drum rhythms ... through a mindset permanently altered by exposure to the multidirectional polyrhythms developed by Elvin Jones and Rashied Ali in John Coltrane's groups.

Listening to the collectively improvised passages ...the 'dense, multiple erupting thicket of sound--and feeling,' ... you instinctively grasp what Donald Ayler was getting at when he gave instructions on how to listen to this music: 'Don't focus on the notes. Follow the sound, the pitches, the colours, you have to watch them move.' And from there it is just a short leap of the imagination to understanding how this music ... knew of the potential for revelation through noise.[28]

The band had stayed with Ayler's parents throughout these engagements. After the concerts, Ayler said to Samson, 'We'll play at Slugs' in New York on May 1. Will you be there with us?'[29] The reformed quintet returned to New York (with Samson moving into the Aylers' apartment and treated as part of the family), where Donald remembered little itty-bitty things crawling around their room at 133rd and St. Nicholas. Hearing these descriptions of the bad living conditions dissuaded Clyde Shy from relocating to live with the roaches, mice, and rats, so he decided to stay in Cleveland and come in and play when he was needed.[30]

CHAPTER XVI

Slugs'

S eeking more popular appeal, Ayler took on an even simpler style than before, his melodies becoming more composition-oriented, with preplanned themes, harmonies, and tempos. And New York, a city that had long resisted him, offered opportunities for him to try this development out on live audiences.

On May 1, the band played Slugs' Saloon. Home to the new music as played by the likes of Ayler, Cecil Taylor, and Sun Ra, Slugs' also booked more traditional jazz musicians such as hard bop progenitors Lee Morgan and Art Blakey. A *Village Voice* review by Michael Zwerin (a trombonist who had played with Miles Davis in 1948) captured Ayler's return to the East Village:

> For all his frenetic and energetically abstract noises, Ayler is in many ways an old-fashioned tenor player. The ensembles were primitively tonal, falling somewhere in between a 20s German brass band, calypso music, and a turn-of-the-century funeral in New Orleans. They were articulated with a good-old-time staccato by his brother Don on trumpet and Michel Samson on violin. … Albert Ayler's improvisations traveled from the nostalgia of these ensembles into a future where time, notes, and dynamics hardly matter. Consistently intense—inhumanly, irrevocably, eternally intense—the variety of sounds merged into one screaming note. Sometimes he held his horn way up, kind of

kissing it, and his involvement with the music was total, almost frightening. Vital, nerve-searing, teeth-chattering, and forever loud, it was the best possible artistic reflection of the worst part of my life.[1]

That Sunday afternoon concert was recorded by an audience member and released, over fifteen years later, as the two-volume set *Albert Ayler Quintet Live at Slug's Saloon* [sic] by the Italian imprint Base Records, which had licensed material from the then-dormant ESP-Disk'. Forty years later, the recording still impressed Chris Kelsey of *JazzTimes*:

> The music's lost none of its power. It's still astonishing: the complexity that springs from the march-like, nursery-rhyme motifs; the lyrical grace that's too seldom commented upon; the link that existed, unobstructed, between inspiration and expression. I doubt even Coltrane was more connected to his primal self.[2]

Opening the set, 'Truth Is Marching In' possesses a 'footstomping swagger.'[3] Ayler shaved his line to the barest essentials, and his saxophone achieves an 'almost speech-like quality by using a vocalized instrumental dialect that goes back to Congo Square.'[4] It is likely based on the spiritualism described in the book *Up From The Cradle Of Jazz*, a history of New Orleans music penned by Jason Berry, Jonathan Foose, and Tad Jones. According to the authors, this spiritualism spread across North America, where the New Orleans ceremonies reflected Christianity's assimilation of Caribbean religions—African gods became Christian saints—in outbursts of energy, talking in tongues, and spirit visitations.[5]

In John 4:24, it is said, 'God is a spirit and they that worship him must worship him in spirit and truth,' and 'Truth Is Marching In' finds Ayler trying to convey this through his music. Barry McRae of *Jazz Journal* believed this was Ayler's quest for a human truth, basing his opinion on Ayler's *DownBeat* interview with Nat Hentoff:

> To begin with, we are the music we play. And our commitment is to peace,

to understanding of life. And we keep trying to purify our music, to purify ourselves, so that we can move ourselves—and those who hear us—to higher levels of peace and understanding. You have to purify and crystallize your sound in order to hypnotize. I'm convinced, you see, that through music, life can be given more meaning ... and we're trying to bring about peace.[6]

Even though the first theme from 'Truth Is Marching In' is lifted from Stephen Foster, Ayler never mentioned it when he discussed the piece with Nat Hentoff, preferring instead to describe it in more religious terms:

When there's chaos, which is now, only a relatively few people can listen to the music that tells of what will be. You see, everyone is screaming 'Freedom' now, but mentally, most are under a great strain. But now the truth is marching in, as it once marched back in New Orleans. And that truth is that there must be peace and joy on Earth. I believe music can help bring that truth into being because music really is the universal language. That's why it can be such a force.[7]

Ten months after the performance, a byline appeared in *IT* magazine that described Ayler's beliefs as follows:

Those who have found Truth are able to communicate Love, to help those who suffer, people of the Earth as I call them. That the will of God be done, not that of men and women. The will of God is always loving and truthful; it includes harmony and generosity; it permits freedom and is always constructive.[8]

The religious fervor on display at Slugs' continues in Donald's composition 'Our Prayer,' which seems to be linked thematically to 'Truth Is Marching In,' though Albert denied the connection. 'It's a prayer to the Creator,' he told Hentoff. 'A song about the spiritual principles of the universe.'[9]

According to *New York Times* jazz writer and Coltrane biographer Ben Ratliff, 'Our Prayer' is based on a traditional Thanksgiving hymn. Revealing a Native American influence in Ayler's new sound, the piece was—as with most of Donald's music—based on a five-note scale, which had certain advantages in jazz music, namely a harmonic ambiguity that makes it simpler to superimpose changes on top of the chords than it had been in previous styles of jazz, such as bebop.[10]

'Bells' gets a 'rip-roaring treatment' that highlights the dueling relationship between the Aylers before violinist Samson steps into the fray. Both this composition and the following piece, 'Ghosts,' illustrate just how repetition had come to dominate Ayler's style, as if he were using incantations to increase the tension. In what is one of his liveliest interpretations of 'Ghosts,' once the free opening relaxes, a 'plaintive, almost tentative' Ayler presents the theme for the first time, before he begins the rapid repetitions. Another Ayler trademark is present, too, as Ayler contrasts the stark differences between the dense group sections and the light solos.[11]

Chris Sheridan of *Jazz Journal International* was one of a number of critics to note this trait in Ayler's work. However, he felt the Slugs' performance of 'Ghosts' to be weak, 'showing signs of a somewhat off-handed approach.' And yet he believed the group that backed him on this performance to be Ayler's greatest band, revealing 'different faces of the same entity, their overlapping melodic and polyphonic layers linked and punctuated by common rhythmic devices and interludes, often of elemental simplicity.' Ayler is in charge all the way—albeit supported by Donald and Samson, who become equal partners in the polyphony with the rhythm section. These multilayered textural improvisations are fed by a constant free-flowing rhythm that lacks the constraints of a formal beat. Whether this truly was the work of Ayler's greatest group is debatable, but it is great. Despite the rapidly changing moods that border on anarchy, the musicians' energy holds the music together, as Ayler sets the moods, controlling beat and tempo. And despite the melancholy that underlies his 'cry,' he and the musicians are having fun, and it shows.[12]

This is best heard in passages dominated by Albert and Donald, in which, as Milo Fine later wrote in a review for *Cadence*, 'The brothers swoop and tear, Albert with roars and squeals and Donald with those piercing machine gun-like staccato blasts.' Ayler's expression required a communal experience, as when drummer Ronald Jackson made 'sensitive drops in volume' from his 'energetic flailing polyrhythm[s]' in order to make way for Samson to play his 'raw-edged' style unamplified.[13]

Samson's addition to the group solidified the changes that stressed composition in Ayler's music, as on 'Truth is Marching In.' Albert's newer pieces featured multi-part themes, harmonies, and predetermined tempo changes, leading critics such as Schwartz to note the presence of the chorale and march sections that precede the solo sections.

Ayler discussed his transition toward favoring form—along with his move toward simplicity—with Nat Hentoff:

> I'm using modes now because I'm trying to get more form in the free form. Furthermore, I'd like to play something—like the beginning of 'Ghosts'—that people can hum. And I want to play songs like I used to sing when I was real small. Folk melodies that all the people would understand. I'd use those melodies as a start and have different simple melodies going in and out of a piece. From simple melody to complicated textures to simplicity again and then back to the more dense, the more complex sounds. I'm trying to communicate to as many people as I can. It's late now for the world. And if I can help raise people to new plateaus of peace and understanding I'll feel my life has been worth living as a spiritual artist, that's what counts.[14]

Also present in this music was the 'silent scream'—a new mode of expression that had developed away from the more abrasive type of scream Ayler had played earlier in his work, as he explained to Val Wilmer:

> The scream I was playing then [1964–65] was peace to me at that time. That was the way it had to go then. Whatever was inside of me, something was happening, and I did not know exactly what it was. America was going through such a big change, and I'd been travelling all over, seen it all, and had to play it out of me. But now it's peaceful. It's more like a silent scream.[15]

Donald described the spiritual dimension of the 'silent scream' in an unpublished 1976 interview with Wilmer:

I guess he was trying to say it as spiritually as he possibly could. And I guess every man have a way of screaming, too, but a lot of them don't have the outlet of music. Or—you can look at it as being a prayer, or something sacred, and that [is] how I look at it.[16]

A week later, on Sunday, May 8, Ayler's band was once again at Slugs'. They also played the Village Vanguard around this time, in a gig reviewed favorably by *DownBeat*'s Elisabeth van der Mei. While noting the presence of an untitled tune that 'could have been an East European folk song, full of nostalgia, during which sometimes the sound of the tenor and of the violin could hardly be distinguished,' and praising his latest evolution for the way in which it left 'more room for lyrical moments and getting closer to a direct translation of emotion into sound,' she gave special praise to 'Ghosts':

> A dexterous player, in no way slowed by technical shortcoming, Ayler extracted from his tenor saxophone a wildly varied series of sounds, making 'ghosts' travel through an abundance of emotions, playing freely at a height most tenor players can hardly reach and then diving deep into the huskiest ranges of his instrument, coming back to the theme, from which a sparkling trumpet solo grew into a crashing wildfire of sound. Tenor then joined trumpet, surging into a splashing waterfall of music. Once one learns to listen, patterns become apparent, and their intricacy can be astounding. Technically brilliant, Sampson [*sic*] was remarkable in showing how two different worlds of music blended into a new sound so exciting and with such a forceful feeling of joy for life that it literally stirred a cheering audience to its feet.'[17]

Ayler spent the rest of the spring playing around the city, making a notable appearance with the Coltrane Quintet at the Village Vanguard, opening at the New Jazz Sound Festival, at the Astor Place Playhouse, on the evening of Friday, May 20, and heading further afield to the Cellar in Newark, New Jersey, a venue operated by a local bass player, Art Williams, and which had begun drawing the avant-garde players from New York.

At around this time, Donald returned to Cleveland, and on August

17 he applied for a marriage license. His intended bride was Constance Thomas, a playground supervisor four years his junior, but for some reason the marriage never took place. (It's possible that Donald got caught up in preparations for a forthcoming European tour and simply let the application expire.) Nine days later, the group was engaged to play the last of three concerts organized by Lovebeast Enterprises under the concept of 'The Avant Garde: A Perspective In Revolution,' during which they performed a new, multi-themed composition, 'Light In Darkness.' But despite reaching new creative heights, Ayler's band—one of his most creatively and critically successful—was about to fall apart.

'The Avant Garde' was held at the Village Theatre, with the Archie Shepp Quintet and the Frank Smith Sextet also on the bill. In his review for *DownBeat*, Don Heckman made clear Ayler's rising stock among critics who had previously dismissed him:

> Albert Ayler impresses me more every time I hear him. His music reaches toward what seems to me one of the profound innovations of recent jazz history. In the most basic sense, he is returning to fundamental jazz elements— melody, a rudimentary I–V or I–IV–V harmonic pattern, and a tireless re-examination of the major triad. One would assume that the familiarity of these elements would make Ayler's music accessible to a wide audience, and I suspect that such, indeed, may be the case as his music receives better exposure. The problem, of course, is that other aspects of Ayler's music are considerably less accessible. These are the parts that are more typically avant-garde—waves of high harmonies, rattling rhythms, and dense textures. Yet even these parts of Ayler's music seem to have a point and a focus that similar sounds from many other new groups do not. I think, perhaps, this may be due to the interconnection between the two principal forces in Ayler's music—the clear, quasi-primitive basic elements and the whirling energies of the new music style. … In the final piece, 'The Light In The Darkness,' the group gradually worked its way into a stunning flow of rhythmic power, the sound pulsating in swirls of vibrant force—a brilliant example of the new music's ability to sustain interest with few familiar jazz elements other than a primal stream of rhythm.[18]

Three years later, Ayler wrote a letter he titled 'To Mr. Jones—I Had A Vision,' which Amiri Baraka published in issue four of *The Cricket: Black Music In Evolution!!!* In apocalyptic terms, Ayler, quoting heavily from *The Book Of Revelations*, describes a disturbing encounter he and his brother had with a flying saucer one night in New Jersey (only weeks after the Ohio incident):

> Anyway, it was revealed to me that we had the right seal of God almighty in our forehead …
>
> In the forehead of Satan written across his forehead the word blasphemy is there. This is his name also so be very careful and respect God's laws, so you won't receive the devil's mark in your forehead or your right hand. I have seen a few people with the mark already so be very careful and God's angels will be with you even unto the end. Eat only the green things and no meat at all if possible …
>
> We live in darkness now; God Almighty is the God of lights. You see there are mighty angels from Heaven, and they are very large. Bright as the sun. Another way to describe it is like the color of lightening magnified ten times. So, you'd better get ready for the bright lights that will appear in the sky. It has been written on the wall of the universe by God Almighty for me to see and give you this message. So, don't transgress any of God's Laws. The time is at hand. Make up leaflets and pass out to all people Revelation 14, verse 7 to 10. This is very important that everybody should know this will save your soul and you will see a beautiful eternity …[19]

Just as *Revelations* augers the beginning of the end, with mysterious signs and wonders, it is easy to view Ayler's letter as the beginning of the end of his grasp on reality. But, in context, this vision occurred at the height of the UFO phenomenon, and Albert was hardly the only person to report seeing flying saucers at this time. Others reportedly had seen them.

Donald later described the experience in his own words:

> It was a star that came down in our backyard. It was red and green. … It came down as low as the trees—and then went back up. Made a complete turn. … That's where the angels are at. I think the angels are there.[20]

Whatever the brothers saw—or thought they saw—made a deep impression. But while many people found it delightfully hip to accept Sun Ra as an alien from Saturn on a mission to preach peace, a number of those same critics and fans scorned Ayler for his visions. But while some, such as *The Village Voice*'s Richard Mortifoglio, believed that Ayler was struggling with mental illness, he also felt that Ayler 'was able to harness his schizophrenia for coherent social ends … A great moral artist, Ayler, like [the poet and novelist Rainer Maria] Rilke, experienced these historical fissures deep enough to resolve them in an art of healing, compensation, and growth.'[21]

It is also possible to miss the sincerity in Ayler's account. Those who knew him in Cleveland, such as Bobby Few, recalled buying books on UFOs while still at high school, and, later on, going to 'flying saucer meetings' with Albert and Donald:

> They used to have them down at the Sheraton Hotel. That's when I was really believing in that. Don had me convinced that he had seen the men in black. I remember we used to go—down there to the Sheraton and the speaker and the committee of the speakers were all dressed in black—and Don would say, 'That's them, Few, that's them.'[22]

Albert's father discussed *The Book Of Revelations* in an interview with me for WCSB-FM, adding an important religious context to his son's experience:

> It's terrible and it's full of chaos and it's all kind of trouble. As I read it, I say destiny is in the sands of time, and we find that the sands of time is running out. We are on the edge of doom and eternity. In fact, some of them will be condemned to eternal punishment and some will be blessed to everlasting life. This is the summation I explained to the boys. … You want to be a part of those who are going to be away with Christ. … You might get right with God that you won't have to go down into the Lake of Fire that you be able to spend eternity with Jesus.[23]

Albert had grown up in a culture that embraced visions and speaking in tongues, and as his music made clear, he was a man of determined faith. The question is whether the letter marked the beginning of a supposed mental deterioration or was simply a reiteration of his religious faith.

•

Though Ayler was gaining greater recognition in the press, there remained a lot of empty seats at his gigs. Despite the exhilarating musical challenge of playing with Albert, drummer Ronald Jackson quit the band in search of a better-paying gig, admitting, 'We was just working. It was for the love of music. We'd get a few gigs, but nobody would come.'[24] And yet the experience changed his life:

> Albert really opened me up as far as playing. I had never experienced *totally playing* before. Up until then my work had been playing background, the 'ching-ching-a-ding' line, where you played like this person or that person. … You played like them or you weren't playing! Albert was the type of person who wouldn't say, 'I want this,' or, 'I want that.' He'd just say, 'Play! Fill it up with sound!' So from that being ingrained in me, it allowed me to just play. It was a very good experience of my life.[25]

Shortly after Jackson's exit, Ayler also parted ways with his bassist, Lewis Worrell. Roswell Rudd, himself a doyen of the avant-garde scene, later explained to Val Wilmer, in *The Wire*, why he felt Ayler's group began to implode at this time:

> He was like the lead dog and everything sort of followed in his wake. I think Lewis felt a lot of the times in some of these other bands that too much of the responsibility was coming down on the bass. Everybody would be looking around and expecting more from the bass, some kind of conventional stuff that Lewis wasn't providing because he was looking for the lead dog. … Lewis was a good musician, but he didn't evolve to the extent that Albert did at the same time. Lewis evolved more slowly, and there were other bass players that were more proficient than he was. But he sounded great. He and Albert

sounded great together, I mean he really knew how to play a part for Albert. But he needed Albert there, he needed somebody to react to. It wasn't like he could be a catalyst.[26]

Around this time, Ayler met Mary Maria Parks at Count Basie's (now known as Wells Supper Club), a late-night Harlem haunt for jazz musicians which was famous for its chicken and waffles. If records at the US Copyright Office are to be believed, Mary was about sixteen years older than him; some would report that she had a reputation for being controlling, but others would see her as a stabilizing influence. She 'wanted him to make something out of himself,' said Donald, who described her as having 'a straight nose and a pretty good grade of hair … was kinda nice-looking in a country kind of way.'[27]

Originally from Alabama, Parks was living in Brooklyn and working for New York Bell Telephone at the time she met Albert:

My girlfriend was a wildflower. She was hitting on him. But he was looking at me from the corner of his eye. I sat down and he kissed me on the cheek. 'Nice meeting you,' I told him, but I had to get home to Brooklyn. 'I'm going there, too,' he told me. Soon after, I received a note from him saying he had to see me again.[28]

Parks was the opposite of the type of person Ayler usually hung out with. According to Michel Samson, he surrounded himself with flatterers and avoided hiring musicians with strong personalities; as evidenced by his treatment of Sunny Murray, he would try to sidestep conflict by letting his sidemen go without communicating his decision. And yet he ultimately surrendered control of his life to Parks. It may have been the right time: he was frustrated with the way his music was being received, and Parks pushed him in another direction. As she herself put it to Val Wilmer, 'I would like to think that I was a force who continually inspired him on when at times he only wanted to meditate.'[29]

european tour

n the past, friends and relatives had tried to dissuade Ayler from playing
engagements in Europe, but now things seemed to be on an upswing,
with the prestigious Newport Jazz Festival inviting him to be a part of
the line-up for its European shows, bringing Ayler back to a continent
that had been more open to the avant-garde jazz movement. Released
the previous year, *Ghosts* had won an award from one of the European
magazines—though Ayler told Nat Hentoff that Debut, the Danish label
that had released it, had never even told him—and the British jazz press
had begun to refer to him as a 'star,' though Ayler claimed he could not
afford to play there.

Ole Vestergaard, Debut's owner, denied Ayler's accusations, claiming
that he had notified Ayler of the award, and, having recently sold Debut
Records to British businessman Alan Bates, forwarded him $2,000 in back
royalties, air fare, and advances. The same itinerant lifestyle that may have
made it difficult for Vestergaard's messages to get through to Ayler certainly
challenged promoter/critic Joachim-Ernst Berendt, who, as director of the
1966 Berlin Jazz Festival, was looking for an avant-garde artist to replace
his first choice, John Coltrane, who had declined the invitation to perform
due to health problems. Struggling to locate Ayler, Berendt asked Newport's
founder, the legendary George Wein, to bring Ayler with him.

Ayler had been without a gig since the May engagements at Slugs' and had not even practiced for three weeks when Wein called him. Despite being namechecked in *Time* and *Vogue*, his spirits were low. Unable to get Henry Grimes to travel to Europe with him at such short notice, Ayler recruited Bill Folwell, whom he knew through clarinetist Perry Robinson. Folwell was a member of the UNI trio and had picked up playing the bass while stationed in the army. He wound up being one of the few white musicians on the tour: 'They'd make jokes about me, to get to the back of the bus,' he recalled. 'Like in the South. They made those jokes because I was the only white guy on that half of the tour. But I was just in heaven; that was great.'[1]

The same whims that could lead Ayler to fire one musician could also lead him to hire another just as reflexively, and he brought in Folwell without ever hearing him play. As the bassist told Ben Young, for WKCR radio:

> I rehearsed with Albert, and I met the guys. I think we rehearsed down at the Village Gate … I just did what I thought needed, and I played the bow. … The bow seemed to work, and Albert was happy with it. … I think Albert and Donald, they were their tunes … it's just my conjecture that they were so simple … it was something they could play together … it was basically I–IV–V chord structures … and then it would just go off and make as much energy as you can.[2]

At this time in jazz, it was unusual to give the bass a sustaining voice by using a bow (as opposed to plucking), but this again illustrates Ayler's conception of the bass as a melodic instrument, as opposed to one that would reinforce the rhythm-chord structure.

To play on drums, Ayler hired an old army buddy he'd met while stationed at Fort Knox and with whom he'd gigged while on leave in Louisville. William Godvin 'Beaver' Harris, who earned his nickname playing for Negro American League baseball team the Indianapolis Clowns, was born in Pittsburgh in 1936 and also played clarinet and alto sax. 'We would always get along,' Harris recalled of their earlier time together.

'Some musicians will play in a way that the technique will dominate the soulfulness. Albert had the technical ability that dominated his soulfulness at times.'[3]

By the time he received Ayler's call, Harris had about eight years of experience playing with musicians such as Archie Shepp, making a name for himself with the 'powerfully squat physique' he'd inherited from an athletic father and a dancer mother. Like Sunny Murray before him, Harris's style moved away from bebop, replacing the time-keeping roles of the bass drum and hi-hat with a use of ride and crash cymbals. But though his playing was described as a 'fountain of noise' that seemed disconnected from the others in the quintet, Harris always managed to hold the music together.[4]

The group's first concert was in Berlin, on November 3, with the Kurt Edelhagen Band and Willie 'The Lion' Smith opening. The show was reviewed by local newspaper *Die Zeit*, for whom Siegfried Schmidt-Joos wrote:

> Albert and Donald Ayler ... offer the oldest and dustiest hats from Moravian folk coffeehouses, but dressed fashionably with free jazz feathers, as 'uncompromising modernity' for sale. Their collage of marketplace and circus sounds, located in the narrow space between tonic, dominant and subdominant, hit through tunes such as 'The Sandman Is There,' 'Long, Long Is Here,' and 'I Came From Alabama With The Banjo On My Knee.' And, after several minutes of these feathers, a short burst takes place in the language of free jazz, and prevailed in the arbitrariness of the solos.[5]

The concert was recorded for a television broadcast, and video footage still exists in its entirety; excerpts are seen in Kasper Collin's documentary *My Name Is Albert Ayler*. Whatever songs Schmidt-Joos thought he heard, the audio released several years later, as *The Berlin Concerts—1966*, on the Italian label Relyable, reveals the setlist to have been 'Our Prayer,' 'Ghosts/ Bells,' 'Truth Is Marching In,' and 'Omega Is The Alpha.'

Reviewing the 1990 Philology release *Albert Ayler*—which included three of the Berlin tracks alongside recordings from his 1964 residency at

Jazzhus Montmartre, in Copenhagen—jazz musician Milo Fine felt that Ayler's latest group seemed 'formally organized to a greater degree' than the Ayler quartet he'd last taken to Europe. But, he added:

> the expression is just as strong. Harris propels the music with an aggressive style that breaks apart rather than redefines jazz drumming. The Ayler brothers soar, as does Sampson [sic], whose drone-based, slippery, glissandi-drenched outing on 'Ghosts-Bells' is outstanding. Fowell [sic] is only heard in a supporting role, but he acquits himself well. Fittingly enough, the LP ends as it began, with an unembellished eloquent reading of an Ayler theme.[6]

Elsewhere, reviewers such as *Jazz Journal International*'s Chris Sheridan felt that the Berlin recordings represented the perfect statement of Ayler's art, even though their influence wasn't as great as that of the landmark albums *Spiritual Unity* and *Ghosts*.

Heading west through Germany, the band recorded a set (now lost) at the SWF television studio in Munich on November 4, 5, or 6, before moving on to Lörrach on November 7. As the fifteen-day tour continued, it seemed to take on the shape of one of Ayler's own compositions: the group concentrated on a core set of pieces established in Berlin but added new works in each city, as if the first show were a theme and the following performances variations on that theme. Reviewing the Lörrach performance in *Cadence*, Larry Hollis felt the set offered a 'montage of the tenor-saxophonist's thought-provoking compositions and an overview of his radical approach to his instrument.'[7] *JazzTimes*'s Francis Davis noted the stylistic change that had taken place since Ayler had last visited Europe, writing, 'His solos here (and those of his brother, the volleying trumpeter Donald) are short and sudden and ecstatic, with the stridently lovely clashes of horns and rhythm and Sampson's [sic] firefly violin, on the expansion and contraction of Donald's written lines.'[8]

This is illustrated by the changing moods throughout the concert—found even within the same section of a work—as when Ayler is at the height of originality in what Barry McRae called 'a multi-structured piece like "Holy Ghosts," in the frenzied passion of "Jesus," or in the folky, chuckle tune atmosphere of "Bells," with its Scottish skirl.'[9] Typical of an Ayler performance of the era and yet also an example of the saxophonist at the peak of his creativity, the Lörrach show captured him 'full of swaggering confidence, very much in charge of his instrument and able to build solos with ease and creativity.'[10]

Expanding on this thought in 1983, McRae wrote, 'He is majestic. Whether stating his quirky chuckle tunes with leathery authority, playing dirge-like moans, or roaring freely in the pantonal hinterland, he takes control … he shows us how to solo with inspiration.'[11]

But while McRae would praise the rhythm section of Folwell and Harris—here given the only solo spots in all their recordings with Ayler—for making 'a major contribution' to his music, 'whether dragging at a dirge, putting the backbone in a march sequence or indulging in arhythmic extravagance behind solos,' he initially found violinist Michel Samson to be 'not quite as convincing as a soloist in this company.'[12] He revised his opinion seven months later, writing that Samson:

> fits in better here than on previous releases, and he does so, not by providing a contrast to his wild colleagues, but by joining them in some headlong and ferocious improvising. His near demonic outbursts on 'Bells' and 'Jesus' are as apposite as are his studied ensemble parts on 'Our Prayer,' and throughout, he plays with a chromatic abandon and soulfulness.[13]

This change in group dynamics had occurred at the start of the tour: Gary Giddins noted in his review of *Holy Ghost* that Samson had been a 'fifth wheel' at the La Cave shows but had now evolved into a 'plucky disciple' and 'emphatic collaborator' with Ayler.[14] It was, however, ironic that Samson, who had received technical training from established conservatories, had to find a way of fitting into Ayler's style, yet the relatively untutored Donald fell instinctively into place. Indeed, where some critics had at first been underwhelmed by the younger Ayler sibling, McRae felt Donald had grown in stature, declaring that he 'belongs naturally in this music':

His instrumental limitations matter little because it is difficult to imagine a more ideal partner for the tenor giant. He is at his best when forthright, as on 'Prayer' and 'Holy Ghost,' but throughout he pitches in with flurryingly free solos, distinguished more by their fire and rhythmic impetus than by their melodic ingenuity.[15]

After Germany, Ayler moved on to the Netherlands, playing at the Doelen Jazz Festival in Rotterdam on November 8. A spurious twelve-minute excerpt alleged to be the Rotterdam performance was shown on the Dutch show *Jazz Is Niet Dood* on July 15, 1970. It seems that the footage has since been lost, but the audio recording has survived; it was released by Revenant Records as part of the *Holy Ghost* box set. Reviewing that release in *Coda*, Art Lange noted that Ayler's band 'sounded better' than they had at La Cave, noting that Folwell was more audible than Clyde Shy had been, and that Samson was:

more comfortable within the ensemble, his violin amplified properly so that his important contribution is equal to the others, coloring the music, droning, soloing with greater nuance, and caressing the horn lines. At the Rotterdam concert, Beaver Harris, the new drummer, attacked the drums with a violence unimaginable during Sunny Murray's reign, reconfiguring the group dynamic in keeping with the more dramatic ambiance of the full ensemble.[16]

Over thirty years earlier, *Coda* had run a very different account of the gig in a quasi-obituary of Ayler written by the expatriate US poet Ted Joans. Something of a bridge between the New American poetry and the Black Arts movement, Joans's poetry derived from the Black avant-garde tradition and was characterized by an 'edgy, jazz-influenced surrealism' that owed as much to Langston Hughes as it did to French surrealists such as André Breton or Paul Éluard. His derision of white musicians such as Bill Folwell—'yes ANOTHER white bass player. … He didn't or couldn't take care of bass biz like Gary Peacock had done. But he was up there going through the motions'—made clear that his politics aligned with Amiri Baraka's, but, artistically, Joans sided with Ayler, who, he said, emerged 'the victor' in the face of a hostile audience that was 'unprepared and reacted to the first half with boos,' which 'quickly changed to screams of ecstasy. Some even wept ... Albert Ayler and his group triumphed.'[17]

After the Rotterdam show, Ayler's group visited a tiny jazz club owned by promoter Paul Kartig, where Joans read poems in their honor. Their next stop was Helsinki, Finland (an audio tape of their performance survives in the Finnish Radio archives), before they moved on to Stockholm for a show on November 10. Recorded for broadcast, the audio was issued decades later as part of Hat Hut's *Stockholm, Berlin 1966*. Michael Tucker of *Jazz Journal* felt that:

> the (often heterophonic) group textures and dynamics are particularly good on these sessions, with Dutch violinist Samson contributing many an adroitly keening accent and Folwell's arco bass offering broad swathes of grounded color within the multi-directional drive supplied throughout ... by the excellent Beaver Harris. Ayler really did have an extraordinary, barn-door wide yet densely-grained sound on tenor, combined with an irruptive labile facility in the extreme upper register; hear him explode on 'Truth' and 'Prayer' or embroider the clearly stepped, folk-like melody of Pharoah Sanders's 'Jesus' [aka 'Japan']. Brother Donald contributes chromatically vivid waves of sound to the kind of diatonically sprung program.[18]

By now, the old guard were beginning to realize how much respect the avant-gardists commanded. In Stockholm, drummer Jo Jones, who had played with everyone from Ella Fitzgerald to Duke Ellington, Count Basie, and Art Blakey, was impressed that Harris's playing was so powerful his drums had to be nailed to the stage. Harris recalled that Ayler's growing stature allowed him to make such demands:

> They didn't want to nail the drums into the concert hall and ... Albert said, 'We're not going to perform until it's done right.'... I said, 'I can't play with the drums sliding around.' And they tried to put weights on the drums and

everything. … There was an evolution in the way that we were treated—
opposed to the way some of our great musicians in the past [were]. … It's a
funny thing. They would sit and watch … these old masters, they were in touch
with the music. Not once had I heard them complain that it was nothing.[19]

On November 11, the quintet then played a concert in Copenhagen (of
which a twenty-six-minute tape of bad quality survives), before two shows
at the Salle Pleyel, in Paris, on November 13. Ayler later told Frank Kofsky
how audiences had begun to applaud him just for walking onstage: 'I
didn't have to play at all, and all these people were clapping, thousands of
people, you know what I mean?'[20]

A poor-quality bootleg of the first Paris show survives, while a better
recording of the midnight show was broadcast and later issued as *Lörrach/
Paris 1966* on Hat Hut. But while none of that release's reviewers picked up
on Albert's vocals at the start of 'Ghost (First Variation),' a quarter-century
later, the performance still amazed Larry Hollis in *Cadence*, who called it
'quintessential Ayler … thoroughly possessed by the high energy spirit feel
and blowing snakes for us all to still try and catch.'[21] Jeff Schwartz cites
'Ghosts' as a standout for the way in which Ayler maintained the freedom
of the piece by ordering the fixed sections at will, with the improvisatory
solos falling between them.[22]

Critic Guy Kopelowicz, who had witnessed the *Spirits Rejoice* session,
was also at the Paris shows. He recalled:

> The whole audience was stunned. A number of people could not stand the
> intensity of the music and booed but most of the audience just enjoyed it and
> Ayler and his musicians got a lot of applause. … The second [concert], which
> was held very late in the evening, was sparsely attended. Cecil Taylor was at
> the concerts. He congratulated Ayler at length when they met after Ayler's
> appearance.[23]

Ted Joans wrote about the Paris gig in *Coda*, once again expressing Amiri
Baraka's view that avant-garde jazz should have been the exclusive domain

of Black musicians. But with a tasteless reference to Samson's ethnicity (not to mention misspelling his name), Joans revealed prejudices of his own:

> On stage at the Salle Pleyel that night Albert's group was joined by a young Dutch Jew with his violin, Micheal Sampson [*sic*]. He had studied the traditional European violin techniques and it all had been shattered after he heard brother Ornette Coleman. He sat in with Ornette in Amsterdam, and now he was still in his parasitic-bag by intruding on Ayler's scene. But he didn't disturb brother Albert, naw sir. Brothers Albert and Don just took care of their musical biz like Sampson wasn't even there.'[24]

Joans claimed that Ayler triumphed over 'arrogant motherfuckers'— meaning white French jazz critics such as Jef Gilson and Claude Lénissois, or 'Lemoison' in Joans's screed—who he felt were trying to crush the new jazz scene through, for example, a negative review of Ayler's Paris concert under their joint byline in the December 1966 issue of *Jazz Hot*. Meanwhile, his own racist leanings caused him to target 'jive master' George Wein, despite Wein's credentials as a longtime supporter of Black jazz artists through his Newport Folk Festival—and Beaver Harris's account of Wein giving Ayler money after he was robbed. And yet, despite his jaded stance, Joans was a sensitive enough listener to hear how Ayler 'was about rearticulating the spiritual in a music that, even today, often gets marketed as merely sexy and cool. Ayler asserted with terrifying but tender force that jazz was emphatically not "devil's music," that the cry of the blues was the same shriek he heard in the sanctified church.'[25] It was music that, as Joans wrote in a different piece, for *IT* magazine, 'shattered' the Parisians' 'entire preconceived concept of Black American music' while also presenting something that transcended both race and geography: 'They witnessed not only black America of the past, present and the future, but also what's happening in Vietnam, Berlin, Barcelona, Baton Rouge.'[26]

Three nights later, Ayler was in Bordeaux for the Sigma Festival, a six-minute video excerpt of which was broadcast on November 28 as part of *Carte Blanche À Nicolas Schöffer: Spectacle Audiovisuel Expérimental.*

Reviewing Ayler's slot in the newspaper *Sud-Ouest*, M.-C. Icre wrote, 'It squeaks, it squeals, it screams, it screeches, it blows, it smokes: it plays the buffoon! The Albert Ayler quintet lashes out: collective madness at its paroxysm. It is, as it seems, "free jazz."' Questioning 'the lack of formal, rhythmic and harmonic research' in the music, Icre did not know whether the music was destroying jazz or reinventing jazz by abusing it.[27]

The final engagement of the tour brought Ayler to London for the first time, but his long-awaited UK debut was beset with problems from the moment they landed, according to Beaver Harris:

> They stopped us at the airport and made us all go in the back room and take our clothes off. There wasn't drugs, we drank, but no drugs or anything. Maybe some cats would come along and give us something to smoke, but that band was a healthy band, we just drank too much. That's why they stopped us at the airport there, they thought that we were drunk on the plane, Don Ayler standing up on his head in the plane.[28]

Bill Folwell felt the rest of the group had been stopped because they were Black. 'I went through customs without a problem, and I'm sitting out in the bus. Like an hour and a half later … they finally came out, and they were just mad as hell.'[29]

Further problems arose with their accommodation:

> Albert and Beaver and Donald … didn't like the hotel where we were staying. It was just cold … they went off into London, disappeared … and we had a rehearsal for a TV show, and there wasn't any Donald or any Albert or any Beaver there for the rehearsal. … Nobody knew where they were … we never had rehearsed with Albert.[30]

On November 15, the quintet recorded two half-hour sessions at the London School of Economics for the BBC Two series *Jazz Goes To College*. According to Val Wilmer, the tapes were subsequently destroyed because Ayler's music horrified the powers that be, but there were also technical difficulties that left the results less than satisfactory: the microphones often missed Folwell's bass, and the BBC's sound engineers stopped the session at least once throughout a 'perpetual dispute over the positioning of the microphones.'[31]

And yet the performance itself received positive reviews, with *IT*'s Alan Beckett writing:

> On record, it sometimes sounds angry, arrogant, far off, but in person it was nothing like this, it was full of life, positive, immediately relevant. Ayler and his colleagues are trying to present an original musical experience using "original" in its literal sense … the BBC seemed to patronize the group and treat them like strange animals. It was unfortunate that this was Ayler's only appearance, and that the group could not play before a more open audience. Some people present seemed determined not to let the music go any further into the world.[32]

Elsewhere, *Jazz Journal*'s Alan Barton felt that Ayler offered a window back in time to the days of the collective improvisation of King Oliver.[33] Summing up Ayler's career to this point, W.A. Baldwin believed the reason for this to be that Ayler had recognized the failure of the totally free improvisation he had recorded on *New York Eye And Ear Control*, and reverted to the classic New Orleans model of collective improvisation. Baldwin concluded that this was the logical outgrowth of Ayler's earlier works, such as *Spirits*, on which he had evoked memories of Congo Square on that album, and *Bells*, on which Ayler affectionately parodied the Crescent City's marching bands.[34] Now the parody had become serious and 'quite profound,' used as light relief to contrast and separate the brief, intense solos which revealed the improvisational possibilities in the old models Ayler had once eschewed.[35]

The comparisons to New Orleans were typical of the UK press, with *Jazz Monthly*'s Ronald Atkins noting how, though the London School Of Economics show featured 'dissonant moments that naturally reflected the sophisticated musicianship of the 1960s:

Each item performed followed a basic pattern. The front-line played a
succession of themes, each introduced by Albert Ayler; then, perhaps, a round
of brief solos and finally a partial recapitulation. The nature of the themes
and their interpretation can only be compared to a New Orleans band, in
particular to the marches and dirges of a brass band of the Eureka type.

Praising Samson's violin for taking 'the clarinet's role, weaving around and
above the other two' horns, Atkins also felt that Donald 'asserted himself
more convincingly than on record,' noting that his tone—'not so coarse
as expected but still closer to that of a parade trumpet than to anyone
else'—stood at odds with the New Orleans sound: 'It completely lacks the
declamatory brilliance and rich vibrato of the post-Armstrong era.' And
yet, Atkins conceded:

The solos of the Ayler brothers cannot possibly be judged by the standards
of Armstrong. ... Now there is absolutely no attempt at the merest kind of
structure; what they play is unmitigated, relentless noise. Compared with the
function of the bass and drums, the solos provide the emotional colouring—
violent and often hysterical—to contrast with the sobriety of the thematic
material.

But though Atkins concluded that the ensemble playing—including the
'rhythmic colouring' of Harris's drums and the 'background of swirling
colours' provided by Folwell's bowed bass—was 'everything one could
wish for: clean, well-integrated, and with untold imaginative touches,' the
audience's reception was mixed: 'Some hated the music; some thought
it limited,' Atkins reported, while seeming to concur. Though suggesting
that nothing could 'mask the present validity of their music,' he ultimately
decided that Ayler's group were 'innovators suddenly stumbling upon a
self-contained form. ... Ayler now needs to expand, and there is every
reason to suppose that he will.'[36]
  While many musicians in the audience laughed at Ayler's performance
(British jazz figurehead Humphrey Lyttleton later recalled pianist Gordon

Beck asking where the fruit market was, in order to throw fruit at the stage[37]), others, such as South African pianist Chris McGregor, were fascinated by it.[38] After the show, McGregor hosted the group at his flat. 'They played together, and the Americans expressed a desire to stay on and work with Chris in England,' wrote Val Wilmer, who had introduced Ayler to McGregor and his wife, Maxine, 'But their concert promoter dismissed the idea. He said it would be "bad for their image."'[39]

•

Despite ending on such a chaotic note, the European tour marked a watershed moment in Ayler's quest to recast the most elemental ingredients of his music. This, according to an interview Ayler gave with the US magazine *Newsweek*, was his attempt to cut through the noise and distractions of a club and communicate the sound of human possibility: 'Yeah, yeah, that's it. Right after that first sound comes, I just give all that's in my heart to give—just give it all,' Ayler said. 'I'm livin' it, breathin' it, drinkin' it. I'm out in another dimension and I'm hummin' a tune. I never stop. I'm hummin' a tune when I'm talkin' to you.'[40]

The group returned to New York in time to play at the Village Vanguard on December 18—a show that John Coltrane attended. For this engagement, Ayler added Henry Grimes on bass, and the difference was immediately apparent. According to Richard Cook and Brian Morton, authors of *The Penguin Guide To Jazz On CD, LP, And Cassette*, the second bass 'actually sharpens the sound considerably, producing a rock-solid foundation for Ayler's raw witness.'[41]

The group recorded five pieces at this date—'Truth Is Marching In,' 'Spirits Rejoice,' 'Our Prayer,' 'Divine Peacemaker,' and 'Angels' (actually a revision of 'Prophecy,' according to Jeff Schwartz)—but only 'Truth Is Marching In' and 'Our Prayer' were released during Ayler's lifetime, as part of the 1967 release *Albert Ayler In Greenwich Village*. Praised by *Cadence* for being 'one of the more rewarding documents of Albert Ayler's unique music,'[42] these recordings also received a warm reception from the formerly skeptical *DownBeat*, with Pete Welding writing:

The music is vividly alive, churning, full of colors and textures, and relentlessly moving. There is a great deal of energy, and relentless passion to it, yet it doesn't sound 'disturbed' or otherwise disoriented. Ayler's music is not at all incomprehensible or difficult of access. All it requires is a pair of open ears, a willingness to enter a world of musical thought that might on the surface seem alien and uncomfortable. It's not, though. The vistas are fresh, the natives friendly.[43]

With thirty years of hindsight at his disposal—and evidence of another show, held at the Village Theatre the following February and given a posthumous release as part of *The Village Concerts*—*The Wire*'s Art Lange felt that the Vanguard performances ranked alongside Ayler's epochal ESP-Disk' sessions of 1964 and 1965 for 'the nearly hysterical urgency of "Holy Ghost," the transcendent talking in tongues on "Truth Is Marching In," and the gravity defying solos amid frantic fanfares and folk song fragments of "Spirits Rejoice."' Decades after it was seemingly co-opted by Amiri Baraka, Lange sought to separate Ayler's music 'from the ideological protests of the Black nationalist vanguard of the free jazz movement'; he defended Donald from accusations of being 'an amateur or, worse a psychotic' while praising 'the ensemble texture ... of those harrowing horns, the alternately articulate and thudding basses of Henry Grimes and Bill Folwell, Michel Sampson's [*sic*] razor-edged violin, and Beaver Harris's rollicking drums.' From his vantage, Lange concluded that the full concert was 'capable of evoking uninhibited expressions of wonder, lamentation, and rapture. But not aggression. In its overwhelming intensity, Ayler's music sought out extremes of passion, never anger or frustration.'[44]

In a different vein, Barry McRae, of *Jazz Journal International*, was drawn to the pathos of Ayler's music:

It is perhaps an oversimplification, however, to think of headlong tirades as the only basics of his style. The pathos in his essentially simple solo on 'Spirits Rejoice' or his realization of the New Orleans funeral fanfare and dirge ... provide evidence of his broader stylistic range. This ... underlines the fact that he had as much in common with the music's primitives as he did with contemporary saxophonists.[45]

Ayler's expanded line-up offered the ideal setting for him to roar his overtones against the sound of the bassists playing in the upper harmonic range. The continued presence of Michel Samson also illustrated the excellent way in which strings could be integrated into jazz, as if picking up the baton from Charlie Parker's experiments in 1949–50.

In a 1987 interview with WKCR-FM, Beaver Harris suggested that Ayler's use of strings sought to create a trance-like state in the listener, reminiscent of the religious experiences that were a daily part of life in his parental home:

> I stayed at his mother's and dad's house there. … They would have visions and different things. … So, a lot of what Albert was doing was natural to him, but it was odd to people around him. … The strings, it had something to do with … a drone. It goes … more or less into a chant or a repeat of a theme … but it evolves out of that one point. … It gives feeling of the ghosty … mysterious type feelings. … He figured that he had to utilize certain instruments in order to get his feelings across, and evidently the strings had a lot to do with his feelings. It was an open thing. Everything was based on the Biblical connotations as we know them.[46]

The trance-type feeling that Ayler sought was complemented by the way his instruments seemed to be speaking in tongues, as heard on 'Light In Darkness,' from the Village Theatre performance.

Writing in the liner notes to *The Village Concerts*, Robert Palmer felt that 'Angels,' the final performance of the December 1966 show, was 'the major discovery on this major addition to the Ayler discography.'[47] A duet with a pianist suspected to be Call Cobbs, it finds Ayler playing with a style that's tragic yet lacking in sentimentality against the pianist's comical, almost silent-film-like piano accompaniment. Palmer felt that the unconfirmed identity of the pianist, who had helped Ayler deliver such a crucial performance was a mystery second only to the cause of Ayler's strange death.[48]

Part of the reason for Ayler's rise in popularity was that he spoke for his times. With the world on the cusp of the Summer of Love, hurtling toward the worst of the Vietnam War, and soon to be propelled along by a generation demanding social and political change, Ayler's music was, as Joe Pinelli wrote in *Sounds & Fury*, capable of expressing emotions that had not been expressed before: 'This, the new music, is life music. It's dirt and gristle and blood and the catalyst is the sheer animal joy of being alive.'[49]

CHAPTER XVIII

back to the village

S ettling back in New York, Ayler moved into Mary Parks's apartment at 1055 Dean Street, at the corner of Franklin Avenue in Crown Heights, Brooklyn, but his relationship with her gave many of his associates concern. Though she would handle Ayler's business affairs and later collaborate with him on his music, Michel Samson believed that Parks 'was simply an office worker who would stand on the stage.' Others felt that she was using Ayler to further her own ambitions, despite having no real comprehension of his music.[1] Don told Peter Niklas Wilson, 'Mary kept him at home with her. She kept him away from everyone else and monopolized him. She knew a little about music, but I never liked it. Especially after all that real music we had played. I thought that Al was going in a wrong direction—which he was.' Sunny Murray felt that Parks was 'opportunistic,' but he may have been envious of the privileged position she now held in Ayler's life: 'I had never before known a woman to have so much power over him.'[2]

Tellingly, Parks seemed to alienate Albert not only from other musicians, but from his brother, who would reflect:

> She was a rock'n'roller, and at the same time I was no rock'n'roller. ... The reason why she had got away with what she had got away with [was] she was dealing with my brother. My brother was always looking for someone to be a

brother, sister, mother, and all that stuff. Lookin' for a family, rather than his own family.[3]

Many of Albert's friends would also come to resent her influence: Albert no longer hung out in Harlem; instead of visiting jazz clubs or meeting up for drinks on street-corner bars, he spent his time in Brooklyn's Prospect Park, practicing with Mary—on one occasion they were forcibly ejected by the police. But despite the misgivings of some, Bobby Few remembered, 'She always encouraged him, she was always there for him.'[4]

For Ayler, it may have been a relationship as much of convenience as romance. The jazz scene was notoriously misogynistic, and Ayler, who felt that meeting Parks was 'a blessing,' was all too happy to let her handle the parts of life he didn't want to, admitting, 'I met Maria and she takes care of writing, talks to people, business, and everything. I sleep and take care of my music.'[5]

One of the few females to interview and write about Ayler during his lifetime, Val Wilmer observed first-hand the 'disparaging remarks about Mary and the influence she had on Albert.' Noting that Call Cobbs was an exception, she herself defended Parks while calling out the sexism that characterized the jazz scene at the time:

> While I agree that she is an unusual woman—and one that doubtless had considerable attraction for Albert, as otherwise, why would he have chosen to withdraw from many of his associates and to live with her—I dislike the 'demonizing' of her that has often surfaced. In my experience of over forty years of writing about Black music and society, I have frequently encountered disparaging remarks about women who took their husbands away from the music in order to concentrate on the family and the domestic sphere. I'm not saying that Mary did not have a negative influence on Albert, for I know nothing about that, but she surely does not need to be misrepresented.[6]

Indeed, it was possible for jazz visionaries to lead fulfilling artistic and domestic lives, as with John Coltrane, whose wife, Alice, was also a creative partner. An accomplished musician in her own right, Alice had studied classical music, and had established a career in jazz prior to meeting John. Coltrane cut a path for others to include wives and girlfriends in their band, and Ayler, who had already taken Donald under his wing, had long been open to giving novice talents a platform. As Parks told Wilmer, 'I would rather think that Albert influenced me in that he awakened in me a sleeping ambition.'[7]

Despite what some disgruntled musicians said, Ayler felt Parks understood his music just fine, as he told Kiyoshi Koyama shortly before his death:

> [Mary] and myself have a good relationship. … I was married, but I had a divorce. My wife didn't understand my music. She jumped up in a club and ran out. … She wanted big money, see, she was a glamour girl. … Maria is a brilliant woman, probably the smartest woman I could meet—or anyone else could meet.[8]

In fact, according to Don and Edward, Albert had procured a Mexican divorce, which was not worth the paper it was printed on.

Certainly, Parks helped take Ayler's music in a different direction. She also took charge of booking concerts for him, including the December Village Vanguard date. In January 1967, she accompanied Ayler back to Cleveland and met his family. Staying in town for a week, Ayler booked a benefit show for the Cleveland Music School Scholarship Fund on Saturday, February 4, at the WHK Auditorium, and staged a warm-up concert the night before, at Kelly Hall, Antioch College, in Yellow Springs, Ohio. According to Jon Goldman, who reviewed the warm-up in *Coda*, an audience of over 600 students gave Ayler three standing ovations.

With Bill Folwell acting in an Arthur Miller play back in Brooklyn and Samson absent for unknown reasons, Ayler asked Clyde Shy to sit in on bass. (Folwell would rejoin the band for the Saturday concert, although Samson absented himself from both engagements.) He later recalled the warm-up:

[Albert] had something in mind about Spanish music … and he wanted that kind of influence … if somebody seemed like they were getting tired or seemed like they were gonna slow down—he would get behind them with the horn and you could actually feel the force of the horn in your back. … We played for four hours—one song, and my bass broke in the middle of the thing, and I had enough time to fix it and get back to play again. So what I had to do was improvise—I would … like play the bass like a bongo and then pull the string and pluck it—and make a noise and a sound, and it would go from there until I got it fixed.[9]

Though Shy was fully operational in time for the benefit show itself, Ethel Boros, writing in the *Plain Dealer*, was unconvinced by Cleveland's hometown star. Despite praising the group as 'excellent instrumentalists' who 'complement each other nicely,' she concluded:

Some of the songs sound as though he had listened to foreign language radio programs and put down what he heard on an aural canvas in a somewhat satiric fashion. He even sings a wordless, high-pitched song which could be Polish or Serbian or even Indian. The best part of the music is the kind of synthesis that the Aylers are able to do, reflecting the world around them. The worst part is the kind of frenzy that turns a recognizable melody and rhythm into honking, overblown notes which express pure frustration. It is a tantrum set to music. It is unmusical, undisciplined. And discipline is necessary if their music is ultimately to mean something. The Aylers have something but it is not yet a finished product.[10]

Jon Goldman, who MC'd the concert, felt the problems were due to Ayler's ad-hoc line-up, plus the venue's poor sound, which 'did not allow much of the basses or harpsichord to be heard, so the complete textures so necessary to an understanding and appreciation of Ayler's concept were missing.' Still, he asserted, 'the love that Albert generates through his songs can overcome even these difficulties,' and, in a set that included 'Bells,' 'Angels,' and 'Spirits Rejoice,' he singled out a new song, titled 'All,' as a piece that, played twice that evening, 'stood out from the rest':

Albert, his face screwed up with tension and suffering cried into the microphone, uttering sounds of vocal anguish from the roots of his soul. Don played a simple line which along with Beaver Harris's percussion figures produced memories of certain movies featuring an African locale—*Tarzan*, and all that.

Presciently, Goldman predicted a 'small period of adjustment, before the next development in Ayler's music, which … may now go into an incubation period where current ideas will be refined and new ideas generated.'[11]

The Ayler brothers, along with Call Cobbs, then performed in a classroom at Western Reserve University's Thwing Hall after local radio DJ Bill Randle, who had championed their music on his WERE show, asked them to guest during one of the Popular Culture classes he taught. The audience fled their not-so-popular music, and the trio wound up playing to a single student. After Ayler returned to New York, Shy stayed in Cleveland, where he eventually sought a new audience. Converting to Islam, he changed his name to Mutawaf Shaheed and became an imam at the Kinsman Road mosque.

•

Ayler's first recorded performance of the new year was on Saturday, February 25, at the Village Theatre, a show that was later issued on *The Village Concerts*. Advertised as 'Music of the Year 2000!!,' it saw Albert perform with Donald, trombonist George Stell, a returning Michel Samson on violin, cellist Joel Freedman, bassists Bill Folwell and Alan Silva, and drummer Beaver Harris. Yet Michael Zwerin, writing in the *Village Voice*, observed the disarray that plagued Ayler's affairs while Mary Parks was at the helm:

> The concert looked like a total economic disaster. The theatre was maybe ten per cent filled and a good deal of those seemed to be the Ayler family. The 25th was a very cold night and the prices were an absolutely frigid $3, $4, and $5. There had been little advertising other than the posters in front of the theatre, which has a capacity of about 2,500. Whoever booked it was an optimist with a poor

memory because only two months ago, when Ayler played the Village Vanguard, even that little room was far from packed. … Beforehand, in the lobby, Cobbs said he wasn't playing because he had just found out there was no harpsichord in the place. 'The music wouldn't sound right on piano,' he explained.

So Cobbs absented himself, Mary Parks described as an 'avant-garde chick' opened the concert forty-five minutes late as she showed up in a golden sequined gown, welcoming the audience, 'Good evening—space friends … tonight— we—will—hear a—concert—of—music—of the—year two—thousand.'[12]

Reviewing the concert for *DownBeat*, George Hoefer made no mention of the year but noted that 'the sources for Ayler's music are likely to come from almost anywhere. There was Eastern European folk-dance music (polkas and schottisches) and mariachi music, as well as the marching band sound.' A self-confessed 'old-time jazz listener' who had been writing for magazines since before World War II, Hoefer was one of the rare traditionalists who praised Ayler's music while recognizing its lineage:

> The group has a valid 'sound' of its own. It's still experimental, far from perfect, and sometimes tedious (as in the concert's overlong performance of 'Truth Is Marching In'), but … we experienced moments of high stimulation and excitement. … Absent from the music was the nihilistic impulsiveness that has been saxophonist Ayler's on some of his recordings. His harsh sounds are being replaced by a much more lyrical approach. His brother, with whom he is in close musical alliance, performs with thought waves that emulate, but also offer contrast to, Albert's playing. Rather the most significant facet of Albert's current group is the rapport and inspiration between the horns and the strings. … One got the impression that the unfamiliar sounds could become quite pleasant when one is used to them through experience. Only a saxophonist with mastery of his instrument could possibly play in this register with the control evidenced by Ayler.[13]

According to *The Wire*'s Art Lange, this show marked the beginning of the second half of Ayler's career, 'as he broke away from the rigorous quest for freedom toward a simpler type of expression, still seeking transcendence but grounded in the accessible forms of spirituals, R&B and finally (and most controversially), rock'n'roll.' Lange continued:

> The first steps in this direction may be heard on the February 67 Village Theatre performances, where explosive outbursts are held to a minimum, and the singsong themes are not savaged but sanctified, and a devout hymn like 'Spiritual Rebirth' is juxtaposed with the loose, high energy hoedown of 'Infinite Spirit.' If Ayler now sounds somewhat naïve in comparison to his more flamboyant period, he is totally without guile or artifice ... especially in his eerie sax homage/elegy 'For John Coltrane' ... and his remarkable solo in 'Omega Is The Alpha,' a statement in pure, near white sound.[14]

The incomplete performance was released across two collections, *Albert Ayler In Greenwich Village* and *The Village Concerts*, and then collected together on *Albert Ayler In Greenwich Village: The Complete Impulse Recordings*, though it has been speculated that the tape ran out during 'Universal Thoughts.'

Opening the performance, 'For John Coltrane' was titled following Coltrane's death later that summer. A tribute played by Ayler's alto and strings, it possesses intense melodies, as seen at the work's beginning, before the dense movement of the lower textures in the strings. While Freedman concentrates on the melody, Silva explores the upper ranges of his instrument; as Ayler explained to Nat Hentoff: 'The point of having two basses, is that, thereby you can go in two different harmonic directions which are, however, integrally connected, so that you remain in organic unity.'[15] Yet while critics such as Art Lange heard a borderless new beginning, Ekkehard Jost felt the piece crossed the line into banality through Ayler's mixture of simplicity and pathos. In particular, Jost cites the merging of theme and improvisation as tonal phrases enter into improvisations, as well as the increasing use of unbroken triads—in this case a B-flat major triad.[16]

After Coltrane's death, Ayler spoke about the saxophonist's significance in his life, citing him as a man of peace who sought music as a means to becoming closer to the creator:

All I do is meditate—I practice and I meditate. You have to go all the way, because that's what Coltrane did. The picture that he showed me when I looked into his eyes, that was universal man. That's the whole thing about it. It could only be the natural force of God. It had to be. Because the natural force, the true spiritual force, it was God, through a man, who was playing an instrument. … To listen to him play was just like he was talking to me, saying, 'Brother, get yourself together *spiritually*.' Just one sound; that's how profound this man was.[17]

Of the next piece, 'Change Has Come'—performed a little over two years after Sam Cooke released his anthem of resistance, 'A Change Is Gonna Come'—Ayler told Nat Hentoff that he was playing 'about the beauty that is to come after all the tensions and anxieties. Foreshadowing the title of his 1968 album *Love Cry*, he continued, 'I mean the cries of love that are already in the young and that will emerge as people seeking freedom come to spiritual freedom.' Writing in *Cadence*, Robert Iannapollo felt it was a 'rather intense performance that emphasizes emotion,'[18] while Barry McCrae, in *Jazz Journal*, heard Ayler taking a 'flight into the false upper register that sounds so human as to be considered a sexual shout.'[19]

The title of 'Infinite Spirit' was one of Ayler's catchphrases, something he dropped into an interview with Frank Kofsky:

You have to evolve, though, to get that *mental* thing together; try to live with each other… just tell the truth to each other, without lying to each other because only true vibrations will build each other. … We have to love the infinite spirit first. Then, when we can love the infinite spirit, we can talk to each other, be truthful to each other. That's what it's all about, you know. You want to be as truthful as you possibly can. You tell your truth and really try to communicate with someone … 'cause we all have to pay for what we do here.[20]

So, too, was 'Universal Thoughts,' which provided another link to Coltrane:

Ask Coltrane about that, because his whole thing was giving past reflections. Like universal thoughts. You know, we just can't take earthly thoughts anymore, because it's uncomfortable to do this. … Those who are true artists, they know why they are here, what their job is to do, and this is the job of a master. Spiritual duties to be performed.[21]

The other selections performed during the show—'Light In Darkness,' 'Heavenly Home,' 'Spiritual Rebirth,' and 'Omega Is The Alpha'— hearken back to the singing evangelist tradition of Blind Willie Johnson and others who used two types of vocalizations, Ayler mimicking this with his use of a 'deep, raspy sound and a high, round, liquid sound.' American ethnomusicologist Robert Palmer compared the ecstatic over-blowing of Ayler to a recording of a Black healing service in rural Mississippi. Palmer concluded that even though Donald attempted to achieve his own instrumental take on the religious phenomenon of talking in tongues, it was Albert who precisely captured the vocal characteristics, particularly in his solo on 'Light In Darkness,' which featured a 'high, ululating tone quality, rapid-fire glottal articulation, restricted pitch range, fervent machine-gun delivery.' The Blind Willie Johnson song 'Dark Was The Night,' which Palmer compared to Ayler's compositions, also possessed 'simple triadic melody,' 'sumptuous tone quality,' a 'robust, apocalyptic growl,' and a 'floating out-of-tempo time feeling,' as did these Ayler compositions.[22]

Johnson's lyrics prophesized the same visions that were found in Ayler's prose writing, as in his letter 'To Mr. Jones—I Had A Vision':

> Remember he said you know not the minute nor the hour, so let's be obedient children to God's laws. We live in darkness now; God Almighty is the God of lights. You see there are mighty angels from Heaven and they are very large. Bright as the sun. Another way to describe it is like the color of lightening [*sic*] magnified ten times. So you'd better get ready for the bright lights that will appear in the sky.[23]

The title 'Light In Darkness' symbolized the polar opposites found in Ayler's music, which are a naïve simplicity and an overpowering force; a simple melody distilled into a complex texture by added complexities and added densities. Rather than shy away from European influences, Ayler utilized them (as did Duke Ellington and Cecil Taylor) to enhance his interpretations of the integral elements that are present in the existence of Black America.

Despite the outer-space broadsides and archaic tone, the Village Theatre recordings prove that Ayler was working within the jazz tradition of improvisation.[24] Pete Welding, who had panned *Bells* in *DownBeat*, praised Ayler for doing as much in his review of the 1967 release of *Albert Ayler In Greenwich Village*:

> The music of the various groups Ayler has spearheaded has represented some of the most perfect realizations of the artistic goals of the avant-garde. ... In this, Ayler's music has represented the fullest realization of the play principle as well. ... And that's what Ayler has always striven for in his music—a total spontaneity of group utterance, 'absorbing the player intensely and utterly' and at the same time proceeding 'within its own proper boundaries of time and space according to fixed rules and in an orderly manner.' Ayler's music goes this one better, for it fixes those boundaries and sets those rules in the very heat of play itself ... Ayler and his confreres are creating their own ordered cosmos in their music, *as* they make that music. And this album offers the best, fullest, most perfect view of that musical cosmos.[25]

Yet still some felt that Ayler represented the putative 'charlatanry' of the 'New Thing,' his agonized sound approaching an 'eerie desolation' despite his 'rhetoric of peace and joy.'[26] He was still up against this view when he went through the efforts of organizing the Village Theatre show, and was distressed that only thirty or forty people came—especially in light of his success in Europe. As bassist Alan Silva said, 'That was, I believe, a heart rending experience for him. His depression developed from the rejection. He tried to present something to the people what he had himself produced—and he was rejected, and he felt that.'[27]

•

In March 1967, a translation of the article Ayler had written for the French magazine *Jazz* appeared in the British publication *IT* (*International Times*). Ayler's band went through more personnel changes in the months that followed as he himself switched saxophones, replacing his Selmer with a Buffet as part of an endorsement deal that would see him mention Buffet's horns on the back of his record sleeves. This change seems to have affected his timbre; Peter Niklas Wilson attributes this to a switch in both saxophones and mouthpieces (from a Berg Larsen to an Otto Link), which would cause him to roughen his style through growls. It would be more noticable in the shows later in the year.[28]

Meanwhile, Beaver Harris had returned to touring with Archie Shepp; he was replaced by Milford Graves, an on-off Ayler sideman who had played with Albert during the Black Arts parade of two years earlier. Donald Ayler would call Graves 'the greatest drummer I ever, ever played with.'[29] Albert explained why he made the right fit at this time:

> That's the extension, and the extension was through the folk music, which is primitive music. And that was the extension for all of it to unite with everyone. Because the spiritual forces are uniting through the folk. … My drummer, Milford Graves, he plays rhythms from all over the world.[30]

Comparing Ayler's new drummer to one of his greatest, Sunny Murray, Alan Silva explained the stylistic change that took place now that Graves was behind the kit:

> I'd been working with [Albert] off and on for the last three to four years, and Sunny Murray is involved with swing, but [Albert's] swing has not been felt yet by the people. That's his biggest problem … that drums and rhythm have to be feeled by the people, before they're understood—that is communicatable. You can't feel the beats or the pulse, or the total swing of the energy of the drum until you can identify with it totally. And I felt … that Milford is punctuating, you know, where like Sunny lifts … up the horn player. It did change Albert's playing in a sense.[31]

Graves, a music teacher at the Black Arts Repertory Theatre, also noted how Albert's style shifted, telling Daniel Caux that the music 'became a lot more intense':

> The energy level went ... a step higher, then what it was before. ... I would
> say controlled emotion ... without trying to balance each other out no matter
> how loud we went ... a lot of people can't do that with drums. You know,
> if the drums reach a certain point volume-wise, where it just drowns out
> everybody else ... that wasn't with him, 'cause I've heard him play with about
> two, three drummers on stage, and he played alto man, and you heard him
> over everybody else. I mean that's something he just had. He didn't really have
> to have amplifiers. He didn't need that. He already had it natural in him.[32]

Indeed, this was music that needed to be experienced, not analyzed, and the first chance that Ayler had to present it to an audience was at Newport Jazz Festival on Friday, June 30. Not usually given to rehearsing his music, Ayler felt the opportunity was important enough for his band to have to rehearse—albeit without him or Donald.

Having attracted commercial sponsorship for the first time—the Schlitz Brewing Company had put up $25,000 for the event—the Newport Jazz Festival gave its 1967 event a theme: 'The History Of Jazz.' Among a line-up of artists who had pointed toward new directions at various times in history, Ayler represented the avant-garde—what Newport organizer George Wein called 'an example of the jazz of the present scene, and something for the future.'[33] But where past audiences had left venues because of his music, here the crowd—a reduced number of 5,000, one third of the festival's capacity—stayed away because of the weather.

Despite being the height of summer, it rained steadily all day, finally letting up in time for Ayler to take the stage along with Donald, Michel Samson, Bill Folwell, and Milford Graves. Speaking to WCSB-FM, Donald recalled the physical challenge of playing under conditions that made it hard 'to blow just get a true note': 'It was a little cool. I wasn't really prepared for it. I just wore a suit ... the instruments are very cold, and yet ... Milford was playing on time—I mean, he's putting the beat down there so tough.'[34]

The group's set—'Truth Is Marching In/Omega,' 'Japan/Universal Indians,' and 'Our Prayer'—was broadcast over the Voice Of America. The experience of being among the jazz establishment at Newport made an impression upon Albert:

> I had a certain feeling about Max Roach, Percy Heath, and all the old greats, they were still around to give their message. It was very cold at Newport that night, and you had to like play something altogether out of sight to get the people around you. But there was a certain amount of young people there who waited all the way through for the end. And when I finished, George Wein, he asked me like, 'Are you finished now?' And that's beautiful, because he has a certain respect for the new music, in a sense, because he knows that a few were given the spirit; and he knows that, because it's the same as it was in the past and as it will be in the future. It is infinite.[35]

The Ayler brothers closed their set seventy minutes past the midnight curfew, earning George Wein a fine for $2,000—'an insult to the festival.'[36]

DownBeat's Dan Morgenstern felt that year's line-up 'failed' in its 'pretentions to being an "informal" panorama of jazz history.' But while he offered Ayler faint praise—'there can be no doubt that he plays the way he does because he feels it'—Morgenstern sneered that, 'Sincerity, alas, has never yet sufficed to make notable art.'[37]

Writing in the *New York Times*, John J. Wilson drew comparisons between Ayler's music and Babatunde Olatunji's percussion ensemble, famous for their 1959 album *Drums Of Passion*: 'Mr. Olatunji's primitivism was so sophisticated and Mr. Ayler's sophistication was so primitive that they seemed to occupy the same piece of ground in the jazz spectrum.'[38] The connection was pertinent: Donald mentioned the influence of sub-Saharan Africa on his performance, recalling that he began to sing a tribal song 'in the middle of the music' before stopping.[39] It's possible that the influence came from Coltrane, who was a collector of African music, and used the Folkways record *The Pygmies Of The Ituri Forest* as a reference point for the piece 'Africa,' on his 1961 album *Africa/Brass*.

Later released in the *Holy Ghost* box set, the Newport performance was recognized by some critics as delivering on the promise of Ayler's European tour in 1966. Writing in *Coda*, Art Lange noted:

> The band's heaven-storming potential seems to have reached fruition seven months later at, of all places, a Newport Jazz Festival appearance. With Milford Graves behind the drum set, there is a palpable boost of energy that inspires a looser, freer exchange of individual components—Samson flies over his fingerboard with a wider-than-usual range of details. Ayler vocalizes with abandon, brother Donald's trumpet blasts puncture the ensembles, and the sounds blister the air. Again, the horns exaggerated vibrato and the barrage of drums reinforce the oft-quoted parallels to the raw, immediate, folk and spiritual-inspired origins of New Orleans brass band music.[40]

The Wire's Tony Herrington heard in the recording evidence of a reinvigorated Ayler 'who grips the imagination' on 'Our Prayer':

> Here he also plays alto and transposes the pitch of the instrument into the knife-point attack of a ney [a Persian flute] or shenai [an Indian double reed instrument]. But he moves this needling sound through such extreme registers that the fidelity, the envelope of the recording, is barely able to contain the expanse of the soundfield staked out by what might be the most amazing section of music he ever produced.[41]

Having contributed so much to Ayler's music in just a little over a year, violinist Michel Samson left the band after Newport in order to return to a career in classical music. In an interview with the Dutch magazine *Jazz Bulletin*, he revealed how exasperated he had become with Ayler, who refused to let him play with other musicians:

> A removal began to arise between Albert and me. … He was jealous. As for myself, I got increasingly fed up with the pseudo-religious and would-

be philosophical bullshit that Albert came up with. The rhythm section was constantly changing. The dialogue would go: 'Well, man, Sunny [Murray] … he doesn't have that energy, man.' One month later it was: 'Well, Beaver [Harris], he is a funny cat, but he doesn't have that energy.' The musical judgment had nothing to do with knowledge or rationality. Or it was expected that the sidemen would take a very humble stance.

Though he acknowledged that Ayler's music 'woke up something in me,' Samson felt that thing 'didn't need to be woken up anymore.' He also hinted that he'd felt like an outsider in Ayler's band: 'I could as well have come from another planet.' This feeling provides the subtext to the only Samson interview that survives about his time with Ayler. In an hour's conversation with *Jazzwereld*'s Bert Vuijsje, published under the headline 'Ik Probeer Niet Echt Jazz Te Spelen,' the violinist spoke passionately about the great classical composers but hardly mentioned jazz at all. Following a stint playing with saxophonist John Handy, he 'quit jazz completely. This also had to do with a growing aversion against the opportunistic side of myself. I had other interests. I wanted to paint, perhaps a career as conductor.'[42]

•

Less than three weeks after the Newport show, John Coltrane, one of Ayler's biggest influences and greatest supporters, was dead. He'd been suffering from frequent, sometimes debilitating, headaches since the early months of the year but, rather than see a doctor, he self-medicated with large doses of aspirin. In May, the problem escalated, and he began to experience frequent and severe stomach pains; at Alice's urging, John saw a gastro-enterologist. A biopsy was done, but Coltrane refused additional testing. On July 16, he was admitted to Huntington Hospital, on Long Island, and died from liver cancer at four o'clock the following morning.

Bob Thiele, then Coltrane's producer and the head of Impulse! Records, broke the news to Ayler over the phone: 'You know something, Albert … Coltrane is dead.' Ayler initially thought it was a joke, but Thiele finally convinced him, before attempting to console Albert with one of Coltrane's final wishes: 'His last request was for Ornette Coleman and for you to play at his funeral.'

'How could I do that?' Ayler replied. 'How could I play crying?'

In the days that followed, Milford Graves helped Ayler understand that a funeral didn't have to be a mournful occasion:

> I told him that we should take it to a higher level. I said, 'We should play without worrying about being professional at a funeral in America.' … In other words, I wanted to go forth, I want to really testify. We shouldn't play very soft music. … I actually think that seeing John Coltrane lying in a casket … really hit him … he was, you could say, not scared or nervous, but it seemed like this all of a sudden it got to him. Like, he was saying that he was messing with some forces, he didn't know how to handle this. … So, I told him let's take it right on through. Let the people know that this is really where it was at. You don't have to come here and cry and all that. I said, you know, like that's not what it's about.[43]

Ayler had a deep affection for Coltrane. He shared some of his memories with Frank Kofsky:

> His music was so sincere. Coltrane just gave his all to it. The last time I talked to him, we talked for *hours*, and I could feel that I was talking to a ghost, you know. But he was just the same way he had been for all the time. His pain was too great to feel, too great to feel. Thank God. We don't know how long it was going on for him, you know, because he was only digging the music. Let's face it, there's not too many artist's artists. It's a given thing from God. He picks who his messengers are.[44]

Coltrane's 1966 album *Meditations* opens with the composition 'The Father And The Son And The Holy Ghost.' In an article titled 'Albert Ayler, Breakfast In Montreal … A Reflection,' Stuart Broomer, a former editor of *Coda*, wrote about an impromptu conversation he had with Ayler shortly after Coltrane's death, between sets at club in Montreal:

Albert told me that the last time they'd talked, Coltrane had declared himself the father, Pharoah Sanders the son, and Albert the holy ghost. It was a kind of statement that could send me running, but from Ayler it seemed plausible. There was no arrogance in it, only his wonder at the scale of the music he was playing. It was a way of finding language to give the music its rightful dimension. He had a sense of his own ascendancy, telling me confidently and modestly... that he had to keep working at it as he felt Pharoah Sanders gaining on him.[45]

Ayler made a similar comment to Frank Kofsky:

But when you get spiritual on all levels, it seems you just evolve. That's the only thing. The father, son and holy ghost. What Coltrane was talking about— maybe it was a Biblical term. He was the father, Pharoh was the son, and I was the holy ghost. And only he could tell me things like that. You know, people think in a Biblical sense all the time. But when he said that on that record, *Meditations*, I believe you knew that ... John knew that he was going to die a long time ago. Because God has been very good to him, because he's been one of the most spiritual men.[46]

Ayler bought a white suit for the funeral, which was officiated by the 'jazz pastor'—the Reverend John Garcia Gensel, a Lutheran who ministered to the jazz community in New York City—and took place at St. Peter's Lutheran Church in Manhattan on July 21. Accompanied by Donald, Milford Graves, and bassist Richard Davis, Albert played a medley in front of a thousand mourners, as Donald recalled:

We played ['Truth Is Marching In'] and a spiritual Baptist type of number which my brother just created on the spot. ... Then we went over the 'Father, Son, And Holy Ghost.' The song we trilled on the instrument. My brother would trill, and I would answer him ... then we went into my song 'Our Prayer.'[47]

In *Chasin' The Trane*, his biography of John Coltrane, J.C. Thomas writes, 'During his portion of the music, Ayler stopped, twice and screamed; not with his horn but with his voice, the first scream like a cry of pain and the other like a shout of joy that Coltrane, though dead, would live forever.'[48]

•

Coltrane was gone, but Ayler was at the zenith of his success. John Hammond, producer and impresario at Columbia Records, had been courting him, but Coltrane had lobbied for Ayler to move to Impulse! Bernard Stollman, founder of ESP-Disk', the label that done so much to put Ayler on the map, recalled:

> He said, 'Bernard, I've had an offer to record for Impulse! They're offering me an advance. I don't know what to do.' By 1967, '68, my company was on the way down. Between the industry with all the bootlegging, and the government and our antiwar policy, we were done in. I said, 'Albert they can give you the money and the distribution that I can't give you. It might make very good sense. They'll move your career along.'[49]

But Ayler, lacking business sense, refused to get advice on the contracts that Impulse's parent label, ABC Records, sent over, as Don recalled, 'Coltrane said to get in contact with his lawyer [Harold Lovett] so he could read the contracts that ABC gave to him … and he didn't want to do that. And he could be so stubborn, I tell you. Al could be stubborn as everything.'[50]

Speaking to Bob Rusch of *Cadence*, Donald explained Ayler's aversion to the machinations of the industry, saying, 'Al was a genius, and he didn't know the business angle of it, as far as he was concerned he was an artist.'[51] In conversation with this author, Donald elaborated, revealing that both he and Albert got 'screwed' over royalties:

> I was trying to tell him what to do, like get your music copyrighted. … He was just stupid … [Thiele took] advantage of both of us. We were so hungry, man, and I sold half the rights [to 'Our Prayer'] for $75 to $100 … we signed over so much of a percentage of royalties of different songs so that we'd be able to transfer that into funds.[52]

Ironically, at a time when Ayler was poised to be hailed as Coltrane's successor—newly signed to his label, next in line to become jazz music's highest-profile visionary—the first studio album he recorded for Impulse!, *Love Cry*, would be received, in the words of *Cadence*'s Robert Iannapollo, as both 'Ayler on the decline' and also his 'last great statement … a summation.'[53]

The conflict arises because the album comprised of two sets of very different material, recorded on two dates four and a half months apart (the complete recordings from both sessions were released on CD twenty-three years later). The first session, held on August 31, 1967, took place just five weeks after Coltrane's death, with Ayler still reeling from his loss. Six cuts were recorded that day: 'Love Cry,' 'Ghosts,' 'Omega,' 'Dancing Flowers,' 'Bells,' and 'Love Flower.' Unusually for Ayler, all of these were short enough to be released as singles, leading to some contention over whether that was Ayler's intent. Certainly, some of those close to him felt that Ayler changed direction in order to score hits, which may explain why he remade several of his most famous compositions during the August session. As Bill Folwell claimed, 'He always waited for the big breakthrough.' Milford Graves expressed similar thoughts, feeling that Ayler deliberately played simple, kitschy music in order to get it to stick in listeners' heads.

In line with the cover for *Albert Ayler In Greenwich Village*, which had been released at the end of the previous year, the sleeve for *Love Cry*, which followed in June 1968, featured psychedelic artwork typical of the era—an attempt to appeal to the hippie crowds that gathered at the Fillmore Auditoriums on both coasts to see stars such as Miles Davis and Charles Lloyd. *Love Cry* also features Ayler's first recorded attempts at vocals, with lyrics that did their part to court countercultural record buyers. And yet 'Zion Hill' and 'Universal Indians,' the pieces recorded at the second session, held on February 13, 1968, were lengthier, reasserting Ayler's ties to Coltrane and bringing back to his music an element of what one reviewer described as 'intensity through uncorralled exploration.'[54]

According to the French reviewer Philippe Carles, these differences made *Love Cry*:

more complex, richer in borrowings, quotations, and multiple references (hailing from close horizons—Indian chants on 'Love Cry,' maybe as a tribute to these people first colonized/dispossessed by Europe—or distant—Call Cobbs's harpsichord), more beautiful, violent. From 1967 onward, Ayler's music doesn't deny itself anything, claiming and reclaiming instruments, chants, rhythms and even musicians it had done without until then.[55]

An easy, attractive work in relation to the output that Ayler had made his name with, *Love Cry* was the culmination of everything he'd explored in the Greenwich Village concerts—'a rigorous thematic development' that was modeled after Sonny Rollins.[56] With hindsight, it can be seen as the last of the complicated albums that Ayler recorded for Impulse!, ushering in an era of commercially minded efforts on which he abandoned his over-blowing in favor of playing a soul-based music.[57] At that time of its release, however, the album was received as a signpost toward future groundbreaking evolutions, as Ayler's 'probing, searching saxophone looked into, and sometimes entered the future.'[58] But while some retrospective reviewers found it old fashioned, thanks to its 'chanting quality' and its hints of New Orleans marching bands and the call and response of gospel music, others, such as Derek Ansell, writing in *Jazz Journal International*, heard much to admire in the 'abstract, free floating drum figures and roving bass lines' that gave 'this music a thick density and enhance the fierce alto saxophone arabesques.'[59]

Bassist Alan Silva, who was also a painter, had studied music with John Cage, and in Jeff Schwartz's opinion he brought a painterly aesthetic to his playing. Avant-garde pianist Burton Greene also felt that Silva's style was a musical representation of Jackson Pollock's painting, but others criticized him for his deliberate attempts to make the bass sound as little like a bass as possible.[60] Critics such as Val Wilmer noticed a trend: as his career progressed, Ayler's sidemen became increasingly more mundane by comparison with the greats he had worked with in the past.[61]

Though Ayler had worked with some of the most technically gifted bassists in jazz, such as Gary Peacock and Henry Grimes, his latter-day collaborators created new sounds on their instruments. Silva, who had played with Cecil Taylor and would go on to be a veteran of the Sun Ra Arkestra, explained that, though he was a bass player, 'I never really dug bass-players; I used to dig horn players ... what I am trying to do with the strings now, is to be a multi-string/reed player ... to say something on each of the strings.'[62]

Robert Iannapollo understood what Silva was trying to do, while also noting what Graves brought to Ayler's new music: 'Silva plays his instrument as hard and unorthodoxly as Ayler did his saxophone. And he had a similar "cry" to match. Graves's rumbling polyrhythms seem to push the music more than Murray's cymbals/snare approach.[63]

However, Peter Niklas Wilson—himself a jazz bassist in the avant-garde tradition—feels that Ayler's rhythm section ignored any metrical and harmonic basis in the music. In his eyes, Graves messes up, and sabotages any potential smoothness.[64]

Call Cobbs's harpsichord also split the critics. With its rejection of jazz in favor of the white classical tradition, it was also attuned to the baroque pop leanings of mainstream pop albums such as The Beach Boys' *Pet Sounds* and The Beatles' *Sgt. Pepper's Lonely Hearts Club Band*. But Dave McElfresh, writing for *Coda*, called 'the dreadful harpsichord ... a sad attempt to be hip.'[65] *The Wire*'s Dave Keenan would later view it as the sound of 'choruses of bells in the sky, colouring the atmosphere an unearthly tint.'[66]

Alan Silva felt that Ayler's attempt at making a crossover record was a decision that also involved Bob Thiele:

> This album was very important to Albert, 'cause it was on a major label, and John Coltrane had passed, and I think Impulse! thought that this guy was going to be the next saxophone position. ... You have to realize that Ayler, for me, was one of the possible crossover artists, especially in this period, when rock was just beginning to formulate. ... I think Bob Thiele thought that Albert, with his blues base and his jazz base, could reach out to a broader audience. And Albert had a spiritual message; at the time of the Vietnam War

and the whole anti-war movement, I felt that, as a social artist, he was very important. … I think Albert had a real accessible saxophone style at the time, and even the band we had was accessible.[67]

Opening the album, 'Love Cry' itself features Ayler's first recorded vocal. As one critic noted, his singing is very much in the style of his saxophone playing: 'long phrases, deep vibrato, and sudden register leaps.'[68]

Silva suggested why Ayler chose to start singing:

> When he used his voice, it showed the quality which is necessary. … Because for him to sing … especially the shouts, the shouts was for the people to know that like that was coming out of the horn. … So, I think he was trying to make a sort of statement that, 'Look, I can sing what I play.'[69]

Instead of the tenor sax, Ayler plays alto, and he's backed by his brother on trumpet, Silva on bass, Cobbs on harpsichord, and Graves on percussion. The piece layers ecstasy in pure jubilation: Ayler makes the call, his brother's response follows, and then he vocalizes the theme.[70]

Call Cobbs absented himself from the re-recordings of 'Ghosts'—which continued Ayler's variations on that theme—and 'Bells.' And, unusually, Donald's participation on *Love Cry* was kept to a minimum—he lays out on several cuts. If Impulse! sought to reduce the more abrasive side of Ayler's music, Donald's 'limited range of gutteral squawking' would have been one of the elements in need of toning down. Ironically, however, he received good reviews when the album was released, with *DownBeat*'s Bill Quinn noting, 'Brother Don has greatly improved over the last couple of years. … The brothers' musical interactivity suggests images in a house of mirrors, magnified and multiplied in a kind of cubistic situation wherein all sides of the phrase at any given moment are played as near simultaneously as possible. The cumulative effect is one of continuous revelry.'[71]

Don was also absent from 'Dancing Flowers' and 'Love Flower,' two songs, along with the remake of 'Bells,' that were also favorably reviewed in *DownBeat*:

'Dancing Flowers,' featuring Albert alone in front, begins with a parody of Wayne King's alto sound, tripping through the ricocheting vibrations of Cobbs's harpsichord and the pulsating rhythm unit. 'Bells' retains its happy, ringing instrumental chant. The theme figure races up and down, working its way out of a maze. 'Love Flower' is a plaintive tapestry decorated with filigree of harpsichord and percussion.[72]

The balance of the *Love Cry* material was drawn from the February session, during which Ayler recorded 'Love Cry II' along with two takes of 'Zion Hill' and 'Universal Indians.' Despite its title, 'Love Cry II' bore no relation to its predecessor. It was first released on the 1991 CD reissue that collected the complete album sessions together, causing Robert Iannapollo to reassess Don's contribution to the album and call him the 'real surprise … His expressive power finally matches his brother's with broad, carefully shaded strokes and pithy contrapuntal phrases.'[73] As in August, Ayler did a vocal, and Wilson notes that he increased the fierce energy of sound volumes in which he plays in the high alto range of his tenor.[74]

Titled after the home of God in the Books of Psalms, Isaiah, and Joel, 'Zion Hill,' links back to the Biblical roots that never left Ayler. He would return to the idea in his letter to Amiri Baraka:

> In a night vision I saw a very dark sky and I looked up and saw a large star falling as fast as it could move. Brothers and Sisters you see there is only Heaven and Earth. There is no other planets. The planet that they call Venus is Zion Hill, the home of God Almighty.[75]

The piece inspired further praise from Bill Quinn, while Barry McRae of *Jazz Journal* felt that it 'proved to be one of the most poignant records made by Ayler … the tenor has strength, obvious direction, and impetus, yet it also has a tranquility that can move the listener rather than embarrass him.'[76]

Ayler laid down another vocal on the album's closing cut, 'Universal Indians,' which is the only piece on the original album release to feature extended soloing. As a variant of 'Love Cry,' it uses the same two notes (F# and B) as thematic material, as well as Ayler's vocals, whose falsetto reinforces the song's connection with Native American music. The theme is played by Donald Ayler and balanced by a contrapuntal moan by Albert, which blends with Silva's bowed glissandi. Albert then performs a tenor solo before the composition closes as Silva and Graves engage in a duet of continuous movement, featuring Silva's glissandi against Graves's accompaniments on 'world' instruments such as a conga, gong, and tabla.[77] These percussions also reflect the African influence that Donald says was the idea behind the work (as well as reinforcing the two-note theme).[78]

Bringing the album to a close, the piece was, for Quinn, 'a prolonged assault on apathy' on which 'Albert … furiously overblows at the top of the horn. He seems to want another register at the upper end and, finding none, forces the top one to extend itself to those heights anyway. A bugling Donald brackets Graves's calibrated efforts and Silva's bow-swoops, and dives to the returning onslaught of the front line.'[79]

Writing shortly after the release of the expanded 1991 reissue, Richard Cook and Brian Morton felt that 'Zion Hill' and 'Universal Indians' provided 'the clearest indications on the set of where Ayler was headed next.'[80]

•

Between the two sessions that resulted in *Love Cry*, Ayler made a number of live appearances. During a residency at Slugs' from September 12 to 17, which likely had the same small attendance as that of the earlier Village Theatre engagement, the depression that Alan Silva had noted in Ayler, seemingly stemming from the rejection of his music, grew worse. Annette Peacock, now married to pianist Paul Bley, remembered an ominous encounter after one of the shows:

> The last time I saw him was at Slugs' Saloon. … He'd just finished a set, and he was surrounded by a small group of sycophants. He turned away from the group, and said the last words he would ever speak to me. 'I'm not even here,' he said. I realized that his spirit was broken.[81]

Ayler then supposedly toured Upstate New York and Canada, but the only documentation is of a late August 1967 Canadian concert in Montreal, at L'Atelier Au Jazz, in the early hours of the morning. He brought his usual corps of musicians, including brother Don and Call Cobbs. They were augmented by Rashied Ali (whom Ayler had known from his friendship with Coltrane) and bassist Bill Davis. A review by the actor-writer Patrick Straram, published in France's *Jazz Magazine*, felt the show was 'a physical and mental ordeal in self-discovery':

> I didn't know that Albert Ayler played soprano. A soprano of febrile and haughty sharpness. … On tenor, he extracts from himself a flood of sharp fragments, bordering on the most demented cacophony, in relief over a kind of bizarre, primary, punctuation for popular dance, half-creole half-suburban waltz: exposition and progressions. … Don Ayler: pneumatic drill. Howls of a man being tortured. Immaterial outbursts as beautiful as certain moments of violin in Bartók. Vitality inside excess. Suddenly, an unbearable discant from Albert spurts out, before he takes his chorus. Insane, mad, sublime high-pitched notes.'[82]

Years later, Stuart Broomer detailed just how intimate the concert was:

> It was an after-hours coffee house, a few steps below street level. The band was already playing, the music seeping outside, but when I went through the door Ayler's tenor hit like a wall, not violence or anger or any of those things, but a wall of impossible sweetness. … The band was a quintet with Ayler's brother Don on trumpet and Call Cobbs playing an apartment-size piano. I recognized Rashied Ali on drums. … The bass player … turned out to be… Bill (not Steve, not Art, and not Richard) Davis. I'm not sure now if the band didn't outnumber the audience even at the start of the night, when the club was as crowded as I would see it. The music was extraordinary … Coltrane had died only a few weeks before, and his presence could be felt in the way that Albert and Rashied played that night. … The performance ended around 4:30. By the end of the last set, I was an audience of one.[83]

Before re-entering the studio to finish *Love Cry*, Ayler made a live recording with Pharaoh Sanders during a gig at New York's Renaissance Ballroom on January 21, 1968—a 'Night Of Soul-African Culture' sponsored by the *New Amsterdam News*. Ayler sat in on the last number, 'Venus/Upper And Lower Egypt,' which went unreleased until it surfaced on the *Holy Ghost* box set over thirty years later. Sanders's set was originally planned for the first side of a forthcoming release on Amiri Baraka's Jihad label, *Black Renaissance* (Jihad 1003) which would have featured a speech by Amiri Baraka on the second side.

When 'Venus/Upper And Lower Egypt' finally saw release, Francis Davis, writing in the *Village Voice*, described it as an 'unexpected revelation … though virtually a sideman in a Harlem encounter with Pharaoh Sanders, Ayler is the one whose screams pierce the heavens.'[84] It is also likely that Ayler and Sanders made some trio recordings around this time, with percussionist Juma Sultan at Sultan's house on the Lower East Side.

Donald, too, made sessions outside of his brother's group, recording a solo record for the same label. Though it featured esteemed musicians such as saxophonist Noah Howard, pianist Don Pullen, and bassists Reggie Workman and Sirone, it too remained on the shelf—not that Donald was concerned. 'I paid all the men seventy-five dollars apiece,' Donald told Val Wilmer in 1976, 'but it never did materialize because there was a lot of conflict between the people that was playing. I don't think [Baraka] was going to put the record out, but I wasn't satisfied.'[85]

Ayler was back with his own group at the Albright-Knox Gallery in Buffalo on Saturday, March 9, airing works from the yet-to-be-released *Love Cry*. Their performance was part of the second Buffalo Festival Of Arts Today, a sixteen-day festival in which new developments in art, music, drama, movies, poetry, and literature were showcased. Despite being filmed for the program *Who's Afraid Of The Avant-Garde*, Ayler did not appear in the final edit, though it's possible the footage exists in director D.A. Pennebaker's archives. Nonetheless, Ayler's inclusion on the bill— alongside Cecil Taylor and Charles Lloyd, plus performances of works by leading avant-garde classical musicians such as Taduesz Baird, Lejaren

Hiller, Iannis Xenakis, and Krzysztof Penderecki, and the premiere of Henri Pousseur's opera *Votre Faust*—was a surefire indication that he had arrived. Despite faulting the sound and the 'too blatant drum work' of Graves, David P. Prizinsky, reviewing Ayler's show in the *Buffalo Courier-Express*, felt that 'a new vocabulary must be invented' to describe the type of music he heard.

According to Alan Silva, in a *Cadence* interview with Larry Nai, a full Ayler tour had been planned in support of *Love Cry*:

> I only know that, after we finished *Love Cry*, we were supposed to begin a tour. And Bob Thiele liked this record a lot, and the reason some of the tunes were real short was that we wanted to be on the radio. … We were told to go to California to do his big concert at the Fillmore West, at this time. You have to realize that Ayler, for me, was one of the possible crossover artists, especially in this period, when rock was just beginning to formulate … I think Bob Thiele thought that Albert, with his blues base and his jazz base, could reach out to a broader audience.[86]

The album didn't garner anything like the sort of airplay needed to make it a hit, however, and the tour never materialized.

In the decades that followed, the album proved no less divisive than any of Ayler's previous recordings: where some critics, such as *Stereo Review*'s Chris Albertson (also Bessie Smith's biographer), heard an 'audio nightmare … the jazz equivalent of the chimpanzee paintings that are said to have fooled some art critics many years ago,' others heard the future.[87] Whether it was the 'fierce tenor lines' on 'Ghosts,' or the tenderness in 'Dancing Flowers' and 'Love Flower,' it was easy to see what Ayler's most famous successor, David Murray, chose to take, and what was left behind.[88]

CHAPTER XIX

beginning of the end?

n the wake of John Coltrane's death, the jazz world fell into a silence not seen since the loss of Charlie Parker, over a decade earlier. Beaver Harris discussed the void that Coltrane left behind, and how Ayler sought to fill it:

> Evidently John Coltrane had said that he felt that Albert was the next horn player in line ... Albert was so different, and he was searching for newer ideas along the line that could fit his music. Trane was also searching in his music for newer ideas so ... Albert felt that he and Trane were the two chosen. ... Trane's death affected Albert. ... I remember hearing him say, 'I guess it's only me now.' ... He knew that he had to change to keep that whole thing going on, along with his thing. He couldn't keep his brother with him and do that change, so they were beginning to part, and his mother, through being highly spiritual, thought that Albert was cracking up because of what he had received from the other sound ... so, she would somewhat torment him because she wanted for he and Don to play together endlessly, and Albert wanted to [move] on.[1]

At the same time, the college kids that had once made up a large part of the jazz audience were shifting away to rock music, which was then gaining stature as a serious art form. There was no room here for jazz visionaries such as Charles Mingus and Ornette Coleman, and Miles Davis's electric experiments, deemed more percussive than lyrical, went too far out for many, although it should be stated that Davis made the idea of crossing over into rock acceptable at this time. While the purveyors of free-jazz abstractions struggled to find new fans, the music's older traditionalists abandoned the US for Europe; some of them even sought to reach an accommodation with rock and pop music, with old-guard innovators such as Duke Ellington, Count Basie, and Ella Fitzgerald recording Beatles tunes.

Love Cry was Ayler's initial attempt to merge jazz and rock, but Impulse! treated it as a failure and never gave him a second chance. Had the label stuck by him, it's possible that *Love Cry*'s disastrous follow-up, *New Grass* (and its successor, *Music Is The Healing Force Of The Universe*), may have been succeeded by something with the crossover appeal of Herbie Hancock's jazz-funk landmark *Head Hunters*. As producer Ed Michel observed of *Music Is The Healing Force Of The Universe*—a record he worked on, and the final album released during Ayler's lifetime, 'Back then, I wouldn't have thought of Albert as a fusion guy, but now, looking back, that music with [guitarist Henry] Vestine, it does seem like that's what he was doing … Maybe a failed attempt at fusion.'[2]

On the other hand, Ayler could have achieved what critic Kevin Whitehead referred to as a 'reverse crossover': a music too tainted by pop to be appreciated by jazz aficionados, yet too weird to be embraced by rock fans. As examples of these types of records, Jeff Schwartz cites Archie Shepp's Impulse! output of 1971 and 1972: *Things Have Got To Change*, *Attica Blues*, and *The Cry Of My People*. He believes that Ayler's final albums are of a piece with them: that is, Ayler was not trying to achieve commercial success, but, instead, trying to bring his message to a larger audience.[3] Yet still other critics, among them Cook and Morton, felt that Ayler had 'moved with unnerving swiftness from the torrential outpourings of *Bells* and *Spirits Rejoice* towards the irredeemably banal R&B of *New Grass*.'[4]

•

And so Ayler began his freefall. Some have suggested that the pressures of Impulse!'s corporate structure are evident in Ayler's later recordings—and there are some clues to suggest as much, including Impulse!'s alleged demands on Ayler's line-up. With Donald seemingly being edged out of the picture, drummer Milford Graves, hailed as 'a percussionist of inexhaustible resource, who could call up anything from huge tribal calls-to-arms to quiet filigreed patterns,' was also targeted for dismissal after Impulse! executives considered him to be too political—he spoke up for musicians' independence from record companies and promoters, and championed Black pride.[5] According to Mary Parks, Ayler received a phone call from the label with orders to drop both Graves and his brother from the group; based upon his past behavior, though, it seems far more likely that Albert wanted a change of direction and made Impulse! the villain.

Graves has been said to have stood in the way of Thiele's corporate makeover of Ayler, but other evidence suggests otherwise. Judging from his work with Coltrane, Bob Thiele was a hands-off producer. Furthermore, Thiele could not reasonably control Ayler when it came to assembling his live band (and it should be recalled that similar accusations were made about Bernard Stollman's alleged interference regarding Sunny Murray). And yet Donald put the blame on both Parks and Thiele, asserting that the decision was a 'combination of both of them. They wanted rock'n'roll. They wanted Al to play rock'n'roll. They wanted to eliminate me and Milford. So that's the way it went.'[6]

Another source, Sonny Simmons, weighed in on the controversy:

> Donald complained of suspicious characters around Albert, shadowy figures and record-industry people telling his brother what to do and turning Albert against him. 'Donnie was kind of losing it during that period, which was real sad,' says Simmons. 'The white boys would come over in their suits and ties like Madison Avenue lawyers and tell Donald, "Get out. We want to talk to your brother." I thought it was strange. I wouldn't let those cats talk to my little brother like that. Donald was very upset, and it fucked him up mentally. Here

was the big brother Donnie grew up with, and Albert discarded him once they got to New York and he gets a big contract.'[7]

Other one-time members of Ayler's circle had different opinions: some felt that Donald had expressed a drinking problem which had gotten out of hand, while Bobby Few told me, 'I had thought maybe it was for financial reasons—booking a large group became more difficult.'

Mutawaf Shaheed felt that even greater business conflicts were at play:

I don't know if it's true or not, that Donny began to believe that he was calling the shots over Al, and that he was better than Albert, and that this had been goin' on for a while. And that it had come to a head. Plus Albert knew that with the change in direction that he was getting ready to make that it would be difficult for Donny to make that change because of the way and the kind of music that Donny played.[8]

The brothers remained in touch after Donald's firing, though they were never again as close as they had been. In an interview shortly before his passing, Albert hinted at a dispute, telling Daniel Caux, 'When we talk, he doesn't hear me, and I don't hear him. We just be screaming at each other like the music was.' What is not disputed, however, is that Ayler respected Donald's talent. He was, Albert said, 'a very great artist in his own right.'[9]

One of the last times Donald and Albert played together was at the only performances of Albert's *Songs Of Zion—New Opera: Universal Message: Songs Of David* at the Grand Ballroom of the Hotel Diplomat, in New York, on Sunday, April 28. Two performances of this lengthy, expansive show were held, at 6:30 and 10pm. For this ambitious undertaking, Ayler's core group of Don, Call Cobbs, Mary Parks, percussionist Paul Smith, and, during the second show only, Milford Graves, were augmented by five singers: Vicki Kelley, Janet Rose, Charlotte Richardson, Tamam Tracy, and Grace Joyce. Donald read poetry at the event, which was covered by the Dutch publication *Jazzwereld* in one of the only surviving accounts of the show:

The organization of the event didn't go smoothly … but the music was stunning. At the moment, Ayler uses many voices in his music. He had four female singers, who didn't sing words, only sounds, incorporated in the music as instruments. Only brother Don was on stage during the entire concert … there were three different bassists … four different drummers … who each took their turn and of whom I didn't know anyone, all unknown musicians, who fitted in Ayler's music in different ways … but most of the time Albert didn't know their name himself … 'doesn't make any difference … they feel my music so I play with them.' And there was the Ayler magic. Said someone in the audience, 'Wow, that guy only needs to play one note to get me excited.' Many melodies, almost no solos, seemingly unorganized music, which nevertheless leaves a feeling of unity in the end.

Clearly, Albert was moving in another new direction. Supporting Shaheed's view on Donald's firing is the fact that Albert did not replace Donald with another trumpeter. Instead, his band became keyboard-based—something that he had avoided with his previous groups, because the fixed tones of the instrument got in the way of his earlier approach of playing 'shapes.' Never one for communicating honestly with his sidemen, it's likely that Albert used Bob Thiele as a scapegoat for his own need to change things up. He explained to Daniel Caux his need to keep evolving his band:

You feel different things at different times and when it's time for a record to be made, I'll practice with a certain musician to see if I can use him for the date, if he can feel somewhat what I can feel for the date. And if OK, I'll use him and if not, I'll move around to different musicians because I believe music could never be made with one steady group all the time. You have to have different people to help you make the music for it to be new music.[10]

To Val Wilmer, he connected this impulse with his spiritual beliefs: 'You have to make changes in life just like dying and being born again, artistically speaking. You become very young again through this process, then you grow up and listen and grow young again.'[11]

This time, however, and on the evidence of some of the *Love Cry* material, it is likely that Ayler also had an eye on delivering what he believed the public wanted in order to score a hit record. Writing about his final two records, *New Grass* and *Music Is The Healing Force Of The Universe*, John Litweiler heard 'a crisis in his conception,' adding:

> Among some Free musicians there is a need to 'meet the public'—to emphasize features of their music that appear to have wide popular appeal. It may be conscious or an unconscious need, but it has nothing to do with selling out or going commercial; a musician *can* attempt to present a broad message without debasing or falsifying it. The most likely explanation for his last two LPs is that this philosophically assured revolutionary was convinced of his ability to communicate within any medium.[12]

Ayler was not alone in seeking new, potentially lucrative, ways of connecting with his audiences. Miles Davis's legendary crossover success, *Bitches Brew*, was just a year away, and it is not inconceivable that Ayler would have sought to create his own kind of jazz fusion. Unfortunately, however, he chose to explore this through merging R&B rhythms with hippie-era lyrics written by novice songwriter Mary Parks. Could he have been more successful if an assured songwriter such as Laura Nyro or Joni Mitchell—both with strong affinities for jazz music—had been collaborators? Or if he had worked with a rock-oriented producer such as Al Kooper, who, with Blood, Sweat & Tears, succeeded where Ayler had failed? Perhaps. But though Ayler had a sound idea, he was never quite able to unshackle himself from his old style. As Ekkehard Jost would later observe, 'The tragedy of Albert Ayler's musical evolution is that in trying to communicate with his listeners he wasted his strength on platitudes. He first replaced complexity by simplicity, and then simplicity by vacuity. In seeking to escape from the cliches he had himself created over the years, he reduced his musical language rather than expanded it.'[13]

For its part, Impulse! should have known better than to think Ayler would deliver truly commercial material. As a producer, Bob Thiele had been making hits since the 1950s, and there were many other saxophonists out there with greater exposure outside the jazz press. However, according to Peter Niklas Wilson, it was Thiele who agreed to let Ayler use Mary Parks as a songwriter on his material, on the condition that Ayler sing on the records.

Ayler recalled it differently, while admitting that he was reluctant to use any musicians outside of his own handpicked circle:

> [Mary] had the idea for the *New Grass* album. Bob Thiele wanted me to make the *New Grass* album. He said he wanted me to play with a young group for just a couple minutes. … I said, 'No, I would like to stick with my own thing if I can—if I have to play pop music let me get the men together and play the music.' So he said, 'OK, it's time for you to make *New Grass*. You have to sing.' … So, I played in a club in the Village … and then the first couple of nights, I started getting real hoarse. I said, 'Playing was bad enough, but to sing too?' Then it was time for us to go into the studio, and Mary started thinking … and she started writing, going crazy running all round the house all night long. And I wrote [the posthumously released song] 'Thank God For Women' myself. … After that, I figured, well, America, I can play pop, I can play free, I can play anything. I can play a variety of music so maybe it will be OK.[14]

Ayler had recently visited Bill Folwell, who had moved to Hoboken, New Jersey, where he was rehearsing his own group, Insect Trust. Folwell was experimenting with an electric bass when Albert dropped by, and Ayler was impressed by what he heard. In need of something different for a forthcoming residency at the Café Au Go Go, Ayler enlisted Folwell and his new instrument as part of a revamped quartet that included Call Cobbs and Beaver Harris.

Across July 19–21 and 23–25, Ayler alternated the opening-act slot with the West Coast fusion band Seatrain. During the second evening, he announced that he would sing—a shock to his new group, who'd never head him sing before, and to ESP-Disk' founder Bernard Stollman, who walked out once Ayler started: 'It was dark and he was totally absorbed and he was … singing in tones or in tongues. I was amazed. But for whatever reasons I fled.'[15]

Further surprises were in store—if not necessarily for Albert. He'd kept the shows a secret from Donald, who turned up after Beaver Harris told him about them. According to Peter Niklas Wilson, this caused an irreparable breach between Albert and Harris, though Harris would remain part of Ayler's group through to an engagement at Slugs' later in the summer.

An underwhelmed Elisabeth Van Der Mei reviewed the weeklong residency in *Coda*. Feeling that Cobbs was too docile and Harris too straight, and that Folwell's electric bass degraded Ayler's sound, she concluded that 'the result was not as glorious as I had expected … Frankly, Ayler did not do as well as he could have, but this is mainly the fault of the combination with which he played—it was not strong enough to defend this experiment.'[16]

Roy Blumenfeld, Seatrain's drummer, had an altogether more startling experience when he sat in with Albert sets after Harris turned up late: 'My style was more straight-up blues, R&B, jazz rock and eclectic Seatrain style (rock/classical pieces),' he recalled. 'Albert's was definitely avant-garde jazz … I played about three tunes and his drummer showed up and took the stage. I was relieved.'[17]

Harris thought the group 'had that potential, we could have been … anything at that time, 'cause that's how the avant-garde was.'[18]

•

Two members of the Cafe Au Go Go group—Cobbs and Folwell—would join Ayler in the studio in the first week of September, recording what would become *New Grass*. He'd cut four demos at the end of the previous month; one of them, a six-minute blues number on which he used a raspy tone over a walking bass line, attracted praise from Harvey Pekar, who reviewed the demos when they were released as part of the *Holy Ghost* box set. However, Pekar felt that the balance of the material was 'aesthetically

insubstantial,' with two of the pieces, 'Thank God For Women' and 'New
Ghosts,' only redeemed by Ayler's playing.[19]

Ayler revisited both pieces on September 5, when he recorded the basic
tracks for *New Grass*. Though 'Thank God For Women' wouldn't make the
final cut, the other eight numbers did, including 'Message from Albert,'
'New Grass,' 'New Generation,' 'Sun Watcher,' 'Heart Love,' 'Everybody's
Movin',' and 'Free At Last.' For this session, Ayler was on tenor sax, ocarina,
and lead vocals, with Call Cobbs on piano, organ, and harpsichord, Bill
Folwell on electric bass, Bernard 'Pretty' Purdie on drums, plus Rose Marie
McCoy and Mary Parks on vocals (credited as The Soul Singers on the
final record). Seemingly lost in the mists of time was the fact that Rose
Marie McCoy was a very famous singer/songwriter whose songs were
recorded by James Brown, Ike & Tina Turner, and Elvis Presley.

If *New Grass* was Ayler's opportunity—or obligation—to record music
that would attract airplay, Ayler himself felt there was nothing lacking in
the musicianship, even if he was, in his telling, pushed toward coming up
with something suitable for a single release. Speaking to Kiyoshi Koyama
shortly before his death, he asserted that Bob Thiele 'told me to do this':

> He said, 'Well look, Albert. You gotta get with the young generation now and
> see what you can do.' … They promised me they was gonna put a record on
> 45 for years and it never happened yet. … But when I made it, I made it as
> good or better than they ever heard before … I know it was good. On 'New
> Generation' we was cooking.[20]

Whatever Thiele's involvement in the decision, Ayler's girlfriend, Mary
Parks, had certainly begun to influence his music. Ever since Ayler
discovered a notebook of her poems, the pair had been playing together—
Parks on vocals, piano, harp, and, later, the soprano saxophone, Ayler on
tenor. Parks would earn writing and performance credits across *New Grass*
and its follow-up, *Music Is The Healing Force Of The Universe*, but while
some saw her as an opportunist from the moment she got together with
Albert, Donald Ayler told Bob Rusch of *Cadence* that her involvement

in his music grew over time: 'At the period [when] her and him got together ... she wasn't pushing music, you know? ... I mean she wasn't trying to put her own talents out here at that period of time.'[21]

Call Cobbs suggested it was Parks, not Bob Thiele, who encouraged Ayler to begin singing on his records:

> We heard some of the critics say he was beginning to get a little bit too conventional, but then it was selling, and they [the recording company] liked that. He didn't want to sing but he started to on *New Grass* because his friend Mary Maria suggested it. She had written some lyrics to tunes, so they sang something together and asked me how does it sound? I said it sounds good and it was original, and so I wrote the music out for him.[22]

According to Bill Folwell, Parks originally intended for some neighborhood girls to sing on the record with Ayler (likely the singers who had appeared at the *Songs Of Zion* show), but Thiele enlisted her and Rose Marie McCoy instead.[23] On September 6, the day after the initial *New Grass* session, the producer also overdubbed a horn section consisting of trumpeters Burt Collins and Joe Newman, trombonist Garnett Brown, tenor saxophonist and flautist Seldon Powell, and baritone saxophonist Buddy Lucas. The session was arranged and conducted by Bert DeCoteaux—a renowned producer in the disco/soul/funk genres, later associated with Sister Sledge and Main Ingredient—and carried out in Ayler's absence.

'I never saw him,' Seldon Powell told *Cadence*. 'The rhythm was already on the track with Albert playing solos—we "sweetened the date" as it was known in those days. We horns were put on to support spots on the record which they thought should be enhanced.'[24]

Critic Barry McRae bemoaned the results as a mix of Motown clichés. Elsewhere, *DownBeat*'s Alan Heineman praised Ayler's 'absolutely unique and compelling' tone, but found that *New Grass* didn't live up to expectations:

> For sheer shock value, this may be worth five stars. ... Some of the tenor work is delightful ... Unfortunately, the vocals aren't terribly good. Not bad, but not

good. His voice is slightly reminiscent of the early Jackie Wilson, but rougher and less sure. The arrangements are mostly dull, and the lyrics, especially those to 'Generation,' 'Heart Love,' … and 'Movin',' are atrocious. … One would like to like the record a great deal more. It shows innumerable possibilities. But except for some flashes by the leader's tenor, that potential is largely unfulfilled.[25]

Ayler opens the title cut with what Jack Cooke would call 'one of his finest improvisations,' then breaks the news that the avant-garde is over.[26] On 'New Grass,' he returns to the blues of his Little Walter days, as he romanticizes it in the song's spoken-word introduction, titled 'Message From Albert': 'The music I have played in the past I know I have played in another place and a different time.' He then returns to the stomping blues beat, the simple structure, and the catalog of rhythm-and-blues clichés.[27]

Rather than transform R&B into his own style, Ayler subjugates himself to R&B, resulting in a disorderly mix that, with its banal lyrics, failed to advance R&B, jazz, or Ayler himself. Yet, writing almost three decades later, *Jazz Journal International*'s Graham Colombé heard much to enjoy in the song:

> His singing in a high-toned tenor voice contrasts with the rough-hewn saxophone sound which … derives from the rhythm-and-blues honkers. 'New Ghosts,' once the vocal introduction is out of the way, presents a logically developed tenor solo over a calypso rhythm and is the most successful track [on the album] but, in keeping with the overall brevity, it fades out with Ayler in full flow.[28]

Elsewhere, however, Colombé felt that 'the poverty of the material and the frequent divergence between Ayler's abstractions and the over-simple support' meant that that only the most dedicated Ayler collectors would be interested in *New Grass*.

Other critics also picked up on Ayler's simplified sound, with Gary Giddins of *JazzTimes* feeling that Bernard Purdie's rock-oriented drumming left him 'a fish out of water,'[29] forcing the music away from Ayler's notion of playing around the beat.

Writing in *The Cricket* at the time of the album's release, Larry Neal described the album as 'shitty':

> The rhythm on this album is shitty. There are no shadings, no implied values beyond the stated beat. The guitar is shitty. Most of the singing is shitty, especially the songs 'Heart Love' and 'Everybody's Moving.' The Sister sounds like she is straining, trying to find some soul in a dead beat. There are no kinds of nuianees [*sic*] on the drums. Hard rock, death chatterings.

In essence, Neal concluded, there was little to offer beyond the beats.[30]

A more careful understanding of Neal's criticism is that he condemned not the concept behind *New Grass* but rather the manner in which Ayler approached it: whether it was Thiele's or Parks's idea for Ayler to take lead vocals on a bland attempt at true R&B music, Ayler was a willing participant in this attempt to reach a wider audience. Among 'some good, some heart-stoppingly bad' moments,[31] some critics singled out 'isolated peaks in a plain of mediocrity,'[32] even if no one could praise the album as a whole. Alan Heineman highlighted 'New Generation' for its 'chorus of raunchy R&B, a chorus of free playing, in rhythm, then two choruses in the upper register which relate sensibly and provocatively to the tune,[33] while *Jazz Monthly*'s Jack Cooke liked other cuts, such as 'New Grass' and 'Sun Watcher.' Both of those pieces had fewer people involved, and, as a result, gave listeners a chance to focus in on Ayler's high register technique.[34] Almost a quarter-century later, Cooke reflected that the album was one of the 'great lost recordings' in Ayler's catalogue.[35]

Indeed, though many contemporary critics scorned the backing, they liked Ayler's contributions to the record. Among them was John Litweiler, who concluded that *New Grass* was 'good Ayler' if listeners could 'overlook the accompanying sinners':

> The very dark and shocking near-unaccompanied tenor solo in the title track is essential Ayler art; solos in 'Heart Love,' 'Sun Watcher,' 'New Generation' additionally present a somewhat more determinedly lyrical approach to the

basic Ayler style, and they are also valuable. 'New Ghosts,' a calypso, is played in the tone of the nastiest early 50s R&B tenors, but the phrasing is remarkably Rollins-like—indeed, except for the tone this could pass for a Rollins solo. There is, Ayler's own singing 'in tongues' here, too, with traces of his saxophone approach in the quavery vocal—a nice diversion.[36]

Alan Heineman was also on hand to praise Ayler himself, and even heard a humorous reference to a brand of dog food:

'Sun' has some nice tenor work, too, particularly the opening few bars, with Ayler producing an amazingly rich, dark tone in the lower and middle ranges, which he then contrasts to some more screeching. … 'Ghosts' begins with Ayler chanting glossolalia extended by loop echoes. Nice effect. The tune moves to a sort of conga rhythm, and Albert takes tenor in hand and trucks right on down, demonstrating his wit with a longish quote from the Ken L Ration TV jingle ['My dog is better than your dog'], complete with variations. He stays almost entirely within the middle register on the solo, a welcome contrast to the two previous tracks. 'Free' is potentially the most exhilarating cut, but it sounds as if it were rather badly edited. It has an authentic Baptist meeting sound, but Ayler's tenor solo slows down in the middle, and the accumulated propulsion is thereby damaged.[37]

A decade and a half later, 'Sun Watcher' took on a different meaning to Litweiler: '[Ayler] peeps an ocarina solo, and that instrument's poverty of sound symbolizes his decline.'[38] And yet in other recordings from this era, there are hints of a different path he could have taken. Writing about the blues demo that later surfaced on the *Holy Ghost* box set, Giddins heard a 'stunning' hint at what might have been: 'it's a straightforward ride through the basic twelve[-bar], except that Ayler rings compound overtones and undertones while maintaining steady intonation at the center. The Ayler captured here … might have won him the larger audience he coveted.'[39]

•

When he was still part of Albert's band, two years before the *New Grass* sessions, Donald had offered the somewhat prophetic opinion that Ayler's music would outlast his life, and that the different path he took in life was a sign of artistic and spiritual growth. Wearing a green suit that matched his brother's, he told Val Wilmer:

> Perhaps they think [Albert's] someone who's going to drop off on the way. But it's not going to be that way and I think they've recognized this. ... If you stop an artist somewhere down the line when you know that he's growing—after a while everybody wakes up to the fact that you have let the man go.[40]

Albert's firing of his brother overshadowed the upcoming controversy over the style change, but, like Albert, Donald had moved on: he played an engagement with his own quartet at Slugs' on September 21, as part of the 'Jazz On A Saturday Afternoon' series.[41] Despite the firing, Albert still maintained some contact with his brother and appeared at the gig.

A few months later, around the beginning of 1969, Albert hung out for the last time with Sunny Murray, the drummer who had been such an important part of his artistic breakthrough. Though they lived only a few blocks away from each other, the pair hadn't spent any time together for over a year; Murray later recalled that Donald asked if he and Albert could swing by. When they arrived, Albert pulled out a set of bagpipes, though he admitted that he did not know what to do with the instrument. After half an hour of playing together, Albert lost consciousness from the column of air while playing; after he finally worked out how to play the instrument, they jammed together for three and a half hours.

Throughout the afternoon, Ayler talked about seeking a new spiritual beginning and forged plans to record together as a trio with the energy of the old quartet. Murray, however, came away feeling that Ayler was deep in the web of Mary Parks and her family and friends. 'As they say among teenagers, he had joined the wrong gang,' Murray recalled. 'These people took advantage of Albert, his warmth, his kindness. There was a lot of opportunism involved. It was like a band of bandits.[42]

Years later, in 2011, Murray offered further insight into the way the brothers' relationship had declined:

> For Donnie, it was like his brother disappeared in the ground. … And then he got kind of lost somewhere in New York. He went further out, I think, and then that depression and the medicine. Just before that, him and Albert came to my house, but Albert didn't tell him where he lived in Brooklyn.[43]

Despite their differences, Albert continued to join Donald onstage. During a show on Saturday, January 11, at the Town Hall on West 43rd Street, he appeared on two songs, 'Prophet John' and 'Judge Ye Not.' Donald's band was styled after the group that Albert had abandoned a year earlier, and, according to *The Wire*'s Tony Herrington, who reviewed the two tunes when they were released on the *Holy Ghost* box, the music the brothers played together was 'the most apocalyptic ten minutes of music ever recorded.' He continued:

> The opening trumpet fanfare is leveled in the direction of Jericho, and the rest of the track, a cataclysmic combination of ferocious percussion onslaughts from drummer Mohammad [sic] Ali, whooping sounds of alarm from the saxophones of Ayler and Sam Rivers … sounds like the walls themselves being razed to the ground.[44]

At this time, Donald was living in Amiri Baraka's basement in New Jersey. According to original handbills, Albert was slated to play with him on April 4 and 5—two ultimately disastrous shows sponsored by the Committee For A Unified Newark in a series of Black Arts/Soul Culture events. Alleging that his trumpet was stolen, Donald played an Indian oboe the first night, and also borrowed—and broke—an alto sax. The following night, he came onstage with a trumpet for a show that was reviewed anonymously in Baraka's publication *The Cricket*:

> drunk, zipper open, staggering, he call his self a musician. Really just a cheap

version with no identity, purpose and direction. … We had to suffer, his 'playing' one beatup note all night, which would have probably been the same on alto … played the same big ass run, the whole set.

Adrift, Donald returned to Cleveland and began to exhibit the bizarre behavior that would eventually lead to a nervous breakdown. Claiming that he felt 'negative vibes' from Albert, he also lamented the rift between him and the older brother that 'looked out for me a lot of times':

When you get egotistical you burn bridges, and that's what happened. He'd think he was doing it all by himself—he didn't think it takes a group of people to make a band sound. … I called Mary [Parks] up and I told her what I felt, and she said just go on back to Cleveland. So she gave me enough money to take the bus and she drove all the way over from Brooklyn to the Bronx. So Mary wasn't really too bad.[45]

Back home, though Albert's parents found that contact with their son was irregular, they kept in touch through letters. His father, Edward, recalled that when he later spent some time in the hospital, Albert 'called me from New York—practically called directly to the hospital—he kept up with our condition.'[46]

•

The negative reaction to *New Grass* deepened Albert's isolation from his friends and colleagues. He stopped returning phone calls, and when Milford Graves visited him at his apartment in Brooklyn, Albert sat quietly, surrounded by thick clouds of smoke from countless burning incense sticks. If he did answer the telephone, he would lift the receiver, say nothing, listen to the caller, then put the receiver back down. Graves later recalled their final interaction, at a demonstration at 125th Street in Harlem: 'We walked up to each other, and he sort of smiled at me. And I just walked right past him. I didn't want anything more to do with it.'[47]

Ayler was suffering a spiritual crisis. He returned to Cleveland seeking religious instruction from his father, who recalled that his son had begun to have visions, as later recounted in the letter 'To Mr. Jones—I Had A Vision,' published in *The Cricket* in 1969.

Sometime in the summer, Ayler made his final live appearance in Cleveland, playing with guitarist Jimmy Landers's band at Sir-Rah's House, 4170 Lee Road. 'Him and Bobby Few came and played with me,' Landers recalled. 'I think it was the song Gene Ammons played, "Blue Greens And Beans" … we do that song all the time and he sat in with us, and he soloed on it … that's the last time I saw him.'[48]

Back in New York on August 26, 1969, Ayler recorded four cuts— 'Music Is The Healing Force Of The Universe,' 'A Man Is Like A Tree,' 'Again Comes The Rising Of The Sun,' and 'Desert Blood'—at Plaza Sound Studios, with Bobby Few on piano, Bill Folwell on electric bass, Stafford James on double bass, and Muhammad Ali, who had played with Ayler in Montreal in August 1967, on drums.

The group recorded an additional ten cuts the following day, among them 'Birth Of Mirth,' 'Oh! Love Of Life,' 'Island Harvest,' 'Masonic Inborn' (on which Ayler played ocarina and bagpipes), 'All Love,' 'Poetic Soul,' and 'Water Music.' Guitarist Henry Vestine of the boogie-rock band Canned Heat joined for the day's final three cuts, 'Drudgery,' 'Toiling,' and 'Joining Forces,' the last of which remains unreleased. Vestine was also on hand to record a final, untitled duet with Ayler August 29; it was released on *The Last Album*.

Six of the August cuts made up for the final album issued in Ayler's lifetime, 1970's *Music Is The Healing Force Of The Universe*, and six more were given a posthumous release on the following year's *The Last Album*. Ayler would once again blame Bob Thiele for the direction this material took, but Thiele had left Impulse! earlier that year. Producer Ed Michel said the music was all Ayler's idea:

> He was definitely interested in a rock'n'roll audience, and he thought that Mary Parks … was writing commercial songs. Because a lot of tunes had lyrics, there was probably more organization in his head than other dates. But Albert talked

a lot and didn't say much, if you know what I mean; he didn't lay out a deep philosophical road map. It was, 'This is what we're going to do,' and bam![49]

Critic Robert Palmer saw Ayler for the final time during the *Music Is The Healing Force Of The Universe* sessions and noted that he was dressed in a fringed jacket, as if he were a rock musician. With hippie-style long hair, Vestine, too, looked the part; when Archie Shepp walked in while the group was listening to a rough cut of 'Drudgery,' he told the guitarist—a white musician playing the blues—'I'd have liked your playing a lot better … if I hadn't seen what you looked like.'[50]

Ayler's friend since the early 50s, Bobby Few met Mary Parks for the only time while recording the album. Contrary to the opinion of many of Ayler's former sidemen, he found her 'very sweet' and 'very kind' during the sessions, which put Ayler in mind of the music they made together as kids. He recalled:

> She was always very nice to me. I never saw any bad signs. She wrote the words, as far as I know, to the songs. The music, I believe, was credited to Ayler. He was giving the directions for that, and she was only singing … I remember very well they told him he had had to sing on this. And Albert looked around at me—he got the tune together; he whispered to me, 'Just like Cleveland, huh.' I said, 'Yeah, Albert.' That was the rock thing on there—the guitars and all that stuff. … He didn't like it, but he did it.[51]

In a letter to the German critic Gudrun Endress, Ayler expounded on the thoughts behind the album's title: 'I would like to leave Politics to the politicians. Also music to the Artists. All I want is peace enough to create beauty in my music.'[52] Released later in 1969, *Music Is The Healing Force Of The Universe* maintained the philosophical outlook that ran throughout Ayler's prior work, yet it also continued his latest trend of catering to the rock generation. But Robert Rouda of *Coda* suggested that he might have felt more positive about the record had Parks's vocals been omitted: 'In brief, her singing leaves much to be desired, and the lyrics, in this person's opinion, are inane ("Tree is like a man"?). Most of the time, her singing is involuntarily flat and/or off key.' But where some critics had felt Ayler's playing at least transcended the low points on *New Grass*, Rouda felt that Ayler was being dragged down by his surroundings on *Music Is The Healing Force Of The Universe*: 'self-derivative playing seems to be demeaned even more from the weakness in song.'[53]

DownBeat's Larry Kart called the album 'an almost unlistenable disaster' and gave it one and a half stars:

> Miss Maria chants tautological slogans and in comparison to *Spiritual Unity*, *Bells*, and *Ghosts* Ayler's playing is so crudely simplified that one can hardly believe this to be the same man. It seems likely that the absence or suppression of an inner censor enabled Ayler to 'hear through' fifty-odd years of musical sophistication and magnificently rediscover … the preharmonic 'innocence' of jazz, but that same quality has led to such sorry efforts as this LP. Either there are extra-musical factors at work or Ayler is simply unable to judge the virtues of his own music. Certainly the elaborate motivic constructions, the sudden contrasts of emotion, and the soaring melodies that once distinguished his playing are nowhere apparent here.[54]

Though Parks was the dominant vocalist on the album, Ayler sang on one cut, 'Oh! Love Of Life,' but his voice wasn't much better received: Rouda described his singing as 'a bit too dramatic for my taste, although his vocalizing, interestingly, reflects his sustained vibrato horn playing.'[55]

Across the Atlantic, where fans and critics had been quicker to embrace Ayler, *Music Is The Healing Force Of The Universe* left *Melody Maker*'s Richard Williams 'worried about the state of the avant-garde in New York.' Though he was seemingly one of the few critics to feel it improved on *New Grass*, and he clung on to a belief that 'every note Albert plays, in whatever context, is valuable,' Williams ultimately felt that Ayler had become 'a pale carbon-copy of Pharoah Sanders … he seems to have lost the purity and strength which once characterised his music, and there are too many intentions behind this music to make it successful … I can only hope that he finds a rather better context for the future than that displayed here.'[56]

Amid the scorn, however, Rouda did note that Ayler was beginning to explore new terrain, such as using his recently-mastered bagpipes on 'Masonic Inborn'—though that didn't save the piece from being 'very derivative of the early Coltrane total-energy sound.'[57] Elsewhere, Ekkehard Jost felt the piece was an 'isolated peak in a plain of mediocrity'[58]—perhaps because of what John Litweiler described as its 'dervishlike bagpipe solo,'[59] and a self-duet created through overdubbing. Producer Ed Michel felt that Ayler's decision to play the bagpipes was in keeping with the times:

> things were spacy, experimental. Albert played bagpipes on one track, but it didn't sound far out enough, so I said, 'Well, let's do something I've done on a rock'n'roll record—let's turn the tape over. We can play the bagpipes backwards.' And we did.[60]

The cuts that were held over for *The Last Album* ran the intellectual range from what Barry McRae in *Jazz Journal* called the 'naive religious sentiments' of 'Desert [Blood]' to the 'sixth-form philosophy' of 'Again Comes The Rising Of The Sun.' To some ears, 'Birth Of Mirth' showed that Ayler was still exploring and 'extending the scope of his music,' as heard in his 'torrential solo' and 'free blowing in the non-developmental sense.' Indeed, whatever the quality of his material, Ayler never lets the listener forget his great technique. As McRae put it, he 'creates brilliantly, at even this inhibiting tempo, and his control in the false upper register is daunting.'[61]

Released just a year after Ayler's death, *The Last Album* was received more favorably than it might have been. Writing in 1972, McRae felt it offered a synthesis of the old and new Ayler styles, but every positive view, such as Robert Rouda's assertion that 'Drudgery' exhibited 'some spark with free-form blues playing,'[62] had its opposite, with Jack Cooke describing Ayler's solo on the cut as sounding 'as though he's auditioning not too successfully for a job with an organ combo.'[63] And yet, Ayler's solo on 'All Love' was enough, McRae opined, to make *The Lost Album* a worthwhile purchase; it was, he said, a never-ending cadenza—a superbly rambling tenor excursion, drawing constantly on the theme, yet continually setting out on its own detours.'[64]

As time passed, however, critics became more hostile toward Ayler's last recordings, possibly viewing his changing style as fatal to the development of free jazz. As critics have pondered what could have been, many have come to view his final efforts as a greater creative tragedy than Ayler's contemporary critics did. Writing in *Coda* in 1997, Dave McElfresh is particularly hard on Ayler, while also claiming that his latter-day change was a rejection of his father. As Richard Cook wrote, 'There is an almost Aeschylean inevitability to Albert Ayler's life and death, a downward trajectory of neglect and misprision.'[65] But why are these recordings now held in such a lowly regard? According to John Litweiler, it's because Ayler once was great:

> Ayler's creations, even at the end, were far larger than life; his conflict and pain and poverty were those of a hero albeit Albert was a hero unfortunately like you and me in outward appearance. His was a classic art. His strange death prematurely deprived American music of all kinds of one of its outstanding vital forces. If we are to become a civilization, Ayler's kind of humanist understanding, his depth and complexity, even his kind of contrasting simplicities and innocences, must become part of our character. We cannot all be heroes, but it may be that we can someday be the more sensitive individuals that Albert Ayler thought we might be.[66]

CHAPTER XX

france 1970

A yler's final year began with bad news: his father was seriously ill and needed surgery. Albert went home for about two months to be with his family, and Mary came, too. While in Cleveland, however, he told his cousin Sandy Wright that Parks was crowding him and that he was planning to cut his ties with her. He also told his family that he was preparing to tour Japan. But then Impulse! chose not to renew its contract with him, leaving him to find a new plan. Once again, salvation seemed to come from Europe.

•

Albert had entered a new phase of depression and began locking himself in his room, playing his saxophone alone and talking to himself. Sometimes, he would reminisce about his Quartet's first European tour—a success a lifetime away from his current state of affairs. Besides his worries about his brother, there was the oblivion to which his spiritual message had been consigned. He would tell Daniel Caux:

> Maybe the American people just don't understand. … After I made *New Grass*, I should maybe have been in Europe … [I thought] I'm going to give the American people another chance. They deserve that. They deserve another chance. So, I stayed, and, the next record I made, nothing happened with that.[1]

Based in France, Caux was a painter associated with the mid-60s Fluxus movement who had championed the revolutionary music coming from ESP-Disk' and other labels out of New York. As a journalist for *Jazz Hot* and music editor of art dealer Aimé Maeght's publication *Chroniques de l'art vivant*, he became involved in concert promotion; it was Maeght who suggested that Caux promote some of the new musicians at Les Nuits de la Fondation Maeght, an arts festival held at Fondation Maeght, in Saint-Paul De Vence in the south of France. The theme of that year's exhibition was the United States, so the organizers needed American musicians to come and perform.[2]

Ayler was one of Caux's initial choices—Caux remembered Ayler's two November 1966 shows at the Salle Pleyel—but the Maeght line-up was not without controversy; producer and Verve Records founder Norman Granz, who had organized the legendary series of Jazz At The Philharmonic concerts of the 40s and 50s, complained that Ayler was neither a serious musician nor, indeed, an artist.

As soon as the shows looked certain, Caux contacted Mary Parks, who began to make arrangements for Ayler to travel, and helped put together his band, which consisted of Call Cobbs on piano, Steve Tintweiss on bass, and Allen Blairman on drums, with Parks herself providing soprano sax and vocals. Ayler played soprano and tenor, and performed only limited vocals.

Tintweiss, whom Ayler had known from a jam at Slugs' Saloon four years earlier, later recalled the short-notice circumstances: 'Mary seemed to function as Albert's business manager for the French trip at least. She was the one who called me, at Albert's request. With only a few days notice she went with me to obtain an emergency passport.'[3]

Donald recalled Albert asked him to accompany him on the French trip—a claim partly substantiated by advertisements referring to the Albert Ayler Sextet (as opposed to the quintet that eventually performed). But Donald was 'fed up with his messin' with Mary Parks singing that rock'n'roll. I don't fit into nothing like that,' he said, so he declined.[4]

Ayler's two shows, on July 25 and 27, 1970, should have been a new beginning for Ayler, who hadn't played live since the summer of 1968. Fondation Maeght, where the gig would be held, was a far cry from the clubs of New York. Since opening in 1964, the Maeght had been in the front rank of the world's smaller museums, and its galleries and sculpture gardens had played host to many of the world's leading creatives, John Cage and Picasso among them. For this festival, the Karlsruhe-born, Paris-based architect Hans-Walter Müller had constructed a pear-shaped inflatable structure designed to hold five hundred people. Venue aside, the US musicians weren't used to the level of hospitality and friendliness the European organizers extended: the musicians were presented to the artists whose original lithographs were on display in the Maeght Fondation; Ayler and his group were invited to attend receptions and parties.

Despite the way his latest music had been received by some US jazz critics, Ayler was considered cool by the international avant-garde, and he shared the Nuits de la Fondation Maeght bill with other boundary-pushing artists such as Sun Ra, Terry Riley, La Monte Young, and Pandit Pran Nath. His appearances could have been a disaster; his bagpipes were lost in transit, and pianist Call Cobbs missed his flight, and the first performance, while he sat in the airport bar. When he landed the following day, as Jacqueline Caux explained to me, 'He found himself in front of Albert and as he wanted to explain himself, Albert stopped him, laughing, and said, Don't say a word. I know the story!'[5]

Wearing a broad-brimmed hat and a long white robe, Ayler overcame these obstacles, and it seemed as though the Impulse! disasters may have been behind him. Steve Tintweiss recalled that the first night 'was even less structured, in a rhythm & blues sense,' than the second, 'and more free-form improvisational without the piano; and also due to the fact that we had never performed as a group before (not even a single rehearsal); I had played with Albert only once before.'[6] The performances were recorded by three separate parties, Tintweiss, the Fondation Maeght, and Radio Belgium; eight selections from the July 27 recording were released in 1971 as *Nuits de la Fondation Maeght*.

Issued on the Shandar label—set up by Daniel Caux with the help of

Chantal Darcy, a friend of Aimé Maeght—the live recording received more praise than Ayler's most recent studio albums. Writing in *DownBeat*, John Litweiler felt that it was 'superior to most Ayler Impulses,' and captured

> the matured Ayler style undergoing profound reassessment. Some of the material is long familiar, but the relaxed self-consciousness of Ayler's playing here brings a new introspective quality to his art. For example, the original *Spirits Rejoice* (ESP 1020) is wild and exuberant, with frantic solos. Nothing could be more different than this marvelous new version, with Ayler's out-of-tempo decorated free-association restatements of the several themes. Frequently they remain unfinished, unresolved, as Ayler begins a new theme with yet more variations.[7]

Clifford Allen of *Paris Transatlantic* praised Tintweiss and Blairman as 'the closest approximation of the Grimes-Murray team that graced some of his earlier recordings.'[8] Parks, too, received positive notices: R. Szyfmanowicz of *Jazz Hot* felt that she was a favorable replacement for Donald, while Harald Schönstein of *Jazz Podium* wrote:

> The singer Mary Maria then followed in the same intensity, even possession, with the soprano sax, and Albert Ayler played on the tenor with churning on the intensity in the rising phrases of his free improvisation. As a singer Mary Maria is not agitated in the least. Just the same, she had an expressive voice at her disposal. She knew how to use it.

Schönstein also had praise for Ayler:

> He had relied on his earlier concept of long-march-like introductions with transition-less shattering improvisations, and, so began his pieces in accordance with swinging jazz. Yet, he hardly used the folk-song and march-music based elements, but he didn't place them beyond the midpoint—instead he used them here and there as accessories. … And he played with a clearer, stronger voice, as phrased on the tenor sax, yet with an uncommon vibrato. With a

cracking voice here and there, he also pushed the boundaries to hysteria, and then let this furiousness slowly subside again.[9]

As Ayler ended that evening, he was a model of humility, according to critic Gérard Noël of the French magazine *Jazz*. As he put his instruments away, he told his group, 'I'm so happy, my friends, I want you to know … my music is a music of love … thank you … thank you.'[10]

Steve Tintweiss recalled the scenes that greeted them after the final night's show:

> They didn't want us to stop after the very long set until they heard from Albert after Mary's parting announcement of, 'We love you,' in English. Albert took the mic and said, 'I've been playing so hard I can't talk.' There was a big roar to hear him speak … the fans gathered outside … and stood in front of our car in an adoring mob scene as we were trying to leave.'[11]

John Litweiler heard 'a renewed sense of purpose in this final concert,' as if Ayler were turning 'away from rock and modal dabbling' toward 'possibly some major changes in his art.'[12] Tintweiss, however, had a different explanation for Ayler's more carefree mood: along with titles from *Music Is The Healing Force Of The Universe*, Ayler leaned on many older compositions, among them 'Spirits Rejoice,' 'Holy Family,' and 'Truth Is Marching In.'

'Albert told us that we would only be playing his previously released compositions,' the bassist recalled, 'as he feared getting ripped off.'[13]

The concert was recorded by the Fondation on both film and audio. The film, *Albert Ayler, Le Dernier Concert*, was shown throughout Europe and is still extant.[14] Directed by Jean-Michel Meurice, the fifty-one-minute film was shown at the Fondation in March 2015. The entire concerts were released in a deluxe set of five LPs or four CDs in 2022.

The day after closing his festival engagement, Ayler performed before a small impromptu audience where the group were staying. Tintweiss remembered:

It was an add-on performance at 'Villages Vacances Tourisme' which was a retreat of tourist villas outside of Saint-Paul De Vence ... where we were staying. Although the management did not want to open up the attendance to our fans who were not guests there, we insisted, so they were allowed in. It was all by word-of-mouth, but the news spread quickly. There was an informal set-up, an upright piano, no bass amplification at all, and only one ancient PA microphone which we didn't really use.[15]

Ayler's final recorded performance, it was reviewed in *Jazz Hot* as 'three hours of spontaneous, euphoric, swinging music,'[16] forty minutes of which were subsequently released in the *Holy Ghost* box. Tony Herrington of *The Wire* felt that Ayler was 'working with a new group of musicians that are so far behind him in terms of his musical conception it's like hearing Jimi Hendrix jamming with The Dave Clark Five.'[17]

Art Lange wrote in *Coda*:

Ayler playing extended solos once again, ornamenting the melodies 'Mothers' and 'Children' along arpeggiated, sometimes modal contours. More interestingly, on three untitled pieces Ayler seems to be reverting back to an earlier (circa '64) approach, on one subverting Call Cobbs's romantic, harmonically conservative piano with intense upper-register overtones, and imposing an aharmonic improvisation onto a Sephardic sounding melody on another ... yet it's ironic that the last music we have from Ayler is neither visionary nor compromised, but the flamboyant, exhilarating, intently personal manner of improvising he made his mark with, and is now established as a continuing force in creative music.[18]

Nuits de la Fondation Maeght received the Charles Cros Academy's Grand Prix International Du Disque and *Swing Journal*'s Silver Award, but while the recordings captured Ayler in a more creatively satisfying place than the two studio albums that preceded them, they also raise questions about the future that might have been: was he consolidating his past, or ready to move into another new phase? Was he about to start concentrating on interpretation rather than improvisation? To Litweiler's ears, Ayler's soloing 'had lost nothing of technique and creativity':

> Fortunately, Ayler takes by far the greatest solo space in both sets. The listener senses here an ego as massive as Armstrong's and a mind twice as sentimental. Along with the brilliance one hears cautious but definite change. The Ayler tragedy is compounded by the unavoidable feeling … that the successes of his past were only an indication of the potential of his future.[19]

If any of these reviewers could have seen the future, they would have known that their opinions would be held by others—such as Richard Brody's praising of the deluxe edition of *Revelations: The Complete ORTF 1970 Fondation Maeght Recordings* in the *New Yorker*.[20]

•

Before flying back home, Ayler gave the final interview of his life to Daniel Caux. Caux had plans for Ayler to return in January, for a concert in which he would have been accompanied by an orchestra of bagpipes. Albert still spoke favorably about his brother, and Caux would remember a friendship forged in the days following the Fondation Maeght shows:

> He stayed with me for six days, just hanging out. Maeght had given him the use of a car so that he could drive around if he wanted. He was very gentle, very intelligent, and the concerts he played were very special. I liked him very much and we connected.[21]

If the reactions of the French audiences were anything to go by, Ayler could be said to have accomplished the mission he felt he was on. 'It's late now for the world,' he said. 'And if I can help raise people to new plateaus of peace and understanding, I'll feel my life has been worth living as a spiritual artist.'[22]

'another afro sound—gone'[1]

I n early August 1970, dressed in a black suit, a silk shirt, and a pork-pie hat, Ayler dropped by Kunle Mwanga's Liberty House on Bleeker Street. Liberty House was the New York retail outlet for the Poor People's Cooperation, a Mississippi-based cooperative that supported female African American artisans. It was also a mecca for avant-garde musicians. Albert had heard about the violinist Leroy Jenkins, who was an employee of the store, from the widow of Charles Clark, a Chicago bassist. Ayler dropped by Liberty House to hear Jenkins for himself.

Like Clark, Jenkins was from Chicago, where he'd played with the Creative Construction Company, an experimental jazz ensemble. Keeping with the collectivist theme, Jenkins was also a member of the Association For The Advancement Of Creative Musicians, a flagship not-for-profit founded in Chicago which promoted African American experimental music. Jenkins told Art Sato of San Francisco's KPFA about meeting Ayler:

> He told me he had a gig coming up and he wanted to … see if we could get our vibrations together … he didn't have any place to rehearse. So, I said, 'I have this place upstairs in the store, so, Kunle at that time closed the place early that afternoon. … We just started playing 'Ghosts' … and he taught it to me, man. We played that, man, 'bout an hour or so. … After we got through it, he said,

'Yeah man, you and me, we're all right.' He says, 'Look, I got this gig, man, Sunday [sic] ... so, I'll be 'round to pick you up,' and, so I said, 'OK, man.'

On the morning of Saturday, August 8, 1970, a large limo pulled up at Liberty House. Inside were Ayler, Maria Parks, drummer Allen Blairman, a pile of instruments, and an English chauffeur. Jenkins got in, and the band drove to Springfield, Massachusetts, arriving at the DeBerry School in the afternoon for a concert held under the joint sponsorship of the local Parks Department and the federal-aid Model Cities Program. In front of an open-air audience of five hundred people, the bands Souls Unlimited (formerly the Soul Ignitions) and the Dynamite performed as the opening acts and then, without any rehearsal, Ayler played several selections from *Music Is The Healing Force Of The Universe*.

Jenkins described the audience's reaction to the 'bizarre' music:

> When we first started playing, the audience ... split up like, like if it was the Red Sea. That was the kind of expression, man. It was as if they was running ... we just kept playing. I guess they saw these guys are serious. And they came back, man. ... I closed my eyes after I saw the sea split like that. ... I said, 'Well, you know, it didn't look like it was gonna work.' ... By the time I opened my eyes up again, you know, it was packed—they were all in front ... Albert said, 'Hey man, we're definitely gonna get together some more soon. I'm gonna make a record.'[2]

The concert was reviewed in the *Springfield Union* a few days later:

> It sounded a little like a Negro spiritual, bound up in some Basin street blues and tied together with a calypso beat, all rolled into a jam session. With flashing strobe lights alternately silhouetting the band, plunging them into darkness and then multi-colored light, it looked like an old-time movie. ... Ayler, who sports a half white and half black goatee and huge round-rimmed glasses, said he recently returned from a European tour. ... His style of music is reminiscent of Bohemian experiments heard in the Latin Quarter of Paris. ... The audience thought he was tuning up. He had been playing for fifteen minutes. The sound

was new and strange, but the audience slowly got into it, most appreciably when singer Mary Maria, dressed in a gold lame pants-suit, came on stage.[3]

Peter Niklas Wilson's interview with Leroy Jenkins revealed that the show left Ayler fully spent, and that he sweated so heavily that his face turned into a 'black sea.'[4] It was a disconcerting image, the likes of which others witnessed in New York. Poet Ted Joans claimed to see the first indications of a worrying shift in Ayler's behavior when he spotted him standing at the intersection of 125th Street and Eighth Avenue, accompanied by a woman likely to have been Parks; both were wearing winter clothing. In a velvet suit, ascot tie, and beaver hat, Ayler was sweating profusely, the sweat accumulating in his beard.[5]

Writing in *As Serious As Your Life*, Val Wilmer recounted a similar experience of saxophonist Noah Howard, who claimed to have seen Ayler in a 'full-length fur coat and gloves, and his face covered in Vaseline.' The reason for the Vaseline, Ayler said, was, 'Got to protect myself.'[6] Bobby Few remembered, 'All the girls were scared to kiss him because it would take off their makeup. I think it was some type of spiritual thing he had going on. He would shine like a spirit, or an angel. Maybe, he felt he looked good. He was caked with it.'[7]

Certainly, in Psalm 23 there is the commandment, 'Thou shall anoint thy head with oil.' However, Donald Ayler offered a different insight into why Ayler may have started rubbing himself in Vaseline: their mother regularly put olive oil on their foreheads in order to make their skin shine; and it seems as though Ayler may have had the skin condition vitiligo. His former fiancée Carrie Lucas told me, 'I saw him with Vaseline on his face a few times, especially when this thing seemed to be spreading … that was pink around his lips, and he kept Vaseline on it.'[8] Another source said that the white spot on his chin was a blessing from where God had touched him, but that when his brother's problems began, Albert began to feel that the 'divine seal' was instead a mark of sin.[9]

•

Around September 1970, having exhibited bizarre behavior for the past two years, Donald was hospitalized with what he referred to as a problem with chemical imbalance. Discussing it at length with Bob Rusch of *Cadence*, he said:

> I had a nervous breakdown simply because I was into yoga too deep … standing on my head six hours a day, and half lotus maybe four hours a day. I just went to the extremes. At that period of time there were so many vibrations out there not knowing what it was all about. I guess I had been feeling something as far as my brother's life was concerned. All I could do was be in prayer, Yoga, you know. I was in the institution not very long though, a period of maybe a couple of months. Eventually I got out of it, returned back. I was feeling something at that period of time, I guess I couldn't put my finger on it and when my brother passed, then I realized why I felt the way I felt.[10]

This was the first of intermittent hospitalizations for Donald, who began to take medication for the problem. During this stay, he received a phone call from Albert, who told him, 'Man, all you need to do is be up there in New York, you'll be all right—'cause everybody up there is supposed to be crazy anyway.'[11]

Albert himself paid what would be his final visit to Cleveland at this time. He exhibited a marked physical and mental deterioration that caused concern among his family. Though Donald's hospital records indicate that he was under care while Albert visited, Donald says he tried to help his brother through exercise, suggesting that they run 'from 40th and Kinsman to Ripley Road' (around four miles). 'We won't stop,' Donald told him.

'He stayed there about two or three months,' Donald recalled, 'and he was okay after that. Mind untightened, and he wasn't paranoid or anything like that. We worked on him. He was OK.'

According to Donald, this would be the last time he saw his brother— something the younger Ayler sibling had already intuited:

> I knew it was the last time I was gonna see him. I said, 'Al, play "Jesus" one last

time.' I grabbed the trumpet to brace it up, and he had a horn lying in my bed to brace it up. I looked at his fingers. His hands just moved. You could see he was all artist—you know what I'm trying to say, his hands just moved over his instrument, just moving.[12]

Albert also attempted to visit his son, Curtis, at his former fiancée Carrie Lucas's house in the early hours of the morning. She, too, witnessed the change in Albert, who told her about his planned tour of Japan, and 'a lady'—most likely Mary Parks—who he didn't want to go with him:

He was nervous. It was like he had to go, he had to hurry up. But he had to stop by for some reason. … But he did mention, 'I put some numbers under my mother's hot water tank.' And I'm not thinking to ask what the numbers are for. … I said, 'Why don't you stay?'—it was, like, two o'clock in the morning. 'We could have some coffee. We could have sit here and talk, you know. You could leave before my kids wake up.' But, it was like maybe somebody hit him, and he thought about it, and he had to go. He left without putting his jacket on. And I never saw him again.[13]

Ayler returned to New York and paid a visit to Ornette Coleman, according to violinist Leroy Jenkins, who had been hanging out with Coleman:

I was going over there a lot, so I said, 'Man, you and Ornette ought to get together.' … So, he said, 'Yeah, I'd like to check Ornette out.' … He came over to Ornette's house and they rapped … they were sorta warming up to each other. Him and Ornette were talking about some stuff that had gone down during their little heyday, before either one of them had got to be known. They were talking, laughing, joking about that, man.[14]

Toward the end of October, he paid a visit to Bernard Stollman, the ESP-Disk' founder who had showed such crucial belief in Ayler's work. Stollman felt that Ayler—who claimed to have secured a quarter of a million dollars to play Japan—appeared to be disappointed, rather than depressed:

I think he was hoping I could give him some money, but ESP was closing. … He was his typical self, not at all ruffled. He played me a cassette of gospel songs that he had modified to the point that they were unrecognizable. He just took it way, way out. I never heard anything like it before or again. It was gorgeous, but I was flabbergasted. But it didn't matter how I felt, as I was in no position to help him. … He told me that his brother, Don, was going to the hospital, and he somehow had to help him. Who would have imagined that two weeks later he'd be dead![15]

Albert disappeared on November 5. Mary Parks told Daniel Caux that, during this time, he called her for a week or two. Claiming to be in Canada, he told her, softly and serenely, to be calm—that he was going to disappear, but it wasn't important; he wanted her to be happy. Three weeks later, at 9:15am on Wednesday, November 25, his body was found floating in the East River, at the foot of Brooklyn's Congress Street Pier. He was identified by the passport in his back pocket and taken to the Kings County Hospital morgue.

Violinist Leroy Jenkins recalled the confusion that followed:

We were supposed to meet for a gig or something that day, or later on, and he never showed up … the drummer [Allen Blairman] called up Maria … to find out what was happening. And she was—she said something like she was scared or something. … And man, we were shook up by that … I called [a woman at *DownBeat*] … and she said that he gotten mixed up with some bad people or something.[16]

The gig would have been at the Village East, where Ayler had been booked for three nights, December 25 through to December 27. Archie Shepp wound up playing in Ayler's absence.

Back in Cleveland, Albert's family weren't even aware that he'd gone missing. Though his parents received a letter claiming to be from their son, but according to Donald, who had returned home to them, it didn't seem to be written in Albert's style or even his handwriting. The family flew to

New York, and while Albert's mother, Myrtle, stayed in the car, Donald, his father, and Call Cobbs identified the body; Donald recalled that it was so decomposed it had turned black, but they identified that it was Albert from the white patch of skin near his mouth. In line with the autopsy, the New York Medical Examiner ruled that Albert had died by 'asphyxia by submersion—circumstances undetermined.'[17]

•

Such an open-ended and unexplained death has inevitably led to rumors surrounding Ayler's final days. Mary Parks's statements to the police have led to the logical conclusion of suicide, and, after such a long time in the water before discovery, Albert's body showed no other evidence to disprove this. And yet, rumors of foul play persisted among musicians, including a fatal shooting by, variously, the police, the Mafia, or drug dealers—despite there being no reports, either officially or from those who identified Albert's body, of bullet holes in his corpse. Another rumor connected him with the mistress of a Mafia boss; eventually, an urban myth had him tied to a jukebox and dumped in the river. His one-time associate, Gary Peacock, connected all these threads when he told *Hot House* magazine, 'Someone had shot him in the back of the head. Some said it was drugs. But my experience was that he wasn't a druggie. My own suspicion is probably female-related, in a way.'[18] Donald would fan the flames of the latter element by claiming, 'He was messing with an Italian girl in New York, I heard.'[19]

Since it was first suggested in print, in the February 1971 issue of *Jazz & Pop* magazine, that Albert had killed himself, many theories have arisen as to why he would have done so. In the British edition of *As Serious As Your Life*, Val Wilmer expresses the opinion that Albert blamed himself for Donald's breakdown after firing him from his band. Writing to *The Wire*'s Mike Hames in 1984, Mary Parks—who, in Donald's words, had come 'out of the blue' and then 'disappeared out of the blue' following Albert's death[20]—went so far as to suggest that Albert's mother had put the blame on her son, and that both Myrtle and Donald had spent the two years leading up to Albert's death pressuring him to re-hire Donald. She had, she said, remained silent for so long in order to avoid embarrassing the Ayler family, but that, after 'much meditation and prayer,' she wanted to put an end to the spurious rumors surrounding Albert's death. His hometown friend Jon Goldman also felt this to be the case, adding that they had pressured Albert to hire Donald in the first place.

Dave McElfresh of *Coda* believed that Parks wanted to downplay Ayler's mental-health issues, which would explain her delay in coming forth. According to Parks, she had asked Albert's father to talk some sense into his son, but Edward seemed unconcerned; she also had her sister try to talk Albert out of killing himself. Apparently, after a brief moment of success, he told her one evening, 'My blood has got to be shed to save my mother and my brother,' and then smashed his saxophone across the television set and left. But though Parks had said she called the police after this, Ayler's cousin Sandy Wright has claimed that Parks was less forthcoming with Albert's family, and that she stonewalled attempts to get information about Albert's whereabouts after Parks first informed them that he was missing.[21]

At odds with the picture this paints of Albert's family dynamic, Michael Drexler, writing in the *Plain Dealer*, claimed that Ayler visited his family often, and that it was always financial concerns that forced him to return to New York. According to Albert's late maternal cousin, Edward, Albert visited his apartment after his altercation with Parks and claimed that she had threatened him and thrown him out of the apartment—he grabbed his passport before leaving, so that he could travel to Japan in December, and pawned his saxophone in order to get some funds to live on. (Donald retrieved it following Ayler's death.)

Clearly, based on the recollections of Carrie Lucas and others, Albert and Mary's relationship was frayed. Indeed, critics such as Ben Young have suggested that Ayler was in a calmer state of mind when he was away from her—as he was during his relatively relaxed interview with Kiyoshi Koyama.[22] But drummer Milford Graves suggested that Ayler was struggling with the pressures of the music industry, as he told Mitch Goldman and Andy Rotman of WKCR radio:

> Albert was very depressed at the end and, this was because of business deals with Impulse! ... Albert was totally aware, but you had to listen to Albert because he was very subtle sometime, and he was quick. [Recording vocals] was not something that Albert wanted to do. It was on paper that certain things should be done.[23]

And yet Ayler had his new gospel records, as described by Bernard Stollman, and the forthcoming tour of Japan. In conversation with Koyama, he sounded positive about his future—he was enthusiastic about playing the Maeght Festival, and he felt he was at a stage in his career where he could fill bigger venues rather than the smaller jazz clubs he'd more often played:

> I've been just staying at home and getting my music together. It's either big or nothing. And we live the best way we can until we make it big. ... And now, I see things are getting better. The better you are, the harder it is to make it, but when you make it, you make it big.[24]

In 2010, a French book, *Albert Ayler: Témoignages Sur Un Holy Ghost*, featured an article by Daniel Caux, who, after conducting his own independent investigations, not unreasonably concluded that a combination of family strains, relationship pressures, and concerns over his career had taken their toll on Ayler's wellbeing. Caux believed that the loss of his Impulse! contract had not only hurt Albert's pride but also exacerbated concerns that he would always be seen as a marginal figure. Additionally, he felt that Ayler struggled with the perception that certain musicians and critics had that he was a traitor to the Black cause. After returning to New York following his triumph in France at Fondation Maeght, all these problems seem to have come to a head.

Newly brought to light in Caux's article was a discussion that Caux and his wife had in Paris with Anthony Braxton.[25] A saxophonist, composer, and leading light of the avant-garde, Braxton had seen Ayler shortly before his death, and he claimed that Ayler had spoken to him of suicide. Additionally, Caux revealed that, though he had attempted to visit Ayler's family in Cleveland two years after Albert's death, they refused to see him; however, in a phone conversation with Caux's wife, Jacqueline, Myrtle Ayler is said to have stated, 'I wish he had never been born.'[26]

Over forty-eight years later, Jacqueline Caux still recalls the brief conversation:

> It was a strange, and for me, violent conversation. She was obviously very hostile, the voice was very unpleasant, a voice like a crazy person, really angry, indeed regretting that her son was born and that he did not take enough care of his brother—which made us think that the pressure on Albert must have been really strong![27]

Donald, however, would suggest that he was the one who carried the familial burden, saying, 'My mother needed me more than my brother did. She could hardly get around the house.'[28]

It is easy to see how Ayler, burdened with family guilt, could see his situation in terms of the religious beliefs that coursed through his music. His letter 'To Mr. Jones—I Had A Vision' is steeped in Old Testament imagery and reinforces the notion of blood atonement that he is said to have expressed to Mary Parks. His former bandleader Charles Tyler noted the connection:

> Al was really a sad person despite his charisma and everything. That 'old-time religion' was what caused his sadness; it was in his music. Al was a heavy guy, and there won't be nobody like him. And it seems that in his death he's going to be more so … someone said Al got depressed and jumped off the bridge. I wouldn't be surprised his religious background followed him through to the end.[29]

According to the Coast Guard, Ayler had jumped from a ferry boat near the Statue Of Liberty—a symbolic end for the creator of free jazz who couldn't free himself from his own demons. Apparently, had he chosen any other spot, the currents would have carried Ayler's body out to sea, further deepening an already tragic mystery. And yet some, such as drummer Beaver Harris, believe that Ayler's death was an accident:

> I think that maybe by some freak accident Albert just drowned. Maybe he was on the bridge. ... Accidents happen. No, he didn't do anything to himself, that was an accident. ... This man knew how great he was.[30]

In conversation with this author—and confirmed by Sandy Wright— Bernard Stollman revealed that Ayler actually suffered from a fear of water.[31] But while this seems to make it doubtful whether Ayler would have gone near a ferry or lingered long on a bridge, a pathologist believed that any suicidal urges would have overcome his phobia; conversely, however, a psychiatrist would suggest that his phobia would have overcome any impulse to jump. Statistically, too, suicide by drowning is a rare phenomenon in African Americans—its victims are typically Caucasian males over forty.[32]

Shortly after I interviewed Albert's father and brother, in September 1997, a *Plain Dealer Sunday Magazine* article proffered the theory that Albert was killed over a drug debt. Claiming insider knowledge from Willie Smith—a Cleveland saxophone player and a supposed friend that neither Edward nor Donald Ayler had heard of—reporter Michael Drexler wrote that Ayler's 'drug habit' had begun in 1965 and progressed until his death. Smith felt that Ayler would eventually be killed because he was selling drugs to support his own addiction.[33] But while the story created plenty of controversy, Donald was adamant that the only drug Ayler evert touched was marijuana—'And who didn't mess around with marijuana in the 60s?'[34] Admittedly, the cocaine use at the *Spirits Rejoice* session casts some doubt on this denial, but Ayler's public statements about drug use reinforce the author's beliefs in Ayler's spiritual message. It seems more likely that Drexler, a freelance writer, simply met a local musician who repeated and embellished a variant of the jukebox canard over a round of drinks so it could be published as a puff-piece in the paper's Sunday supplement.

Even Drexler wrote that Edward confirmed Ayler's use of marijuana but denied that his son ever used hard drugs.[35] On the other hand, Donald admitted to his own later cocaine use. Before his final hospitalization, he was visited by some musician fans from California and, in this author's presence, told them how cocaine had messed up his life and destroyed his marriage, but it is unclear when his habit began. Despite this, everyone who was close to Albert denies that he used hard drugs, and Albert himself made several assertions that he did not touch them.

Bobby Few was emphatic in this:

> I had heard through the grapevine about some kind of drug problem, but, I refused to believe it … he was too healthy. He was too spiritual. … And I knew Albert all the way up until his death. Sometimes he would smoke, you know, but never saw any hard stuff around him.[36]

Ayler seemed to have had no financial incentive to deal drugs. And while Edward asserted that he never sought to make money from his art—'He was truly a genius … he didn't want to push out in front. That's all he wanted—to play. He had all the titles but not a dime'[37]—in conversation with both Kiyoshi Koyama and Daniel Caux, Ayler claimed he had plenty of money from a $10,000 advance that Impulse! had given him, as well as his fees for appearing at the Maeght festival. Indeed, Albert felt he was now big enough to turn down fees that he felt were beneath him. His former drummer Sunny Murray, who believed Ayler's death to be linked to drugs and hoodlums, had heard from Mary Parks that Ayler was due to get $250,000 for his tour of Japan, while Steve Tintweiss, who played bass with Ayler in France, was sure that his money problems were coming to an end.[38] According to a conversation he had with Columbia Records' legendary A&R man John Hammond, the label had once again made overtures to Ayler:

> John Hammond himself told me that Albert was being groomed to be the next Miles Davis … mass-audience jazz artist, with a tour of Japan being scheduled for January 1971! Those kinds of statements I would take with a grain of salt

if it weren't John Hammond. … John had offered Albert $2,000 to record him for this experimental project which Columbia had him produce, but John told me that Albert wouldn't do it for that amount.[39]

•

Whatever confluence of pressures Ayler felt had become too burdensome, Donald felt that life in the white-hot crucible of New York—a city that had repeatedly rejected him and his music—would have done nothing to ease his troubles:

> You can't stay in New York for a year or two, especially if you're under pressure of producing an artistical talent … you got to take a break away. I'd step away for five months … and my brother stayed up there a year … a couple years. And see, that's a rubber room for you there.[40]

And yet Albert's hometown didn't do much to mark the passing of one of its heroes. A bona-fide jazz great, he received no obituary in the *Cleveland Press*; the only story that ran in the local media was by Bernard Lairet in the weekly *Cleveland Scene*:

> The new jazz loses one of its principal exponents, and an exciting creative spirit. One of Cleveland's own, he seems almost ignored in his native town, though recognized in music spheres all around the world. … Albert Ayler has altered all the conventional landmarks: rhythm nearly becomes melody; harmony has rediscovered the kind of innocence it had in the early days of jazz; traditional musical organization has been rejected and the expressive potential of the sound itself has been examined differently. An expression of purity, his music has transmitted the new messages required of a new sensibility. … Now we have lost the father AND the holy Ghost.[41]

Ayler's body was returned to Cleveland for burial. The final service was held during a sunny afternoon at 3:30pm on Friday, December 4, at the Memorial Chapel at Highland Park Cemetery. Before a gathering of fifty-five mourners, Albert was buried in Grave 3, Lot 6, Tier 7, near the eleventh hole of the Red Course of the Highland Park Golf Course, where, as an adolescent, he had developed his love of golf. His father called him 'a swell, quiet guy, easy to get along with.'[42]

On the night of the funeral, the Ayler family staged a more intimate, invite-only event. As Jon Goldman later recalled, he visited the family home to pay his respects but was asked to leave because the Aylers were expecting a visit from a medium who would contact Albert's spirit. For a man often described as living life on a different plane, this seemed fitting—and perhaps was a natural development from an experience his twelve-year-old son Curtis had. As Carrie Lucas recalled it, she only heard of Ayler's death after the funeral, through a mutual friend. When she got home, however, she discovered that her son had found out in an altogether different way after he made a strange reference to his father's shiny leather suit:

> When I walked in the door, Curtis was crying, 'Mom, somebody killed my dad—they pushed him down a hill, and he rolled into the water. And he had something really shiny on.' I said, 'What? Somebody call here and told you that, or what?' And, he said, 'No, I just saw it. Mom, I just saw it.'[43]

Despite the lack of local press attention, Ayler's life and work would be eulogized in the mainstream jazz press that had once treated him with confusion and derision, with *Jazz Journal*'s Barry McCrae asserting that 'the main body of his work … must be considered along with the very best in jazz.'[44] Having been an outsider for so long, Ayler was now hailed as a true influence, his use of the false upper register now part of the common language of a jazz world he had redefined.

Before Albert Ayler, jazz musicians followed a long-established tradition: music was based on rhythm and scales. But he saw a bigger picture—one in which music was based on the notion of sound. While parallel developments in Western music by the likes of Cage and Varèse were developed from theory, Ayler played emotion and senses, laying new foundations for what would come in his wake .

As John Litweiler put it:

> Charismatic, with an ego as vast as Armstrong's or Parker's, he could not
> conceive of his new idiom without his total destruction of the jazz heritage.
> Nonetheless, it was left to others to build with Ayler's new resources amid the
> rubble he left; poignantly, their finished structures began to appear while he
> was losing faith in his art.[45]

Ayler himself was not unaware that future generations of musicians would
build upon what he had started—as happened with all the jazz greats:

> But even when they pass away, somebody else will come along who'll be
> playing the true message from their heart. It's just like the person is still here
> and it's one continual flowing thing.[46]

Some of those torch-bearers performed at a benefit concert, held in New
York, on December 7, for Albert's wife, Arlene, and daughter, Desiree.
Saxophonists Gary Bartz, Arthur Jones, Frank Wright, Noah Howard, and
Marzette Watts; pianist Ron Burton; drummers Elvin Jones, Rashied Ali,
and Sunny Murray; and the Art Ensemble all paid tribute. On April 11
the following year, Cleveland hosted a fund-raising concert of its own,
at Karamu House, to raise money for an Albert Ayler Memorial Fund.
Sponsored by the Organization For The Development And Advancement
Of The Cultural Black Arts, the event was broadcast on WCUY-FM and
sought to raise money for the benefit of 'musically talented, underprivileged
Black youths.'[47] Former Ayler sideman Bobby Few and his group The
Sound Bomb were received as a highlight of what critic Bernard Lairet
called 'a spectacle of extraordinary quality.'[48]

Nor was Ayler forgotten in France, the scene of his final triumph: on
the first anniversary of his death, the French Broadcasting System aired a
pair of three-hour programs in his memory. Closer to home, New York
radio station WKCR, owned by Columbia University, played a fifteen-
hour program about Ayler's music and life. Marking the fifth anniversary

of his death, Ayler's spiritual descendent David Murray—an artist who 'created a synthesis of the radical experimentation of John Coltrane and ... Albert Ayler with the classic jazz tradition'[49]—released a memorial album, *Flowers For Albert*.

As Barry McRae noted in *Jazz Journal*, 'The death of an outstanding revolutionary often encourages the reactionaries to consider a reappraisal.'[50] Though his final albums still divide critics, that has, broadly speaking, been the case with Ayler, whose influence has spread not only beyond jazz and into the rock world but beyond music and into poetry, inspiring a collection by the poet F.A. Nettelbeck, *Albert Ayler Disappeared*. By the time that Revenant Records' *Holy Ghost: Rare & Unissued Recordings (1962–1970)* box set was released in 2004, his work was regarded highly enough to receive a Grammy nomination.

How to close this final chapter? I think Litweiler's summation is the best:

> Everything about Albert Ayler's music was astonishing. With him, the new music broke its last lingering ties with not just bop but the entire jazz tradition. Every one of the noisy horrors the first Free wave was accused of, he gladly embraced. He screamed through his tenor saxophone in multiphonics and almost uncontrolled overtones, absolutely never in a straight saxophone sound or in any identifiable pitch. His ensembles really did improvise with utter abandon, and they related their music to each other's in the most primal, irregular ways--when they related at all. Among the great jazz musicians, Ayler's emotional range may be the most limited: In his most creative years, frenzied ecstasy in the fastest tempo that's humanly possible alternated with the most maudlin ballads imaginable, and these two forms of hysteria were the sole content of his soloing. He never swung, not even in the standard settings of his earliest recordings; instead, his fastest solos acquired momentum through the kinetic energy of his tornado speed lines. Indeed, he bypassed the entire history of jazz to go back to attitudes and ideas about music that predated the art's inception; he then built up his own art out of primitive discoveries.[51]

postscript

Albert Ayler was survived by his parents, brother, son, daughter, and his grandmother, Mrs Augusta Kennedy. His widow, Arlene, still lives in Cleveland, and their daughter, Desiree Fellows, works in Beachwood; she herself now has a daughter, who has begun a nursing career, and a son, Melvin Fellows, who attended The Ohio State University on a football scholarship. He was a defensive end and played in the 2010 Rose Bowl.

Edward Ayler retired from TRW in July 1977. Myrtle Ayler died in 1985, following a steep decline in her physical health. Edward remarried three years later—his second wife was named Edith, and, in a strange coincidence, she shared a surname with Mary Parks. He knew her from his childhood days on Woodland Avenue.[1]

Ayler's only son, Curtis Roundtree, inherited his father's musical talents. A cement truck driver by profession—working for his own company, Advanced Quality Concrete LLC—he has released several twelve-inch singles as part of a hip-hop group formed with his siblings. He plays saxophone.

Donald Ayler took the loss of his brother hard. It was nearly three years after Albert's death before he picked up a horn. In the decades that followed, his own battles with mental health led to multiple hospitalizations, yet he helped keep the legacy alive. In September 1997, I contacted him and asked if he would consent to give an interview on WCSB-FM. Donald was floored that someone still remembered him.

Weeks later, near the anniversary of Albert's death, the *Plain Dealer* published Michael Drexler's story about Albert in their Sunday magazine, with the headline 'Gone But Not Forgotten.' The Ayler family had mixed feelings about it. At last, Albert had received recognition in his hometown— but at the price of being labeled a drug dealer. In a subsequent interview, Donald agreed to tell more of the story how he saw it, filling in the gaps of a life lived with and without his brother.

After the failed New Jersey gig of April 1969—drunk, zipper open, as *The Cricket* reported—Donald didn't play much for several years. In 1973, he began performing occasional gigs around Cleveland, heading up to Kinsman Grill on Sunday and jamming with the band Days Of Wine And Roses—though his free style was in a sharp contrast with the straight-ahead styles of organist Eddie Bacchus and drummer Jack Singleton. In 1977, he told Bob Rusch of *Cadence* magazine, 'Well, I would like to eventually get myself a recording session, put some music out there and play music every day. The more I play, the better the chops get.'[2]

In April that year, Donald sat in with Pharaoh Sanders's band at Fat Glenn's, a Cleveland State University bar, on April 15 and 16. People still respected his talent and his style of playing. He made three appearances at Peabody's Café on Cedar and Taylor Road for the Northeast Ohio Jazz Society, June 14, September 6, and November 12, 1979. The group was jointly led by Don and Otis Harris. As more gigs followed, Donald regained his chops, and in November he sat in with bassist Kevin Muhammad's band, Altotude, at Kay's Casablanca Club at 3520 Lee Road; Muhammad later admitted that his crew was blown away with his technique.

The closest thing that Donald had to a job in music was working at a record store, Robert Johnson's Buckeye Music, where he was employed for six months as a cashier. Despite being twice admitted to Fairhill Hospital, in 1980 and 1981, he continued to return to music. On May 3, 1981, he played a concert (on cornet) at Cleveland State University in the Sundown Jazz series with a small group composed of David Thomas, piano, Ed McEachen, guitar, Kip Reed on bass, Marty Barker on drums, and Frank Doblekar on sax.[3] Doblekar replaced the original sax player,

Rex Cowen. Don also performed as a soloist backed by the Cleveland State University Jazz Ensemble. Donald wanted to use that line-up for his forthcoming Italian tour, but everyone but Doblekar dropped out.[4] That was a warm-up for his subsequent booking to perform in Florence, Italy, though Donald felt that the musicians he recruited were too lazy to practice, and only good for keeping time. Rather than play against them, however, Don played straight as well. The concert was recorded and issued on the Frame label as a three-record set, *Don Ayler In Florence 1981*. It was favorably reviewed by Jon Goldman, the Ayler brothers' Cleveland friend, in *Coda*, who wrote, 'Despite the lack of any substantial rehearsal time and the thrown-together nature of the group, the results are somewhat more than satisfying ... some of the new faces really shine.'[5]

Donald's style had changed since his time with Albert, but though he took a more conventional approach in his later years, he finally began to receive overdue respect, with avant-garde composer and trumpeter Wadada Leo Smith considering Donald to be the main influence on his style. Jon Goldman observed how Donald's original material followed in the same vein as the praised 'Our Prayer,' a centerpiece of his performances with Albert:

> Don's compositions tend to be jumping off points for long improvisations by all of the members of the group and provide a level of emotional framework variously interpreted. Most of Don's tunes by their nature require modal frameworks, yet the freely arranged accompaniments by the rhythm section lend an unusual flavor to the totality of the performances.[6]

Yet Donald's fortunes remained mixed. During one show, in a bar on Prospect Avenue in Cleveland, only his family turned up. But it was here, however, that Donald met Letty Lucille 'Dolly' Harris. Almost two decades earlier, as a sixteen-year-old accompanied by two friends, she had seen Donald perform with Albert at the WHK Auditorium; Dolly's brother Otis was now in Donald's band. With his mother's health failing, Donald was of a mind to start settling down: 'Lots of guys was gettin' the chicks, and I got my horn. And, then I got lonely later on in life.'[7] He and Dolly married on August 18, 1984, in the backyard of his cousin Robert Johnson's house.[8]

Shortly after this, Donald was hospitalized again—this time at Northcoast Behavioral. A social worker assigned to look after him noted that he had been off psychotropic drugs for about five months, and Donald's hospital records also indicate that he was drinking two quarts of beer a day, about two or three times a week, as well as smoking marijuana. Donald also tested positively for cocaine. Further hospitalizations occurred into the mid-90s; Donald and Dolly moved around the Cleveland area, finally settling on South Moreland Boulevard. After another hospitalization in late 1999, Dolly left him. With Donald convalescing, no one paid the rent nor answered the subsequent eviction notice. Everything he owned wound up on the curb.

After Dolly left, an application was made in the Cuyahoga County Probate Court in August 2003 for Donald's involuntarily commitment, with Kerry Formica and Jude Troha appointed as guardians.[9] Donald eventually took up residence in a social-service facility in the Rose Home (in Cleveland Heights), where he met a new girlfriend, Marlene. On my visits to him, I found him to be quite happy but restless; though he had swollen ankles—a side effect of diabetes—he used to like walking to the local Bruegger's Bagels down the block, and he enjoyed going shopping for clothes, attending films, and receiving family visits. Despite the nice surroundings, Donald was probably the youngest person in the home, and he shared space with other residents in various stages of dementia.

Around November 2001, Donald was a guest of honor at the Cleveland Cinematheque, receiving a standing ovation when he spoke to the audience gathered to watch a movie about the free-jazz movement, *Inside Out In The Open*, directed by local filmmaker Alan Roth. Later, a Swedish film crew interviewed him for another film, *My Name Is Albert Ayler*, but he passed away before he had the chance to see it.

In the years leading up to his death, Donald's hospitalizations had become more frequent, and his behavior more dangerous—to himself and others. In November 2003, while at Northcoast, he was arrested for sexual assault and charged with sexual battery and gross sexual imposition. The following spring, he was deemed incompetent to stand trial; he was prescribed various antipsychotic medications and mood stabilizers, and eventually diagnosed with schizophrenia.[10] His attending physician at Northcoast, Dr Sirkin, noted 'evidence of grandiose delusions (especially regarding multiple advanced degrees) and disorganized thinking.'

Donald often avoided taking his medication because it caused him to gain weight—though this, in turn, precipitated his relapses. His latest prescription lessened his agitation, but it didn't help with the psychosis or the grandiose moods. He also began to put on weight, which exacerbated his diabetes, caused high blood pressure, and put a strain on his heart.

One moment euphoric, the next irritable, Donald became 'quick to take offense at questions.' He accused the doctors of holding him against his will in order to hoard his 'great wealth' for themselves. Increasingly delusional, he insisted that the year was 2020; that he 'was a white man; 'pushing on his eyes,' he said, he could 'make the lights in the building go out.'

Later, he was God, the President of the United States, and the President of the Federation of the Universe. He insisted that the charges against him had been dropped because 'he hadn't been taking his medication at the time,' and he'd 'been dead twenty-three years in the morgue.' During one evaluation session, he asked Dr Hatters-Friedman why she thought he would have committed a sex crime when he had two beautiful daughters of his own, then showed her his 'daughters': a photo of two white models taken from a magazine. Convinced that he was both his own defense attorney and the jury that would decide his case, he asserted that the case would be closed 'when I play "Embraceable You" on my trumpet.'[11]

Eventually, the charges were downgraded to attempted sexual battery and gross sexual imposition. Donald was re-arrested and re-indicted on May 31, 2005, and confined to the Cuyahoga County Jail. I visited him there twice in July 2005. After I told him that Luther Vandross had passed away earlier that month, he began to sing one of Vandross's songs through the glass partition; he told me that he liked it in jail—the food there was better than at the hospital, and he was friendly with the guards. This was the last time I saw him.

Further examinations painted a sorry picture of Donald's mental decline, though the charges against him were dismissed without prejudice in August, and Donald was recommended for 'placement in a crisis stabilization unit or a group home for the mentally ill.'[12] Weakened by a stroke and a double pneumonia, he passed away at 5:05am on October 21, 2005, at BraeView Manor Health Care Facility in Euclid. The official cause of death was given as hypertensive and dilated cardiomyopathy.[13] Donald was buried nine days later at a sparsely attended funeral. Joining the family and friends who gathered to pay their respects—among them his father, who would outlive him for five years, before passing away on December 14, 2011, aged ninety-eight; cousins Claytene Wright, Sandra Wright, and Robert Johnson; Albert's children, Curtis and Desiree; and Mutawaf Shaheed—I helped carry Donald's coffin from the hearse to his graveside.

In death, Donald received some recognition for his contribution to jazz. Val Wilmer wrote a nice obituary in the *Guardian*,[14] and Tom Feran wrote an extensive article in the *Plain Dealer*.[15] Both writers recognized him not just as Albert Ayler's brother, but as a talent in his own right.

•

Donald's death brought back memories of when I first met him. A two-minute walk away from the majestic houses that lined Van Aken Boulevard there sat an apartment building with boards covering a broken window in the front door. Up three flights of stairs was a tiny apartment that Donald kept. Having sold the royalties to 'Our Prayer' for a pittance during a period of hunger, he had received no future income for the part he had played in changing the course of jazz. He'd received session fees for his performances, nothing more. But he had his memories, and he still went to see old friends perform in the clubs—Beaver Harris had died, but he kept him laughing until the end, and Donald was ecstatic when Sunny Murray called him from Paris. But no one was calling to book Donald for gigs. In those final years, he only played when he dreamed of Albert:

> It always happens that we are going on tour, to one of the concerts, playing the music. But I never see him, and I don't hear his horn. But I know we are going to play.[16]

Donald still wrote music, and he had written a song named for his brother. No longer in possession of a trumpet, he softly sang 'Albert Ayler' to me: the beautiful lyricism was recognizably in the style of 'Our Prayer.' He was optimistic that he could play again:

> I know it's gonna be a little rough trying to get back there, but as long as I've been there, I can always get back … I'm still into music, even if I never picked a horn up again, 'cause that sound goes out there in space forever. I hope to get back again.[17]

And Ayler's influence keeps growing. As the poet Ted Joans wrote:

> Angels of jazz, they don't die, they live, in hipsters like you and I.[18]

acknowledgments

I want to acknowledge those who helped me, including my agent, Lloyd Jassin; my publisher, Tom Seabrook of Jawbone Press; and my editor, Jason Draper; as well as my friends Patrick Regan and Pierre Crépon, who supplied me with material and also contributed their input (and Pierre, who helped me with translations). I am indebted to those writers who encouraged me from the start, such as Gary Giddins, Scott Yanow, John Litweiller, Val Wilmer, Lewis Porter, and John Szwed. Obviously, I am indebted to the publications who granted me permission to use material, and to those researchers into Ayler material who had gone before, such as Peter Niklas Wilson, Val Wilmer, and Jeff Schwartz, as well as Bengt Nordström; Bernard Stollman, who took the chance and had the vision; and my friend Donald Ayler, RIP, who gave me the idea to do the book.

bibliography

BOOKS

Michael Baden and Marion Roach, *Dead Reckoning: The New Science Of Catching Killers* (New York: Simon & Schuster, 2001)

Michael Baden, *Unnatural Death: Confessions Of A Medical Examiner* (New York: Random House, 1989)

Whitney Balliett, *Collected Works: A Journal Of Jazz, 1954–2001* (New York: St. Martin's Griffin, 2001)

Amiri Baraka, *The Autobiography Of LeRoi Jones* (Chicago: Lawrence Hill Books, 1997)

— *Black Music* (New York: Da Capo Press, 1998)

Jason Berry, Jonathan Foose, and Tad Jones, *Up From The Cradle Of Jazz: New Orleans Music Since World War II* (Athens: University Of Georgia Press, 1986)

Jason C. Bivins, *Spirits Rejoice! Jazz And American Religion* (New York: Oxford University Press, 2015)

Paul Bley and David Lee, *Stopping Time: Paul Bley And The Transformation Of Jazz* (Montreal: Vehicule Press, 1998)

Cleveland Baseball Federation, Annual Report, 1958 (Cleveland: The Federation, 1958)

The Cleveland Directory Co.'s Cleveland (Ohio) City Directory, various volumes (Cleveland: The Cleveland Directory Company, 1919–68)

Bill Cole, *John Coltrane* (New York: Da Capo Press, 2001)

Michel Contat (ed.), *Les treize morts d'Albert Ayler* (Paris: Gallimard, 1996)

Richard Cook and Brian Morton, *The Penguin Guide To Jazz On CD, LP, And Cassette* (Harmondsworth: Penguin Books, 1992)

Stanley Crouch, *Considering Genius* (New York: Basic Civitas Books, 2006)

Francis Davis, *In The Moment: Jazz In The 1980s* (Oxford: Oxford University Press, 1986)

Miles Davis, *Miles: The Autobiography* (New York: Simon And Schuster, 1989)

Robert B. Dickerson, Jr., *Final Placement: A Guide To The Deaths, Funerals, And Burials Of Notable Americans* (Algonac, Michigan: Reference Publications, 1982)

Bill Dixon, *L'Opera: A Collection Of Letters, Writings, Musical Scores, Drawings And Photographs (1967–1986)* (North Bennington: Metamorphosis Music, 1986)

Louis Dompierre, *Walking Woman Works: Michael Snow 1961–67. New Represented Art And Its Uses* (Kingston, Ontario: Agnes Therington Art Centre, 1983)

Hans Dulfer, *Jazz In China En Andere Perikels Uit De Geimproviseerde Muziek* (Amsterdam: Bert Bakker, 1980)

Colin Evans, *The Casebook Of Forensic Detection: How Science Solved 100 Of The World's Most Baffling Crimes* (New York: Berkley Books, 2007)

Karl Evanzz, *The Messenger: The Rise And Fall Of Elijah Muhammad* (New York: Pantheon, 1999)

Leonard Feather, *The Encyclopedia Of Jazz In The Sixties* (New York: Horizon Press, 1966)

James Feeney, *A History Of Jazz In Cleveland: The Feasibility Of An All Jazz Format Commercial Station In Metropolitan Cleveland* (Cleveland: 1976–77)

Dick Fiddy, *Missing Believed Wiped: Searching For The Lost Treasures Of British Television* (London: BFI Publishing, 2001)

Yasuhiro Fujioka, *John Coltrane: A Discography And Musical Biography* (Lanham, Maryland: Scarecrow Press, 1995)

Alf Gabrielsson, *Strong Experiences With Music: Music Is Much More Than Music* (Oxford: Oxford University Press, 2011)

John Gennari, *Blowin' Hot And Cool: Jazz And Its Critics* (Chicago: The University Of Chicago Press, 2006)

Gary Giddins, *Visions Of Jazz: The First Century* (New York: Oxford, 1998)

Mike Hames, *Albert Ayler, Sunny Murray, Cecil Taylor, Byard Lancaster & Kenneth Terroade: On Disc & Tape* (Wimborne, Dorset: Hames, 1983)

Mike Heffley, *Northern Sun, Southern Moon: Europe's Reinvention Of Jazz* (New Haven: Yale University Press, 2005)

Fredrick A. Jaffe, *A Guide To Pathological Evidence For Lawyers And Police Officers* (Scarborough, Ontario: Thomson Professional Publishing Canada, 1991)

Ekkehard Jost, *Free Jazz* (New York: Da Capo Press, 1981)

Ashley Kahn, *The House That Trane Built: The Story Of Impulse Records* (New York: W.W. Norton & Co., 2006)

Frank Kofsky, *Black Nationalism And The Revolution In Music* (New York: Pathfinder Press, 1970)

— *Coltrane And The Jazz Revolution* (New York: Pathfinder Press, 1998)

Bettye Lavette, *A Woman Like Me* (New York: Blue Rider Press, 2012)

Daniel Lewis, *A Guide To The Microfilm Edition Of The Black Power Movement. Part 1: Amiri Baraka From Black Arts To Black Radicalism* (University Publications Of America, undated)

John Litweiler, *The Freedom Principle: Jazz After 1958* (New York: William C. Morrow, 1984)

Graham Lock, *Chasing The Vibrations: Meetings With Creative Musicians* (Devon: Stride, 1994)

Humphrey Lyttleton, *Take It From The Top* (London: Robson Books, 1975)

Guerino Mazzola and Paul B. Cherlin, *Flow, Gesture, And Spaces In Free Jazz. Towards A Theory Of Collaboration* (Berlin: Springer, 2009)

Franck Médioni, *Albert Ayler: Témoignages sur un Holy Ghost* (Marseille: Le mot et le reste, 2010)

William Parker, *Conversations* (Paris: RogueArt, 2011)

Brian Priestley, *John Coltrane* (London: Apollo, 1978)

Ben Ratliff, *Coltrane: The Story Of A Sound* (New York: Farrar, Straus & Giroux, 2007)

Jane Martha Reynolds, *Improvisation Analysis Of Selected Works Of Albert Ayler, Roscoe Mitchell And Cecil Taylor* (Madison: University Of Wisconsin, 1993)

Perry Robinson and Florence Wetzel, *Perry Robinson: The Traveler* (San Jose: Writers Club Press, 2002)

Randall Sandke, *Where The Dark And The Light Folks Meet: Race And The Mythology, Politics, And Business Of Jazz* (Lanham, Maryland: The Scarecrow Press, 2010)

Jeff Schwartz, *New Black Music: Amiri Baraka (LeRoi Jones) And Jazz, 1959–1964* (Bowling Green, Ohio: Schwartz, 2004)

Ben Sidran, *Talking Jazz: An Illustrated Oral History* (San Francisco: Pomegranate Books, 1992)

James Edward Smethurst, *The Black Arts Movement: Literary Nationalism In The 1960s And 1970s* (Chapel Hill: The University Of North Carolina Press, 2005)

A.B. Spellman, *Four Lives In The Bebop Business* (New York: Pantheon Books, 1966)

Frederick J. Spencer, *Jazz And Death: Medical Profiles Of Jazz Greats* (Jackson: University Press Of Mississippi, 2002)

Jan Ström, *Jimmy Lyons: A Sessionography* (Sweden: Ayler Records, 2000)

John F. Szwed, *Space Is The Place: The Life And Times Of Sun Ra* (New York: Pantheon Books, 1997)

J.C. Thomas, *Chasin' The Trane* (Garden City, New York: Doubleday, 1975)

W.S. Tkweme *Vindicating Karma: Jazz And The Black Arts Movement* Thesis (Amherst: University Of Amherst, 2007)

David Toop, *Ocean Of Sound: Aether Talk, Ambient Sound And Imaginary Worlds* (New York: Serpent's Tail, 1995)

Norman C. Weinstein, *A Night In Tunisia: Imaginings Of Africa In Jazz* (Metuchen, New Jersey: Scarecrow Press, 1992)

Jason Weiss, *Always In Trouble: An Oral History Of ESP-Disk', The Most Outrageous Record Label In America* (Middletown, Connecticut: Wesleyan University Press, 2012)

Val Wilmer, *As Serious As Your Life* (Westport, Connecticut: Lawrence Hill, 1980)

— *Mama Said There'd Be Days Like This: My Life In The Jazz World* (London: Women's Press, 1989)

Peter Niklas Wilson, *Spirits Rejoice! Albert Ayler Und Seine Botschaft* (Hofheim: Wolke, 1996)

— *Spirits Rejoice! Albert Ayler And His Message* (Hofheim: Wolke, 2022)

Ben Young, *Dixonia* (Westport: Greenwood, 1990)

ARTICLES EXCERPTED FROM BOOKS

Amiri Baraka, 'You Think This Is About You?' in *Albert Ayler: Holy Ghost* (Austin, Texas: Revenant Records, 2004)

— [as LeRoi Jones] 'The Need For A Cultural Base To Civil Rites & Bpower Mooments,' in *Raise, Race Rays Raze: Essays Since 1965* (New York: Random House, 1971) and in Floyd B. Barbour (ed.), *The Black Power Revolt: A Collection Of Essays* (Boston: Porter Sargent, 1968)

Bob Blumenthal, 'Albert Ayler,' in John Swenson (ed.), *The Rolling Stone Jazz Record Guide* (New York: Random House, 1992)

Walter Bruyninckx, 'Ayler, Albert' and 'Ayler, Donald,' in *60 Years Of Recorded Jazz* (Mechelen, Belgium: Bruyninckx, 1979)

Daniel Caux, 'Apparitions Of Albert The Great In Paris And Saint-Paul de Vence,' in *Albert Ayler: Holy Ghost* (Austin, Texas: Revenant Records, 2004)

— 'Qui a tué Albert Ayler?' in Franck Médioni, *Albert Ayler: Témoignages sur un Holy Ghost* (Marseille: Le mot et le reste, 2010)

Marc Chaloin, 'Albert Ayler In Europe: 1959–62' in *Albert Ayler: Holy Ghost* (Austin, Texas: Revenant Records, 2004)

Christopher A.Colombi, Jr., 'Jazz' in David D. Van Tassell and John J. Grabowski, *Encyclopedia Of Cleveland History* (Bloomington: Indiana University Press, 1987)

Diedrich Diederichsen, 'Jazz As Concept Art,' in Wolfram Knauer (ed.), *Jazz Goes Pop Goes Jazz. Der Jazz Und Sein Gespaltenes Verhältnis Zur Popularmusik* (Hofheim: Wolke, 2006)

Gary Giddins, 'Titans Of The Tenor,' in Sean Manning (ed.), *The Show I'll Never Forget: 50 Writers Relive Their Most Memorable Concertgoing Experience* (Cambridge: Da Capo Press, 2007)

Wolfram Knauer, 'Healing Force Of The Universe? Warum Der Free Jazz Zahm Wurde,' in Wolfram Knauer (ed.), *Jazz Goes Pop Goes Jazz. Der Jazz Und Sein Gespaltenes Verhältnis Zur Popularmusik* (Hofheim: Wolke, 2006)

'Michael Snow,' in *17 Canadian Artists: A Protean View* (Vancouver: The Vancouver Art Gallery, 1976)

Ingrid Monson, 'Jazz Improvisation,' in Mervyn Cooke and David Horn, *The Cambridge Companion To Jazz* (Cambridge: Cambridge University Press, 2002)

Peter Morris, 'Snow Place For A Lady: The Early Films Of Michael Snow,' in Louis Dompierre, *Walking Woman Works: Michael Snow 1961–67. New Represented Art And Its Uses* (Kingston, Ontario: Agnes Therington Art Centre, 1983)

Stuart Nicholson, 'Fusions And Crossovers,' in Mervyn Cooke and David Horn, *The Cambridge Companion To Jazz* (Cambridge: Cambridge University Press, 2002)

Harvey Pekar and Gary G. Dumm, 'Albert Ayler And Joe Lovano: A Study In Contrasts,' in *American Splendor: Our Movie Year* (New York: Ballantine Books, 2004)

David Toop, 'Frames Of Freedom: Improvisation, Otherness And The Limits Of Spontaneity,' in Rob Young (ed.), *Undercurrents: The Hidden Wiring Of Modern Music* (London: Continuum, 2002)

Val Wilmer, 'Cobbs, Call,' in Barry Kernfeld (ed.), *New Grove Dictionary Of Jazz* (Oxford: Oxford University Press, 2003)

Ben Young, 'Tracks,' 'Whence,' and 'Witnesses,' in *Albert Ayler: Holy Ghost* (Austin, Texas: Revenant Records, 2004)

Ben Young, Tom Greenwood, and Matt Konttinen, 'Sidemen,' in *Albert Ayler: Holy Ghost* (Austin, Texas: Revenant Records, 2004)

PERIODICALS

Simon Adams, '[Review of] *In Memory Of Albert Ayler,' Jazz Journal International* vol. 45, no. 12 (December 1992)

'Advertisement,' *OrkesterJournalen* vol. 30, no.10 (October 1962)

'Advertisement,' *Jazz Hot* no. 225 (November 1966)

'L'album anniversaire: Albert Ayler,' *Jazz Magazine* no. 334 (December 1984)

'Albert Ayler 1936–1970,' *Jazz & Pop* vol. 10, no. 2 (February 1971)

'Albert Ayler Dead,' *Melody Maker* no. 45 (December 12, 1970)

'Albert Ayler Dead: Drowning,' *Rolling Stone* (December 24, 1970)

'Albert Ayler Dies,' *Down Beat* vol. 38, no. 1 (January 7, 1971)

'Albert Ayler In Die Hall Of Fame Gewahlt,' *Jazz Podium* vol. 32, no. 10 (October 1983)

'Albert Ayler Program,' *Scene* (Cleveland) vol. 2, no. 14 (April 8–14, 1971)

Chris Albertson, '[Review of] *Love Cry,' Stereo Review* vol. 57, no. 4 (April 1992)

Clifford Allen, 'Juma Sultan,' *The New York City Jazz Record* no. 126 (October 2012)

— 'On ESP,' *Paris Transatlantic* (April 2005)

Pascal Anquetil, 'Nuits de la Fondation Maeght,' *Jazz Magazine* no. 674 (July 2015)

— 'Albert Ayler,' *Jazz Magazine* no. 685 (July 2016)

Derek Ansell, '[Review of] *Love Cry,' Jazz Journal International* vol. 45, no. 7 (July 1992)

Ronald Atkins, 'Albert Ayler At L.S.E.,' *Jazz Monthly* vol. 12, no. 11 (January 1967)

— 'Albert Ayler Tuned Out,' *Jazz Journal* vol. 69, no. 8 (August 2016)

— '[Review of] *Nuits de la Fondation Maeght, Vol. 1,' Jazz & Blues* vol. 3, no. 3 (June 1973)

Jeff Atterton, 'Ayler, Coleman Quartets Play For Trane Funeral,' *Melody Maker* (August 5, 1967)

Albert Ayler, '26 jazzmen nouveaux A la question' *Jazz Magazine* no. 165 (December 1965)

— 'Albert Ayler,' *IT* (13 March 1967)

— 'To Mr. Jones—I Had A Vision,' *The Cricket* no. 4 (1969)

Duck Baker, 'ESP: Even Now You Never Heard Such Sounds,' *Coda* no. 325 (January 2005)

— '[Review of] *Spiritual Unity (50th Anniversary Edition),' The Absolute Sound* no. 250 (February 2015)

— 'A Whole Lot Of Cannonball, Fantasy 20-Bit Remasters, V.S.O.P., Albert Ayler's New Leaf,' *Coda* no. 325 (January 2005)

W.A. Baldwin, 'Albert Ayler: Conservative Revolution? (1)' *Jazz Monthly* vol. 13, no. 7 (September 1967)

— 'Albert Ayler: Conservative Revolution? (2),' *Jazz Monthly* vol. 13, no. 8 (October 1967)

— 'Albert Ayler: Conservative Revolution? (3),' *Jazz Monthly* vol. 13, no. 9 (November 1967)

— 'Albert Ayler: Conservative Revolution? (4)' *Jazz Monthly* vol. 13, no. 11 (January 1968)

— 'Albert Ayler: Conservative Revolution? (5)' *Jazz Monthly* vol. 13, no. 12 (February 1968)

Whitney Balliet, 'Musical Events: Jazz Concerts,' *New Yorker* vol. 39, no. 47 (January 11, 1964)

Dan Barbiero, 'The Village Concerts: Al Ayler At His Best,' *The Hoya* (January 26, 1979)

Paul de Barros, '[Review of] *Lörrach, Paris 1966,' DownBeat* vol. 69, no. 10 (October 2002)

Alan Barton, 'The Ayler Enigma,' *Jazz Journal* vol. 20, no. 2 (February 1967)

James Beaudreau, '[Review of] *The Copenhagen Tapes* [and] *Nuits de Fondation Maeght,' Signal To Noise* vol. 29 (Spring 2003)

Alan Beckett, 'Ayler At LSE,' *IT* 4 (November 28–December, 1966)

Daniel Berger, 'Les Frères Ayler et la tradition destructive,' *Jazz Hot* 222 (July–August 1966)

— '[Review of] *Spirits Rejoice,' Jazz Hot* (1966/67)

Ralph Berton, 'Conversations With Bernard Stollman,' *Sounds And Fury* vol. 2, no. 2 (April 1966)

Dan Bilawsky, 'Healing Force: The Songs Of Albert Ayler,' *Jazz Improv* vol. 8, no. 10 (December 2007)

Billboard Campus Attractions (March 28, 1970)

Jean-Pierre Binchet, '[Review of] *Love Cry,' Jazz Magazine* no. 157 (July/August 1968)

'Bitstream,' *The Wire* no. 286 (December 2007)

Jason Bivins, '[Review of] *Live On The Riviera,' Cadence* vol. 40, no. 1. (January–March 2014)

R. Blome, '[Review of] *New York Eye And Ear Control,' Sounds* no. 3 (1967)

Chris Bohn, '[Review of] *My Name Is Albert Ayler,' The Wire* no. 266 (April 2006)

Sven Boija, '*Albert Ayler: Holy Ghost,' Orchester Journalen* vol. 73, no. 1 (January 2005)

Brian J. Bowe, '*Albert Ayler: Holy Ghost,' Creem Magazine* (November 2004)

Richard Brody, 'My Name Is Albert Ayler,' *The New Yorker* (November 12, 2007)

— 'His Name Is Albert Ayler,' *The New Yorker* (January 19, 2011)

— 'The Jubilant Glory Of Albert Ayler's *Revelations*,' *The New Yorker* (April 26, 2022)

Stuart Broomer, 'Albert Ayler, Breakfast In Montreal … A Reflection,' *Coda* 272 (March–April 1997)

— '[Review of] *Spiritual Unity*,' *Coda* vol. 6, no. 5 (December 1965–January 1966)

Stuart Broomer and Mike Hames, 'An Albert Ayler Discography,' *Coda* 272 (March–April 1997)

Yves Buin, 'Le musée imaginaire d'Albert Ayler,' *Jazz Hot* no. 34/243 (1968)

Pat Buzby, '[Review of] *New York Eye & Ear Control*,' *Signal To Noise* no. 38 (Summer 2005)

Philippe Carles, 'La bataille d'Ayler n'est pas finie,' *Jazz Magazine* 185 (January 1971)

— 'Disques du mois,' *Jazz Magazine* 190 (June–July 1971)

— '[Review of] *Albert Ayler: Holy Ghost—Rare And Unissued Recordings (1962–1970)*,' *Jazz Magazine* no. 552 (October 2004)

— '[Review of] *The Last Album*,' *Jazz Magazine* no. 191 (August 1971)

— '[Review of] *Spirits Rejoice*,' *Jazz Magazine* no. 135 (October 1966)

— 'Tribute To Albert Ayler Live At The Dynamo,' *Jazz Magazine* no. 609 (December 2009)

Philippe Carles and Jean-Louis Comolli, 'Les secrets d'Albert le Grand,' *Jazz Magazine* 142 (May 1967)

Brian Case, '[Reviews of] *Albert Ayler At Slug's Saloon Vol. 1 & 2*, *Albert Ayler Lörrach/Paris*, [and] *Swing Low Sweet Spiritual*,' *The Wire* no. 3 (March 1983)

— 'Special Ayler,' *Melody Maker* no. 56 (January 31, 1981)

Jacqueline Caux and Daniel Caux, 'Les secrets du Grand Albert,' *Jazz Magazine* no. 552 (October 2004)

— 'My Name Is … Albert Ayler,' *Chroniques de l'art vivant* XVII (February 1970)

— 'The Road To Freedom,' *The Wire* no. 227 (January 2003)

Eugene Chadbourne, '[Review of] *Albert Ayler Live At St. Paul De Vence*,' *Coda* vol. 11, no. 10 (June–July 1974)

Marc Chaloin, 'Bill Folwell: An Interview With Marc Chaloin,' *Point Of Departure: An Online Music Journal* (2019)

A.Chenal, 'Hommage a Albert Ayler,' *Jazz Magazine* no. 402 (March 1991)

Aaron Cohen, '[Review of] *Spiritual Unity*,' *Coda* no. 252 (November–December 1993)

Byron Coley, '[Review of] *Stockholm/Berlin 1966*,' *The Wire* no. 334 (December 2011)

Graham Colombé, '[Review of] *New Grass*,' *Jazz Journal International*, vol. 59, no. 8 (August 2006)

Jean-Louis Comolli, '[Review of] *Albert Ayler In Greenwich Village*,' *Jazz Magazine* no. 162 (January 1969)

Thomas Conrad, 'Earshot Jazz Festival,' *JazzTimes*

— 'Playing It With Love,' *JazzTimes* vol. 37, no. 10 (December 2007)

Richard Cook, 'My Name Is Albert Ayler,' *The Wire* no. 58–59 (December 1988–January 1989)

Jack Cooke, 'Great Lost Recordings,' *The Wire* 106/107 (December 1992–January 1993)

— '[Review of] *New Grass*,' *Jazz Monthly* no. 177 (November 1969)

— '[Review of] *Nuits de la Fondation Maeght, Vol. 2*,' *Jazz & Blues* III/3 (June 1973)

— '[Review of] *Ghosts*,' *Jazz Monthly* vol. 16, no. 10 (January 1970)

— '[Review of] *Music Is The Healing Force Of The Universe*,' *Jazz Monthly* 186 (August 1970)

— '[Review of] *Spirits*,' *Jazz Monthly* vol. 12, no. 1 (March 1966)

John Corbett, 'Ayler's Wings/Multipli,' *DownBeat* vol. 59, no. 11 (November 1992)

— 'Flowers For Albert: Reconsidering The Legacy Of Albert Ayler,' *DownBeat* vol. 71, no. 10 (October 2004)

— 'Gone: Aylers Letzte Tage: Isolierte Stille, Verschwörungs-Theorien, Eine Kosmiche Subversion, Unwahrheit Inmitten von Friedhofsruhe [I],' *Jazz Podium* (February 2020)

— 'Gone: Aylers Letzte Tage Teil 2: Coltrane Und Dessen Tod, Die Vermissten Und Verschundenen, Henry Grimes, Giuseppe Logan, Und Charles Gayle Zum Beispiel,' *Jazz Podium* (March 2020)

— 'Pulseology: Down In The Basement With Milford Graves,' *DownBeat* vol. 69, no. 2 (February 2002)

Alain Corneau, '[Review of] *Bells*,' *Jazz Hot* (1966)

Peter Cousaert, 'Albert Ayler: Get Back To The Melody,' *White Heat* (September 2006)

David Cristol, *'Bells/Prophecy (Expanded Edition)*,' *Jazz Magazine* no. 681 (March 2016)

Ian Crosbie, 'Didn't They Ramble,' *Jazz Journal* (London, England) vol. 24 (August 1971)

Stanley Crouch, 'Albert Ayler: Talking In Tongues,' *Soho Weekly News* vol. 3, no. 18 (February 5, 1976)

— 'Coltrane Derailed,' *Jazz Times* vol. 32, no. 7 (September 2002)

Wolfgang Dauner, '[Review of] *Spiritual Unity*,' *Jazz Podium* vol. 14, no. 10 (October 1965)

Sam Davies, 'The Art Of The Improvisers,' *Sight & Sound* vol. 17, no. 3 (March 2007)

Francis Davis, 'The Fire That Time,' *Village Voice*, vol. 49, no. 41 (October 5, 2004)

— '[Review of] *Albert Ayler Lörrach/Paris 1966*,' *Jazz Times* vol. 12 (October 1982)

'Die Like A Dog: Fragments Of Music, Life And Death Of Albert Ayler/Never Too Late But Always Early,' *The Wire* no. 345 (November 2012)

Bill Donaldson, '[Review of] *The Copenhagen Tapes*,' *Cadence* vol. 29 (June 2003)

Kenny Dorham, 'Two Views Of Three Outer Views,' *DownBeat* vol. 32, no. 15 (July 15, 1965)

'Down By The Sea,' *Jazziz* vol. 33, no. 6 (Summer 2016)

David Dupont, 'Mind Games/Tribute To Albert Ayler: Live At The Dynamo. Live In Nickelsdorf,' *Cadence* vol. 36, no. 7–9 (July–September 2010)

— 'Roswell Rudd Interview II,' *Cadence* vol. 18, no. 11 (November 1992)

Alex Dutilh, '[Review of] *The Village Concerts*,' *Jazz Hot* (May 1978)

— '[Review of] *Witches & Devils*,' *Jazz Hot* no. 287 (October 1972)

John Elsasser, 'The Life Of A Free Jazz Legend,' *Magnet* vol. 16, no. 78 (January 2008)

Gudrun Endress, 'Albert Ayler: We Play Peace,' *Jazz Podium* (October 1966)

Gilbert M.Erskine, 'Two Views Of The New Wave,' *DownBeat* vol. 33, no. 2 (January 27, 1966)

Gene Feehan, 'Black Baseball To Black Music,' *DownBeat* vol. 40 (March 15, 1973)

Gordon Hilton Fick, 'Blues For Albert Ayler,' *Cadence* vol. 38, no. 4 (October–December 2012)

Milo Fine, '[Review of] *Albert Ayler*,' *Cadence* vol. 18, no. 5 (May 1992)

— '[Review of] *In Memory Of Albert Ayler*,' *Cadence* vol. 17, no. 8 (August 1991)

Mike Fitzgerald, 'Into Thin Air,' *Signal To Noise* XXVIII (Winter 2003)

'Flashes,' *Jazz Magazine* no. 186 (February 1971)

Colin Fleming, 'Copenhagen 1964,' *JazzTimes* vol. 47, no. 7 (September 2017)

Chris Flicker, 'A la recherche du temps perdu,' *Jazz Hot* (January 1971)

Phil Freeman, 'Albert Ayler Festival,' *The Wire* no. 320 (October 2010)

— 'Black Fire! New Spirits! Radical And Revolutionary Jazz In The USA 1957–1872 / 90 Degrees Of Shade: Hot Jump-Up Island Sounds From The Caribbean,' *The Wire* no. 370 (December 2014)

David Fricke, 'Speaking In Tongues,' *Mojo* no. 132 (November 2004)

Gary A. Galo and Vincent Pelote, '*Holy Ghost*,' *ARSC Journal* vol. 36, no. 1 (Spring 2005)

Peter Gamble, '*Spiritual Unity*,' *Jazz Journal* vol. 67, no. 11 (November 2014)

James Gavin, 'The Most Democratic Music? Homophobia In Jazz,' *Jazz Times* vol. 31, no. 10 (December 2001)

Alain Gerber, '[Review of] *New York Eye And Ear Control*,' *Jazz Magazine* no. 141 (April 1967)

Gary Giddins, 'The Night Coltrane Terrorized Philharmonic Hall,' *Village Voice* (December 1, 1975)

— 'Fresh Flowers For Albert,' *Jazz Times* vol. 34 (November 2004)

— 'Post-War Jazz: An Arbitrary Road Map,' *Village Voice* Jazz Supplement (June 11, 2002)

Ira Gitler, 'Newport Echoes,' *DownBeat* (September 7, 1967)

Laurent Goddet, 'Noah Howard From New Orleans,' *Jazz Hot* (April 1976)

Jon Goldman, 'The Albert Ayler Sextet In Concert—Cleveland—February 4, 1967,' *Coda* vol. 8, no. 1 (April–May 1967)

— '[Review of] *Don Ayler In Florence 1981*,' *Coda* 187 (December 1, 1982)

Jon Goldman and Martin Davidson, 'Albert Ayler Life And Recordings,' *Cadence* vol. 1, no. 4 (April 1976)

'Gossip (Note From Cleveland),' *The Cricket* (1969)

Kurt Gottschalk, '[Review of] *Spiritual Unity*,' *Signal To Noise* no. 38 (Summer 2005)

Mark C. Gridley, 'Misconceptions In Linking Free Jazz With The Civil Rights Movement,' *College Music Symposium* vol. 47 (2007)

Pat Griffiths, 'The Silva Lining,' *Melody Maker* (May 15, 1971)

Paul Gros-Claude, '[Review of] *La saga héroïque d'Albert Ayler*,' *Jazz Magazine* no. 192 (September 1971)

Willie Gschwendner, '[Review of]Albert Ayler *The Hilversum Session*,' *Jazz Podium* vol. 41 (February 1992)

Evan Haga, 'Our Prayer,' *JazzTimes* vol. 37, no. 20 (December 2007)

— 'You Have To Be Proud Of Having This History: An Interview With Sunny Murray,' *JazzTimes* vol. 42, no. 9 (November 2012)

Paul Haines, 'Ayler, Peacock & Murray: You And The Night And The Music,' *Coda* no. 378 (November–December 2004)

Mike Hames, 'The Death Of Albert Ayler,' *Wire* 6 (Spring 1984)

Max Harrison, 'Letter,' *Jazz Monthly* vol. 15, no. 1 (March 1969)

— '[Review of] *Sonny's Time Now*,' *Jazz Monthly* vol. 14, no. 3 (May 1968)

— '[Review of] *Spirits Rejoice!*,' *Jazz Monthly* vol. 12, no. 11 (January 1967)

Ed Hazell, 'Beaver Harris,' *Modern Drummer* 13 (November 1989)

— 'Free Spirit: Rediscovering Albert Ayler,' *Boston Phoenix* II/4 (December 4–10, 1998)

Don Heckman, 'A Perspective In Revolution,' *DownBeat* vol. 33, no. 21 (October 20, 1966)

Alan Heineman, '[Review of] *New Grass*,' *DownBeat* vol. 36, no. 15 (July 24, 1969)

Mike Hennessey, 'Cherry's Catholicity: The Kalideoscopic View Of Jazz,' *DownBeat* vol. 33, no. 15 (July 28, 1966)

Nat Hentoff, 'The New Jazz,' *Vogue* (February 1, 1966)

— 'The Truth Is Marching In,' *DownBeat* vol. 33, no. 23 (November 17, 1966)

— 'The Truth Is Marching In,' *DownBeat* vol. 76, no. 5 (May 2009)

Scott Herha and Matthew Sumera, '*Holy Ghost*,' *One Final Note: Jazz & Improvised Music Webzine* (November 2004)

Tony Herrington, '[Review of] *Albert Ayler. Holy Ghost: Rare & Unissued Recordings (1962–70)*,' *The Wire* no. 249 (November 2004)

'Hie Logan Da Ayler: Gesprach um das New Thing,' *Jazz Podium* vol. 14, no. 7 (July 1965)

'High Wire: My Name Is Albert Ayler,' *Coda* no. 273 (May–June 1997)

Aaron Hillis, 'My Name Is Albert Ayler,' *The Village Voice* vol. 45, (November 7, 2007)

George Hoefer, '[Review of] Albert Ayler Village Theater, New York City,' *DownBeat* vol. 34, no. 10 (May 18, 1967)

— 'Caught: Ayler At The Village,' *DownBeat* vol. 66, no. 7 (July 1999)

Larry Hollis, '[Review of] *Albert Ayler Live In Lörrach, Germany, And Paris, France, 1966*,' *Cadence* vol. 16, no. 11 (November 1990)

Walter Horn, '[Review of] *The Hilversum Session*,' *Cadence* vol. 24, no. 11 (November 1998)

Bob Houston, 'Ayler: What Will Mrs W Make Of All This?' *Melody Maker* (November 2, 1966)

Robert Iannapollo, '[Review of] *Albert Ayler In Greenwich Village*,' *Cadence* vol. 16, no. 1 (January 1990)

— '[Review of] *Love Cry*,' *Cadence* vol. 18, no. 5 (May 1992)

Dick Idestam-Almquist, '[Review of] *The First Recordings*,' *OrkesterJournalen* vol. 37, no. 10 (October 1969)

Michael James, 'Don Cherry In Amsterdam,' *Jazz Monthly* vol. 10, no. 11 (January 1965)

— '[Review of] *New Wave In Jazz*,' *Jazz Monthly* (April 1966)

— '[Review of] *Witches & Devils*,' *Melody Maker* (February 24, 1979)

Edward Jarvis, 'Albert Ayler,' *OrkesterJournalen* vol. 55, no. 9 (September 1987)

— 'Albert Ayler,' *OrkesterJournalen* vol. 55, no. 8 (July–August 1987)

Ted Joans, 'AA! AA? Yeah, AA!,' *IT* no. 5 (December 12–26, 1966)

— 'Alphabet Ayler,' *Jazz Magazine* 189 (May 1971)

— 'Spiritual Unity: Albert Ayler,' *Coda* vol. 10, no. 2 (July–August 1971)

LeRoi Jones, 'Apple Cores: Strong Voices In Today's Black Music,' *DownBeat* vol. 33, no. 3 (February 10, 1966); reprinted in Amari Baraka, *Black Music*

— 'Caught In The Act,' *DownBeat* (February 27, 1964)

— 'Jazz And The White Critic: A Provocative Essay On The Situation Of Jazz Criticism' *DownBeat* (August 15, 1963)

Max Jones, 'Avant Garde? Are There Enough Fans For Concert Dates?' *Melody Maker* (July 23, 1966)

Rudie Kagie, 'Avonturen In De New Thing,' *Jazz Bulletin* 83 (June 2012)

Ashley Kahn, 'The House That Trane Built: The Impulse Records Story,' *JazzTimes* vol. 32, no. 7 (September 2002)

Larry Kart, '[Review of] *Music Is The Healing Force Of The Universe*,' *DownBeat* vol. 37, no. 20 (October 15, 1970)

David Keenan, 'The Primer,' *The Wire* no. 208 (June 2001)

Chris Kelsey, '[Review of] *Albert Ayler: Slug's Saloon: May 1, 1966*,' *JazzTimes* vol. 36, no. 3 (April 2006)

— '[Review of] *The Hilversum Session*,' *JazzTimes* vol. 38, no. 2 (March 2008)

Rupert Kettle, 'The New Jazz,' *The East Village Other* (15 March 1966)

Wolfram Knauer, '*Albert Ayler: Holy Ghost: Rare And Unissued Recordings*,' *Jazz Podium* vol. 53, no. 11 (November 2004)

Reiner Kobe, 'European Radio Studio Recordings 1964,' *Jazz Podium* vol. 65, no. 9 (September 2016)

— '[Review of] *Stockholm/Berlin 1966*,' *Jazz Podium* vol. 60, no. 12 (December 2011/ January 2012)

— '[Review of] *Lörrach/Paris 1966*.' *Jazz Podium* vol. 63, no. 4 (April 2014)

— '[Review of] *Spirits Rejoice! Albert Ayler und Seine Botschaft* von Peter Niklas Wilson,' *Jazz Podium* vol. 46 (January 1997)

Frank Kofsky, 'An Interview With Albert And Donald Ayler,' *Jazz & Pop* vol. 7, no. 9 (Sept. 1968)

— 'John Coltrane And The Jazz Revolution: The Case Of Albert Ayler, Part One' *JAZZ* vol. 5, no. 9 (1965)

— 'John Coltrane And The Jazz Revolution: The Case Of Albert Ayler. Part Two,' *JAZZ* vol. 5, no. 10 (1965)

— 'Revolution, Coltrane And The Avant-Garde, Part I,' *JAZZ* vol. 5, no. 7 (July 1965)

— 'Revolution, Coltrane And The Avant-Garde, Part II,' *JAZZ* vol. 5, no. 8 (August 1965)

Guy Kopelewicz, 'Autumn In New York,' *Jazz Hot* no. 215 (December 1965)

Kiyoshi Koyama, 'Interview With Albert Ayler,' *Swing Journal* (October 1970)

John Kruth, 'The Healing Force Of The Universe: Albert Ayler's Life And Legacy (34 Years Hence),' *Signal To Noise* no. 36 (Winter 2005)

— 'One Nation Underground,' *Signal To Noise* no. 38 (Summer 2005)

Bernard Lairet, 'Albert Ayler Memorial Concert,' *Jazz Hot* 273 (June 1971)

— 'Albert Ayler: The Holy Ghost Is Dead,' *Scene* (Cleveland) (December 10–16, 1970)

— 'Jazz,' *Scene* (Cleveland) (April 22–28, 1971)

Steve Lake, '[Review of] *Vibrations*,' *Melody Maker* 49 (July 27, 1974)

Art Lange, 'Ayler Resurrected, A Look Into Revenant's *Albert Ayler Holy Ghost*,' *Coda* no. 378 (November–December 2004)

— '[Review of] *Albert Ayler Live In Greenwich Village: The Complete Impulse! Recordings*,' *The Wire* no. 178 (December 1998)

— '[Review of] *The Hilversum Session*,' *Coda* no. 177 (February 1, 1981)

Daniel Lazro, 'Ayler 66,' *Jazz Magazine*

Gayle Lemke, *The Art Of The Fillmore* (Petaluma, CA: Acid Test Productions, 1997)

Jean Levin, '[Review of] *Spirits Rejoice*,' *Jazz Magazine* no. 222 (May 1974)

Robert Levin, 'Some Observations On The State Of The Scene,' *Sounds And Fury* vol. 1 (July–August 1965; retracted in December 1965)

— 'The Third World,' *Jazz & Pop* vol. 10, no. 1 (January 1971)

John Lewis, 'My Name Is Albert Ayler,' *Sight & Sound* vol. 17, no. 4 (April 2007)

John Litweiler, 'The Legacy Of Albert Ayler,' *DownBeat* vol. 38, no. 7 (April 1, 1971)

— '[Review of] *Albert Ayler Vol. 1* [and] *Albert Ayler No. 2*,' *DownBeat* vol. 39, no. 12 (June 22, 1972)

— '[Review of] *Spirits Rejoice*,' *Sounds* 2 (1967)

— 'Charles Tyler,' *DownBeat* vol. 51, no. 5 (May 1984)

— '[Review of] *The Hilversum Sessions*,' *DownBeat* vol. 49, no. 2 (February 1982)

Graham Lock, 'Bill Dixon,' *JazzTimes* vol. 31, no. 4 (May 2001)

Don Locke, 'The New Conservatism,' *Jazz Monthly* vol. 14, no. 3 (May 1968)

Allen Lowe, '[Review of] *Albert Smiles With Sunny*,' *Cadence* vol. 22, no. 9 (September 1996)

Godehard Lutz, 'Albert Ayler Quartett,' *Jazz Podium* vol. 66, no. 9 (September 2017)

Kerstan Mackness, 'My Name Is Albert Ayler,' *Time Out London* no. 1903 (February 7–13, 2007)

Mort Maizlish, '[Review of] *Spiritual Unity*,' *Sounds And Fury* vol. 2, no. 2 (April 1966)

Lucien Malson, 'Sur quelques oeuvres contemporanies,' *Jazz Magazine* no. 176 (March 1970)

Marshall Marrotte, 'Henry Grimes: The *Signal To Noise* Interview,' *Signal To Noise* XXVIII (Winter 2003)

— 'Surviving Albert Ayler (bassist Henry Grimes),' *The Wire* no. 227 (January 2003)

François de Marsan, '[Review of] *Witches & Devils*,' *Jazz Magazine* no. 206 (December 1972)

Terry Martin, '[Review of] *Bells*,' *Jazz Monthly* vol. 11, no. 10 (December 1965)

— '[Review of] *My Name Is Albert Ayler*,' *Jazz Monthly* vol. 12, no. 1 (March 1966)

Bill Mathieu, '[Review of] *My Name Is Albert Ayler*,' *DownBeat* vol. 32, no. 24 (November 18, 1965)

— '[Review of] *Spiritual Unity*,' *DownBeat* vol. 72, no. 1 (January 2005)

— 'Two Views Of The New Wave,' *DownBeat* vol. 33, no. 2 (27 January 1966)

— 'Two Views Of Three Outer Views,' *DownBeat* vol. 32, no. 15 (15 July 1965)

Dave McElfresh, 'The Truth Is Marching In,' *Coda* 272 (March–April 1997)

Barry McRae, 'Albert Ayler: An Obituary,' *Jazz Journal* vol. 24, no. 2 (February 1971)

— 'Avant Courier: Message From Albert,' *Jazz Journal* vol. 25, no. 9 (September 1972)

— 'Avant Courier,' *Jazz Journal* vol. 26, no. 3 (March 1973)

— '[Review of] *Albert Ayler Live In Greenwich Village*,' *Jazz Journal International* vol. 52, no. 5 (May 1999)

— '[Review of] *Jesus*,' *Jazz Journal International* vol. 45, no. 6 (June 1982)

— '[Review of] *Lörrach/Paris 1966*,' *Jazz Journal International* vol. 36, no. 1 (January 1983)

— '[Reviews of] *Love Cry* [and] *The Last Album*,' *Jazz Journal* vol. 65, no. 1 (January 2012)

— '[Review of] *The First Recordings* / Albert Ayler (Sonet SNTCD 604),' *Jazz Journal International* vol. 44, no. 7 (July 1991)

— '[Review of] *The Hilversum Sessions*,' *Jazz Journal* vol. 34, no. 5 (May 1981)

— '[Review of] *The Last Album*,' *Jazz Journal* vol. 24 (December 1971)

— '[Review of] *Swing Low, Sweet Spiritual*,' *Jazz Journal International* vol. 37, no. 1 (January 1984)

Franck Médioni, Alexandre Pierrepont, and Gérard Rouy, 'Albert Ayler Message Reçu,' *Jazz Magazine* no. 462 (September 1996)

Bill Meyer, 'Endless Possibilities,' *DownBeat* vol. 81, no. 4 (April 2014)

Thomas Millroth, 'Ayler's Dilemma,' *OrkesterJournalen* vol. 40, no. 11 (November 1972)

Richard Mortifoglio, 'Albert Ayler As Angel Of History,' *Village Voice* (August 7, 1978)

Dan Morgenstern, 'Caught In The Act,' *DownBeat* vol. 32, no. 15 (15 July 1965)

— 'Sense Of Fairness,' *DownBeat* vol. 82, no. 10 (October 2015)

— 'Titans Of The Tenor Sax,' *DownBeat* vol. 33, no. 7 (April 7, 1966)

Dan Morgenstern and Ira Gitler, 'The Newport Jazz Festival,' *DownBeat* vol. 34, no. 16 (August 10, 1967)

Brian Morton, 'Dear Old Stockholm,' *Jazz Journal* vol. 67, no. 6 (June 2014)

— 'Flowers For Albert,' *Nation* vol. 279, no. 17 (November 22 ,2004)

— 'The Story Of Albert Ayler / *Spiritual Unity*,' *The Wire* no. 366 (August 2014)

Jean-Pierre Moussaron, '[Review of] *Live In Lörrach/Paris 1966*,' *Jazz Magazine* no. 393 (May 1990)

Lars Movin, 'My Name Is Albert Ayler,' *Jazz Special* (Denmark)

Charles Shaar Murray, 'Shots From The Hip,' *New Musical Express* (October 23, 1976)

Mitch Myers, '[Review of] *Nuits de la Fondation Maeght 1970*,' *DownBeat* vol. 70, no. 7 (July 2003)

Larry Nai, 'Alan Silva Interview,' *Cadence* vol. 25, no. 7 (July 1999)

— 'Marzette Watts Interview,' *Cadence* vol. 24, no. 8 (August 1998)

— 'Noah Howard Interview,' *Cadence* vol. 24, no. 1 (January 1998)

Larry Neal, 'New Grass,' *The Cricket* (1969)

Gérard Noel, 'L'art admirable d'Albert le temraire,' *Jazz Hot* (January 1971)

John Norris, 'Three Notes With Albert Ayler,' *Coda* vol. 7, no. 1 (April–May 1966)

'Obituaries,' *Cadence* vol. 34, issues 1–3 (January–March 2008)

Stéphane Ollivieri, 'Albert Ayler et Sun Ra sont d'extraordinaires voyageurs interstellaires,' *Jazz Magazine* no. 685 (July 2016)

— 'Ayler Records,' *Jazz Magazine* no. 625 (May 2011)

'Passed Away,' *Jazz Forum* no. 11 (Spring 1971)

Harvey Pekar,'[Review of] *Spirits Rejoice!*' *DownBeat* vol. 33, no. 18 (September 8, 1966)

Harvey Pekar and Gary Dumm, 'Albert Ayler And Joe Lovano: A Study In Contrasts,' *Cleveland Free Times* vol. 10, no. 38 (June 5–11, 2002)

Joe Pinelli, 'Joy In The New Music,' *Sounds And Fury* vol. 2, no. 2 (April 1966)

Edwin Pouncey, 'Life With The Lions,' *The Wire* no. 227 (January 2003)

— '[Review of] *Lörrach/Paris 1966*,' *The Wire* no. 359 (January 2014)

— 'Trane Was The Father, Pharaoh Was The Son, I Was The Holy Ghost,' *Jazz Special* no. 79 (December 2004–January 2005)

Brian Priestley, '[Review of] *Ghosts*,' *Jazz Monthly* vol. 12, no. 1(March 1966)

— '[Review of] *Spiritual Unity*,' *Jazz Monthly* 179 (January 1970)

— '[Review of] *The First Recordings*,' *Jazz Monthly* vol. 16, no. 7 (Sept. 1970)

Thierry Quenum, '[Reviews of] *Love Cry* [and] *The Last Album*,' *Jazz Magazine* no. 631 (November 2011)

Benoît Quersin, 'Ayler et l'avant garde,' *Jazz Magazine* (February 1965)

Bill Quinn, 'Four Modernists,' *DownBeat* vol. 35, no. 12 (13 June 1968)

— '[Review of] *Sunny's Time Now*,' *DownBeat* vol. 34, no. 6 (23 March 1967)

Erik Raben, 'Albert Ayler På Skiva,' *OrkesterJournalen* XXXV (June 1967)

Boris Rabinowitsch, 'Aylers Musik Utan Fast Struktur,' *OrkesterJournalen* vol. 32, no. 10 (October 1964)

Mac Randall, 'Children Of The Revolution,' *JazzTimes* vol. 46, no. 8 (October 2016)

Jacques Réda, 'Le cri d'Albert Ayler,' *Jazz Magazine* no. 399 (December 1990)

— 'PARIS JAZZ FESTIVAL, 4e VOLET Le Lion, Illinois, et ses amis, Max Roach, Sonny Rollins, Albert Ayler,' *Jazz Magazine* 137 (December 1966)

— '[Review of] *New Grass*,' *Jazz Monthly* no. 171 (1969)

James Renner, 'Strangers In The Night,' *Scene* (Cleveland) vol. 35, no. 13 (March 31–April 6, 2004)

'[Review of] *Albert Smiles With Sonny*,' *Jazz Podium* vol. 45 (May 1996)

'[Review of] *Ghosts*,' *Cadence* vol. 17 (October 1991)

'[Review of] *Going Home*,' *Coda* no. no. 266 (March–April 1996)

'[Review of] *Albert Ayler Live In Greenwich Village: The Complete Impulse Recordings*,' *Coda* no.285 (May/June 1999)

'[Review of] *Lörrach/Paris 1966*,' *DownBeat* vol. 49, (October 1982)

'[Review of] *Love Cry*,' *DownBeat* vol. 59, no. 5 (May 1992)

'[Review of] *Vibrations*,' *Jazz Journal International* vol. 41 (April 1988)

'[Review of] *Witches & Devils*,' *Jazz & Blues* vol. 2 (May 1972)

'[Review of] *Witches & Devils*,' *Melody Maker* vol. 47 (May 25, 1972)

'[Review of] *Les treize morts d'Albert Ayler*,' *JazzMagazine* no. 466 (January 1997)

Philippe Richard and Yves Sportis, 'My Name Is Albert Ayler,' *Jazz Hot* (special issue 2001)

Roger Riggins, '[Review of] *The Hilversum Session*,' *Coda* 177 (February 1, 1981)

Richard J. Rosen, '[Review of] *Holy Ghost*,' *Stereophile* vol. 28, no. 2 (February 2005)

Michael Rosenstein, 'Healing Force: The Songs Of Albert Ayler,' *Cadence* vol. 34, no. 4–6 (April–June 2008)

Richard Rouda, '[Review of] *Music Is The Healing Force Of The Universe*,' *Coda* vol. 9, no. 11 (1971)

Bob Rusch, 'Beaver Harris Stories II,' *Cadence* vol. 9, no. 3 (March 1983)

— 'Beaver Harris Stories III,' *Cadence* vol. 9, no. 4 (April 1983)

— 'Donald Ayler: Interview,' *Cadence* vol. 5, no. 2 (February 1979)

— '[Review of] *Prophecy*,' *Cadence* (March 1976)

— 'Seldon Powell Interview,' *Cadence* (November 1989)

Geert Ryssen, 'Powerjazz à la Ayler,' *Jazzmozaiek* no. 1 (2017)

Jamie Saft, 'Spiritual Jazz,' *JazzTimes* vol. 48, no. 1 (January–February 2018)

Harald Schönstein, 'Die Nachte der Fondation Maeght,' *Jazz Podium* (October 1970)

Martin Schouten, '[Review of] *Spirits Rejoice*,' *Jazz Wereld* (January 1967)

Han Schulte, 'De Schreeuw van Albert Ayler: Notities Over de Belangrijkste Jazz-Improvisatoruit de Periode 1960–1970,' *Jazz Nu 3 Jahr* no. 2 (November 1968)

Jeff Schwartz, 'Healing Force: The Songs Of Albert Ayler,' *American Music* vol. 27, no. 1 (Spring 2009)

'A Severe Case Of Fraud,' *Blues & Soul* no. 998 (June 22, 2007)

Keith Shadwick, 'Rise And Fall Of Albert Ayler,' *Music Maker* (December 1971)

Chris Sheridan, '[Review of] *Lörrach/Paris 1966*,' *Jazz Journal International* vol. 43, no. 6 (June 1990)

— '[Reviews of] *Truth Is Marching In* [and] *Black Revolt*,' vol. 42, no. 7 *Jazz Journal International* (July 1989)

Bill Shoemaker, 'Ayler And Beyond,' *DownBeat* vol. 58, no. 4 (April 1991)

— '[Review of] *Albert Ayler Live In Greenwich Village: The Complete Impulse Recordings*,' *JazzTimes*, vol. 29 (April 1999)

— '*The Holy Ghost:* Bill Shoemaker revisits The Albert Ayler Legacy In The Light Of A New Multi-Disc Archive Of Rare Recordings,' *Jazz Review* no. 62 (November 2004)

François-René Simon, '[Review of] *Stockholm/ Berlin 1966*,' *Jazz Magazine* no. 632 (December 2011)

— 'Ghosts,' *Jazz Magazine* no. 692 (March 2017)

Frank Simpson, 'Pop Saves The Avant Garde,' *Melody Maker* (April 13, 1968)

Heinrich Smejkal, *Info From Saturn* archives no. 190 (February 2002)

Bill Smith, 'The Truth Is Marching In,' *The Wire* no. 3 (Spring 1983)

Frank Smith, 'His Name Is Albert Ayler,' *JAZZ* vol. 4, no. 11 (December 1965)

Daniel Soutif, '[Review of] *Albert Ayler In Greenwich Village*,' *Jazz Magazine* no. 349 (April 1986)

'Statue To A Negro,' *Children's Magazine* (March 16, 1946)

Aaron Steinberg, 'The Ghost In The Guitar: Marc Ribot & Spiritual Unity Explore The Haunted Music Of Albert Ayler,' *JazzTimes* vol. 35 (July–August 2005)

Ira Steingroot, '[Review of] *Vibrations*,' *DownBeat* vol. 42, no. 14 (August 14, 1975)

Ulrich Steinmetzger, 'Blues For Albert Ayler,' *Jazz Podium* vol. 61, no. 9 (September 2012)

Lennart Stenbeck, 'New Orleans—Jazzen och Albert Ayler,' *OrkesterJournalen* vol. 35, no. 5 (May 1967)

Jesse Stewart, 'Improvisation, Representation, And Abstraction In Music And Art: Michael Snow And Jesse Stewart In Conversation, Toronto. 12 November 2005,' *Critical Studies In Improvisation* vol. 3, no. 1 (2007)

Patrick Straram, 'Jazz libre en Quebec,' *Jazz Magazine* 148 (November 1967)

John Sutherland, '[Review of] *Swing Low Sweet Spiritual* / Albert Ayler,' *Coda* 191 (August 1, 1983)

Jean Szlamowicz, '[Review of] *Nuits de la Fondation Maeght 1970*,' *Jazz Hot* no. 635 (December 2006/January 2007)

R. Szyfmanowicz, 'Les Nuits de la Fondation Maeght,' *Jazz Hot* 264 (September 1970)

Derek Taylor, 'A Bouquet For Albert,' *Dusted Magazine* (October 2004)

— '[Review of] *Albert Ayler: Live On The Riviera*,' *Dusted* (April 12, 2005)

James Taylor, '[Review of] *Albert Ayler: Live On The Riviera*,' *All About Jazz* (April 24, 2005)

Barry Tepperman, '[Reviews of] *Witches & Devils* [and] *Prophecy*,' *Coda* 152 (December 1976)

Alain Tercinet, 'Une Vie,' *Jazz Hot* (January 1971)

Samuel Thiebaut, 'Le monde selon Cecil,' *Jazz Magazine* no. 609 (December 2009)

'Time listings: [Review of] *The New Wave In Jazz*],' *Time* (December 17, 1965)

David Toop, 'Sonic Archaeologist: What Unearthly Music Is Harold Budd Exhuming Now?' *The Wire* no. 124 (June 1994)

Mike Trouchon, 'John Tchicai,' *Oppobrium* no. 3

Michael Tucker, '[Review of] *Stockholm, Berlin 1966*,' *Jazz Journal* vol. 65, no. 3 (March 2012)

François Tusques, 'Un soir autour d'Ayler,' *Jazz Magazine* no. 193 (October 1971)

Elisabeth Van der Mei, 'Caught In The Act. Albert Ayler,' *DownBeat* vol. 33, no. 14 (July 14, 1966)

— 'Ayler's Voices,' *Jazzwereld* no. 19 (August 1968)

— 'The New Music,' *Coda* (November–December 1968)

Ole Vestergaard, 'Chords & Dischords: Spirited Reply To Ayler,' *DownBeat* vol. 34, no. 3 (February 9, 1967)

Luciano Viotto, 'Discografia Completa di Albert Ayler,' *Musica Jazz* vol. 46, no. 11 (November 1990)

Jean Wagner, 'Ayler: La cause du peuple,' *Jazz Magazine* 182 (October 1970)

Tim Wall, 'David Murray: The Making Of A Progressive Musician,' *Jazz Research Journal* vol. 1, no. 2 (November 2007)

Dan Warburton, *'Albert Ayler: Holy Ghost,' Paris Transatlantic Magazine* (November 2004)

— 'Expatriate Act,' *Signal To Noise* no. 33 (Spring 2004)

— 'Interview with Sunny Murray,' *Paris Transatlantic*; Abridged version in *Signal To Noise* no. 23 (February 2001)

— 'Invisible Jukebox,' *The Wire* no. 199 (September 2000)

— 'Pour Albert Ayler,' *The Wire* no. 324 (February 2011)

— 'Pour Albert Ayler,' *Paris Transatlantic* (Winter 2010)

Francis Ward, '[Review of] *The New Wave In Jazz*,' *Negro Digest* (September 1966)

Charles Waring, 'Albert Ayler,' *Mojo* no. 271 (June 2016)

— '[Review of] *Albert Ayler Holy Ghost—Rare & Unissued Recordings 1962–1970*,' *Blues & Soul* no. 984 (November 22, 2006)

Ken Waxman, '[Review of] *Live On The Riviera*,' *The New York City Jazz Record* (November 2013)

Norman Weinstein, 'Sunny Murray: The Creation Of Time,' *Village Voice* (August 30, 1988)

Jason Weiss, 'You Have To Be Proud Of Having This History: An Interview with Sunny Murray,' *JazzTimes* vol. 42, no. 9 (November 2012)

Pete Welding, '[Review of] *Albert Ayler In Greenwich Village*,' *DownBeat* vol. 35, no. 14 (July 11, 1968)

—'[Review of] *Bells*,' *DownBeat* vol. 32, no. 20 (September 23, 1965)

Lars Werner, 'Reflektioner Kring Cecil Taylor,' *OrkesterJournalen* vol. 30, no. 10 (October 1962)

— '[Review of] *Something Different*,' *OrkesterJournalen* vol. 31, no. 2 (February 1963)

Spencer Weston, 'Sunny Murray Interview,' *Coda* vol. 5, no. 6 (June 1979)

Kevin Whitehead, 'Death To 'The Avant-Garde,' *Village Voice* XL (March 21, 1995)

— '[Review of] *Swing Low Sweet Spiritual*,' *Cadence* IX (April 1983)

Richard Williams, 'Ayler: Beyond This World,' *Melody Maker* 45 (December 12, 1970)

— '[Review of] *The New Wave In Jazz*,' *Melody Maker* 46 (April 3, 1971)

— 'Running Down The Ayler,' *Melody Maker* vol. 45 (June 20, 1970)

— 'Stollman And ESP: A Label Without Myopia,' *Melody Maker* (June 5, 1971)

Val Wilmer, 'Albert & Don Ayler Talk To Val Wilmer,' *Jazz Monthly* vol. 12, no. 9 (December 1966)

— 'Albert Ayler sur paroles,' *Jazz Magazine* no. 462 (September 1996)

— 'Ayler: Mystic Tenor With A Direct Hot Line To Heaven?' *Melody Maker* (October 15, 1966)

— 'Caught In The Act. Berlin Jazz Festival,' *DownBeat* vol. 34, no. 1 (January 12, 1967)

— 'Controlled Freedom Is The Thing This Year,' *DownBeat* vol. 34, no. 6 (March 23, 1967)

— 'Conversation with Call,' *Melody Maker* (August 21, 1971)

— 'L'Enfer d'Ayler,' *Jazz Magazine* 292 (December 1980)

— 'Free Spirit,' *Mojo* no. 78 (May 2000)

— 'A Legend In His Own Time,' *Time Out* (September 14–20, 1979)

— 'Music As An Escape From The Ghetto,' *Jazz Journal International* vol. 31 (November 1978)

— 'Ronald Shannon Jackson: A Shaman For The 80s,' *DownBeat* vol. 49, no. 8 (August 1982)

— 'Roswell Rudd And The Chartreuse Phantasm,' *The Wire* no. 249 (November 2004)

— 'Spirits Rejoice! Albert & Don Ayler,' *Coda* 272 (March–April 1997)

Peter Niklas Wilson, '[Review of] *Goin' Home*,' *Jazz Podium* vol. 44, no. 1 (January 1995)

— 'Die Sphinx des Free Jazz. Albert Ayler zum 20. Todestag,' *Jazz Podium* vol. 39, no. 12 (December 1990)

— 'Shapes From Notes To Sounds,' *Jazz Podium* vol. 45, no. 10 (October 1996)

D.P. Wirthwein and Bernhard J.J. Prahlwo, 'Suicide By Drowning: A 20 Year Review,' *Journal Of Forensic Sciences* no. 74/1 (2002)

Barry Witherden, 'Live On The Riviera,' *Jazz Journal* vol. 67, no. 5 (May 2014)

Carlo Wolff, 'Ghost Story,' *Scene* (Cleveland) (September 29, 2004)

— 'The '60s, Inside & Out,' *DownBeat* vol. 83, no. 6 (June 2016)

Josef Woodard, 'Jazz & The Abstract Truth,' *Option* (November/December 1989)

Henry Woodfin, 'The New Jazz 2. The Breakthrough,' *Sounds & Fury* (April 1966)

— 'Whither Albert Ayler?' *DownBeat* vol. 33, no. 23 (November 17, 1966)

Scott Yanow, '[Review of] *Holy Ghost*,' *Cadence* vol. 30, no. 10 (October 2004)

— '[Review of] *My Name Is Albert Ayler*,' *Cadence* vol. 23, no. 6 (June 1997)

— '[Review of] *The First Recordings, Volume 2*,' *Cadence* vol. 17, no. 5 (May 1991)

Ben Young, 'Ist Er Das? Neuendecktes Von Jung-Ayler Eine Spurensuche,' *Jazz Podium* (February 2020)

Rafi Zabor and David Breskin, 'Ronald Shannon Jackson: The Future Of Jazz Drumming,' *Musician* (June 1981)

Stefano Zenni, 'Il Testamento di Ayler,' *Musica Jazz* vol. 48, no. 5 (May 1992)

Paul D. Zimmerman and Ruth Ross, 'The New Jazz,' *Newsweek* (December 12 1966)

Michael Zwerin, 'Elmer's Tune And Ayler's Song,' *Village Voice* (May 19, 1966): 22, 25

— 'Jazz Journal: Space Friends,' *Village Voice* (March 9, 1967)

NEWSPAPERS

'17th Ward Pct. O Republican Club,' *Cleveland Call & Post* (August 31, 1940)

'125 To Compete For Caddie Title,' *Plain Dealer* (Cleveland) (July 11, 1954)

Bill Adler, '[Review of] *Albert Ayler: Reevaluations—The Impulse Years*,' *Ann Arbor Sun* (February 8, 1974)

Jan Aghed, 'My Name Is Albert Ayler,' *Sydsvenska Dagbladets AB* (May 20 2005)

'Albert Ayler, 36, Jazz Saxophonist,' *New York Times* (December 4, 1971)

'Albert Ayler Quintet In Kelly Hall,' *Antioch College Record* (February 3, 1967)

'Albert Ayler vier dagen hier Sterren sterretjes' *Het Vrije Volk* (November 5, 1964)

'Annual Golf Assn. Tournaments Tops,' *Cleveland Call & Post* (January 1, 1955)

'Augusta Kennedy Death Notice,' *Plain Dealer* (Cleveland) (October 15, 1977)

Edward Ayler, 'Letters To The Editor,' *Cleveland Call & Post* (June 15, 1940)

Bruce Bennett, 'There's No Catching Up With Albert Ayler,' *New York Sun* (November 7, 2007)

Rita Bergman and Oscar Bergman, 'Christmas Comes Early To The Thoughtful,' *Plain Dealer* (Cleveland) (August 25, 1953)

Bill Beuttler, 'Box Sets: Five From The Vaults,' *Boston Globe* (October 29, 2004)

Bob Blumenthal, 'Swing Low On High,' *Boston Phoenix* (January 11, 1983)

Ethel Boros, 'Clevelander's New Sound: A Mute Note Here,' *Plain Dealer* (Cleveland), *Friday Magazine* (January 27, 1967)

— 'Devotees Hail Aylers' 'Free' Jazz,' *Plain Dealer* (Cleveland) (February 5, 1967)

Luc Bouquet, '*Albert Ayler: Holy Ghost*,' *Jazz Break* (November 19, 2004)

Maartje den Breejen, 'Muziek Uit Een Kistje,' *Het Patrool* (October 12, 2004)

Greg Burk, 'The Sound Of Truth,' *LA Weekly* (November 4, 2004)

Christian Broecking, 'Zwischen Vision und Wirrnis,' *Neue Zürcher Zeitung* (November 11, 2004)

E.M. Burrus, 'The Sound Of … Something Different!' *Cleveland Call & Post* (July 24, 1965)

'Called To Colors,' *Cleveland Press* (September 23, 1958)

Tim Campbell, 'My Name Is Albert Ayler,' *Star Tribune* (Minneapolis–St. Paul)

Nate Chinen, 'Albert Ayler: Holy Ghost,' *Philadelphia City Paper* (November 24, 2004)

Chris Colombi, Jr., '"Sound Bomb" Reverberates At Concert,' *Plain Dealer* (Cleveland) (April 12, 1971)

'Coltrane Is Given A Jazzman's Funeral Here,' *New York Times* (July 22, 1967)

'Columbia U Student Takes Post In Japan,' *New York Age* (April 13, 1949)

'Death Notices,' *Plain Dealer* (Cleveland) (December 3, 1970)

Ellen Delmonte, 'Saxophonist's Body Found In New York's East River,' *Call & Post* (Cleveland) (December 12, 1970)

'Denk Fires Two Straight Birdies To Win District Caddie Title with 77,' *Plain Dealer* (Cleveland) (July 13, 1954)

'District Caddie Golf,' *Plain Dealer* (Cleveland) (July 13, 1954)

'Dit en volgend weekend Jazzconcerten,' *Leeuwarder Courant Hoofdblad van Friesland* (November 5, 1966)

'Doelen Zeer Geschikt Hoogte en dieptepunt besluiten Newport," *De Tijd* (November 9, 1966)

Michael Drexler, 'Gone But Not Forgotten,' *Plain Dealer* (Cleveland) *Sunday Magazine* (November 23, 1997)

Tom Feran, 'Silent Solo,' *Plain Dealer* (Cleveland) January 21, 2008

'First Sergeant Clarence E. Thomas,' *Cleveland Call & Post* (December 5, 1942)

John Fordham, 'The Holy Ghost Of Jazz,' *Guardian* (January 31, 2007)

Michael Fox, 'Miles Ahead,' *SF Weekly* vol. 27, Issue. 6 (March 5, 2008)

'Free Music ... Discorded Chaos?' *Cleveland Call & Post* (February 9, 1963)

Phil Gallo, 'My Name Is Albert Ayler,' *Daily Variety* (March 7, 2008)

Jon Garelick, 'A Tale Of Two Saints: Albert Ayler And Lenny Bruce Get Boxed,' *Portland Phoenix* (December 16, 2004)

Eva Af Geijerstam, 'My Name Is Albert Ayler,' *Dagens Nyheter*

Ryan Gilbey, 'Love, Loss And All That Jazz,' *New Statesman* (February 12, 2007)

Max Goldberg, 'My Name Is Albert Ayler,' *San Francisco Bay Guardian* (March 5, 2008)

'Golfers vie with Orange,' *John Adams Journal* (May 8, 1953)

'Goodbye Cleveland, Hello Sweden,' *Cleveland Call & Post* (April 21, 1962), 3-B

'Goodson's Great Finish Wins Golf Tourney,' *Cleveland Call & Post* (August 21, 1954)

Annie Gray, 'Star's Ray On The John Hay,' *Cleveland Call & Post* (December 4, 1954)

Joe Gross, 'The Legend: Albert Ayler,' *Palm Beach Post* (October 17, 2004)

'Hampton Concert Is Given Applause,' *Plain Dealer* (Cleveland) (December 17, 1945)

'Hampton Settlement Sponsors Series Of Sunday Pop Concerts,' *Cleveland Call & Post* (April 14, 1945)

'Hampton Social Settlement News,' *Cleveland Call & Post* (May 5, 1945)

'Hampton Social Settlement News,' *Cleveland Call & Post* (July 14, 1945)

Ron Hart, '*Albert Ayler: Holy Ghost*,' *Billboard* (November 24, 2004)

Andrey Henkin, 'Albert Ayler: *Holy Ghost*,' *All About Jazz* (October 31, 2004)

Nat Hentoff, 'The New Jazz—Black, Angry And Hard To Understand,' *New York Times* (December 25, 1966)

W. Kim Heron, 'New Doc Raises The Ghost Of Albert Ayler,' *Metro Times* (March 12 2008)

Dylan Hicks, 'My Name Is Albert Ayler,' *CityPages* (Minneapolis–St. Paul)

'His First Birthday Party Is Lawn Fete,' *Cleveland Call & Post* (August 24, 1946)

Demètre Ioakimidis, 'Le voix de l'avant-garde du jazz,' *Tribune de Lausanne* (April 17, 1966)

William D. Jackson, 'Detroit Golfers Tops In 6th City,' *Cleveland Call & Post* (July 10, 1954)

'Jazzartiesten In Nederland voor festival,' *Het Vrije Volk* (November 2, 1966)

'Jazzfest In De Doelen Newport: Surrogaat In Rotterdam,' *De Tijd* (November 8, 1966)

'Jazzman Ayler's Rites Tomorrow,' *Plain Dealer* (Cleveland) (December 3, 1970)

Derek Jewell, 'This Way Out,' *Sunday Times* (November 20, 1966)

David Brent Johnson, '*Holy Ghost: Albert Ayler*,' *WFIU Public Radio* (December 25, 2004)

Phil Johnson, 'Talk Of The Town: Holy-Rolling Hymns Unwilling To Swing,' *Independent* (October 10, 2004)

Timo Kangas, 'My Name Is Albert Ayler,' *Lira Musikmagasin*,

David Keenan, 'Spirit In The Sky,' *The Sunday Herald* (October 3, 2004)

'Kinsman Area News,' *Cleveland Call & Post* (May 22, 1948): 10-B

Bernard Lairet, 'Ayler: Still Unsung In His Home Town,' *Cleveland Press. Showtime* (December 10, 1971)

— 'Who Was Albert Ayler?' *Cleveland Press. Showtime* (April 2, 1971)

Stewart Lee, 'Pop CD Of The Week,' *Sunday Times* (October 24, 2004)

— 'The World Is Ready For Ayler—At Last,' *Sunday Times* (November 5, 2006)

Sheri Linden, 'My Name Is Albert Ayler,' *Los Angeles Times* (7 March 2008)

'Little Daisy Carr Gets Birthday Party,' *Cleveland Call & Post* (September 27, 1947): 16-B

'Live Wire Social Club,' *Cleveland Call & Post* (February 16, 1935)

Bernard Loupias, 'Albert Ayler, le revenant,' *Le Nouvel Observateur* (November 4, 2004)

Derek Malcolm, 'Jazz Documentary Is Worth The Wait,' *Evening Standard* (London (February 8, 2007)

'Max Roach, Albert Ayler En Sonny Rollins Op Jazzfestival: Laatste Concert Hoogtepunt,' *Het Vrije Volk* (November 9, 1966)

Bill Meyer, 'Spirit Of Ayler's Music Lives On In *Holy Ghost*,' *Chicago Tribune* (October 24, 2004)

Brian Morton, 'Spiritual Renaissance,' *The Scotsman* (October 9, 2004)

'Music Notes,' *New York Times* (May 7, 1965)

Chris Mudede, 'My Name Is Albert Ayler,' *The Stranger* (October 26, 2005)

Hernán Muleiro, 'Mi música refleja el sufrimiento, dice a La Jornada Archie Shepp,' *La Jornada* (March 4, 2021)

'Musicians Boost Scholarship Fund,' *Call & Post* (Cleveland) (March 6, 1971)

'My Name Is Albert Ayler,' *Kultureflash: Headlines From London* (February 11, 2007)

'My Name Is Albert Ayler,' *Heuriskein* (November 24, 2006)

'Nellie Thompson Thrills Audience In First Recital at Liberty Hill,' *Cleveland Call & Post* (May 10, 1947)

'Newpoort Jazzfestival 1966: Geslaagd Festijn In Rotterdam,' *De Waarheid* (November 9, 1966)

'Newport Jazz Festival Drie Dagen In Doelen' *Het Vrije Volk* (September 30, 1966)

Stuart Nicholson, '*Albert Ayler: Holy Ghost*,' *The Observer Music Monthly* (December 12, 2004)

Magnus Olsson, '*Albert Ayler: Holy Ghost*,' *Svenska Dagbladet* (November 19, 2004)

'One "Hometown Boy" That's Making Good,' *Call & Post* (Cleveland) (February 1, 1964)

Robert Ostermann, 'The Moody Men Who Play The New Music,' *National Observer* (June 7, 1965)

Gilles Ouellet, 'Albert Ayler: Je ne suis pas de ce monde,' *La Presse* (Montreal) (September 9, 1967)

Dan Ouellette, 'Ayler's Passionate Blast From The Past,' *Billboard* (October 30, 2004)

Robert Palmer, 'The Gospel, According To Saxophones,' *New York Times* (March 6, 1987)

Anastasia Pantsios, 'Uninhibited Rocker Still Packs Power,' *Plain Dealer* (Cleveland) (July 10, 2000)

'Pct. O Republican Club,' *Cleveland Call & Post* (August 17, 1940)

Harvey Pekar, '*Holy Ghost*: Revenant Records Returns with Free-Jazz Specter Albert Ayler,' *Austin Chronicle* (October 8, 2004)

Lennart Persson, 'My Name Is Albert Ayler,' *Sydsvenskan*

Jens Peterson, 'My Name Is Albert Ayler,' *Aftonbladet* (March 25, 2005)

'Picard Leads Local Caddies To Nationals,' *Cleveland Press* (August 4, 1953)

'Picard Snares Caddie Crown,' *Plain Dealer* (Cleveland) (August 4, 1953)

'Pittsburgh Rookies Work Out With Clowns,' *Cleveland Call & Post* (April 9, 1955)

Tom Place, 'Rangers Show Their Best In News Tourney,' *Cleveland News* (June 7, 1954)

Sam Prestianni, '*Albert Ayler: Holy Ghost*,' *SF Weekly* (December 22, 2004)

David P. Prizinsky, 'Quintet Is Strong In "New" Sound,' *Buffalo Courier-Express* (March 10, 1968)

Glenn C. Pullen, 'Band Really Jumps In Poolside Version Of 'Rain,' *Plain Dealer* (Cleveland) (July 13, 1965)

Andrew Pulver, 'My Name Is Albert Ayler,' *The Guardian* (February 9, 2007)

Anthony Quinn, 'My Name Is Albert Ayler,' *The Independent* (February 9, 2007)

Ben Ratliff, 'Make Him Wanna Holler,' *The New York Times* (October 24, 2004)

— 'Tribute For A Birthday That Never Arrived,' *New York Times* (September 23, 1996)

'Rawlings P. T. A. Has Musical Tea' *Cleveland Call & Post* (October 20, 1945)

'Returns From Unveiling Of Memorial For Kin,' *Cleveland Call & Post* (June 8, 1946)

Françoy Roberge, 'Ayler et frère: Le jazz filmique,' *Le Devoir* (Quebec), (August 29, 1967)

John Robinson, 'Free Radical,' *Guardian* (April 15, 2006)

'Rotterdam In teken van jazz,' *De Tijd* (November 4, 1966)

Luca Sabbatini, 'Prophète du jazz, Albert Ayler ressuscite enfin,' *24 Heures* (October 31, 2004)

Magnus Säll, 'En Ursinnigt Klagande Sax' *Dagens Nyheter* (March 25, 2005)

Sukhdev Sandhu, 'My Name Is Albert Ayler,' *Daily Telegraph*, (February 9, 2007)

Bret Saunders, 'New Light On Mystery Man,' *Denver Post* (October 10, 2004)

Richard Scheinen, 'A Startling Rediscovery Of A Jazz Original,' *San Jose Mercury News* (December 5, 2004)

Siegfried Schmidt-Joos, 'Organisierte Originalität,' *Zeit* (November 18, 1966)

Karel Scholten, 'Weinig beweging bij kwartet Albert Ayler,' *Het Vrije Volk* (November 9, 1964)

Matt Zoller Seitz, 'Free-Jazz Pioneer, Aware Of His Legacy,' *New York Times* (November 8, 2007)

Gene Seymour, 'Blowing Sax And Minds,' *Newsday* (November 28, 2004)

Archie Shepp, 'Albert Ayler 1934–1970,' *New York Times* (December 20 1970)

— 'Black Power And Black Jazz,' *New York Times* (November 21, 1967)

Jeff Simon, 'My Name Is Albert Ayler (4/4),' *The Buffalo News* (13 February 2009)

Matthew Simpkins, '*Albert Ayler: Holy Ghost*,' *Double Bassist* no. 33 (Summer 2005)

Linda Siteman, 'Band Concerts End With Music By Ayler,' *Springfield Union* (August 11, 1970)

'Slotconcert Was Subliem: Albert Ayler Met Muzikale Collage In Doelen,' *Utrechts Nieuwsblad* (November 9, 1966)

John Soeder, 'A New Light,' *Plain Dealer* (Cleveland) (September 26, 2004)

'South, Lincoln Near Showdown,' *Plain Dealer* (Cleveland) (June 3, 1955)

Mikhael Strömberg, 'Ayler och den Helige Ande,' *Aftonbladet* (March 25, 2005)

Rui Tentúgal, 'O Grito,' *Expresso* (November 27, 2004)

'To Far East,' *Cleveland Call & Post* (August 20, 1949)

'Top Arts Figures For Buffalo Fest,' *Buffalo Evening News* (January 20, 1968)

Athina Rachel Tsangari, 'Expanding Cinema,' *Austin Chronicle* (September 17, 1999)

'Two Promising Pittsburgh Youngsters, Contenders For Berths With Famous Clowns, In Camp Here,' *Carolina Times* (April 9, 1955)

'Uniek drie-daags jazz-festijn In de Rotterdamse 'Doelen',' *Nieuwsblad Van Het Noorden* (November 3, 1966)

Bert Vuijsje, 'Een Opname-Session Met Albert Ayler En Don Cherry,' *Vrij Nederland* (December 5, 1964)

Jari-Pekka Vuorela, 'Muistomerkki vapauden profeetalle kostuttaa silmät,' *Aamulehti* (4 November 2006)

Eric Waggoner, 'Silent Scream,' *Metro Times Detroit* (November 17, 2004)

'We hadden aardig succes In Newport,' *Het Vrije Volk* (July 12, 1966)

'Wedding Bells,' *Cleveland Call & Post* (January 30, 1965)

Kevin Whitehead, '*Albert Ayler: Holy Ghost*,' National Public Radio (December 14, 2004)

Peter Whittle, 'My Name Is Albert Ayler,' *Sunday Times* (February 11, 2007)

'William "Beaver" Harris, Drummer [Obituary],' *Boston Herald* (January 8, 1992)

Richard Williams, 'Blowing In The Wind,' *Guardian* (November 24, 2000)

— 'Free Rage,' *Guardian* (September 25, 2004)

— 'Jazz: The Obituary,' *Guardian* (May 25, 2001)

'Willoughby Is Favorite In News Golf Tourney,' *Cleveland News* (June 4, 1954)

Val Wilmer, 'Obituary: Donald Ayler: "Free" Jazz Trumpeter Forever In His Older Brother's Shadow,' *Guardian* (November 16, 2007)

John S. Wilson, 'Albert Ayler Octet Plays Jazz Concert,' *New York Times* (February 27, 1967)

— 'Black Arts,' *New York Times* (March 26, 1965)

— 'Bud Powell Heard With 3 Jazz Groups,' *New York Times* (May 2, 1965)

— 'Buddy Rich Star Of Jazz Festival,' *New York Times* (July 3, 1967)

— 'Newport Begins Its Jazz Festival,' *New York Times* (July 1, 1967)

— 'Newport Offers History Of Jazz,' *New York Times* (July 2, 1967)

Douglas Wolk, 'The Ayler Set: Revenant's Monument To A Minor Musician,' *Seattle Weekly* (November 9, 2004)

'Young Adult Group Sponsors Playground Dance,' *Cleveland Call & Post* (August 13, 1949)

LINER NOTES

Joachim-Ernst Berendt, *Lörrach/Paris 1966* (Hat ART Records, 1990)

Michael Cuscuna, *Vibrations* (Arista Records, 1975)

— *Saga Of The Outlaws* / Charles Tyler (Nessa N-16)

— *The Gentle Side Of John Coltrane* / John Coltrane (Impulse 9306-2)

Ray Funk, *Cleveland Gospel* (Gospel Heritage HT 316, 1948)

Nat Hentoff, *Live In Greenwich Village: The Complete Impulse Recordings* (Impulse IMPD2-273, 1998)

Steve Holtje, *Spiritual Unity: 50th Anniversary Edition* (ESP-Disk' WEP-1002, 2014)

David Keenan, *Nuits de la Fondation Maeght 1970* (Water Records 103, 2002)

Barry McRae, *Goin' Home* (Black Lion CD BLCD 760197, 1994)

Robert Palmer, *Live In Greenwich Village: The Complete Impulse Recordings* (Impulse IMPD-2-273, 1998)

Mary Parks (Mary Maria), *The Last Album* (Impulse As-9208, 1998)

— *Live In Greenwich Village: The Complete Impulse Recordings* (Impulse IMPD2-273, 1998)

Bernard Stollman, 'ESP Fax interview (April 92) Between Bernard Stollman And Tom "Tornado" Klatt,' in *College Tour* / Patty Waters (ESP CD 1055-2)

John F Szwed, *The Magic City* / Sun Ra (Evidence ECD 22069-2, 1993)

Dan Warburton, *The Copenhagen Tapes* (Ayler Records CD-0033, 2002)

FILMS

Kasper Collin, *My Name Is Albert Ayler* (2005)

Alan Roth, *Inside Out In The Open* (2001)

Tom Surgal, *Fire Music* (2021)

DOCUMENTS

American Federation Of Musicans (Cleveland Chapter, Local #4)

City Of Cleveland. Department Of Parks And Public Property. Division Of Cemeteries. Register Of Internments. Highland Park Cemetary 1948

Cuyahoga County, Ohio Certificate Of Death #1808-2007000337 October 31, 2007 (Don Ayler)

Cuyahoga County Juvenile Court Case no. 179765

Cuyahoga County Ohio Probate Court case 2003GRD79166 (August 5, 2003)

Cuyahoga County Ohio Probate Court case 2004GRD79166B (May 5, 2004)

Cuyahoga County Ohio Probate Court case 2003GRD79166C (February 17, 2006)

Cuyahoga County Probate Court Marriage Licenses, vol. 169

Cuyahoga County Probate Court Marriage Licenses, vol. 689

Cuyahoga County Probate Court Marriage Licenses (Application), vol. 728

Cuyahoga County Probate Court Marriage Licenses, vol. 964

Cuyahoga County Probate Court Marriage Licenses, vol. 985

'Don Ayler Joins CSU Jazz Ensemble For May 3 Date,' News Release, April 17, 1981 (#4818), Cleveland State University Office Of Information Services

Susan Hatters-Friedman, M.D., Competency Restoration Report (letter To Judge Burt Griffin, August 23, 2004)

Marvin Chernin vs. Donald Ayler (Cleveland Municipal Court Case 1999 CVG 027648)

New York City Department Of Health, Bureau Of Records And Statistics. Death certificate (Albert Ayler) 156-70-223868

Dr. Stephen Noffsinger, Competency report (letter to Judge John D. Sutula), August 5, 2005

Ohio. Department Of Health, Division Of Vital Statistics. Certificate Of Birth. File no. 50076. Registered no. 8044 (Albert Ayler)

Ohio Department Of Health, Vital Statistics, Supplemental Medical Certification, January 2, 2008

Ohio Rev. Code 2907.03

Ohio Rev. Code 2907.05

State Of Ohio, City Of Cleveland vs. Donald Ayler Cleveland Municipal Court case 2003 CRA 045807

State Of Ohio vs. Donald Ayler. Cuyahoga County Court Of Common Pleas Case, CR-04-447191

State Of Ohio vs. Donald Ayler. Cuyahoga County Court Of Common Pleas. Case, CR-05-466737-A

United States Armed Forces Enlistment Record

United States Congress House Committee On Un-American Activities, *Communist Youth Activities* (8th World Youth Festival, Helsinki, Finland, 1962): hearings, 87th Congress, 2nd session, April 25–October 4, December 21, 1962 (Washington, DC, 1962)

WEB PAGES

www.allaboutjazz.com

www.ancestry.com

www.aylerrecords.com

www.findagrave.com

www.insideoutintheopen.net

www.jazzdisco.org

www.mindspring.com/murray.html

www.mindspring.com/~scala/Graves.html

www.mynameisalbertayler.com

www.ohiostatebuckeyes.com
www.revenantrecords.com
www.tributes.com

Clifford Allen, 'Bernard Stollman, The ESP-Disk'
Story,' www.allaboutjazz.com (November 2005)
Pierre Crépon, 'Avant Garde Jazz And Black
Rights Activism In 1960s Cleveland, Ohio:
An Interview With Mutawaf A. Shaheed,'
www.thewire.co.uk (March 2019)
'Donald Ayler, 1942–2007,' *The Wire*
Phil Freeman, '*Holy Ghost*,'
www.culturevulture.net (October 2004)
Jack Gold-Molina, '[Review of] *My Name Is
Albert Ayler*,' www.allaboutjazz.com
(February 1, 2006)
Billy Bob Hargus, 'The Real Godfathers Of
Punk' www.furious.com/perfect
Reverend Inergy, 'My Name Is Albert Ayler:
Who The Hell Is Albert Ayler, And Why
Should I Care?' www.hybridmagazine.com
(June 2001)
Mark Jacobson, 'The Heartbeat Of Queens:
Milford Graves,' www.jazzhouse.org (2001)
Fred Jung, 'A Fireside Chat with Gary Peacock,'
www.jazzweekly.com
— 'A Fireside Chat with Ronald Shannon
Jackson,' www.jazzweekly.com (March 31,
1999)
Thom Jurek, 'Albert Ayler: Holy Ghost,'
www.allmusicguide.com (November 2004)
Robert Levin, 'Cecil Taylor At The Take 3,
1962–63,' www.allaboutjazz.com
Matt McNally, 'My Name Is Albert Ayler,'
www.bbc.co.uk (January 30, 2007)
Philippe Méziat, 'Le Jazz à Sigma—Une
chronologie commentée,' www.citizenjazz.com
Philip Moore, 'My Name Is Albert Ayler,'
www.dfgdocs.com
Joe Mosbrook, *Jazzed In Cleveland*,
www.cleveland.oh.us
Billy Mowbray, 'My Name Is Albert Ayler
Review,' www.channel4.com
'The Music Of George Frederick Root (1820–
1895),' www.pdmusic.org
Brian Nation, 'Albert Ayler: Beat The Devil,'
www.boppin.com (November 2006)
Jimmy Razor, 'My Name Is Albert Ayler,'
www.filmexposed.co.uk
Patrick Regan, 'Albert Ayler,' www.ayler.co.uk
Jeff Schwartz, *Albert Ayler: His Life And Music*,
www.reocities.com/jeff_l_schwartz

Matthew M. Sumera, 'Spiritual Unity And The
Resurrection Of Albert Ayler,'
www.tc.umn.edu/~sumer001/
Remco Takken, 'Albert Ayler: Holy Ghost,'
www.ayler.co.uk
Seth Tissue, 'Ken Vandermark: Discography
1984–2007,' tisue.net/vandermark/
'Who's Afraid Of The Avant Garde,'
www.paleycenter.org

INTERVIEWS, CORRESPONDENCE, AND LECTURES

'Albert Ayler: Music, Spirituality And Freedom,'
Cleveland Museum Of Art, panel discussion
(March 17, 2011)
Donald Ayler interviews (WCSB-FM, October
22, 1997; WCSB-FM, December 4, 1997;
April 5, 1998; May 24, 1998; August 2, 1998;
October 25, 1998; November 25, 1998;
April 3, 1999; June 19, 1999; July 3, 2000);
conversation (March 1, 2002)
Daniel Caux, 'My Name Is Albert Ayler,
1: Spiritual Unity,' Atelier de création
radiophonique, *France Culture* (November
28, 1971)
— 'My Name Is Albert Ayler, 2: Love Cry,'
Atelier de création radiophonique, *France
Culture* (December 5, 1971)
Edward Ayler interviews (WCSB-FM, October
22, 1997; WCSB-FM, December 4, 1997; July
3, 2000)
Roy Blumenfeld email correspondence (January
26, 2001)
Jacqueline Caux email correspondence (August
24, 2018)
Frank Doblekar email correspondence (April 1,
2002)
Bobby Few interview (August 23, 2000)
Bill Folwell interview with Ben Young (WKCR,
July 29, 2007)
Jon Goldman phone conversation (February,
2000)
Milford Graves interview with Mitch Goldman
and Andy Rothman (WKCR, July 13, 1987)
Larry Hancock interview (WCSB-FM, December
24, 2007)
Beaver Harris interview with Elliott Bratton
(WKCR-FM, July 13, 1987)
Terry Hynde conversation (October 29, 2005)
Jimmy Landers interview (September 24, 2000)
Joëlle Léandre and Franck Médioni, *Albert Ayler
Tribute Concert*

Carrie Lucas interview (June 6, 2002)

Kevin Muhammad interview (WCSB-FM, February 2007)

Velibor Pedevski email correspondence (2003)

Lewis Porter email correspondence (May 30, 2012)

Bill Randle conversations (various)

Art Sato, 'In Your Ear,' radio interview with Leroy Jenkins (KPFA, 1987)

Jeff Schwartz email correspondence (May 4, 2000)

— '"You Never Heard Such Sounds In Your Life": ESP-Disk And The Business Of Free Jazz,' Experience Music Project (February 26, 2011)

Mutawaf Shaheed interview (WCSB-FM, January 10, 2001); conversation (February 10, 2008); email correspondence (various)

Sune Spångberg written statement, 'Albert Ayler's First Recording Session' (Stockholm, February 19, 1992)

Robert Strassfeld, 'How The Cleveland Bar Became Segregated,' Cleveland City Club (February 8, 2012)

Steve Tintweiss email correspondence (April 26, 2000; September 11, 2013)

Tony Viscomi interview (WCSB-FM, April 2, 2003)

Richard Wedler phone conversation (July 3, 2000)

Val Wilmer correspondence (January 6, 2002; August 28, 2004)

— unpublished interview with Donald Ayler (November 2, 1976)

Sandy Wright phone conversation (December 2007)

Ben Young conversation (August 2003)

endnotes

INTRODUCTION

1 Peter Niklas Wilson, 'Die Sphinx des Free Jazz'
2 Charles Shaar Murray, 'Shots From The Hip'

CHAPTER I

1 Gudrun Endress, 'Albert Ayler: We Play Peace'
2 *The Cleveland Directory Co.'s Cleveland City Directory Name Index* vol. 1943–1944
3 'Hampton Settlement Sponsors Series Of Sunday Pop Concerts
4 'Hampton Social Settlement News'
5 'Hampton Social Settlement News'
6 'Hampton Concert Is Given Applause'
7 *Cleveland Call & Post*, June 5, 1948
8 Donald Ayler interview
9 Bobby Few interview
10 Val Wilmer, *As Serious As Your Life*
11 Val Wilmer, 'Spirits Rejoice!'
12 Val Wilmer, private correspondence
13 Stanley Crouch, 'Albert Ayler: Talking In Tongues'
14 Stanley Crouch, 'Albert Ayler: Talking In Tongues'
15 Peter Niklas Wilson, 'Die Sphinx des Free Jazz'
16 Tom Place, 'Rangers Show Their Best In News Tourney'
17 William D. Jackson, 'Detroit Golfers Tops In 6th City'
18 Kiyoshi Koyama, 'Interview With Albert Ayler'
19 Val Wilmer, *As Serious As Your Life*
20 Daniel Caux, 'My Name Is Albert Ayler, 1'
21 Ben Young, 'Ist Er Das?'

CHAPTER II

1 Carrie Lucas interview
2 Carrie Lucas interview
3 Kiyoshi Koyama, 'Interview With Albert Ayler'
4 Carrie Lucas interview
5 Daniel Caux, 'My Name Is Albert Ayler, 1'
6 Carrie Lucas interview
7 Nat Hentoff, 'The Truth Is Marching In'
8 Marc Chaloin, 'Albert Ayler In Europe: 1959–62'
9 Edward Ayler interview
10 Peter Niklas Wilson, 'Die Sphinx des Free Jazz'
11 Francis Davis, 'The Fire That Time'
12 Perry Robinson and Florence Wetzel, *Perry Robinson: The Traveler*
13 Francis Davis, *In the Moment*
14 Bill Cole, *John Coltrane*
15 Bobby Few interview
16 Jon Goldman and Martin Davidson, 'Albert Ayler Life And Recordings'
17 Val Wilmer, 'Ayler: Mystic Tenor With A Direct Hot Line To Heaven?'

CHAPTER III

1 Nils Edström, www.aylerrecords.com
2 Sune Spångberg, 'Albert Ayler's First Recording Session.' *See also* Alf Gabrielsson, *Strong Experiences With Music*
3 Sune Spångberg, 'Albert Ayler's First Recording Session'
4 Lars Werner, *'Something Different'*
5 Richard Cook, 'My Name Is Albert Ayler'

6   Ekkehard Jost, *Free Jazz*
7   'Free Music … Discorded Chaos?'
8   Brian Priestley, '*The First Recordings*'
9   Richard Cook, 'My Name Is Albert Ayler'
10 John Litweiler, *The Freedom Principle*
11 John Litweiler, *The Freedom Principle*
12 Brian Priestley, '*The First Recordings*'
13 Peter Niklas Wilson, 'Die Sphinx des Free Jazz'
14 Jeff Schwartz, *Albert Ayler*
15 Barry McRae, '*The First Recordings*'
16 Scott Yanow, '*The First Recordings, Volume 2*'
17 Barry McRae, '*The First Recordings*'
18 Scott Yanow, '*The First Recordings, Volume 2*'
19 Dan Warburton, 'Interview with Sunny
    Murray.' *See also* Jason Weiss, *Always In Trouble*
20 Donald Ayler interview

CHAPTER IV

1   Bill Mathieu, '*My Name is Albert Ayler*'
2   Jeff Schwartz, *Albert Ayler*
3   Amiri Baraka, *Black Music*
4   Ekkehard Jost, *Free Jazz*
5   Terry Martin, '*My Name Is Albert Ayler*'
6   Terry Martin, '*My Name Is Albert Ayler*'
7   Bill Mathieu, '*My Name is Albert Ayler*'
8   Terry Martin, '*My Name is Albert Ayler*'
9   W.A. Baldwin, 'Albert Ayler: Conservative
    Revolution? (1)'
10 Bill Mathieu, '*My Name is Albert Ayler*'
11 Terry Martin, '*My Name is Albert Ayler*'
12 Richard Williams, 'Ayler: Beyond This World'
13 John Litweiler, *The Freedom Principle*
14 John Litweiler, *The Freedom Principle*
15 Bill Mathieu, '*My Name is Albert Ayler*'
16 Donald Ayler interview
17 Jeff Schwartz, *Albert Ayler*
18 W.A. Baldwin, 'Albert Ayler: Conservative
    Revolution? (1)'
19 Ekkehard Jost, *Free Jazz*
20 Nate Horwitz, conversation with Mark
    Gridley (cited in 'Misconceptions In Linking
    Free Jazz With The Civil Rights Movement')
21 Peter Niklas Wilson, 'Die Sphinx des Free Jazz'
22 Frank Kofsky, 'An Interview with Albert and
    Donald Ayler'
23 Jeff Schwartz, *Albert Ayler*
24 Frank Smith, 'His Name Is Albert Ayler'
25 Frank Kofsky, 'John Coltrane And The Jazz
    Revolution'
26 Barry McRae, 'Avant Courier'
27 Ben Sidran, *Talking Jazz*
28 Val Wilmer, *As Serious As Your Life*

CHAPTER V

1   Stanley Crouch, *Considering Genius*
2   Val Wilmer, 'Conversation With Call'
3   Frank Smith, 'His Name Is Albert Ayler'
4   Nat Hentoff, 'The Truth Is Marching In'
5   Frank Smith, 'His Name Is Albert Ayler'
6   Clifford Allen, 'Bernard Stollman, The ESP-
    Disk Story'
7   Val Wilmer, *As Serious As Your Life*
8   LeRoi Jones, 'Caught In The Act'
9   Whitney Balliet, 'Musical Events: Jazz
    Concerts'
10 Paul Bley and David Lee, *Stopping Time*
11 Graham Lock, *Chasing The Vibrations*
12 Jeff Schwartz, *New Black Music*
13 Ben Young, 'Chronology'

CHAPTER VI

1   Barry Tepperman, '*Witches & Devils*'
2   Michael James, '*Witches & Devils*'
3   Marshall Marrotte, 'Henry Grimes: The
    Signal To Noise Interview'
4   'One Hometown Boy'
5   Robert Ostermann, 'The Moody Men Who
    Play The New Music'
6   Donald Ayler interview
7   Peter Niklas Wilson, 'Shapes From Notes To
    Sounds'
8   Gary Giddins, *Visions Of Jazz*
9   Peter Niklas Wilson, 'Shapes From Notes To
    Sounds'
10 John Litweiler, 'The Legacy Of Albert Ayler'
11 Stanley Crouch, *Considering Genius*
12 Val Wilmer, *As Serious As Your Life*
13 Val Wilmer, 'Spirits Rejoice!'
14 Nat Hentoff, 'The Truth Is Marching In'
15 Don Locke, 'The New Conservatism'
16 Val Wilmer, 'Albert & Don Ayler Talk To Val
    Wilmer'
17 Barry Tepperman, '*Witches & Devils*'
18 Nat Hentoff, liner notes to *Live In Greenwich
    Village: The Complete Impulse Recordings*
19 Barry Tepperman, '*Witches & Devils*'
20 Jeff Schwartz, *Albert Ayler*
21 W.A. Baldwin, 'Albert Ayler: Conservative
    Revolution? (1)'
22 Val Wilmer, *As Serious As Your Life*
23 'Albert Ayler Dies'
24 W.A. Baldwin, 'Albert Ayler: Conservative
    Revolution? (1)'
25 Michael James, 'Don Cherry In Amsterdam'
26 Jack Cooke, '*Spirits*'

27 Don Locke, 'The New Conservatism'
28 Nat Hentoff, 'The New Jazz'
29 Philippe Carles and Jean-Louis Comolli, 'Les
    Secrets d'Albert Le Grand'
30 LeRoi Jones, 'Apple Cores'
31 John Litweiler, *The Freedom Principle*
32 Mutawaf Shaheed interview
33 LeRoi Jones, 'Apple Cores'
34 W.A. Baldwin, 'Albert Ayler: Conservative
    Revolution? (1)'
35 Michael James, 'Don Cherry In Amsterdam'
36 W.A. Baldwin, 'Albert Ayler: Conservative
    Revolution? (1)'
37 Barry McRae, 'Avant Courier'
38 John Litweiler, *The Freedom Principle*
39 W.A. Baldwin, 'Albert Ayler: Conservative
    Revolution? (1)'
40 W.A. Baldwin, 'Albert Ayler: Conservative
    Revolution? (1)'
41 W.A. Baldwin, 'Albert Ayler: Conservative
    Revolution? (1)'
42 W.A. Baldwin, 'Albert Ayler: Conservative
    Revolution? (1)'

CHAPTER VII

1 Gary Giddins, *Visions Of Jazz*
2 Peter Niklas Wilson, *Spirits Rejoice!*
3 Peter Niklas Wilson, '*Goin' Home*'
4 Peter Niklas Wilson, *Spirits Rejoice!*
5 Barry McRae, '*Swing Low, Sweet Spiritual*'
6 Peter Niklas Wilson, '*Goin' Home*'
7 Kevin Whitehead, '*Swing Low Sweet Spiritual*'
8 John Sutherland, '*Swing Low Sweet Spiritual*'
9 Barry McRae, liner notes to *Goin' Home*
10 Edward Ayler interview
11 John Sutherland, '*Swing Low Sweet Spiritual*'
12 Kevin Whitehead, '*Swing Low Sweet Spiritual*'
13 John Sutherland, '*Swing Low Sweet Spiritual*'
14 John Sutherland, '*Swing Low Sweet Spiritual*'
15 Barry McRae, liner notes to *Goin' Home*
16 John Sutherland, '*Swing Low Sweet Spiritual*'
17 Peter Niklas Wilson, '*Goin' Home*'
18 Barry McRae, liner notes to *Goin' Home*
19 Kevin Whitehead, '*Swing Low Sweet Spiritual*'
20 Peter Niklas Wilson, '*Goin' Home*'

CHAPTER VIII

1 Richard Williams, 'Blowing In The Wind'
2 Larry Nai, 'Marzette Watts Interview'
3 Ekkehard Jost, *Free Jazz*
4 Ekkehard Jost, *Free Jazz*
5 Ekkehard Jost, *Free Jazz*

6 Dan Warburton, 'Expatriate Act'
7 Clifford Allen, 'Bernard Stollman, The ESP-
   Disk Story'
8 John Kruth, 'One Nation Underground'
9 Bernard Stollman, 'ESP Fax interview (April
   '92) Between Bernard Stollman And Tom
   "Tornado" Klatt'
10 John Kruth, 'One Nation Underground'
11 Val Wilmer, 'Spirits Rejoice!'
12 Jeff Schwartz, *Albert Ayler*
13 Ekkehard Jost, *Free Jazz*
14 Albert Ayler, 'Albert Ayler'
15 Daniel Caux, 'My Name Is Albert Ayler, 1'
16 Ekkehard Jost, *Free Jazz*
17 Peter Niklas Wilson, *Spirits Rejoice!*
18 Hernán Muleiro, 'Mi música refleja el
   sufrimiento, dice a *La Jornada* Archie Shepp'
19 Marc Chaloin, 'Bill Folwell: An Interview
   With Marc Chaloin'
20 Barry Tepperman, '*Prophecy*'
21 Stanley Crouch, 'Albert Ayler: Talking In
   Tongues'
22 Stanley Crouch, 'Albert Ayler: Talking In
   Tongues'
23 Stanley Crouch, 'Albert Ayler: Talking In
   Tongues'
24 Stanley Crouch, 'Albert Ayler: Talking In
   Tongues'
25 Barry Tepperman, '*Prophecy*'
26 Richard Williams, 'Blowing In The Wind'

CHAPTER IX

1 Clifford Allen, 'Bernard Stollman, The ESP-
   Disk Story'
2 Val Wilmer, *As Serious As Your Life*
3 Clifford Allen, 'Bernard Stollman, The ESP-
   Disk Story'
4 Albert Ayler, 'Albert Ayler'
5 John Litweiler, *The Freedom Principle. See also*
   'Hie Logan—Da Ayler'
6 Frank Smith, 'His Name Is Albert Ayler'
7 Stuart Broomer, '*Spiritual Unity*'
8 Jeff Schwartz, *Albert Ayler*
9 Kenny Dorham, 'Two Views Of Three Outer
   Views'
10 Bill Mathieu, 'Two Views Of Three Outer
   Views'
11 Richard Williams, 'Ayler: Beyond This World'
12 Ekkehard Jost, *Free Jazz*
13 Val Wilmer, *As Serious As Your Life*
14 Val Wilmer, *As Serious As Your Life*, citing
   LeRoi Jones, 'Apple Cores'

15 W.A. Baldwin, 'Albert Ayler: Conservative Revolution? (1)'
16 John Litweiler, *The Freedom Principle*
17 Barry McRae, 'Avant Courier: Message From Albert'
18 Robert Ostermann, 'The Moody Men Who Play The New Music'
19 Mort Maizlish, '*Spiritual Unity*'
20 Stuart Broomer, 'Albert Ayler, Breakfast In Montreal ... A Reflection.' *See also* Wolfgang Dauner, '*Spiritual Unity*'
21 W.A. Baldwin, 'Albert Ayler: Conservative Revolution? (1)'
22 Mort Maizlish, '*Spiritual Unity*'
23 Brian Priestley, '*Spiritual Unity*'
24 Jeff Schwartz, *Albert Ayler*
25 Jeff Schwartz, *Albert Ayler*
26 Mort Maizlish, '*Spiritual Unity*'

CHAPTER X

1 Jason Weiss, *Always In Trouble*
2 Jason Weiss, *Always In Trouble*
3 *17 Canadian Artists: A Protean View*
4 Louis Dompierre, *Walking Woman Works*. *See also* Jesse Stewart, 'Improvisation, Representation, And Abstraction In Music And Art'
5 Richard Williams, 'Blowing In The Wind'
6 Val Wilmer, 'Spirits Rejoice!'
7 Jason Weiss, *Always In Trouble*
8 Ekkehard Jost, *Free Jazz*
9 W.A. Baldwin, 'Albert Ayler: Conservative Revolution? (1)'
10 Ekkehard Jost, *Free Jazz*
11 Ekkehard Jost, *Free Jazz*

CHAPTER XI

1 Larry Nai, 'Alan Silva Interview'
2 Val Wilmer, 'Spirits Rejoice!'
3 Clifford Allen, 'Bernard Stollman, The ESP-Disk Story'
4 Peter Niklas Wilson, *Spirits Rejoice!*
5 James Beaudreau, '*The Copenhagen Tapes*'
6 Brian Priestley, '*Ghosts*'
7 Jack Cooke, '*Ghosts*'
8 Barry McRae, 'Avant Courier: Message From Albert'
9 Ira Steingroot, '*Vibrations*'
10 Jack Cooke, '*Ghosts*'
11 Robert Ostermann, 'The Moody Men Who Play The New Music'

12 W.A. Baldwin, 'Albert Ayler: Conservative Revolution? (1)'
13 Ira Steingroot, '*Vibrations*'
14 Jeff Schwartz, *Albert Ayler*
15 W.A. Baldwin, 'Albert Ayler: Conservative Revolution? (2)'
16 Steve Lake, '*Vibrations*'
17 W.A. Baldwin, 'Albert Ayler: Conservative Revolution? (2)'
18 Val Wilmer, 'Mystic Tenor With A Hot Line To Heaven'
19 W.A. Baldwin, 'Albert Ayler: Conservative Revolution? (2)'
20 John Litweiler, *The Freedom Principle*
21 W.A. Baldwin, 'Albert Ayler: Conservative Revolution? (2)'
22 Peter Niklas Wilson, *Spirits Rejoice!*
23 Ben Young, 'Chronology'
24 Robert W. Sabin, *Gary Peacock*
25 Michael James, 'Don Cherry In Amsterdam'
26 Benoit Quersin, 'Ayler et l'avant garde'
27 Hans Dulfer, *Jazz In China En Andere Perikels Uit De Geimproviseerde Muziek*
28 Bert Vuijsje, 'Een Opname-Session Met Albert Ayler En Don Cherry'
29 Bert Vuijsje, 'Een Opname-Session Met Albert Ayler En Don Cherry'
30 Bert Vuijsje, 'Een Opname-Session Met Albert Ayler En Don Cherry'
31 Brian Case, 'Special Ayler'
32 Bob Blumenthal, 'Albert Ayler'
33 Walter Horn, '*The Hilversum Session*'
34 Roger Riggins, '*The Hilversum Session*'
35 Barry McRae, '*The Hilversum Session*'
36 John Litweiler, *The Freedom Principle*
37 Jeff Schwartz, *Albert Ayler*
38 Brian Case, 'Special Ayler'
39 Jeff Schwartz, *Albert Ayler*
40 Brian Case, 'Special Ayler'
41 Hans Dulfer, *Jazz In China En Andere Perikels Uit De Geimproviseerde Muziek*
42 Donald Ayler interview
43 Hans Dulfer, *Jazz In China En Andere Perikels Uit De Geimproviseerde Muziek*
44 Donald Ayler interview
45 Gary Giddins, *Visions Of Jazz*
46 Donald Ayler interview
47 W.A. Baldwin, 'Albert Ayler: Conservative Revolution? (3)'
48 Stefano Zenni, 'Il Testamento di Ayler'
49 Jacqueline and Daniel Caux, 'My Name Is Albert Ayler'

CHAPTER XII
1 Donald Ayler interview
2 John Gennari, *Blowin' Hot And Cool*
3 John Gennari, *Blowin' Hot And Cool*
4 Peter Niklas Wilson, *Spirits Rejoice!*
5 Peter Niklas Wilson, *Spirits Rejoice!*
6 Peter Niklas Wilson, *Spirits Rejoice!*
7 Ana Isabel O, 'Happy 83 Birthday, Maestro Cecil Taylor! Long Life And Love'
8 Peter Niklas Wilson, *Spirits Rejoice!*
9 Marc Chaloin, 'Bill Folwell: An Interview With Marc Chaloin'
10 Peter Niklas Wilson, *Spirits Rejoice!*
11 Kiyoshi Koyama, 'Interview With Albert Ayler'
12 Bobby Few interview
13 Marriage license, Cuyahoga County Probate Court Marriage Licenses, Vol. 689, page 36
14 Carrie Lucas interview
15 Donald Ayler conversation
16 John F. Szwed, liner notes to *The Magic City*
17 John F. Szwed, *Space Is The Place*
18 Kiyoshi Koyama, 'Interview With Albert Ayler'
19 Ekkehard Jost, *Free Jazz*
20 W.A. Baldwin, 'Albert Ayler: Conservative Revolution? (3)'
21 Bob Rusch, 'Donald Ayler: Interview'
22 Milan Simich email correspondence
23 Hentoff, 'The Truth Is Marching In'
24 Ben Ratliff, *Coltrane*
25 Frank Smith, 'His Name Is Albert Ayler'
26 Ekkehard Jost, *Free Jazz*
27 Mutawaf Shaheed interview
28 Frank Smith, 'His Name Is Albert Ayler'
29 Frank Smith, 'His Name Is Albert Ayler'
30 Frank Smith, 'His Name Is Albert Ayler'
31 Randall Sandke, *Where The Dark And The Light Folks Meet*
32 Jeff Schwartz, *Albert Ayler*, citing Amiri Baraka, 'The Fire Must be Permitted To Burn Full Up: Black Aesthetic'
33 Ingrid Monson, 'Jazz Improvisation'
34 Paul de Barros, '*Lörrach, Paris 1966*' and Daniel Caux, 'My Name Is Albert Ayler, 1'
35 Paul de Barros, '*Lörrach, Paris 1966*' and Daniel Caux, 'My Name Is Albert Ayler, 1'
36 Ben Young, 'Chronology'
37 Albert Ayler, 'Albert Ayler'
38 'Time listings: *The New Wave In Jazz*'
39 Gilbert M. Erskine, 'Two Views Of The New Wave'
40 Bill Mathieu, 'Two Views Of The New Wave'
41 Richard Williams, 'Blowing In The Wind'
42 W.A. Baldwin, 'Albert Ayler: Conservative Revolution? (3)'
43 Ira Gitler, '*Straight Ahead*'
44 A. B. Spellman, 'Not Just Whistling Dixie'
45 Amiri Baraka, *The Autobiography Of LeRoi Jones*
46 A.B. Spellman, *Four Jazz Lives*

CHAPTER XIII
1 Frank Smith, 'His Name Is Albert Ayler'
2 Dan Morgenstern, 'Caught In The Act'
3 Barry McRae, 'Avant Courier: Message From Albert'
4 Pete Welding, '*Bells*'
5 Val Wilmer, *As Serious As Your Life*
6 Terry Martin, '*Bells*'
7 W.A. Baldwin, 'Albert Ayler: Conservative Revolution? (3)'
8 W.A. Baldwin, 'Albert Ayler: Conservative Revolution? (3)'
9 Daniel Caux, 'My Name Is Albert Ayler, 1'
10 Donald Ayler interview
11 Val Wilmer, *As Serious As Your Life*
12 W.A. Baldwin, 'Albert Ayler: Conservative Revolution? (3)'
13 Robert Ostermann, 'The Moody Men Who Play The New Music'
14 Val Wilmer, 'Spirits Rejoice!'
15 Mary Maria/Mary Parks, liner notes to *The Last Album*
16 Frank Kofsky, *Black Nationalism And The Revolution In Music*
17 John Litweiler, 'The Legacy Of Albert Ayler'
18 Glenn C. Pullen, 'Band Really Jumps In Poolside Version Of *Rain*'; E.M. Burrus, 'The Sound Of … Something Different!'
19 James Edward Smethurst, *The Black Arts Movement*
20 Lewis Porter email correspondence
21 Randall Sandke, *Where The Dark And The Light Folks Meet*

CHAPTER XIV
1 Patrick Regan, 'Albert Ayler'
2 Patrick Regan, 'Albert Ayler'
3 Max Harrison, '*Spirits Rejoice!*'
4 W.A. Baldwin, 'Albert Ayler: Conservative Revolution? (3)'
5 Peter Niklas Wilson, 'Die Sphinx des Free Jazz'
6 W.A. Baldwin, 'Albert Ayler: Conservative Revolution? (3)'
7 Harvey Pekar, '*Spirits Rejoice!*'

8   Jeff Schwartz, *Albert Ayler*
9   W.A. Baldwin, 'Albert Ayler: Conservative Revolution? (3)'
10 Donald Ayler interview
11 W.A. Baldwin, 'Albert Ayler: Conservative Revolution? (3)'
12 John Litweiler, *The Freedom Principle*
13 Harvey Pekar, '*Spirits Rejoice!*'
14 Val Wilmer, *As Serious As Your Life*
15 Jeff Schwartz, *Albert Ayler*
16 Val Wilmer, 'Conversation With Call'
17 Jeff Schwartz, *Albert Ayler*
18 W.A. Baldwin, 'Albert Ayler: Conservative Revolution? (3)'
19 Donald Ayler interview
20 Val Wilmer, *As Serious As Your Life*
21 *Village Voice* advertisement
22 '26 jazzmen nouveaux a la question'
23 Peter Niklas Wilson, *Spirits Rejoice! See also* James Edward Smethurst, *The Black Arts Movement*
24 Max Harrison, 'Letter'
25 Daniel Caux, 'My Name Is Albert Ayler, 1'
26 John Litweiler, *The Freedom Principle*
27 Bill Quinn, '*Sunny's Time Now*'
28 Max Harrison, '*Sonny's Time Now*'
29 Hentoff, 'The Truth Is Marching In'
30 Frank Kofsky, *Coltrane And The Jazz Revolution*
31 Ekkehard Jost, *Free Jazz*
32 Frank Kofsky, *Black Nationalism And The Revolution In Music*
33 Michael Reagan, 'The Sounds Of Struggle'
34 Barry McRae, 'Avant Courier: Message From Albert'
35 Nat Hentoff, 'The Truth Is Marching In'
36 John Litweiler, *The Freedom Principle*
37 John Litweiler, 'The Legacy Of Albert Ayler'

CHAPTER XV

1   Barry McRae, 'Avant Courier: Message From Albert'
2   Val Wilmer, 'Spirits Rejoice!'
3   Peter Niklas Wilson, *Spirits Rejoice!*
4   Rupert Kettle, 'The New Jazz'
5   Peter Niklas Wilson, *Spirits Rejoice!*
6   Norman C. Weinstein, *A Night In Tunisia*
7   John Norris, 'Three Notes With Albert Ayler'
8   Frank Kofsky, 'An Interview With Albert And Donald Ayler'
9   Michael Cuscuna, liner notes to *The Gentle Side Of John Coltrane* (Impulse 9306-2).
10 Gary Giddins, 'Titans Of The Tenor'

11 Dan Morgenstern, 'Titans Of The Tenor Sax'
12 Frank Kofsky, 'An Interview With Albert And Donald Ayler'
13 Amiri Baraka, *The Autobiography Of LeRoi Jones*
14 Ben Young, 'Witnesses'
15 Ben Young, 'Witnesses'
16 Mutawaf Shaheed interview
17 Michael Drexler, 'Gone But Not Forgotten'
18 Michael Cuscuna, liner notes to *Saga Of The Outlaws*
19 Mutawaf Shaheed interview
20 Donald Ayler interview
21 Nat Hentoff, liner notes to *Live In Greenwich Village: The Complete Impulse Recordings*
22 Rudie Kagie, 'Avonturen In De New Thing'
23 Jon Goldman, 'The Albert Ayler Sextet In Concert—Cleveland—February 4, 1967'
24 Richard Wedler phone conversation
25 Steve Traina conversation
26 Mutawaf Shaheed phone conversation
27 Art Lange, 'Ayler Resurrected, A Look Into Revenants' *Albert Ayler Holy Ghost*'
28 Tony Herrington, '*Albert Ayler. Holy Ghost: Rare & Unissued Recordings (1962–70)*'
29 Rudie Kagie, 'Avonturen In De New Thing'
30 Mutawaf Shaheed interview

CHAPTER XVI

1   Michael Zwerin, 'Elmer's Tune And Ayler's Song'
2   Chris Kelsey, '*Albert Ayler: Slug's Saloon: May 1, 1966*'
3   Simon Adams, '*In Memory of Albert Ayler*'
4   Barry McRae, 'Avant Courier: Message from Albert'
5   Jason Berry, Jonathan Foose, and Tad Jones, *Up From The Cradle Of Jazz*
6   Nat Hentoff, 'The Truth Is Marching In'
7   Nat Hentoff, liner notes to *Live In Greenwich Village: The Complete Impulse Recordings*
8   Albert Ayler, 'Albert Ayler'
9   Nat Hentoff, liner notes to *Live In Greenwich Village: The Complete Impulse Recordings*
10 Ben Ratliff, *Coltrane*
11 Simon Adams, '*In Memory of Albert Ayler*'
12 Chris Sheridan, '*Lörrach/Paris 1966*'
13 Milo Fine, '*In Memory of Albert Ayler*'
14 Nat Hentoff, liner notes to *Live In Greenwich Village: The Complete Impulse Recordings*
15 Val Wilmer, 'Ayler: Mystic Tenor With A Direct Hot Line to Heaven?'

16 Val Wilmer, unpublished interview
17 Elisabeth van der Mei, 'Caught In The Act'
18 Don Heckman, 'A Perspective In Revolution'
19 Albert Ayler, 'To Mr. Jones—I Had A Vision'
20 Donald Ayler interview
21 Richard Mortifoglio, 'Albert Ayler As Angel Of History'
22 Bobby Few interview
23 Edward Ayler interview
24 Josef Woodard, 'Jazz & The Abstract Truth'
25 Val Wilmer, 'Ronald Shannon Jackson: A Shaman For The '80s'
26 Val Wilmer, 'Roswell Rudd And The Chartreuse Phantasm'
27 Donald Ayler interview
28 John Kruth, 'The Healing Force Of The Universe'
29 Val Wilmer, *As Serious As Your Life*

CHAPTER XVII
1   Marc Chaloin, 'Bill Folwell: An Interview With Marc Chaloin'
2   Bill Folwell interview with Ben Young
3   Val Wilmer, *As Serious As Your Life*
4   Alan Barton, 'The Ayler Enigma'
5   Siegfried Schmidt-Joos, 'Organisierte Originalität'
6   Milo Fine, '*Albert Ayler*'
7   Larry Hollis, '*Albert Ayler Live In Lörrach, Germany And Paris France 1966*'
8   Francis Davis, '*Albert Ayler Lörrach/Paris 1966*'
9   Barry McRae, '*Jesus*'
10 Barry McRae, '*Jesus*'
11 Barry McRae, '*Lörrach/Paris 1966*'
12 Barry McRae, '*Jesus*'
13 Barry McRae, '*Lörrach/Paris 1966*'
14 Gary Giddins, 'Fresh Flowers For Albert'
15 Barry McRae, '*Lörrach/Paris 1966*'
16 Art Lange, 'Ayler Resurrected, A Look Into Revenant's *Albert Ayler: Holy Ghost*'
17 Ted Joans, 'AA! AA? Yeah, AA!'
18 Michael Tucker, '*Albert Ayler Stockholm, Berlin 1966*'
19 Beaver Harris interview with Elliott Bratton
20 Frank Kofsky, 'An Interview With Albert And Donald Ayler'
21 Larry Hollis, '*Albert Ayler Live In Lörrach, Germany And Paris France 1966*'
22 Jeff Schwartz, *Albert Ayler*
23 Patrick Regan, 'Albert Ayler'
24 Ted Joans, 'AA! AA? Yeah, AA!'

25 Paul de Barros, '*Lörrach, Paris 1966*'
26 Ted Joans, 'AA! AA? Yeah, AA!'
27 M.-C. Icre 'Au Théâtre Français, rencontre explosive du free jazz et du spectacle total'
28 Bob Rusch, 'Beaver Harris Stories III'
29 Bill Folwell interview with Ben Young
30 Bill Folwell interview with Ben Young
31 Val Wilmer, *Mama Said There'd Be Days Like This*
32 Alan Beckett, 'Ayler At LSE'
33 Alan Barton, 'The Ayler Enigma'
34 W.A. Baldwin, 'Albert Ayler: Conservative Revolution? (1)'
35 W.A. Baldwin, 'Albert Ayler: Conservative Revolution? (4)'
36 Ronald Atkins, 'Albert Ayler At LSE'
37 Humphrey Lyttelton, *Take It From The Top*
38 Val Wilmer correspondence
39 Val Wilmer, *As Serious As Your Life*
40 Paul D. Zimmerman and Ruth Ross, 'The New Jazz'
41 Richard Cook and Brian Morton, *The Penguin Guide To Jazz On CD, LP, And Cassette*
42 Robert Iannapollo, '*Albert Ayler In Greenwich Village*'
43 Pete Welding, '*Albert Ayler In Greenwich Village*'
44 Art Lange, '*Albert Ayler Live In Greenwich Village: The Complete Impulse! Recordings*'
45 Barry McRae, '*Albert Ayler Live In Greenwich Village*'
46 Beaver Harris interview with Elliott Bratton
47 Robert Palmer, liner notes to *Live In Greenwich Village: The Complete Impulse Recordings*
48 Robert Palmer, liner notes to *Live In Greenwich Village: The Complete Impulse Recordings*
49 Joe Pinelli, 'Joy In The New Music'

CHAPTER XVIII
1   Peter Niklas Wilson, *Spirits Rejoice!*
2   Peter Niklas Wilson, *Spirits Rejoice!*
3   Donald Ayler interview
4   Peter Niklas Wilson, *Spirits Rejoice!*
5   Jacqueline and Daniel Caux, 'My Name Is Albert Ayler'
6   Val Wilmer correspondence
7   Val Wilmer, *As Serious As Your Life*
8   Kiyoshi Koyama, 'Interview With Albert Ayler'
9   Mutawaf Shaheed interview
10 Ethel Boros, 'Devotees Hail Aylers' "Free" Jazz'
11 Jon Goldman, 'The Albert Ayler Sextet In Concert—Cleveland—February 4, 1967'
12 Michael Zwerin, 'Jazz Journal: Space Friends'

13 George Hoefer, 'Albert Ayler, Village Theater, New York City'

14 Art Lange, *Albert Ayler Live In Greenwich Village*

15 Nat Hentoff, liner notes to *Live In Greenwich Village: The Complete Impulse Recordings*

16 Ekkehard Jost, *Free Jazz*

17 Nat Hentoff, liner notes to *Live In Greenwich Village: The Complete Impulse Recordings*

18 Robert Iannapollo, '*Albert Ayler In Greenwich Village*'

19 Barry McRae, 'Avant Courier: Message From Albert'

20 Frank Kofsky, 'An Interview With Albert And Donald Ayler'

21 Frank Kofsky, 'An Interview With Albert And Donald Ayler'

22 Robert Palmer, liner notes to *Live In Greenwich Village: The Complete Impulse Recordings*

23 Albert Ayler, 'To Mr. Jones—I Had A Vision'

24 Richard Mortifoglio, 'Albert Ayler As Angel Of History'

25 Pete Welding, '*Albert Ayler In Greenwich Village*'

26 Richard Mortifoglio, 'Albert Ayler As Angel Of History'

27 Peter Niklas Wilson, *Spirits Rejoice!*

28 Peter Niklas Wilson, *Spirits Rejoice!*

29 Donald Ayler interview

30 Frank Kofsky, 'An Interview With Albert And Donald Ayler'

31 Daniel Caux, 'My Name Is Albert Ayler, 2'

32 Daniel Caux, 'My Name Is Albert Ayler, 2'

33 Peter Niklas Wilson, *Spirits Rejoice!*

34 Donald Ayler interview

35 Frank Kofsky, 'An Interview With Albert And Donald Ayler'

36 John S. Wilson, 'Buddy Rich Star Of Jazz Festival'

37 Dan Morgenstern and Ira Gitler, 'The Newport Jazz Festival'

38 John S. Wilson, 'Newport Offers History Of Jazz'

39 Donald Ayler interview

40 Art Lange, 'Ayler Resurrected: A Look Into Revenant's *Albert Ayler: Holy Ghost*'

41 Tony Herrington, '*Albert Ayler, Holy Ghost: Rare & Unissued Recordings (1962–70)*'

42 Rudie Kagie, 'Avonturen In De New Thing'

43 Daniel Caux, 'My Name Is Albert Ayler, 2'

44 Frank Kofsky, 'An Interview With Albert And Donald Ayler'

45 Stuart Broomer, 'Albert Ayler, Breakfast In Montreal … A Reflection'

46 Frank Kofsky, 'An Interview With Albert And Donald Ayler'

47 Donald Ayler interview

48 J.C. Thomas, *Chasin' The Trane*

49 John Kruth, 'The Healing Force Of The Universe'

50 Donald Ayler interview

51 Bob Rusch, 'Donald Ayler: Interview'

52 Donald Ayler interview

53 Robert Iannapollo, '*Love Cry*'

54 Dave McElfresh, 'Albert Ayler, The Truth Is Marching In'

55 Philippe Carles, 'La bataille d'Ayler n'est pas finie'

56 Richard Mortifoglio, 'Albert Ayler As Angel Of History'

57 Edward Jarvis, 'Albert Ayler'

58 Derek Ansell, '*Love Cry*'

59 Derek Ansell, '*Love Cry*'

60 Stuart Broomer, 'Albert Ayler, Breakfast In Montreal … A Reflection'

61 Val Wilmer, *As Serious As Your Life*

62 Pat Griffiths, 'The Silva Lining'

63 Robert Iannapollo, '*Love Cry*'

64 Peter Niklas Wilson, *Spirits Rejoice!*

65 Dave McElfresh, 'Albert Ayler, The Truth Is Marching In'

66 David Keenan, 'The Primer'

67 Larry Nai, 'Alan Silva Interview'

68 Jeff Schwartz, *Albert Ayler*

69 Daniel Caux, 'My Name Is Albert Ayler, 2'

70 Bill Quinn, '*Sunny's Time Now*'

71 Bill Quinn, '*Sunny's Time Now*'

72 Bill Quinn, '*Sunny's Time Now*'

73 Robert Iannapollo, '*Love Cry*'

74 Peter Niklas Wilson, *Spirits Rejoice!*

75 Albert Ayler, 'To Mr. Jones—I Had A Vision'

76 Barry McRae, 'Avant Courier: Message From Albert'

77 Jeff Schwartz, *Albert Ayler*

78 Peter Niklas Wilson, *Spirits Rejoice!*

79 Bill Quinn, '*Sunny's Time Now*'

80 Richard Cook and Brian Morton, *The Penguin Guide To Jazz On CD, LP, And Cassette*

81 Richard Williams, 'Blowing In The Wind'

82 Patrick Straram, 'Jazz libre en Quebec'

83 Stuart Broomer, 'Albert Ayler, Breakfast In Montreal … A Reflection'

84 Francis Davis, 'The Fire That Time'

85 Val Wilmer, unpublished interview

86 Larry Nai, 'Alan Silva Interview'
87 Chris Albertson, '*Love Cry*'
88 Richard Cook, 'My Name Is Albert Ayler'

CHAPTER XIX
1 Beaver Harris interview with Elliott Bratton
2 Ashley Kahn, *The House That Trane Built*
3 Jeff Schwartz, *Albert Ayler*
4 Richard Cook and Brian Morton, *The Penguin Guide To Jazz On CD, LP, And Cassette*
5 Val Wilmer, *As Serious As Your Life*
6 Donald Ayler interview
7 Mitch Myers, 'Spirits, Ghosts, Witches & Devils: The Life And Death Of Albert Ayler'
8 Mutawaf Shaheed interview
9 Daniel Caux, 'My Name Is Albert Ayler, 2'
10 Daniel Caux, 'Apparitions Of Albert The Great In Paris And Saint-Paul De Vence'
11 Val Wilmer, *As Serious As Your Life*
12 John Litweiler, 'The Legacy Of Albert Ayler'
13 Ekkehard Jost, *Free Jazz*
14 Daniel Caux, 'Apparitions Of Albert The Great In Paris And Saint-Paul De Vence'
15 John Kruth, 'The Healing Force Of The Universe'
16 Elisabeth van der Mei, 'The New Music'
17 Roy Blumenfeld email correspondence
18 Bob Rusch, 'Donald Ayler: Interview'
19 Harvey Pekar, '*Holy Ghost*: Revenant Records Returns With Free-Jazz Specter Albert Ayler'
20 Kiyoshi Koyama, 'Interview With Albert Ayler'
21 Bob Rusch, 'Donald Ayler: Interview'
22 Val Wilmer, 'Conversation With Call'
23 Peter Niklas Wilson, *Spirits Rejoice!*
24 Bob Rusch, 'Seldon Powell Interview'
25 Alan Heineman, '*New Grass*'
26 Jack Cooke, 'Great Lost Recordings'
27 Ekkehard Jost, *Free Jazz*
28 Graham Colombé, '*New Grass*'
29 Gary Giddins, 'Fresh Flowers For Albert'
30 Larry Neal, '*New Grass*'
31 Jack Cooke, '*New Grass*'
32 Ekkehard Jost, *Free Jazz*
33 Alan Heineman, '*New Grass*'
34 Jack Cooke, '*New Grass*'
35 Jack Cooke, 'Great Lost Recordings'
36 John Litweiler, 'The Legacy Of Albert Ayler'
37 Alan Heineman, '*New Grass*'
38 John Litweiler, *The Freedom Principle*
39 Gary Giddins, 'Fresh Flowers For Albert'
40 Val Wilmer, 'Spirits Rejoice!'
41 *Village Voice*, September 19, 1968

42 Peter Niklas Wilson (translated by White), *Spirits Rejoice!*
43 William Parker, *Conversations*
44 Tony Herrington, 'Soundcheck'
45 Donald Ayler interview
46 Edward Ayler interview
47 Peter Niklas Wilson (translated by White), *Spirits Rejoice!*
48 Jimmy Landers interview
49 Ashley Kahn, *The House That Trane Built*
50 Robert Palmer, liner notes to *Live In Greenwich Village: The Complete Impulse Recordings*
51 Bobby Few interview
52 Peter Niklas Wilson, 'Die Sphinx des Free Jazz'
53 Richard Rouda, '*Music Is The Healing Force Of The Universe*'
54 Larry Kart, '*Music Is The Healing Force Of The Universe*'
55 Richard Rouda, '*Music Is The Healing Force Of The Universe*'
56 Richard Williams, 'Running Down The Ayler'
57 Richard Rouda, '*Music Is The Healing Force Of The Universe*'
58 Ekkehard Jost, *Free Jazz*
59 John Litweiler, *The Freedom Principle*
60 Ashley Kahn, *The House That Trane Built*
61 Barry McRae, '*The Last Album*'
62 Richard Rouda, '*Music Is The Healing Force Of The Universe*'
63 Jack Cooke, 'Great Lost Recordings'
64 Barry McRae, '*The Last Album*'
65 Richard Cook, 'My Name Is Albert Ayler'
66 John Litweiler, 'The Legacy Of Albert Ayler'

CHAPTER XX
1 Daniel Caux, 'Apparitions Of Albert The Great In Paris And Saint-Paul De Vence'
2 Daniel Caux, 'Apparitions Of Albert The Great In Paris And Saint-Paul De Vence'
3 Steven Tintweiss email correspondence
4 Donald Ayler interview
5 Jacqueline Caux email correspondence
6 Steven Tintweiss email correspondence
7 John Litweiler, '*Albert Ayler Vol. 1*'
8 Clifford Allen, 'On ESP'
9 Harald Schönstein, 'Die Nächte Der Fondation Maeght'
10 Gérard Noël, 'L'art admirable d'Albert le téméraire'
11 Steve Tintweiss email correspondence

ALSO AVAILABLE FROM JAWBONE PRESS